*Spring in Action*

# Spring in Action

CRAIG WALLS
RYAN BREIDENBACH

MANNING

Greenwich
(74° w. long.)

Manning Publications Co.      Copyeditor:  Liz Welch
209 Bruce Park Avenue      Typesetter:  Denis Dalinnik
Greenwich, CT 06830      Cover designer:  Leslie Haimes

ISBN 1-932394-35-4

Printed in the United States of America
2 3 4 5 6 7 8 9 10 – VHG – 09 08 07 06 05

*Maisy Grace, see you soon*
                    *—C.W.*


*For my brother, Lee*
                    *—R.B.*

# brief contents

# contents

ix

# preface

Software developers need to have a number of traits in order to practice their craft well. First, they must be good analytical thinkers and problem solvers. A developer's primary role is to create software that solves business problems. This requires analyzing customer needs and coming up with successful, creative solutions.

They also need to be curious. Developments in the software industry are moving targets, always evolving. New frameworks, new techniques, new languages, and new methodologies are constantly emerging. Each one is a new tool that needs to be mastered and added to the toolbox, allowing the developer to do his or her job better and faster.

Then there is the most cherished trait of all, "laziness." The kind of laziness that motivates developers to work hard to seek out solutions with the least amount of effort. It was with curiosity, a good dose of "laziness," and all the analytical abilities we could muster that the two of us struck out together four years ago to find new ways to develop software.

This was the time when open source software was reaching critical mass in the Java community. Tons of open source frameworks were blossoming on the Java landscape. In order to decide to adopt one, it had to hit the sweet spot of our needs—it had to do 80% of what we needed right out of the box. And for any functionality that was not right out of the box, the framework needed to be easily extendible so that functionality too would be included. Extending didn't mean kludging in some hack that was so ugly you felt dirty afterwards—it meant extending in an elegant fashion. That wasn't too much to ask, right?

The first of these frameworks that gained immediate adoption on our team was Ant. From the get-go, we could tell that Ant had been created by another developer who knew our pain in building Java applications. From that moment on, no more javac. No more CLASSPATH. All this with a straightforward (albeit sometimes verbose) XML configuration. Huzzah! Life (and builds) just got easier.

As we went along, we began adopting more and more tools. Eclipse became our IDE of choice. Log4J became our (and everybody else's) default logging toolkit. And Lucene supplanted our commercial search solution. Each of these tools met our criteria of filling a need while being easy to use, understand, and extend.

But something was lacking. These great tools were designed to help develop software, like Ant and Eclipse, or to serve a very specific application need, like searching in the case of Lucene and logging for Log4J. None of them addressed the needs at the heart of enterprise applications: persistence, transactions, and integration with other enterprise resources.

That all changed in the last year or so when we discovered the remarkable one-two enterprise punch of Spring and Hibernate. Between these two frameworks nearly all of our middle- and data-tier needs were met.

We first adopted Hibernate. It was the most intuitive and feature-rich object/ relational mapping tool out there. But it was by adopting Spring that we really got our code to look good. With Spring's inversion of control, we were able to get rid of all our custom factories and configurers. In fact, that is the reason we first integrated Spring into our applications. Its wiring allowed us to streamline our application configurations and move away from homegrown solutions. (Hey, every developer likes writing his own framework. But sometimes you just have to let go!)

We quickly discovered a nice bonus: Spring also provided very easy integration with Hibernate. This allowed us to ditch our custom Hibernate integration classes and use Spring's support instead. In turn, this led us directly to Spring's support for transparent persistence.

Look closely and you will see a pattern here. The more we used Spring, the more we discovered new features. And each feature we discovered was a pleasure to work with. Its web MVC framework worked nicely in a few applications. Its AOP support has been helpful in several places, primarily security. The JDBC support was quite nice for some smaller programs. Oh yeah, we also use it for scheduling. And JNDI access. And email integration. When it comes to hitting development sweet spots, Spring knocks the ball out of the park.

We liked Spring so much, we decided somebody should write a book about it. Fortunately, one of us had already written a book for Manning and knew how to go about doing this sort of thing. Soon that "somebody who should write a book" became us. In taking on this project we are trying to spread the gospel of Spring. The Spring framework has been nothing but a joy for us to work with—we predict it will be the same for you. And, we hope this book will be a pleasant vehicle for you to get to that point.

# *acknowledgments*

The creation of this book was not just a two-man job. In addition to the two authors, a great number of people were involved in many ways to make this book possible.

First, we'd like to acknowledge the book's behind-the-scenes crew at Manning Publications: publisher Marjan Bace, his assistant Susan Capparelle, our editor Jackie Carter, as well as Denis Dalinnik, Leslie Haimes, Mary Piergies, Liz Welch, Susan Forsyth, and Helen Trimes. We can't imagine working with a better team of professionals. You are all very good at what you do and deserve commendation for producing the best technical books in the world.

We'd also like to thank each of the reviewers who contributed their time to provide us with the feedback, criticism, and inspiration we needed to shape the book: Doug Warren, Muhammad Ashikuzzaman, Ryan Cox, Mojahedul Hasanat, Jack Herrington, Olivier Jolly, William Lopez, Lester Martin, Dmitri Maximovich, Daniel Miller, Christian Parker, Matthew Payne, and Norman Richards. Special thanks to Doug Warren for his technical proofread of the manuscript shortly before it went to press.

And finally, thanks to Rod Johnson and the rest of the Spring team for creating Spring in the first place. We can honestly say that Spring is a pleasure to work with. You guys rock!

## CRAIG WALLS

I want to thank my beautiful and loving wife, Raymie. You're the love of my life, my best friend, and my sweetest dream. Thanks for supporting me and for your patience, and for putting up with another book project—I promise that it's over now.

To my coauthor, Ryan, for getting me started with Spring and for helping me put together this book to tell everyone else about it.

To my team at Michaels—Ryan, Marianna, Van, Tonji, Jeff, Jim, Don, Carol, and Leida—thanks for continuing to demonstrate every day what a world-class software development team is capable of. Now that this book is done, maybe I won't have to decline as many lunch invitations!

To my friends and colleagues whom I've met and chatted with this year as I toured the country with the No-Fluff/Just-Stuff software symposiums: Glenn Vanderburg, Ted Neward, Bruce Tate, Venkat Subramaniam, Ramnivas Laddad, Dave Thomas, Erik Hatcher, Howard Lewis Ship, Neal Ford, Rick Hightower, Ben Galbraith, Stuart Halloway, and Matt Raible. And thanks to Jay Zimmerman for always putting on a great show and inviting me to be a part of it in 2004.

To my friends and neighbors from the 'hood: John, Jennifer, and Tobey for providing Raymie and me with frequent pizza/movie/sit-on-the-driveway breaks.

Thanks to Dick Wolf for creating "Law & Order," the TV show that provided much of the background noise while I was writing.

And everyone else I thanked in *XDoclet in Action*.

## RYAN BREIDENBACH

First, I want to thank my wife Angi. Your limitless patience and encouragement is what kept me going in this endeavor. I promise you will see me smiling more and breathing easier now that this is done.

To my daughter Julia, for helping me keep the pressure of writing a book in perspective. It was always a pleasure to take some time away from writing to visit the web sites of Elmo's World and Jo Jo's Circus.

To my parents, Mark and Lynda, and my brother Lee, for understanding why I kept my head buried in my laptop when I came to visit. I will be a lot less stressed during future visits.

To my in-laws, Stephanie and George, for your pep talks and for occasionally (okay, frequently) babysitting to give Angi and me some time to ourselves.

To my fellow developers out there, Van, Marianna, Tonji, and Jerry, for letting me bounce ideas off you. Sometimes my brain gets going too fast and a swift kick is in order to get me back in line.

To my friends and neighbors, Dave, Javier, Alex, Scott and James for helping me keep my chin up and, every now and then, providing some much needed … levity.

To the folks at CVSDude. Cool CVS hosting name. Great CVS hosting service.

Finally, to Craig for being a mentor and showing me the ropes of how to write a book. There is a lot to know and your help made the process that much easier.

# *about this book*

The Spring framework was created with a very specific goal in mind: to make developing J2EE applications easier. Along the same lines, *Spring in Action* was written to make learning how to use Spring easier. Our goal is not to give you a blow-by-blow listing of Spring APIs. Instead, we hope to present the Spring framework in a way that is most relevant to a J2EE developer by providing practical code examples from real-world experience.

Since Spring is a modular framework, this book was written in the same way. We recognize that not all developers have the same needs. Some may want to learn the Spring framework from the ground up, while others may want to pick and choose different topics and go at their own pace. That way, the book can act as a tool for learning Spring for the first time as well as a guide and reference for those wanting to dig deeper into specific features.

## Roadmap

*Spring in Action* is divided into three parts, plus two appendices. Each of the three parts focuses on a general area of the Spring Framework: the core, middle-tier, and web layer. While each part builds on the previous section, each is also able to stand on its own, allowing you to dive right into a certain topic without starting from the beginning.

In part 1, you'll explore the two core features of the Spring framework: inversion of control (IoC) and aspect-oriented programming (AOP). This will give you a good understanding of Spring's fundamentals that will be utilized throughout the book.

In chapter 1, you'll be introduced to IoC and AOP and how Spring uses them to make developing Java applications easier. You will also see how Spring compares to other frameworks, such as EJB, Struts, and PicoContainer.

Chapter 2 takes a more detailed look at how to configure your application objects using IoC. You will learn how to write loosely coupled components and wire their dependencies and properties within the Spring container using XML.

Chapter 3 explores how to use Spring's AOP to decouple cross-cutting concerns, such as security, from the objects that they service. This chapter also sets the stage for chapter 5, where you'll learn how to provide declarative transaction services with Spring's AOP.

Part 2 builds on the IoC and AOP features introduced in part 1 and shows you how to apply these concepts to the middle tier of your application.

Chapter 4 covers Spring's support for data persistence. You'll be introduced to Spring's JDBC support, which helps you remove much of the boilerplate code associated with JDBC. You'll also see how Spring integrates with several popular object-relational mapping frameworks, such as Hibernate, JDO, OJB, and iBATIS SQL Maps.

Chapter 5 complements chapter 4, showing you how to ensure integrity in your database using Spring's transaction support. You will see how Spring uses AOP to give you the power of declarative transactions without having to use EJBs.

Chapter 6 explores how to expose your application objects as remote services. You'll also learn how to transparently access remote services as though they were any other in your application. Remoting technologies explored will include RMI, Hessian/Burlap, EJB, web services, and Spring's own `HttpInvoker`.

Since most enterprise applications do not exist in a vacuum, chapter 7 shows you how to integrate with other enterprise services. In this chapter, you will learn how Spring makes it easy to integrate with mail services, JMS, and even EJBs.

Part 3 moves out of the middle tier and into the presentation layer used in so many J2EE applications: the Web.

Chapter 8 introduces you to Spring's own MVC web framework. You will discover how Spring can transparently bind web parameters to your business objects and provide validation and error handling at the same time. You will also see how easy it is to add functionality to your web applications using Spring's interceptors.

Building on the foundation of Spring MVC, chapter 9 demonstrates how to move beyond JavaServer Pages and use other templating languages such as

Velocity and FreeMarker. In addition, you'll see how to use Spring MVC to dynamically produce binary content, such as PDF and Excel documents.

Chapter 10 shows you how to integrate Spring with other web frameworks. For those of you who have already made an investment in another framework, Spring provides support for several of the popular web frameworks, including Struts, Tapestry, JavaServer Faces, and WebWork.

Finally, in chapter 11 you will learn how to apply security to your web applications using the Acegi Security System to provide authentication. In addition, you will see how to integrate Acegi with your business objects to apply security at the method level as well.

Appendix A will get you started with your own Spring application, showing you how to download the Spring framework and configure your Ant build file.

Appendix B introduces you to several other open source frameworks related to Spring.

## Who should read this book

*Spring in Action* is for all Java developers, but enterprise Java developers will find it particularly useful. While we will guide you gently through code examples that build in complexity throughout each chapter, the true power of Spring lies in its ability to make enterprise applications easier to develop. As a result, enterprise developers will most fully appreciate the examples presented in this book.

Because a vast portion of Spring is devoted to providing enterprise services, many parallels can be drawn between Spring and EJB. Any EJB experience you have will be useful in making comparisons between these two frameworks. Finally, while this book is not exclusively focused on web applications, a good portion of it is dedicated to this topic. In fact, the final four chapters demonstrate how Spring can support the development of your applications' web layer. If you are a web application developer, you will find the last part of this book especially valuable.

## Code conventions and downloads

There are many code examples in this book. These examples will always appear in a code font. If there is a particular part of an example we want you to pay extra attention to, it will appear in a **bolded code** font. Any class name, method name, or XML fragment within the normal text of the book will appear in code font as well.

Many of Spring's classes have exceptionally long names. Because of this, line-continuation markers (➥) may be included when necessary.

Not all code examples in this book will be complete. Often we only show a method or two from a class to focus on a particular topic.

Complete source code for the application found in the book can be downloaded from the publisher's web site at http://www.manning,.com/walls2 or at http://www.springinaction.com.

## Author Online

Purchase of *Spring in Action* includes free access to a private web forum run by Manning Publications where you can make comments about the book, ask technical questions, and receive help from the authors and from other users. To access the forum and subscribe to it, point your web browser to www.manning.com/walls2. This page provides information on how to get on the forum once you are registered, what kind of help is available, and the rules of conduct on the forum.

Manning's commitment to our readers is to provide a venue where a meaningful dialog between individual readers and between readers and the authors can take place. It is not a commitment to any specific amount of participation on the part of the authors, whose contribution to the AO remains voluntary (and unpaid). We suggest you try asking the authors some challenging questions lest their interest stray!

The Author Online forum and the archives of previous discussions will be accessible from the publisher's web site as long as the book is in print.

## About the authors

**Craig Walls** is a professional software developer with more than ten years' experience developing software solutions in the areas of telecommunications, finance, retail, and e-commerce. He is a frequent presenter at user groups and conferences and a co-author of *XDoclet in Action*. Craig lives in Denton, Texas.

An avid supporter of open source Java technologies, **Ryan Breidenbach** has been developing Java web applications for the past five years. Ryan lives in Coppell, Texas.

## About the title

By combining introductions, overviews, and how-to examples, the *In Action* books are designed to help learning *and* remembering. According to research in cognitive science, the things people remember are things they discover during self-motivated exploration.

Although no one at Manning is a cognitive scientist, we are convinced that for learning to become permanent it must pass through stages of exploration, play, and, interestingly, re-telling of what is being learned. People understand and remember new things, which is to say they master them, only after actively exploring them. Humans learn *in action*. An essential part of an *In Action* guide is that it is example-driven. It encourages the reader to try things out, to play with new code, and explore new ideas.

There is another, more mundane, reason for the title of this book: our readers are busy. They use books to do a job or solve a problem. They need books that allow them to jump in and jump out easily and learn just what they want just when they want it. They need books that aid them *in action*. The books in this series are designed for such readers.

## *About the cover illustration*

The figure on the cover of *Spring in Action* is an "Officer of the Grand Signior." The illustration is taken from a collection of costumes of the Ottoman Empire published on January 1, 1802, by William Miller of Old Bond Street, London. The title page is missing from the collection and we have been unable to track it down to date. The book's table of contents identifies the figures in both English and French, and each illustration bears the names of two artists who worked on it, both of whom would no doubt be surprised to find their art gracing the front cover of a computer programming book...two hundred years later.

The collection was purchased by a Manning editor at an antiquarian flea market in the "Garage" on West 26th Street in Manhattan. The seller was an American based in Ankara, Turkey, and the transaction took place just as he was packing up his stand for the day. The Manning editor did not have on his person the substantial amount of cash that was required for the purchase and a credit card and check were both politely turned down.

With the seller flying back to Ankara that evening the situation was getting hopeless. What was the solution? It turned out to be nothing more than an old-fashioned verbal agreement sealed with a handshake. The seller simply proposed that the money be transferred to him by wire and the editor walked out with the bank information on a piece of paper and the portfolio of images under his arm. Needless to say, we transferred the funds the next day, and we remain grateful and impressed by this unknown person's trust in one of us. It recalls something that might have happened a long time ago.

The pictures from the Ottoman collection, like the other illustrations that appear on our covers, bring to life the richness and variety of dress customs of two centuries ago. They recall the sense of isolation and distance of that period—and of every other historic period except our own hyperkinetic present.

Dress codes have changed since then and the diversity by region, so rich at the time, has faded away. It is now often hard to tell the inhabitant of one continent from another. Perhaps, trying to view it optimistically, we have traded a cultural and visual diversity for a more varied personal life. Or a more varied and interesting intellectual and technical life.

We at Manning celebrate the inventiveness, the initiative, and, yes, the fun of the computer business with book covers based on the rich diversity of regional life of two centuries ago, brought back to life by the pictures from this collection.

# Part 1

# Spring essentials

In part 1, you'll explore the two core features of the Spring framework: inversion of control (IoC) and aspect-oriented programming (AOP). Starting with chapter 1, "A Spring jump start," you'll be given a quick overview of IoC and AOP in Spring and how it can make developing Java applications easier. You will also see how Spring compares to other frameworks such as EJB, Struts, and PicoContainer.

In chapter 2, "Wiring beans," you'll take a more in-depth look at how to keep all of your application objects loosely coupled using IoC. You'll learn how to define your application's objects and wire their dependencies within the Spring container using XML.

Chapter 3, "Creating aspects in Spring," explores how to use Spring's AOP to decouple systemwide services (such as security and auditing) from the objects they service. This chapter sets the stage for chapter 5, where you'll learn how to use Spring's AOP to provide declarative transaction services.

# A Spring jump start

1

## This chapter covers

- Creating simpler J2EE applications using Spring
- Decoupling components with inversion of control
- Managing cross-cutting concerns with aspect-oriented programming
- Comparing the features of Spring and EJB

It all started with a bean.

In 1996 the Java programming language was still a young, exciting, up-and-coming platform. Many developers flocked to the language because they had seen how to create rich and dynamic web applications using applets. But they soon learned that there was more to this strange new language than animated juggling cartoon characters. Unlike any language before it, Java made it possible to write complex applications made up of discrete parts. They came for the applets, but they stayed for the components.

It was in December of that year that Sun Microsystems published the Java-Beans 1.00-A specification. JavaBeans defined a software component model for Java. This specification defined a set of coding policies that enabled simple Java objects to be reusable and easily composed into more complex applications. Although JavaBeans were intended as a general-purpose means of defining reusable application components, they have been primarily used as a model for building user interface widgets. They seemed too simple to be capable of any "real" work. Enterprise developers wanted more.

Sophisticated applications often require services such as transaction support, security, and distributed computing—services not directly provided by the JavaBeans specification. Therefore, in March 1998, Sun published the 1.0 version of the Enterprise JavaBeans (EJB) specification. This specification extended the notion of Java components to the server side, providing the much-needed enterprise services, but failed to continue the simplicity of the original JavaBeans specification. In fact, except in name, EJB bears very little resemblance to the original JavaBeans specification.

Despite the fact that many successful applications have been built based on EJB, EJB never really achieved its intended purpose: to simplify enterprise application development. Every version of the EJB specification contains the following statement: "Enterprise JavaBeans will make it easy to write applications." It is true that EJB's declarative programming model simplifies many infrastructural aspects of development, such as transactions and security. But EJBs are complicated in a different way by mandating deployment descriptors and plumbing code (home and remote/local interfaces). Over time many developers became disenchanted with EJB. As a result, its popularity has started to wane in recent years, leaving many developers looking for an easier way.

Now Java component development is coming full circle. New programming techniques, including aspect-oriented programming (AOP) and inversion of control (IoC), are giving JavaBeans much of the power of EJB. These techniques furnish JavaBeans with a declarative programming model reminiscent of EJB, but without all of EJB's complexity. No longer must you resort to writing an unwieldy EJB component when a simple JavaBean will suffice.

And that's where Spring steps into the picture.

## 1.1 Why Spring?

If you are reading this book, you probably want to know why Spring would be good for you. After all, the Java landscape is full of frameworks. What makes Spring any different? To put it simply, Spring makes developing enterprise applications easier. We don't expect that to convince you at face value, so first let's take a look at life without Spring.

### 1.1.1 A day in the life of a J2EE developer

Alex is a Java developer who has just started on his first enterprise application. Like many Java 2 Enterprise Edition (J2EE) applications, it is a web application that serves many users and accesses an enterprise database. In this case, it is a customer management application that will be used by other employees at his company.

Eager to get to work, Alex fires up his favorite integrated development environment (IDE) and starts to crank out his first component, the CustomerManager component. In the EJB world, to develop this component Alex actually has to write several classes—the home interface, the local interface, and the bean itself. In addition, he has to create a deployment descriptor for this bean.

Seeing that creating each of these files for *every* bean seems like a lot of effort, Alex incorporates XDoclet into his project. XDoclet is a code generation tool that can generate all of the necessary EJB files from a single source file. Although this adds another step to Alex's development cycle, his coding life is now much simpler.

With XDoclet now handling a lot of the grunt work for him, Alex turns his attention to his real problem—what exactly should the CustomerManager component do? He jumps in with its first method, getPreferredCustomer(). There are several business rules that define exactly what a preferred customer is, and Alex dutifully codes them into his CustomerManager bean.

Wanting to confirm that his logic is correct, Alex now wants to write some tests to validate his code. But then it occurs to him: the code he is testing will be running within the EJB container. Therefore, his tests need to execute within the container as well. To easily accomplish this, he concocts a servlet that will be responsible for executing these tests. Since all J2EE containers support servlets, this will allow him to execute his tests in the same container as his EJB. Problem solved!

So Alex fires up his J2EE container and runs his tests. His tests fail. Alex sees his coding error, fixes it, and runs the tests again. His tests fail again. He sees another error and fixes it. He fires up the container and runs the tests again. As Alex is going through this cycle, he notices something. The fact that he has to start the J2EE container for each batch of testing really slows down his development cycle. The development cycle should go code, test, code, test. This pattern has now been replaced with code, wait, test, code, wait, test, code, wait, get increasingly frustrated…

While waiting for the container to start during another test run, Alex thinks, "Why am I using EJB in the first place?" The answer, of course, is because of the services it provides. But Alex isn't using entity beans, so he is not using persistence services. Alex is also not using the remoting or security services. In fact, the only EJB service Alex is going to use is transaction management. This leads Alex to another question: "Is there an easier way?"

### 1.1.2  *Spring's pledge*

The above story was a dramatization based on the current state of J2EE—specifically EJB. In its current state, EJB is complicated. It isn't complicated just to be complicated. It is complicated because EJBs were created to solve complicated things, such as distributed objects and remote transactions.

Unfortunately, a good number of enterprise projects do not have this level of complexity but still take on EJB's burden of multiple Java files and deployment descriptors and heavyweight containers. With EJB, application complexity is high, regardless of the complexity of the problem being solved—even simple applications are unduly complex. With Spring, the complexity of your application is proportional to the complexity of the problem being solved.

However, Spring recognizes that EJB does offer developers valuable services. So Spring strives to deliver these same services while simplifying the programming model. In doing so, it adopts a simple philosophy: J2EE *should* be easy to use. In keeping with this philosophy, Spring was designed with the following beliefs:

- Good design is more important than the underlying technology.
- JavaBeans loosely coupled through interfaces is a good model.
- Code should be easy to test.

Okay. So how does Spring help you apply this philosophy to your applications?

### *Good design is more important than the underlying technology*

As a developer, you should always be seeking the best design for your application, regardless of the implementation you choose. Sometimes the complexity of EJB is warranted because of the requirements of the application. Often, this is not the case. Many applications require few, if any, of the services provided by EJB yet are still implemented using this technology for technology's sake. If an application does not require distribution or declarative transaction support, it is unlikely that EJB is the best technology candidate. Yet many Java developers feel compelled to use EJB for every Java enterprise application.

The idea behind Spring is that you can keep your code as simple as it needs to be. If what you want are some plain-vanilla Java objects to perform some services supported by transparent transactions, you've got it. And you don't need an EJB container, and you don't have to implement special interfaces. You just have to write your code.

### *JavaBeans loosely coupled through interfaces is a good model*

If you are relying on EJBs to provide your application services, your components do not just depend on the EJB business interface. They are also responsible for retrieving these EJB objects from a directory, which entails a Java Naming and Directory Interface (JNDI) lookup and communicating with the bean's EJBHome interface. This is not creating a decoupled application. This is tightly coupling your application to a specific implementation, namely EJB.

With Spring, your beans depend on collaborators through interfaces. Since there are no implementation-specific dependencies, Spring applications are very decoupled, testable, and easier to maintain. And because the Spring container is responsible for resolving the dependencies, the active service lookup that is involved in EJB is now out of the picture and the cost of programming to interfaces is minimized. All you need to do is create classes that communicate with each other through interfaces, and Spring takes care of the rest.

### *Code should be easy to test*

Testing J2EE applications can be difficult. If you are testing EJBs within a container, you have to start up a container to execute even the most trivial of test cases. Since starting and stopping a container is expensive, developers may be tempted to skip testing all of their components. Avoiding tests because of the rigidness of a framework is not a good excuse.

Because you develop Spring applications with JavaBeans, testing is cheap. There is no J2EE container to be started since you will be testing a POJO. And since Spring makes coding to interfaces easy, your objects will be loosely coupled, making testing even easier. A thorough battery of tests should be present in all of your applications; Spring will help you accomplish this.

## 1.2 What is Spring?

Spring is an open-source framework, created by Rod Johnson and described in his book *Expert One-on-One: J2EE Design and Development*.[1] It was created to address the complexity of enterprise application development. Spring makes it possible to use plain-vanilla JavaBeans to achieve things that were previously only possible with EJBs. However, Spring's usefulness isn't limited to server-side development. Any Java application can benefit from Spring in terms of simplicity, testability, and loose coupling.

> **NOTE** To avoid ambiguity, we'll use the term "EJB" when referring to Enterprise JavaBeans. When referring to the original JavaBean, we'll call it "JavaBean," or "bean" for short. Some other terms we may throw around are "POJO" (which stands for "plain old Java object") or "POJI" (which means "plain old Java interface").

Put simply, Spring is a lightweight inversion of control and aspect-oriented container framework. Okay, that's not so simple a description. But it does summarize what Spring does. To make more sense of Spring, let's break this description down:

- *Lightweight*—Spring is lightweight in terms of both size and overhead. The entire Spring framework can be distributed in a single JAR file that weighs in at just over 1 MB. And the processing overhead required by Spring is negligible. What's more, Spring is nonintrusive: objects in a Spring-enabled application typically have no dependencies on Spring-specific classes.

- *Inversion of control*—Spring promotes loose coupling through a technique known as inversion of control (IoC). When IoC is applied, objects are passively given their dependencies instead of creating or looking for dependent objects for themselves. You can think of IoC as JNDI in reverse—instead of an object looking up dependencies from a container, the container gives the dependencies to the object at instantiation without waiting to be asked.

---

[1] In this book, Spring was originally called "interface21."

- *Aspect-oriented*—Spring comes with rich support for aspect-oriented programming that enables cohesive development by separating application business logic from system services (such as auditing and transaction management). Application objects do what they're supposed to do—perform business logic—and nothing more. They are not responsible for (or even aware of) other system concerns, such as logging or transactional support.

- *Container*—Spring is a container in the sense that it contains and manages the life cycle and configuration of application objects. You can configure how your each of your beans should be created—either create one single instance of your bean or produce a new instance every time one is needed based on a configurable prototype—and how they should be associated with each other. Spring should not, however, be confused with traditionally heavyweight EJB containers, which are often large and cumbersome to work with.

- *Framework*—Spring makes it possible to configure and compose complex applications from simpler components. In Spring, application objects are composed declaratively, typically in an XML file. Spring also provides much infrastructure functionality (transaction management, persistence framework integration, etc.), leaving the development of application logic to you.

All of these attributes of Spring enable you to write code that is cleaner, more manageable, and easier to test. They also set the stage for a variety of subframeworks within the greater Spring framework.

### 1.2.1 *Spring modules*

The Spring framework is made up of seven well-defined modules (figure 1.1). When taken as a whole, these modules give you everything you need to develop enterprise-ready applications. But you do not have to base your application fully on the Spring framework. You are free to pick and choose the modules that suit your application and ignore the rest.

As you can see, all of Spring's modules are built on top of the core container. The container defines how beans are created, configured, and managed—more of the nuts-and-bolts of Spring. You will implicitly use these classes when you configure your application. But as a developer, you will most likely be interested in the other modules that leverage the services provided by the container. These modules will provide the frameworks with which you will build your application's services, such as AOP and persistence.

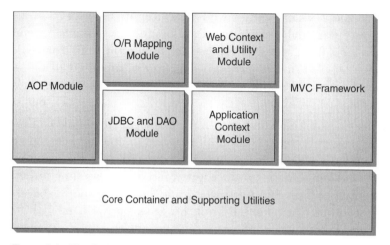

**Figure 1.1    The Spring framework is composed of several well-defined modules.**

### The core container

Spring's core container provides the fundamental functionality of the Spring framework. In this module you'll find Spring's `BeanFactory`, the heart of any Spring-based application. A `BeanFactory` is an implementation of the factory pattern that applies IoC to separate your application's configuration and dependency specifications from the actual application code.

We'll be discussing the core module (the center of any Spring application) throughout this book, starting in chapter 2, when we cover bean wiring using IoC.

### Application context module

The core module's `BeanFactory` makes Spring a container, but the context module is what makes it a framework. This module extends the concept of `Bean-Factory`, adding support for internationalization (I18N) messages, application life cycle events, and validation.

In addition, this module supplies many enterprise services such as e-mail, JNDI access, EJB integration, remoting, and scheduling. Also included is support for integration with templating frameworks such as Velocity and FreeMarker.

### Spring's AOP module

Spring provides rich support for aspect-oriented programming in its AOP module. This module serves as the basis for developing your own aspects for your Spring-enabled application.

To ensure interoperability between Spring and other AOP frameworks, much of Spring's AOP support is based on the API defined by the AOP Alliance. The

AOP Alliance is an open-source project whose goal is to promote adoption of AOP and interoperability among different AOP implementations by defining a common set of interfaces and components. You can find out more about the AOP Alliance by visiting their website at http://aopalliance.sourceforge.net.

The Spring AOP module also introduces metadata programming to Spring. Using Spring's metadata support, you are able to add annotations to your source code that instruct Spring on where and how to apply aspects.

### JDBC abstraction and the DAO module

Working with JDBC often results in a lot of boilerplate code that gets a connection, creates a statement, processes a result set, and then closes the connection. Spring's JDBC and Data Access Objects (DAO) module abstracts away the boilerplate code so that you can keep your database code clean and simple, and prevents problems that result from a failure to close database resources. This module also builds a layer of meaningful exceptions on top of the error messages given by several database servers. No more trying to decipher cryptic and proprietary SQL error messages!

In addition, this module uses Spring's AOP module to provide transaction management services for objects in a Spring application.

### Object/relational mapping integration module

For those who prefer using an object/relational mapping (ORM) tool over straight JDBC, Spring provides the ORM module. Spring doesn't attempt to implement its own ORM solution, but does provide hooks into several popular ORM frameworks, including Hibernate, JDO, and iBATIS SQL Maps. Spring's transaction management supports each of these ORM frameworks as well as JDBC.

### Spring's web module

The web context module builds on the application context module, providing a context that is appropriate for web-based applications. In addition, this module contains support for several web-oriented tasks such as transparently handling multipart requests for file uploads and programmatic binding of request parameters to your business objects. It also cotains integration support with Jakarta Struts.

### The Spring MVC framework

Spring comes with a full-featured Model/View/Controller (MVC) framework for building web applications. Although Spring can easily be integrated with other MVC frameworks, such as Struts, Spring's MVC framework uses IoC to provide for a clean separation of controller logic from business objects. It also allows you to declaratively bind request parameters to your business objects, What's more, Spring's MVC framework can take advantage of any of Spring's other services, such as I18N messaging and validation.

Now that you know what Spring is all about, let's jump right into writing Spring applications, starting with the simplest possible example that we could come up with.

## 1.3  *Spring jump start*

In the grand tradition of programming books, we'll start by showing you how Spring works with the proverbial "Hello World" example. Unlike the original Hello World program, however, our example will be modified a bit to demonstrate the basics of Spring.

> **NOTE**    To find out how to download Spring and plug it into your project's build routine, refer to appendix A.

Spring-enabled applications are like any Java application. They are made up of several classes, each performing a specific purpose within the application. What makes Spring-enabled applications different, however, is how these classes are configured and introduced to each other. Typically, a Spring application has an XML file that describes how to configure the classes, known as the Spring configuration file.

The first class that our Springified Hello World example needs is a service class whose purpose is to print the infamous greeting. Listing 1.1 shows Greeting-Service.java, an interface that defines the contract for our service class.

> **Listing 1.1    The `GreetingService` interface separates the service's implementation from its interface.**

```
package com.springinaction.chapter01.hello;

public interface GreetingService {
  public void sayGreeting();
}
```

GreetingServiceImpl.java (listing 1.2) implements the `GreetingService` interface. Although it's not necessary to hide the implementation behind an interface, it's highly recommended as a way to separate the implementation from its contract.

**Listing 1.2  GreetingServiceImpl.java: Responsible for printing the greeting**

```
package com.springinaction.chapter01.hello;

public class GreetingServiceImpl implements GreetingService {
  private String greeting;

  public GreetingServiceImpl() {}

  public GreetingServiceImpl(String greeting) {
    this.greeting = greeting;
  }

  public void sayGreeting() {
    System.out.println(greeting);
  }

  public void setGreeting(String greeting) {
    this.greeting = greeting;
  }
}
```

The GreetingServiceImpl class has a single property: the greeting property. This property is simply a String that holds the text that is the message that will be printed when the sayGreeting() method is called. You may have noticed that the greeting can be set in two different ways: by the constructor or by the property's setter method.

What's not apparent just yet is who will make the call to either the constructor or the setGreeting() method to set the property. As it turns out, we're going to let the Spring container set the greeting property. The Spring configuration file (hello.xml) in listing 1.3 tells the container how to configure the greeting service.

**Listing 1.3  Configuring Hello World in Spring**

```
<?xml version="1.0" encoding="UTF-8"?>
<!DOCTYPE beans PUBLIC "-//SPRING//DTD BEAN//EN"
    "http://www.springframework.org/dtd/spring-beans.dtd">

<beans>
  <bean id="greetingService"
      class="com.springinaction.chapter01.hello.GreetingServiceImpl">
    <property name="greeting">
      <value>Buenos Dias!</value>
    </property>
  </bean>
</beans>
```

The XML file in listing 1.3 declares an instance of a `GreetingServiceImpl` in the Spring container and configures its `greeting` property with a value of "Buenos Dias!" Let's dig into the details of this XML file a bit to understand how it works.

At the root of this simple XML file is the `<beans>` element, which is the root element of any Spring configuration file. The `<bean>` element is used to tell the Spring container about a class and how it should be configured. Here, the `id` attribute is used to name the bean `greetingService` and the `class` attribute specifies the bean's fully qualified class name.

Within the `<bean>` element, the `<property>` element is used to set a property, in this case the `greeting` property. By using `<property>`, we're telling the Spring container to call `setGreeting()` when setting the property.

The value of the greeting is defined within the `<value>` element. Here we've given the example a Spanish flair by choosing "Buenos Dias" instead of the traditional "Hello World."

The following snippet of code illustrates roughly what the container does when instantiating the greeting service based on the XML definition in listing 1.3:[2]

```
GreetingServiceImpl greetingService = new GreetingServiceImpl();
greetingService.setGreeting("Buenos Dias!");
```

Similarly, we may choose to have Spring set the `greeting` property through `GreetingServiceImpl`'s single argument constructor. For example:

```
<bean id="greetingService"
    class="com.springinaction.chapter01.hello.GreetingServiceImpl">
  <constructor-arg>
    <value>Buenos Dias!</value>
  </constructor-arg>
</bean>
```

The following code illustrates how the container will instantiate the greeting service when using the `<constructor-arg>` element:

```
GreetingServiceImpl greetingService =
    new GreetingServiceImpl("Buenos Dias");
```

The last piece of the puzzle is the class that loads the Spring container and uses it to retrieve the greeting service. Listing 1.4 shows this class.

---

[2] The container actually performs other activities involving the life cycle of the bean. But for illustrative purposes, these two lines are sufficient.

**Listing 1.4   The Hello World main class**

```
package com.springinaction.chapter01.hello;

import java.io.FileInputStream;
import org.springframework.beans.factory.BeanFactory;
import org.springframework.beans.factory.xml.XmlBeanFactory;

public class HelloApp {
  public static void main(String[] args) throws Exception {
    BeanFactory factory =
        new XmlBeanFactory(new FileInputStream("hello.xml"));

    GreetingService greetingService =
        (GreetingService) factory.getBean("greetingService");

    greetingService.sayGreeting();
  }
}
```

The `BeanFactory` class used here is the Spring container. After loading the hello.xml file into the container, the `main()` method calls the `getBean()` method on the `BeanFactory` to retrieve a reference to the greeting service. With this reference in hand, it finally calls the `sayGreeting()` method. When we run the Hello application, it prints (not surprisingly)

```
Buenos Dias!
```

This is about as simple a Spring-enabled application as we can come up with. But it does illustrate the basics of configuring and using a class in Spring. Unfortunately, it is perhaps too simple because it only illustrates how to configure a bean by injecting a `String` value into a property. The real power of Spring lies in how beans can be injected into other beans using IoC.

## 1.4   *Understanding inversion of control*

Inversion of control is at the heart of the Spring framework. It may sound a bit intimidating, conjuring up notions of a complex programming technique or design pattern. But as it turns out, IoC is not nearly as complex as it sounds. In fact, by applying IoC in your projects, you'll find that your code will become significantly simpler, easier to understand, and easier to test.

But what does "inversion of control" mean?

### 1.4.1 *Injecting dependencies*

In an article written in early 2004, Martin Fowler asked what aspect of control is being inverted. He concluded that it is the acquisition of dependent objects that is being inverted. Based on that revelation, he coined a better name for inversion of control: dependency injection.[3]

Any nontrivial application (pretty much anything more complex than Hello-World.java) is made up of two or more classes that collaborate with each other to perform some business logic. Traditionally, each object is responsible for obtaining its own references to the objects it collaborates with (its dependencies). As you'll see, this can lead to highly coupled and hard-to-test code.

Applying IoC, objects are given their dependencies at creation time by some external entity that coordinates each object in the system. That is, dependencies are *injected* into objects. So, IoC means an inversion of responsibility with regard to how an object obtains references to collaborating objects.

### 1.4.2 *IoC in action*

If you're like us, then you're probably anxious to see how this works in code. We aim to please, so without further delay…

Suppose that your company's crack marketing team culled together the results of their expert market analysis and research and determined that what your customers need is a knight. That is, they need a Java class that represents a knight. After probing them for requirements, you learn that what they specifically want is for you to implement a class that represents an Arthurian knight of the Round Table that embarks on brave and noble quests to find the Holy Grail.

This is an odd request, but you've become accustomed to the strange notions and whims of the marketing team. So, without hesitation, you fire up your favorite IDE and bang out the class in listing 1.5.

**Listing 1.5  KnightOfTheRoundTable.java**

```
package com.springinaction.chapter01.knight;

public class KnightOfTheRoundTable {
  private String name;
  private HolyGrailQuest quest;
```

---

[3] Although we agree that "dependency injection" is a more accurate name than "inversion of control," we're likely to use both terms interchangeably in this book.

```
public KnightOfTheRoundTable(String name) {
    this.name = name;
    quest = new HolyGrailQuest();      <— A knight gets its own quest
}

public HolyGrail embarkOnQuest()
        throws GrailNotFoundException {
    return quest.embark();
}
}
```

In listing 1.5 the knight is given a name as a parameter of its constructor. Its constructor sets the knight's quest by instantiating a `HolyGrailQuest`. The implementation of `HolyGrailQuest` is fairly trivial, as shown in listing 1.6.

**Listing 1.6    HolyGrailQuest.java**

```
package com.springinaction.chapter01.knight;
public class HolyGrailQuest {
    public HolyGrailQuest() {}

    public HolyGrail embark() throws GrailNotFoundException {
        HolyGrail grail = null;
        // Look for grail
        ...
        return grail;
    }
}
```

Satisfied with your work, you proudly check the code into version control. You want to show it to the marketing team, but deep down something doesn't feel right. You almost dismiss it as the burrito you had for lunch when you realize the problem: you haven't written any unit tests.

### Knightly testing

Unit testing is an important part of development. It not only ensures that each individual unit functions as expected, but it also serves to document each unit in the most accurate way possible. Seeking to rectify your failure to write unit tests, you put together the test case (listing 1.7) for your knight class.

**Listing 1.7    Testing the KnightOfTheRoundTable**

```
package com.springinaction.chapter01.knight;

import junit.framework.TestCase;

public class KnightOfTheRoundTableTest extends TestCase {

  public void testEmbarkOnQuest() {
    KnightOfTheRoundTable knight =
        new KnightOfTheRoundTable("Bedivere");

    try {
      HolyGrail grail = knight.embarkOnQuest();

      assertNotNull(grail);

      assertTrue(grail.isHoly());
    } catch (GrailNotFoundException e) {
      fail();
    }
  }
}
```

After writing this test case, you set out to write a test case for HolyGrailQuest. But before you even get started, you realize that the KnightOfTheRoundTableTest test case indirectly tests HolyGrailQuest. You also wonder if you are testing all contingencies. What would happen if HolyGrailQuest's embark() method returned null? Or what if it were to throw a GrailNotFoundException?

### Who's calling who?

The main problem so far with KnightOfTheRoundTable is with how it obtains a HolyGrailQuest. Whether it is instantiating a new HolyGrail instance or obtaining one via JNDI, each knight is responsible for getting its own quest (as shown in figure 1.2). Therefore, there is no way to test the knight class in isolation. As it

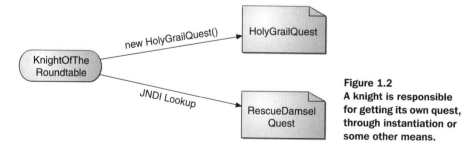

Figure 1.2
A knight is responsible for getting its own quest, through instantiation or some other means.

stands, every time you test `KnightOfTheRoundTable`, you will also indirectly test `HolyGrailQuest`.

What's more, you have no way of telling `HolyGrailQuest` to behave differently (e.g., return `null` or throw a `GrailNotFoundException`) for different tests. What would help is if you could create a mock implementation of `HolyGrailQuest` that lets you decide how it behaves. But even if you were to create a mock implementation, `KnightOfTheRoundTable` still retrieves its own `HolyGrailQuest`, meaning you would have to make a change to `KnightOfTheRoundTable` to retrieve the mock quest for testing purposes (and then change it back for production).

### Decoupling with interfaces

The problem, in a word, is *coupling*. At this point, `KnightOfTheRoundTable` is statically coupled to `HolyGrailQuest`. They're handcuffed together in such a way that you can't have a `KnightOfTheRoundTable` without also having a `HolyGrailQuest`.

Coupling is a two-headed beast. On one hand, tightly coupled code is difficult to test, difficult to reuse, difficult to understand, and typically exhibits "whack-a-mole" bugs (i.e., fixing one bug results in the creation of one or more new bugs). On the other hand, completely uncoupled code doesn't do anything. In order to do anything useful, classes need to know about each other somehow. Coupling is necessary, but it should be managed very carefully.

A common technique used to reduce coupling is to hide implementation details behind interfaces so that the actual implementation class can be swapped out without impacting the client class. For example, suppose you were to create a `Quest` interface:

```
package com.springinaction.chapter01.knight;

public interface Quest {
  public abstract Object embark() throws QuestException;
}
```

Then, you change `HolyGrailQuest` to implement this interface. Also, notice that embark now returns an Object and throws a QuestException.

```
package com.springinaction.chapter01.knight;

public class HolyGrailQuest implements Quest {
  public HolyGrailQuest() {}

  public Object embark() throws QuestException {
    // Do whatever it means to embark on a quest
    return new HolyGrail();
  }
}
```

Also, the following method must also change in KnightOfTheRoundTable to be compatible with these Quest types:

```
private Quest quest;
...
public Object embarkOnQuest() throws QuestException {
  return quest.embark();
}
```

Likewise, you could also have KnightOfTheRoundTable implement the following Knight interface:

```
public interface Knight {
  public Object embarkOnQuest() throws QuestException;
}
```

Hiding your class's implementation behind interfaces is certainly a step in the right direction. But where many developers fall short is in how they retrieve a Quest instance. For example, consider this possible change to KnightOfTheRoundTable:

```
public class KnightOfTheRoundTable implements Knight {

  private Quest quest;
  ...

  public KnightOfTheRoundTable(String name) {
    quest = new HolyGrailQuest();
    ...
  }

  public Object embarkOnQuest() throws QuestException {
    return quest.embark();
  }
}
```

Here the KnightOfTheRoundTable class embarks on a quest through the Quest interface. But, the knight still retrieves a specific type of Quest (here a Holy-GrailQuest). This isn't much better than before. A KnightOfTheRoundTable is stuck going only on quests for the Holy Grail and no other types of quest.

### Giving and taking

The question you should be asking at this point is whether or not a knight should be responsible for obtaining a quest. Or, should a knight be given a quest to embark upon?

Consider the following change to KnightOfTheRoundTable:

```
public class KnightOfTheRoundTable implements Knight {
  private Quest quest;
  ...

  public KnightOfTheRoundTable(String name) {
    ...
  }

  public HolyGrail embarkOnQuest() throws QuestException {
    ...
    return quest.embark();
  }

  public void setQuest(Quest quest) {
    this.quest = quest;
  }
}
```

Notice the difference? Compare figure 1.3 with figure 1.2 to see the difference in how a knight obtains its quest. Now the knight is *given* a quest instead of retrieving one itself. KnightOfTheRoundTable is no longer responsible for retrieving its own quests. And because it only knows about a quest through the Quest interface, you could give a knight any implementation of Quest you want. In a production system, maybe you would give it a HolyGrailQuest, but in a test case you would give it a mock implementation of Quest.

In a nutshell, that is what inversion of control is all about: the responsibility of coordinating collaboration between dependent objects is transferred away from the objects themselves. And that's where lightweight container frameworks, such as Spring, come into play.

### Assigning a quest to a knight

Now that you've written your KnightOfTheRoundTable class to be given any arbitrary Quest object, how can you specify which Quest it should be given?

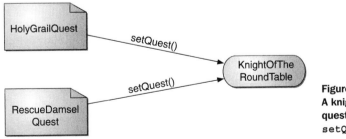

**Figure 1.3**
**A knight is given a quest through its** setQuest() **method.**

The act of creating associations between application components is referred to as *wiring*. In Spring, there are many ways to wire components together, but the most common approach is via XML. Listing 1.8 shows a simple Spring configuration file, knight.xml, that gives a quest (specifically, a `HolyGrailQuest`) to a `Knight-OfTheRoundTable`.

---

**Listing 1.8   Wiring a quest to a knight in knight.xml**

```xml
<?xml version="1.0" encoding="UTF-8"?>
<!DOCTYPE beans PUBLIC "-//SPRING//DTD BEAN//EN"
    "http://www.springframework.org/dtd/spring-beans.dtd">

<beans>                                                    Define a quest
  <bean id="quest"
      class="com.springinaction.chapter01.knight.HolyGrailQuest"/>

  <bean id="knight"
      class="com.springinaction.chapter01.knight.KnightOfTheRoundTable">
                                                           Define a knight
    <constructor-arg>
      <value>Bedivere</value>      <--  Set the knight's name
    </constructor-arg>
    <property name="quest">
      <ref bean="quest"/>          <--  Give the knight a quest
    </property>

  </bean>
</beans>
```

---

This is just a simple approach to wiring beans. Don't worry too much about the details of it right now. In chapter 2 we'll explain more about what is going on here, as well as show you even more ways you can wire your beans in Spring.

Now that we've declared the relationship between a knight and a quest, we need to load up the XML file and kick off the application.

### Seeing it work

In a Spring application, a `BeanFactory` loads the bean definitions and wires the beans together. Because the beans in the knight example are declared in an XML file, an `XmlBeanFactory` is the appropriate factory for this example. The `main()` method in listing 1.9 uses an `XmlBeanFactory` to load `knight.xml` and to get a reference to the "knight" object.

**Listing 1.9  Running the knight example**

```
import org.springframework.beans.factory.BeanFactory;
import org.springframework.beans.factory.xml.XmlBeanFactory;

public class KnightApp {
  public static void main(String[] args) throws Exception {
    BeanFactory factory =
        new XmlBeanFactory(new FileInputStream("knight.xml"));

    KnightOfTheRoundTable knight =
        (KnightOfTheRoundTable) factory.getBean("knight");

    knight.embarkOnQuest();
  }
}
```

Load the XML beans file

Retrieve a knight from the factory

⟵ **Send knight on its quest**

Once the application has a reference to the `KnightOfTheRoundTable` object, it simply calls the `embarkOnQuest()` method to kick off the knight's adventure. Notice that this class knows nothing about the quest the knight will take. Again, the only thing that knows which type of quest will be given to the knight is the `knight.xml` file.

It's been a lot of fun sending knights on quests using inversion of control, but now let's see how you can use IoC in your real-world enterprise applications.[4]

### 1.4.3  IoC in enterprise applications

Suppose that you've been tasked with writing an online shopping application. Included in the application is an `OrderServiceBean`, implemented as a stateless session bean. Now you want to have a class that creates an `Order` object from user input (likely an HTML form) and call the `createOrder()` method on your `OrderServiceBean`, as shown in listing 1.10.

**Listing 1.10  Creating an order using EJB**

```
...
private OrderService orderService;

public void doRequest(HttpServletRequest request) {
  Order order = createOrder(request);
  OrderService orderService = getOrderService();
  orderService.createOrder(order);
}
```

---

[4] This assumes that your real-world applications do not involve knights and quests. In the event that your current project does involve knights and quests, you may disregard the next section.

```
private OrderService getOrderService() throws CreateException {    Get
   if (orderService == null) {                                     the JNDI
      Context initial = new InitialContext();                      Context
      Context myEnv = (Context) initial.lookup("java:comp/env");
      Object ref = myEnv.lookup("ejb/OrderServiceHome");    Retrieve an EJB
      OrderServiceHome home = (OrderServiceHome)            Home from JNDI
            PortableRemoteObject.narrow(ref, OrderService.class);
      orderService = home.create();       Get the Remote object
   }                                      from the Home object
   return orderService;
}
...
```

Notice that it took five lines of code *just* to get your `OrderService` object. Now imagine having to do this everywhere you need an `OrderService` object. Now imagine you have ten other EJBs in your application. That is a lot of code! But duplicating this code everywhere would be ridiculous, so a `ServiceLocator` is typically used instead. A `ServiceLocator` acts as a central point for obtaining and caching EJB-Home references:

```
private OrderService getOrderService() {
   OrderServiceHome home =
      ServiceLocator.locate(OrderServiceHome);
   OrderService orderService = home.create();
}
```

While this removes the need to duplicate the lookup code everywhere in the application, one problem still remains: we always have to explicitly look up our services in our code.

Now let's see how this would be implemented in Spring:

```
private OrderService orderService;

public void doRequest(HttpServletRequest request) {
   Order order = createOrder(request);
   orderService.createOrder(order);
}

public void setOrderService(OrderService orderService) {
   this.orderService = orderService;
}
```

No lookup code! The reference to `OrderService` is given to our class by the Spring container through the `setOrderService()` method. With Spring, we never have to trouble ourselves with fetching our dependencies. Instead, our code can focus on the task at hand.

But inversion of control is only one of the techniques that Spring offers to JavaBeans. There's another side to Spring that makes it a viable framework for enterprise development. Let's take a quick look at Spring's support for aspect-oriented programming.

## 1.5 *Applying aspect-oriented programming*

While inversion of control makes it possible to tie software components together loosely, aspect-oriented programming enables you to capture functionality that is used throughout your application in reusable components.

### 1.5.1 *Introducing AOP*

Aspect-oriented programming is often defined as a programming technique that promotes separation of concerns within a software system. Systems are composed of several components, each responsible for a specific piece of functionality. Often, however, these components also carry additional responsibility beyond their core functionality. System services such as logging, transaction management, and security often find their way into components whose core responsibility is something else. These system services are commonly referred to as *cross-cutting concerns* because they tend to cut across multiple components in a system.

By spreading these concerns across multiple components, you introduce two levels of complexity to your code:

- The code that implements the systemwide concerns is duplicated across multiple components. This means that if you need to change how those concerns work, you'll need to visit multiple components. Even if you've abstracted the concern to a separate module so that the impact to your components is a single method call, that single method call is duplicated in multiple places.

- Your components are littered with code that isn't aligned with their core functionality. A method to add an entry to an address book should only be concerned with how to add the address and not with whether it is secure or transactional.

Figure 1.4 illustrates this complexity. The business objects on the left are too intimately involved with the system services. Not only does each object know that it is being logged, secured, and involved in a transactional context, but also each object is responsible for performing those services for itself.

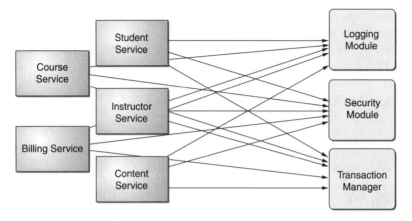

**Figure 1.4   Calls to system-wide concerns such as logging and security are often scattered about in modules where those concerns are not their primary concern.**

AOP makes it possible to modularize these services and then apply them declaratively to the components that they should affect. This results in components that are more cohesive and that focus on their own specific concerns, completely ignorant of any system services that may be involved.

As shown in figure 1.5, it may help to think of aspects as blankets that cover many components of an application. At its core, an application is comprised of modules that implement the business functionality. With AOP, you can then cover

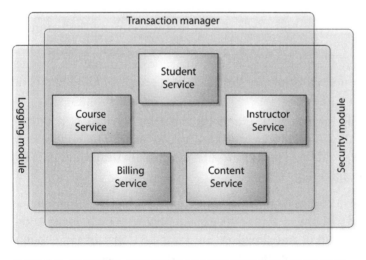

**Figure 1.5   Using AOP, systemwide concerns blanket the components that they impact.**

your core application with layers of functionality. These layers can declaratively be applied throughout your application in a flexible manner without your core application even knowing they exist. This is a very powerful concept.

### 1.5.2 AOP in action

Let's revisit our knight example to see how AOP works with Spring. Suppose that after showing your progress to marketing, they came back with an additional requirement. In this new requirement, a minstrel must accompany each knight, chronicling the actions and deeds of the knight in song.[5]

To start, you create a `Minstrel` class:

```
package com.springinaction.chapter01.knight;

import org.apache.log4j.Logger;

public class Minstrel {
  Logger song = Logger.getLogger(KnightOfTheRoundTable.class);
  public Minstrel() {}

  public void compose(String name, String message) {
    song.debug("Fa la la! Brave " + name + " did " + message + "!");
  }
}
```

In keeping with the IoC way of doing things, you alter `KnightOfTheRoundTable` to be given an instance of `Minstrel`:

```
public class KnightOfTheRoundTable {
...
  private Minstrel minstrel;
  public void setMinstrel(Minstrel minstrel) {
    this.minstrel = minstrel;
  }

...

  public HolyGrail embarkOnQuest() throws QuestException {
    minstrel.compose(name, "embark on a quest");
    return quest.embark();
  }
}
```

---

[5] Think of minstrels as musically inclined logging systems of medieval times.

There's only one problem. As it is, each knight must stop and tell the minstrel to compose a song before the knight can continue with his quest (as in figure 1.6). Ideally a minstrel would automatically compose songs without being explicitly told to do so. A knight shouldn't know (or really even care) that their deeds are being

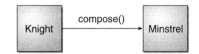

**Figure 1.6   Without AOP, a knight must tell his minstrel to compose songs.**

written into song. After all, you can't have your knight being late for quests because of a lazy minstrel.

In short, the services of a minstrel transcend the duties of a knight. Another way of stating this is to say that a minstrel's services (song writing) are orthogonal to a knight's duties (embarking on quests). Therefore, it makes sense to implement a minstrel as an aspect that adds its song-writing services to a knight. Probably the simplest way to create an aspect-oriented minstrel is to change the minstrel class to be an implementation of MethodBeforeAdvice, as shown in listing 1.11.

**Listing 1.11   An aspect-oriented minstrel**

```
package com.springinaction.chapter01.knight;

import java.lang.reflect.Method;
import org.apache.log4j.Logger;
import org.springframework.aop.MethodBeforeAdvice;

public class MinstrelAdvice
    implements MethodBeforeAdvice {
  public MinstrelAdvice() {}

  public void before(Method method, Object[] args,         Advise method
    Object target) throws Throwable {                       before call

    Knight knight = (Knight) target;

    Logger song =
      Logger.getLogger(target.getClass());                  Get the advised
                                                            class's logger
    song.debug("Brave " + knight.getName() +
      " did " + method.getName());
  }
}
```

As a subclass of `MethodBefore-Advice`, the `MinstrelAdvice` class will intercept calls to the target object's methods, giving the `before()` method an opportunity to do something before the target method gets

**Figure 1.7**
**An aspect-oriented minstrel covers a knight, chronicling the knight's activities without the knight's knowledge of the minstrel.**

called. In this case, `MinstrelAdvice` naively assumes that the target object is a `KnightOfTheRoundTable` and uses log4j as its mechanism for chronicling the knight's actions. As illustrated in figure 1.7, the knight needn't worry about how he is being sung about or even that the minstrel is writing the song.

The knight no longer needs to tell this new aspect-oriented minstrel to sing about the knight's activities. In fact, the knight doesn't even need to know that the minstrel exists. But how does `MinstrelAdvice` know that it is supposed to intercept calls to a `Knight`?

### Weaving the aspect

Notice that there's nothing about `MinstrelAdvice` that tells the `Minstrel` what object it should sing about. Instead, a `Minstrel`'s services are applied to a `Knight` declaratively. Applying advice to an object is known as *weaving*. In Spring, aspects are woven into objects in the Spring XML file, much in the same way that beans are wired together. Listing 1.12 shows the new knight.xml, modified to weave `MinstrelAdvice` into a `KnightOfTheRoundTable`.

> **Listing 1.12   Weaving MinstrelAdvice into a knight**

```xml
<?xml version="1.0" encoding="UTF-8"?>
<!DOCTYPE beans PUBLIC "-//SPRING//DTD BEAN//EN"
    "http://www.springframework.org/dtd/spring-beans.dtd">

<beans>
  <bean id="quest"
      class="com.springinaction.chapter01.knight.HolyGrailQuest"/>

  <bean id="knightTarget"
      class="com.springinaction.chapter01.knight.KnightOfTheRoundTable">
    <constructor-arg><value>Bedivere</value></constructor-arg>

    <property name="quest"><ref bean="quest"/></property>
  </bean>

  <bean id="minstrel"
      class="com.springinaction.chapter01.knight.MinstrelAdvice"/>
```

**Create a minstrel instance**

```
<bean id="knight"
    class="org.springframework.aop.framework.ProxyFactoryBean">
  <property name="proxyInterfaces">
    <list>
      <value>com.springinaction.chapter01.knight.Knight</value>    ◁─┐
    </list>                                                    Intercept calls
  </property>                                                  to the knight
  <property name="interceptorNames">
    <list>
      <value>minstrel</value>    ◁─ Let minstrel handle call first
    </list>
  </property>
  <property name="target"><ref bean="knightTarget"/></property>    ◁─┐
</bean>                                                         Then let the knight
</beans>                                                        handle the call
```

Notice that the id of `KnightOfTheRoundTable` has changed from `knight` to `knightTarget` and now `knight` points to a Spring class called `ProxyFactoryBean`. What this means is that when the container is asked for a `knight` object, it will return an object that intercepts calls to the target `KnightOfTheRoundTable` object, giving `MinstrelAdvice` a shot at handling method calls first. Once `Minstrel-Advice` is finished, control is returned to `KnightOfTheRoundTable` to perform the knightly task.

Don't worry if this doesn't make sense yet. We'll explain Spring's AOP support in more detail in chapter 3. For now, suffice it to say that even though a knight's every move is being observed by a minstrel, the knight's activities are in no way hampered because of the minstrel's presence.

But Spring's AOP can be used for even more practical things than composing ageless sonnets about knights. As you'll see, AOP can be used to provide enterprise services such as declarative transactions and security.

### 1.5.3 AOP in the enterprise

Enterprise applications often require certain services such as security and transactional support. One way of applying these services is to code support for them directly into the classes that use them. For example, to handle transactions, you may place the following snippet throughout your code:

```
UserTransaction transaction = null;
try {
  transaction = ... {retrieve transaction}

  transaction.begin();

  ... do stuff...
```

```
    transaction.commit();
} catch (Exception e) {
    if (transaction != null) transaction.rollback();
}
```

The problem with handling transactions this way is that you may repeat the same transaction handling code several times—once for each time you need a transactional context. What's more, your application code is responsible for more than its core functionality.

EJB simplifies things by making it possible to declare these services and their policies in the EJB deployment descriptor. With EJB it is possible to write components that are ignorant of the fact that they are in a transactional context or being secured and then declare the transactional and security policies for those components in the EJB deployment descriptor. For example, to ensure that a method is transactional in EJB, you simply place the following in the deployment descriptor:

```
<container-transaction>
  <method>
    <ejb-name>Foo</ejb-name>
    <method-intf>Remote</method-inf>
    <method-name>doSomething</method-name>
  </method>
  <trans-attribute>RequiresNew</trans-attribute>
</container-transaction>
```

EJB has hung its hat on how it simplifies infrastructure logic such as transactions and security. But as we discussed in the introduction to this chapter, EJB has complicated matters in other ways.

Although Spring's AOP support can be used to separate cross-cutting concerns from your application's core logic, its primary job is as the basis for Spring's support for declarative transactions. Spring comes with several aspects that make it possible to declare transaction policies for JavaBeans. And the Acegi Security System (another open-source project associated with Spring) provides declarative security to JavaBeans. As with all Spring configuration, the transactional and security policies are prescribed in a Spring configuration file.

**NOTE**    Although the Spring framework comes packed with several frameworks and support for several enterprise-level services, it does not come with much to assist you with security. The Acegi security system uses Spring's AOP support as the foundation of a framework that adds declarative security to Spring-enabled applications. You will learn more about Acegi in chapter 11.

For example, suppose that instead of a knight your application handles student registration for training courses. Perhaps you have a bean called StudentService-Impl that implements the following interface:

```
public StudentService {
  public void registerForCourse(Student student, Course course);
}
```

This bean may be registered in the Spring bean XML file as follows:

```
<bean id="studentServiceTarget"
    class="com.springinaction.training.StudentServiceImpl"/>
```

StudentService's registerForCourse() method should perform the following actions:

1   Verify that there is an available seat in the course.

2   Add the student to the course's roster.

3   Decrement the course's available seat count by 1.

4   Notify the student by e-mail of a successful registration.

All of these actions should happen atomically. If anything goes bad, then all should be rolled back as if nothing happened. Now imagine if instead of a minstrel providing musical logging to this class, you were to apply one of Spring's transaction manager aspects. Applying transactional support to StudentService-Impl might be as simple as adding the lines shown in listing 1.13 to the bean XML file.

**Listing 1.13   Declaring StudentService to be transactional**

```
<bean id="transactionManager" class=
    "org.springframework.orm.hibernate.HibernateTransactionManager">
  <property name="sessionFactory">          Declare transaction manager
    <ref bean="sessionFactory"/>
  </property>
</bean>

<bean id="studentService" class=
"org.springframework.transaction.interceptor.
    TransactionProxyFactoryBean">

  <property name="target">
    <ref bean="studentServiceTarget"/>     <— Apply transactions
  </property>

  <property name="transactionAttributes">
    <props>
```

```
        <prop key="registerForCourse">                        Declare
            PROPAGATION_REQUIRES_NEW,ISOLATION_DEFAULT         transaction
        </prop>
      </props>
  </property>

  <property name="transactionManager">
      <ref bean="transactionManager"/>      <—  Inject transaction
  </property>
</bean>
```

Here we make use of Spring's `TransactionProxyFactoryBean`. This is a convenience proxy class that allows us to intercept method calls to an existing class and apply a transaction context. In this case we are creating a proxy to our `Student-ServiceImpl` class and applying a transaction to the `registerForCourse()` method. We are also using `HibernateTransactionManager`, the implementation of a transaction manager you would most likely use if your application's persistence layer is based on Hibernate.

Although this example leaves a lot to be explained, it should give you a glimpse of how Spring's AOP support can provide plain-vanilla JavaBeans with declarative services such as transactions and security. We'll dive into more details of Spring's declarative transaction support in chapter 5.

## 1.6 Spring alternatives

Whew! After that whirlwind introduction of Spring, you have a pretty good idea of what it can do. Now you are probably chomping at the bit to get down into the details so you can see how you can use Spring for your projects. But before we do that, we need to cover what else is out there in the world of J2EE frameworks.

### 1.6.1 Comparing Spring to EJB

Because Spring comes with rich support for enterprise-level services, it is positioned as a viable alternative to EJB. But EJB, as opposed to Spring, is a well-established platform. Therefore, the decision to choose one over the other is not one to be taken lightly. Also, you do not necessarily have to choose only Spring *or* EJB. Spring can be used to support existing EJBs as well, a topic that will be discussed in detail in chapter 7. With that in mind, it is important to know what these two have in common, what sets them apart, and the implications of choosing either.

### EJB is a standard

Before we delve into the technical comparisons between Spring and EJB, there is an important distinction that we need to make. EJB is a *specification* defined by the JCP. Being a standard has some significant implications:

- *Wide industry support*—There is a whole host of vendors that are supporting this technology, including industry heavyweights Sun, IBM, Oracle, and BEA. This means that EJB will be supported and actively developed for many years to come. This is comforting to many companies because they feel that by selecting EJB as their J2EE framework, they are going with a safe choice.

- *Wide adoption*—EJB as a technology is deployed in thousands of companies around the world. As a result, EJB is in the tool bag of most J2EE developers. This means that if a developer knows EJB, they are more likely to find a job. At the same time, companies know that if they adopt EJB, there is an abundance of developers who are capable of developing their applications.

- *Toolability*—The EJB specification is a fixed target, making it easy for vendors to produce tools to help developers create EJB applications more quickly and easily. Dozens of applications are out there that do just that, giving developers a wide range of EJB tool options.

### Spring and EJB common ground

As J2EE containers, both Spring and EJB offer the developer powerful features for developing applications. Table 1.1 lists the major features of both frameworks and how the implementations compare.

**Table 1.1   Spring and EJB feature comparison**

| Feature | EJB | Spring |
|---|---|---|
| Transaction management | ■ Must use a JTA transaction manager.<br>■ Supports transactions that span remote method calls. | ■ Supports multiple transaction environments through its `PlatformTransactionManager` interface, including JTA, Hibernate, JDO, and JDBC.<br>■ Does not natively support distributed transactions—it must be used with a JTA transaction manager. |

*continued on next page*

**Table 1.1  Spring and EJB feature comparison** *(continued)*

| Feature | EJB | Spring |
|---|---|---|
| Declarative transaction support | ■ Can define transactions declaratively through the deployment descriptor.<br>■ Can define transaction behavior per method or per class by using the wildcard character *.<br>■ Cannot declaratively define rollback behavior—this must be done programmatically. | ■ Can define transactions declaratively through the Spring configuration file or through class metadata.<br>■ Can define which methods to apply transaction behavior explicitly or by using regular expressions.<br>■ Can declaratively define rollback behavior per method and per exception type. |
| Persistence | ■ Supports programmatic bean-managed persistence and declarative container managed persistence. | ■ Provides a framework for integrating with several persistence technologies, including JDBC, Hibernate, JDO, and iBATIS. |
| Declarative security | ■ Supports declarative security through users and roles. The management and implementation of users and roles is container specific.<br>■ Declarative security is configured in the deployment descriptor. | ■ No security implementation out-of-the box.<br>■ Acegi, an open source security framework built on top of Spring, provides declarative security through the Spring configuration file or class metadata. |
| Distributed computing | ■ Provides container-managed remote method calls. | ■ Provides proxying for remote calls via RMI, JAX-RPC, and web services. |

For *most* J2EE projects, the technology requirements will be met by either Spring or EJB. There are exceptions—your application may need to be able to support remote transaction calls. If that is the case, EJB may seem like the the way to go. Even then, Spring integrates with a Java Transaction API (JTA) transaction providers, so even this scenario is cut-and-dried. But if you are looking for a J2EE framework that provides declarative transaction management and a flexible persistence engine, Spring is a great choice. It lets you choose the features you want without the added complexities of EJB.

### The complexities of EJB

So what are the complexities of EJB? Why is there such a shift toward lightweight containers? Here are a few of the complexities of EJB that turn off many developers:

■ *Writing an EJB is overly complicated*—To write an EJB, you have to touch *at least* four files: the business interface, the home interface, the bean implementation, and the deployment descriptor. Other classes are likely to be involved as well, such as utility classes and value objects. That's quite a proliferation of files when all you are looking for is to add some container services to your implementation class. Conversely, Spring lets you define your implementation as a POJO and wire in any additional services needs through injection or AOP.

- *EJB is invasive*—This goes hand in hand with the previous point. In order to use the services provided by the EJB container, you *must* use the `javax.ejb` interfaces. This binds your component code to the EJB technology, making it difficult (if not possible) to use the component outside of an EJB container. With Spring, components are typically not required to implement, extend, or use any Spring-specific classes or interfaces, making it possible to reuse the components anywhere, even in the absence of Spring.

- *Entity EJBs fall short*—Entity EJBs are not as flexible or feature-rich as other ORM tools. Spring recognizes there are some great ORM tools out there, such as Hibernate and JDO, and provides a rich framework for integrating them into your application. And since an entity bean could represent a remote object, the Value Object pattern was introduced to pass data to and from the EJB tier in a course-grained object. But value objects lead to code duplication—you write each persistent property twice: once in the entity bean and once in your value object. Using Spring together with Hibernate or another ORM framework, your application's entity objects are not directly coupled with their persistence mechanism. This makes them light enough to be passed across application tiers.

Again, in most J2EE applications, the features provided by EJB may not be worth the compromises you will have to make. Spring provides nearly all of the services provided by an EJB container while allowing you to develop much simpler code. In other words, for a great number of J2EE applications, Spring makes sense. And now that you know the differences between Spring and EJB, you should have a good idea which framework fits your needs best.

## 1.6.2 *Considering other lightweight containers*

Spring is not the only lightweight container available. In the last few years, more and more Java developers have been seeking an alternative to EJB. As a result, several lightweight containers have been developed with different methods for achieving inversion of control.

Table 1.2 lists the types of IoC. These were first described with the nondescript "Type X" convention, but have since shifted to more meaningful names. We will always refer to them by the name.

**Table 1.2**  **Inversion of Control types**

| Type | Name | Description |
|------|------|-------------|
| Type 1 | Interface Dependent | Beans must implement specific interfaces to have their dependencies managed by the container. |
| Type 2 | Setter Injection | Dependencies and properties are configured through a bean's setter methods. |
| Type 3 | Constructor Injection | Dependencies and properties are configured through the bean's constructor. |

Although the focus of this book is on Spring, it may be interesting to see how these other containers stack up to Spring. Let's take a quick look at some of the other lightweight containers, starting with PicoContainer.

### PicoContainer

PicoContainer is a minimal lightweight container that provides IoC in the form of constructor and setter injection (although it favors constructor injection). We use the word *minimal* to describe PicoContainer because, with it small size (~50k), it has a sparse API. PicoContainer provides the bare essentials to create an IoC container and expects to be extended by other subprojects and applications. By itself, you can only assemble components programmatically through PicoContainer's API. Since this would be a cumbersome approach for anything but the most trivial applications, there is a subproject named NanoContainer that provides support for configuring PicoContainer through XML and various scripting languages. However, at the time of this writing, NanoContainer does not appear to be production-ready.

One of the limitations of PicoContainer is that it allows only one instance of any particular type to be present in its registry. This is could lead to problems if you need more than one instance of the same class, just configured differently. For example, you may want to have two instances of a `javax.sql.DataSource` in your application, each configured for a different database. This would not be possible in PicoContainer.

Also, you should know that PicoContainer is only a container. It does not offer any of the other powerful features that Spring has, such as AOP and third-party framework integration.

### HiveMind

HiveMind is a relatively new IoC container. Like PicoContainer, it focuses on wiring and configuring services with support for both constructor and setter injection. HiveMind allows you to define your configuration in an XML file or in HiveMind's Simple Data Language.

HiveMind also provides an AOP-like feature with its *Interceptors*. This allows you to wrap a service with Interceptors to provide additional functionality. However, this is not nearly as powerful as Spring's AOP framework.

Finally, like PicoContainer, HiveMind is *only* a container. It provides a framework for managing components but offers no integration with other technologies.

### Avalon

Avalon was one of the first IoC containers developed. As with many early entrants into a market, some mistakes were made in its design. Mainly, Avalon provides interface-dependent IoC. In other words, in order for your objects to be managed by the Avalon container, they must implement Avalon-specific interfaces. This makes Avalon an invasive framework; you must change *your* code in order for it to be usable by the container. This is not desirable because it couples your code to a particular framework for even the simplest of cases.

We believe that if Avalon does not adopt a more flexible means of managing components, it will eventually fade out of the lightweight container market; there are other ways of achieving the same results with much less rigidity.

### 1.6.3 Web frameworks

Spring comes with its own very capable web framework. It provides features found in most other web frameworks, such as automatic form data binding and validation, multipart request handling, and support for multiple view technologies. We'll talk more about Spring's web framework in chapter 8. But for now, let's take a look at how Spring measures up to some popular web frameworks

### Struts

Struts can probably be considered the de facto standard for web MVC frameworks. In has been around for several years, was the first "Model 2" framework to gain wide adoption and has been used in thousands of Java projects. As a result, there is an abundance of resources available on Struts.

The Struts class you will use the most is the `Action` class. It is important to note that this is a class and not an interface. This means all your classes that handle input will need to subclass `Action`. This in contrast to Spring, which provides a `Controller` interface that you can implement.

Another important difference is how each handles form input. Typically, when a user is submitting a web form, the incoming data maps to an object in your application. In order to handle form submissions, Struts requires you have `ActionForm` classes to handle the incoming parameters. This means you need to create a class solely for mapping form submissions to your domain objects. Spring allows you to map form submissions directly to an object without the need for an intermediary, leading to eaiser maintenance.

Also, Struts comes with built-in support for declarative form validation. This means you can define rules for validating incoming form data in XML. This keeps validation logic out of your code, where it can be cumbersome and messy. Spring does not come with declarative validation. This does not mean you cannot use this within Spring; you will just have to integrate this functionality yourself using a validation framework, such as the Jakarta Commons Validator.

If you already have an investment in Struts or you just prefer it as your web framework, Spring has a package devoted to integrating Struts with Spring.

Furthermore, Struts is a mature framework with a significant following in the Java development community. Much has been written about Struts, including Ted Husted's *Struts in Action* (Manning, 2002).

### WebWork

WebWork is another MVC framework. Like Struts and Spring, it supports multiple view technologies. One of the biggest differentiators for WebWork is that it adds another layer of abstraction for handling web requests. The core interface for handling requests is the `Action` interface, which has one method: `execute()`. Notice that this interface is not tied to the web layer in any way. The WebWork designers went out of their way to make the `Action` interface unaware that it could be used in a web context. This is good or bad, depending on your perspective. Most of the time it *will* be used in a web application, so hiding this fact through abstraction does not buy you much.

A feature that WebWork provides that Spring does not (at least, not explicitly) is *action chaining*. This allows you to map a logical request to a series of `Actions`. This means you can create several `Action` objects that all perform discrete tasks and chain them together to execute a single web request.

### Tapestry

Tapestry is another open source web framework that is quite different than ones mentioned previously. Tapestry does not provide a framework around the request-response servlet mechanism, like Struts or WebWork. Instead, it is a framework for creating web applications from reusable components (if you are familiar with Apple's WebObjects, Tapestry was inspired by its design).

The idea behind Tapestry is to relieve the developer from thinking about Session attributes and URLs, and instead think of web applications in terms of components and methods. Tapestry takes on the other responsibilities, such as managing user state and mapping URLs to methods and objects.

Tapestry provides a view mechanism as well. That is, Tapestry is not a framework for using JSPs—it is an alternative to JSPs. Much of Tapestry's power lies in its custom tags that are embedded with HTML documents and used by the Tapestry framework. Needless to say, Tapestry provides a unique web application framework. To learn more about Tapestry, take a look at *Tapestry in Action* (Manning, 2004).

### 1.6.4 *Persistence frameworks*

There really isn't a direct comparison between Spring and any persistence framework. As mentioned earlier, Spring does not contain any built-in persistence framework. Instead, Spring's developers recognized there were already several good frameworks for this and felt no need to reinvent the wheel. They created an ORM module that integrates these frameworks with rest of Spring. Spring provides integration points for Hibernate, JDO, OJB, and iBATIS.

Spring also provides a very rich framework for writing JDBC. JDBC requires a lot of boilerplate code (getting resources, executing statements, iterating though query results, exception handling, cleaning up resources). Spring's JDBC module handles this boilerplate, allowing you to focus on writing queries and handling the results.

Spring's JDBC and ORM frameworks work within Spring's transaction management framework. This means you can use declarative transactions with just about any persistence framework you choose.

## 1.7 *Summary*

You should now have a pretty good idea of what Spring brings to the table. Spring aims to make J2EE development easier, and central to this is its inversion of control. This enables you to develop enterprise applications using simple Java objects that collaborate with each other through interfaces. These beans will be wired together at runtime by the Spring container. It lets you maintain loosely coupled code with minimal cost.

On top of Spring's inversion control, Spring's container also offers AOP. This allows you place code that would otherwise be scattered throughout you application in one place—an aspect. When your beans are wired together, these aspects can be woven in at runtime, giving these beans new behavior.

Staying true to aiding enterprise development, Spring offers integration to several persistence technologies. Whether you persist data using JDBC, Hibernate, or JDO, Spring's DAO frameworks ease your development by providing a consistent model for error handling and resource management for each of these persistence frameworks.

Complementing the persistence integration is Spring's transaction support. Through AOP, you can add declarative transaction support to your application without EJB. Spring also supports a variety of transaction scenarios, including integration with JTA transactions for distributed transactions.

Filling out its support for the middle tier, Spring offers integration with other various J2EE services, such as mail, EJBs, web services, and JNDI. With its inversion of control, Spring can easily configure these services and provide your application objects with simpler interfaces.

To help with the presentation tier, Spring supports multiple view technologies. This includes web presentation technologies like Velocity and JSP as well as support for creating Microsoft Excel spreadsheets and Adobe Acrobat Portable Document Format (PDF) files. And on top of the presentation, Spring comes with a built-in MVC framework. This offers an alternative to other web frameworks like Struts and WebWork and more easily integrates with all of the Spring services.

So without further ado, let's move on to chapter 2 to learn more about exactly how Spring's core container works.

# Wiring beans

2

**This chapter covers**

- Wiring bean properties with XML
- Comparing manual wiring and autowiring
- Managing bean life-cycle events
- Publishing and handling application events

Have you ever stuck around after a movie long enough to watch the credits? It's incredible how many different people it takes to pull together a major motion picture. There are the obvious participants: the actors, the scriptwriters, the directors, and the producers. Then there are the not-so-obvious: the musicians, the special effects crew, and the art directors. And that's not to mention the key grip, the sound mixer, the costumers, the makeup artists, the stunt coordinators, the publicists, the first assistant to the cameraman, the second assistant to the cameraman, the set designers, the gaffer, and (perhaps most importantly) the caterers.

Now imagine what your favorite movie would have been like had none of these people talked to each other. Let's say that they all showed up at the studio and started doing their own thing without any coordination. If the director keeps to himself and doesn't say "roll 'em," the cameraman won't start shooting. It probably wouldn't matter anyway, because the lead actress would still be in her trailer and the lighting wouldn't work because the gaffer would not have been hired.

Maybe you've seen a movie where it looks like this is what happened. But most movies (the good ones anyway) are the product of hundreds of people working together toward the common goal of making a blockbuster movie.

In this respect, a great piece of software isn't much different. Any nontrivial application is made up of several components that must work together to meet a business goal. These components must be aware of each other and talk to each other to get their job done. In an online shopping application, for instance, an order manager component may need to work with a product manager component and a credit card authorization component. All of these will likely need to work with a data access component to read and write from a database.

But as we saw in chapter 1, the traditional approach to creating associations between application objects (via construction or lookup) leads to complicated code that is difficult to reuse and unit-test. In the best case, these components do more work than they should, and in the worst case, they are highly coupled to each other, making them hard to reuse and hard to test.

In Spring, components are not responsible for managing their associations with other components. Instead, they are given references to collaborating components by the container. The act of creating these associations between application components is known as *wiring*. And that is what we are going to cover in this chapter—wiring. You will discover that Spring's wiring goes far beyond establishing an association between two objects. You will learn how you can also use Spring to configure all of your beans' properties, externalize deployment configurations in separate files, and manage the life cycle of your beans. Boy, there sure is a lot to this wiring business.

## 2.1  *Containing your beans*

As we promised, we will cover Spring's wiring in depth. But before we go down that road, it is important to understand what is controlling the wiring…and the configuring…and the life-cycle management. Whenever you configure any beans for the Spring framework, you are giving instructions to the Spring container. Understanding the container helps you understand how your beans will be managed.

The container is at the core of the Spring framework. Spring's container uses inversion of control (IoC) to manage the components that make up an application. This includes creating associations between collaborating components. As such, these objects are cleaner and easier to understand, they support reuse, and they are easy to unit-test.

There is no single Spring container. Spring actually comes with two distinct types of containers: Bean factories (defined by the `org.springframework.beans.factory.BeanFactory` interface) are the simplest of containers, providing basic support for dependency injection. Application contexts (defined by the `org.springframework.context.ApplicationContext` interface) build on the notion of a bean factory by providing application framework services such as the ability to resolve textual messages from a properties file and the ability to publish application events to interested event listeners.

> **NOTE**    Although Spring uses the words "bean" and "JavaBean" liberally when referring to application components, this does not mean that a Spring component must follow the JavaBeans specification to the letter. A Spring component can be any type of POJO (plain-old Java object). In this book, assume the loose definition of JavaBean, which is synonymous with POJO.

Beyond these two basic types of containers, Spring comes with several implementations of `BeanFactory` and `ApplicationContext`. Unless there is a need to specifically state which type of container is being used, we'll refer to both bean factories and application contexts synonymously with the word "container."

Let's start our exploration of Spring containers with the most basic of the Spring containers: the `BeanFactory`.

### 2.1.1  *Introducing the BeanFactory*

As its name implies, a bean factory is an implementation of the factory design pattern. That is, it is a class whose responsibility is to create and dispense beans.

But unlike many implementations of the factory pattern, which often dole out a single type of object, a bean factory is a general-purpose factory, creating and dispensing many types of beans.

But there's more to a bean factory than simply instantiation and delivery of application objects. Because a bean factory knows about many objects within an application, it is able to create associations between collaborating objects as they are instantiated. This removes the burden of configuration from the bean itself and the bean's client. As a result, when a bean factory hands out objects, those objects are fully configured, are aware of their collaborating objects, and are ready to use. What's more, a bean factory also takes part in the life cycle of a bean, making calls to custom initialization and destruction methods, if those methods are defined.

There are several implementations of `BeanFactory` in Spring. But the most useful one is `org.springframework.beans.factory.xml.XmlBeanFactory`, which loads its beans based on the definitions contained in an XML file.

To create an `XmlBeanFactory`, pass a `java.io.InputStream` to the constructor. The `InputStream` will provide the XML to the factory. For example, the following code snippet uses a `java.io.FileInputStream` to provide a bean definition XML file to `XmlBeanFactory`:

```
BeanFactory factory =
    new XmlBeanFactory(new FileInputStream("beans.xml"));
```

This simple line of code tells the bean factory to read the bean definitions from the XML file. But the bean factory doesn't instantiate the beans just yet. Beans are "lazily" loaded into bean factories, meaning that while the bean factory will immediately load the bean definitions (the description of beans and their properties), the beans themselves will not be instantiated until they are needed.

To retrieve a bean from a `BeanFactory`, simply call the `getBean()` method, passing the name of the bean you want to retrieve:

```
MyBean myBean = (MyBean) factory.getBean("myBean");
```

When `getBean()` is called, the factory will instantiate the bean and begin setting the bean's properties using dependency injection. Thus begins the life of a bean within the Spring container. We'll examine the life cycle of a bean in section 2.1.3, but first let's look at the other Spring container, the application context.

## 2.1.2 *Working with an application context*

A bean factory is fine for simple applications, but to take advantage of the full power of the Spring framework, you may want to move up to Spring's more advanced container, the application context.

On the surface, an `ApplicationContext` is much the same as a `BeanFactory`. Both load bean definitions, wire beans together, and dispense beans upon request. But an `ApplicationContext` offers much more:

- Application contexts provide a means for resolving text messages, including support for internationalization (I18N) of those messages.

- Application contexts provide a generic way to load file resources, such as images.

- Application contexts can publish events to beans that are registered as listeners.

Because of the additional functionality it provides, an `ApplicationContext` is preferred over a `BeanFactory` in nearly all applications. The only times you might consider using a `BeanFactory` are in circumstances where resources are scarce, such as a mobile device. We will be using an `ApplicationContext` throughout this book.

Among the many implementations of `ApplicationContext` are three that are commonly used:

- `ClassPathXmlApplicationContext`—Loads a context definition from an XML file located in the class path, treating context definition files as class path resources.

- `FileSystemXmlApplicationContext`—Loads a context definition from an XML file in the filesystem.

- `XmlWebApplicationContext`—Loads context definitions from an XML file contained within a web application.

We'll talk more about `XmlWebApplicationContext` in chapter 8 when we discuss web-based Spring applications. For now, let's simply load the application context from the file system using `FileSystemXmlApplicationContext`, or from the class path using `ClassPathXmlApplicationContext`.

Loading an application context from the file system or from the class path is very similar to how you load beans into a bean factory. For example, here's how you'd load a `FileSystemXmlApplicationContext`:

```
ApplicationContext context =
    new FileSystemXmlApplicationContext("c:/foo.xml");
```

Similarly, you can load an application context from within the application's class path using `ClassPathXmlApplicationContext`:

```
ApplicationContext context =
    new ClassPathXmlApplicationContext("foo.xml");
```

The difference between these uses of `FileSystemXmlApplicationContext` and `ClassPathXmlApplicationContext` is that `FileSystemXmlApplicationContext` will look for foo.xml in a specific location, whereas `ClassPathXmlApplicationContext` will look for foo.xml anywhere in the class path.

In either case, you can retrieve a bean from an `ApplicationContext` just as you would from a `BeanFactory`: by using the `getBean()` method. This is no surprise because the `ApplicationContext` interface extends the `BeanFactory` interface.

Aside from the additional functionality offered by application contexts, another big difference between an application context and a bean factory is how singleton beans are loaded. A bean factory lazily loads all beans, deferring bean creation until the `getBean()` method is called. An application context is a bit smarter and preloads all singleton beans upon context startup. By preloading singleton beans, you ensure that they will be ready to use when needed—your application won't have to wait for them to be created.

Now that you know the basics of how to configure a Spring container, let's take a closer look at your bean's existence within the container.

### 2.1.3 *A bean's life*

In a traditional Java application, the life cycle of a bean is fairly simple. Java's new keyword is used to instantiate the bean (or perhaps it is deserialized) and it's ready to use. In contrast, the life cycle of a bean within a Spring container is a bit more elaborate. It is important to understand the life cycle of a Spring bean, because you may want to take advantage of some of the opportunities that Spring offers to customize how a bean is created.

Figure 2.1 shows the startup life cycle of a typical bean as it is loaded into a `BeanFactory` container.

As you can see, a bean factory performs several setup steps before a bean is ready to use. The following list explains each of these steps in more detail:

1 The container finds the bean's definition and instantiates the bean.

2 Using dependency injection, Spring populates all of the properties as specified in the bean definition.

3 If the bean implements the `BeanNameAware` interface, the factory calls `setBeanName()` passing the bean's ID.

4  If the bean implements the `BeanFactoryAware` interface, the factory calls `setBeanFactory()`, passing an instance of itself.

5  If there are any `BeanPostProcessors` associated with the bean, their `post-ProcessBeforeInitialization()` methods will be called.

6  If an `init-method` is specified for the bean, it will be called.

7  Finally, if there are any `BeanPostProcessors` associated with the bean, their `postProcessAfterInitialization()` methods will be called.

At this point, the bean is ready to be used by an application and will remain in the bean factory until it is no longer needed. It is removed from the bean factory in two ways.

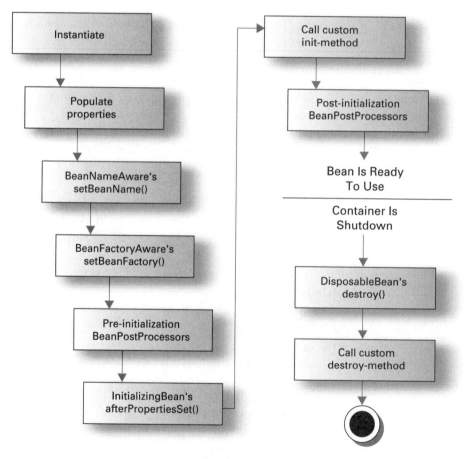

Figure 2.1   The life cycle of a bean within a Spring bean factory container

1 If the bean implements the `DisposableBean` interface, the `destroy()` method is called.

2 If a custom `destroy-method` is specified, it will be called.

The life cycle of a bean within a Spring application context differs only slightly from that of a bean within a bean factory, as shown in figure 2.2.

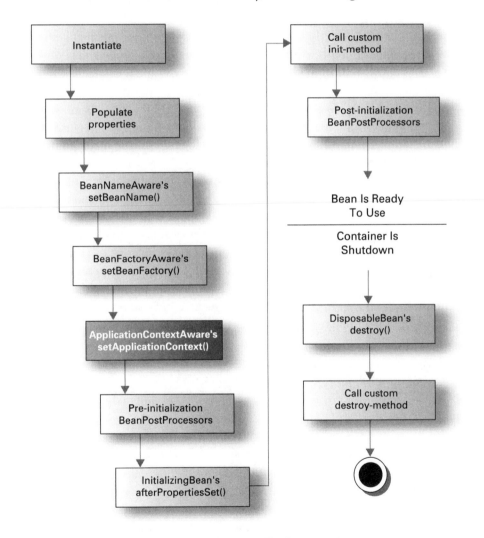

**Figure 2.2  The life cycle of a bean in a Spring application context**

The only difference here is that if the bean implements the `ApplicationContext-Aware` interface, the `setApplicationContext()` method is called.

Regardless of which container you use, you'll need to tell Spring about your application's beans and how they are related. Let's take a look at how to place beans within the Spring container using XML.

## 2.2 *Basic wiring*

Piecing together beans within the Spring container is known as *wiring*. When wiring beans, you tell the container what beans are needed and how the container should use dependency injection to tie them together.

Despite its name, basic wiring doesn't require that you have an electrician's license. You only need to know a little XML. But before we get into the details of wiring beans using XML, let's set the stage for the sample application you'll build while learning how to work with Spring.

Suppose that you're contracted by Spring Training, Inc., a technical training organization. Spring Training wants you to build an application that enables students to register for courses online.

To get started, let's build the service layer of the application. Figure 2.3 shows the objects that make up this portion of the Spring Training application.

There are two service components in the service layer: a student service and a course service. The student service handles all student-related matters, while the course service is responsible for course-related functionality. These services are defined by interfaces. The `StudentService` interface is as follows:

```
public interface StudentService {
  public Student getStudent(String id);
  public void createStudent(Student student);
  public java.util.Set getCompletedCourses(Student student);
}
```

And the `CourseService` looks like this:

```
public interface CourseService {
  public Course getCourse(String id);
  public void createCourse(Course course);
  public java.util.Set getAllCourses();
  public void enrollStudentInCourse(Course course,
      Student student) throws CourseException;
}
```

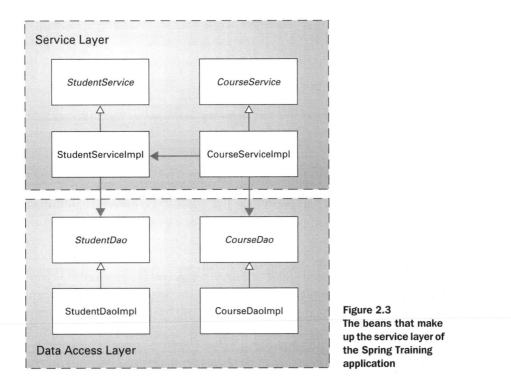

**Figure 2.3**
**The beans that make up the service layer of the Spring Training application**

StudentServiceImpl (listing 2.1) is the implementation of the StudentService interface.

**Listing 2.1  A student service handles student-related functionality**

```
package com.springinaction.service.training;

public class StudentServiceImpl implements StudentService {
  private StudentDao studentDao;

  public StudentServiceImpl(StudentDao dao) {      ⟵ Inject by constructor...
    studentDao = dao;
  }

  public void setStudentDao(StudentDao dao) {      ⟵ Or by setter
    studentDao = dao;
  }

  public Student getStudent(String id) {
    return studentDao.findById(id);
  }
```

```
public void createStudent(Student student) {
  studentDao.create(student);
}

public java.util.Set getCompletedCourses(Student student) {
  return studentDao.getCompletedCourses(student);
}
}
```

StudentServiceImpl delegates much of its responsibility to a StudentDao. A StudentDao handles interaction with the database to read and write student information. The actual implementation of the StudentDao object isn't important right now (we'll flesh it out in more detail in chapter 4 when we talk about working with databases). For the time being, just assume an implementation of StudentDao named StudentDaoImpl.

Notice that there are two ways that a StudentServiceImpl can be given a reference to its StudentDao: either via its constructor or via the setStudentDao() method.

CourseServiceImpl (listing 2.2), the implementation of CourseService, is slightly more interesting than StudentServiceImpl. For the most part, CourseServiceImpl delegates responsibility to a CourseDao object. But the enrollStudentInCourse() method needs to be smarter. Before a student may enroll in a course, he must have completed all of the prerequisite courses.

### Listing 2.2   CourseServiceImpl.java

```
package com.springinaction.service.training;

import java.util.Iterator;
import java.util.Set;

public class CourseServiceImpl implements CourseService {
  private CourseDao courseDao;
  private StudentService studentService;
  private int maxStudents;

  public CourseServiceImpl(CourseDao dao) {          ⟵  Set CourseDao via
    this.courseDao = dao;                                 constructor injection
  }

  public void setStudentService(StudentService service) {
    this.studentService = service;
  }
```

```
      public void setMaxStudents(int maxStudents) {
        this.maxStudents = maxStudents;
      }

      pubic int getMaxStudents() {
        return maxStudents;
      }

      public Course getCourse(String id) {
        return courseDao.findById(id);
      }

      public void createCourse(Course course) {
        courseDao.create(course);
      }

      public void enrollStudentInCourse(Course course,
          Student student) throws CourseException {

        if(course.getStudents().size() >= maxStudents) {
          throw new CourseException("Course is full");
        }

        enforcePrerequisites(course, student);

        course.getStudents().add(student);

        courseDao.update(course);
      }

      private void enforcePrerequisites(Course course,
          Student student) throws CourseException {

        Set completed =
            studentService.getCompletedCourses(student);
        Set prereqs = course.getPrerequisites();

        for(Iterator iter = prereqs.iterator(); iter.hasNext();) {
          if(!completed.contains(iter.next())) {
            throw new CourseException("Prerequisites are not met.");
          }
        }
      }
    }
```

As with StudentServiceImpl, CourseServiceImpl receives its CourseDao reference through its constructor. Again let's just assume an implementation of CourseDao, for now called CourseDaoImpl.

The `enrollStudentInCourse()` method makes a call to `enforcePrerequi-sites()` prior to adding the student to the course. If the student hasn't met the prerequisites, `enforcePrerequisites()` will throw a `CourseException`, which is summarily rethrown by `enrollStudentInCourse()`.

Notice that `enforcePrerequisites()` uses a reference to a `StudentService` implementation to retrieve all of a student's completed courses. This means that in addition to `CourseDao`, `CourseServiceImpl` collaborates with `StudentService` to ensure that the business requirement of prerequisites is met. `CourseServiceImpl` receives its reference to a `StudentService` via the `setStudentService()` method, unlike `CourseDao`, which is set through the constructor. The motivation behind this decision is that the `courseDao` property is used by most of `CourseServiceImpl`, so you shouldn't be able to create a `CourseServiceImpl` instance without setting the `courseDao` property. But only the `enforcePrerequisites()` method requires a reference to a `StudentService`, so it can be optionally set if needed.

Now that the stage has been set, let's see how we can wire our components into our application through a Spring wiring file ("spring-training.xml").

### 2.2.1 *Wiring with XML*

In theory, bean wiring can be driven from virtually any configuration source, including properties files, a relational database, or even an LDAP directory. But in practice, XML is the configuration source of choice for most Spring-enabled applications and is the way we'll wire beans throughout this book.

Several Spring containers support wiring through XML, including

- `XmlBeanFactory`—A simple `BeanFactory` that loads a context definition file by way of a `java.io.InputStream`.

- `ClassPathXmlApplicationContext`—An application context that loads the context definition file from the class path.

- `FileSystemXmlApplicationContext`—An application context that loads the context definition file from the file system.

- `XmlWebApplicationContext`—An application context used with Spring-enabled web applications that loads the context definition file from a web application context. We'll look at this container in chapter 8 when we talk about using Spring with web applications.

All of these XML-oriented containers have their beans defined by a remarkably simple XML file. At the root of the context definition file is the `<beans>` element. This `<beans>` has one or more `<bean>` subelements. Each `<bean>` element (not surprisingly) defines a JavaBean (or any Java object, actually) to be configured within the Spring container.

For example, the XML file in listing 2.3 shows a trivial context definition file for Spring.

---

**Listing 2.3  Configuring beans within a Spring container**

```xml
<?xml version="1.0" encoding="UTF-8"?>

<!DOCTYPE beans PUBLIC "-//SPRING//DTD BEAN//EN"
    "http://www.springframework.org/dtd/spring-beans.dtd">

<beans>    <—  The root element
  <bean id="foo"
      class="com.springinaction.Foo"/>        Bean
                                               instances
  <bean id="bar"
      class="com.springinaction.Bar"/>
</beans>
```

---

This simple bean wiring XML file configures two beans, named `foo` and `bar`, in the Spring container. Let's take a closer look at how the `<bean>` element defines a bean within an application context.

### 2.2.2  *Adding a bean*

The most basic configuration for any bean in Spring involves the bean's ID and its fully qualified class name. Adding a bean to the Spring container is as simple as adding a `<bean>` element to the container's XML file, similar to this:

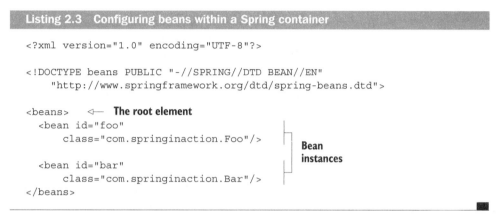

For example, let's start a bean definition XML file for the Spring Training application by adding definitions of the implementations of `CourseDao` and `Student-Dao`, as shown in listing 2.4.

**Listing 2.4    Wiring the DAO beans into the container**

```xml
<?xml version="1.0" encoding="UTF-8"?>

<!DOCTYPE beans PUBLIC "-//SPRING//DTD BEAN//EN"
    "http://www.springframework.org/dtd/spring-beans.dtd">

<beans>                                                Register the courseDao bean
  <bean id="courseDao"
      class="com.springinaction.training.service.CourseDaoImpl"/>
                                                       Register the studentDao bean
    <bean id="studentDao"
      class="com.springinaction.training.service.StudentDaoImpl"/>
</beans>
```

As far as you know, `CourseDaoImpl` and `StudentDaoImpl` have no collaborators or other properties to be configured (that's why they're dummy implementations), so the lines in listing 2.4 are sufficient to tell Spring how to load them into the application context. And as simple as this configuration may be, it still serves as an illustration of how beans are uniquely defined in a Spring container.

### *Prototyping vs. singleton*

By default, all Spring beans are singletons. When the container dispenses a bean (either as the result of a call to `getBean()` or through wiring), it will always give the exact same instance of the bean. But what if you want the context to return a unique instance each time it is asked for a specific bean? What if you need a unique instance of a bean each time it is retrieved from the container?

In this case, you would want to define a prototype bean. Defining a prototype means that instead of defining a single bean, you define a blueprint. Beans are then created based on this blueprint.

The `singleton` property of `<bean>` tells the context whether or not a bean is to be defined as a singleton. By default it is set to `true`, but setting it to `false` results in a bean being defined as a prototype:

```xml
<bean id="foo"
    class="com.springinaction.Foo"
    singleton="false" />
```

The bean is a prototype

Prototyped beans are useful when you want the container to give a unique instance of a bean each time it is asked for, but you still want to configure one or more properties of that bean through Spring. For example, let's change the `studentDao` bean's definition so that a new instance is created every time it is needed:

```
<bean id="studentDao"
    class="com.springinaction.training.service.StudentDaoImpl"
    singleton="false"/>
```

Bear in mind that a new instance of a prototype bean will be created each time `getBean()` is invoked with the bean's name. This could be bad if your bean uses a limited resource such as database or network connections. At a minimum, you may incur a small performance hit each time a new instance is created. Consider these implications of setting `singleton` to `false` and avoid doing so unless it is absolutely necessary.

Configuring a bean as a prototype may be useful if you'd like to use the Spring context as a factory for new instances of domain objects, such as `Student` or `Course` objects. As prototype beans, you would be able to easily configure the objects at the factory level (like any other bean), while still guaranteeing that the factory would dispense a unique instance each time you ask for a domain object.

### Initialization and destruction

When a bean is instantiated, it may be necessary to perform some initialization to get it into a usable state. Likewise, when the bean is no longer needed and is removed from the container, some cleanup may be in order. For that reason, Spring can hook into two life-cycle methods of each of your beans to perform this setup and teardown.

Declaring a custom `init-method` in your bean's definition specifies a method that is to be called on the bean immediately upon instantiation. Similarly, a custom `destroy-method` specifies a method that is called just before a bean is removed from the container:

```
<bean id="foo"
    class="com.springinaction.Foo"
    init-method="setup"  destroy-method="teardown"/>
```

Call setup() when bean is loaded into the container          Call teardown() when bean is unloaded from the container

A typical example of this would be a connection pooling bean:

```
public class MyConnectionPool {
  ...
  public void initialize() {
```

```
    // initialize connection pool
  }

  public void close() {
    // release connections
  }
  ...
}
```

The bean definition would appear as follows:

```
<bean id="connectionPool"
    class="com.springinaction.chapter02.MyConnectionPool"
    init-method="initialize" destroy-method="close"/>
```

Defined in this way, the `initialize()` method will be called immediately after `MyConnectionPool` is instantiated, allowing it the opportunity to initialize the pool. Just before the bean is removed from the container and discarded, the `close()` method will release the database connections.

Spring also provides two interfaces that perform the same functionality: `InitializingBean` and `DisposableBean`. The `InitializingBean` interface provides one method, `afterPropertiesSet()`, that will be called once all of a bean's properties have been set. Similarly, `DisposableBean`'s one method, `destroy()`, will be called when the bean is removed from the container.

The one benefit of this approach is that the Spring container automatically detects beans that implement these interfaces and invokes their methods without any configuration on your part. However, by implementing these interfaces, you tie your beans to Spring's API. Because of this, you should rely on the `init-method` and `destroy-method` bean definitions to initialize and destroy your beans whenever you can. The only scenario where you might favor Spring's interfaces is when you are developing a framework bean that is to be used specifically within Spring's container.

Now you've seen how to configure beans individually within the Spring container. But to paraphrase John Donne, no bean is an island. For a bean to be of any use in an application, it will have to get to know other beans and gain some identity. Let's see how to set bean properties in Spring, starting with setter injection.

### 2.2.3 *Injecting dependencies via setter methods*

Setter injection is not something you need to get every winter to keep from getting the flu. Instead, it is a technique for populating a bean's properties based on standard naming conventions. The JavaBean specification formalized the already well-practiced idiom of having matching "set" and "get" methods that are used to set and retrieve a bean property's value. For instance, a `maxStudents` property may have the following getter and setter methods:

```
public void setMaxStudents(int maxStudents) {
  this.maxStudents = maxStudents;
}

pubic int getMaxStudents() {
  return maxStudents;
}
```

Since bean properties have these methods, why not let Spring use them to configure the bean? Setter injection does just that, and the `<property>` subelement of `<bean>` is the means to inject into a bean's properties through their setter methods. Within the `<property>` element, you can define what property you are configuring and what value you are injecting into this property. And as you will see, you are able to inject just about anything, from primitive types to collections to even other beans within your application.

### Simple bean configuration

It's quite common for a bean to have properties that are of simple types like `int` and `String`. In fact, in the Spring Training application we have a few beans that have such properties. Using the `<value>` subelement of `<property>` you can set properties that are of primitive types, such as `int` or `float`, or are typed as `java.lang.String` in the following way:

```
<bean id="foo"
    class="com.springinaction.Foo"
  <property name="name"><value>Foo McFoo</value>
  </property>
</bean>
```

Set the name property by calling
setName("Foo McFoo")

For example, the `courseService` bean can be configured to limit the number of students enrolled in a course via its `maxStudents` property. To limit the number of students enrolled in any course to no more than 30, change the definition of the `courseService` bean to the following:

```
<bean id="courseService" ...>
  <property name="maxStudents">
    <value>30</value>
  </property>
</bean>
```

Here you are setting an `int` property, but you could set any primitive or `String` property in the same way. Spring will automatically determine the type of the property being set and convert the value appropriately.

At this point you know how to inject simple properties into your beans. But what about properties that are of more complex types, such as other objects? Let's see how you can play matchmaker and introduce your beans to each other.

### Referencing other beans

Believe it or not, socializing your beans doesn't involve sending them on blind dates with your single bean friends or to bean single bars (you just never know who a bean will hook up with there). Instead, beans get acquainted within your application in the same way they are defined—in the container's XML file.

Just as we did previously, we use the `<property>` element to set properties that reference other beans. The `<ref>` subelement of `<property>` lets us do just that:

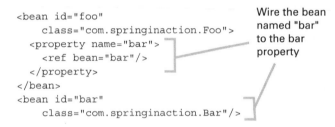

```
<bean id="foo"
    class="com.springinaction.Foo">
  <property name="bar">
    <ref bean="bar"/>
  </property>
</bean>
<bean id="bar"
    class="com.springinaction.Bar"/>
```

Wire the bean
named "bar"
to the bar
property

For example, recall that the `CourseServiceImpl` class uses a reference to a `StudentService` bean when ensuring that a student has met the prerequisites for a course. This reference is wired through the `setStudentService()` method on `CourseServiceImpl` and is declared in XML by changing the `courseService` bean definition to

```
<bean id="courseService"
    class="com.springinaction.service.training.CourseServiceImpl">
  <property name="studentService">
    <ref bean="studentService"/>
  </property>
</bean>
```

The container gives the `courseService` bean a `StudentService` bean (through `setStudentService()`), thereby freeing `CourseServiceImpl` from having to look up a `StudentService` bean on its own.

### Inner beans

Another lesser-used means of wiring bean references is to embed a `<bean>` element directly in the `<property>` element. For example, the `studentService` property of the `courseService` bean could be wired as follows:

```
<bean id="courseService"
    class="com.springinaction.service.training.CourseServiceImpl">
  <property name="studentService">
    <bean
        class="com.springinaction.service.training.StudentServiceImpl"/>
  </property>
</bean>
```

The drawback of wiring a bean reference in this manner is that you can't reuse the instance of `StudentServiceImpl` anywhere else—it is an instance created specifically for use by the `courseService` bean. You may also find that using inner-bean definitions impacts the readability of the XML. On the other hand, this could be beneficial if we don't want an actual bean instance to be accessible without a wrapper bean. For example, if we are creating an AOP proxy, we may not want the target bean to be accessible in our `BeanFactory`. In this case, configuring the proxy's target using an inner bean would achieve this goal.

Now let's take a look at the case where we need to inject not just one object, but a collection of objects.

### Wiring collections

What if you have a property that is a `List` of values? Or a `Set` of bean references? No problem. Spring supports many types of collections as bean properties, as shown in table 2.1.

**Table 2.1  Collections supported by Spring's wiring**

| XML | Type |
| --- | --- |
| `<list>` | `java.awt.List, arrays` |
| `<set>` | `java.awt.Set` |
| `<map>` | `java.awt.Map` |
| `<props>` | `java.awt.Properties` |

Wiring collections isn't much different than wiring singular properties. Instead of using `<value>` or `<ref>` elements, use one of the elements from table 2.1.

### Wiring lists and arrays

Whether you have an array property or a property that's of the type `java.util.List`, you will use the `<list>` element to wire the property in the wiring XML file:

Wire a list
property

```
<property name="barList">
  <list>
    <value>bar1</value>
    <ref bean="bar2"/>
  </list>
</property>
```

List elements can
be any type of element,
including <value>, <ref>, or
even another <list>.

In chapter 4, you'll see how to use Hibernate to persist the objects in the Spring training application. But as a demonstration of how to wire `List` properties using `<list>`, we'll give you a sneak peek now. When using Hibernate with Spring, you'll wire a `LocalSessionFactoryBean` into the container. The `LocalSession-FactoryBean` has a `mappingResources` property that takes a `List` of `Strings` containing the names of Hibernate mapping files. Here's a snippet of XML that we'll introduce to the bean wiring file when we get around to talking about Hibernate:

```
<bean id="sessionFactory" class=
    "org.springframework.orm.hibernate.LocalSessionFactoryBean">
  <property name="mappingResources">
    <list>
      <value>/com/springinaction/training/model/Course.hbm.xml</value>
      <value>/com/springinaction/training/model/Student.hbm.xml</value>
    </list>
  </property>
  ...
</bean>
```

Although the previous snippet wires a `List` of `String` values, you are not limited to using only `<value>`s as entries in a `<list>`. You may use any element that is valid when wiring a singular property, including `<value>`, `<ref>`, or even another collection such as `<list>`. The only limitation is in what your bean's expectations are; you can't wire in a `List` of `Foo`s when your bean is expecting a `List` of `Bar`s.

### Wiring sets

Lists are great, but what if your bean has a `java.util.Set` property to guarantee uniqueness in the collection? That's what the `<set>` element is for:

Wire a set property

Sets, like Lists, can take any type of element

```
<property name="barSet">
  <set>
    <value>bar1</value>
    <ref bean="bar2"/>
  </set>
</property>
```

Notice that you use `<set>` exactly the way you would use `<list>`. The only difference is in how it is wired to a bean property. Where `<list>` wires values to a `java.util.List` or an array, `<set>` wires values to a `java.util.Set`.

### Wiring maps

You can wire `java.util.Map` collections in Spring using the `<map>` element. Map collections are somewhat different than `Lists` and `Sets`. Each entry in a `Map` is made up of a key and a value defined by the `<entry>` element:

The map's keys

The map's entries

```
<property name="barMap">
  <map>
    <entry key="key1">
      <value>bar1</value>
    </entry>
    <entry key="key2">
      <ref bean="bar2"/>
    </entry>
  </map>
</property>
```

The value of a map `<entry>`, just as with `<list>` and `<set>`, can be any valid property element. Again, this includes `<value>`, `<ref>`, `<list>`, or even another `<map>`.

When wiring an `<entry>`, notice that the `key` attribute will also be a `String`. This is a slight limitation over the full functionality of `java.util.Map`, which allows any object to be the key of a map entry. However, this limitation doesn't often present a problem, as `Maps` are typically keyed with `Strings` anyway.

### Wiring properties

A `java.util.Properties` collection is the final type of collection that can be wired in Spring. It is wired with the `<props>` element. Each element of a properties collection is wired with the `<prop>` element.

In many ways, `<props>` works similarly to `<map>`. The big difference is that the value of a `<prop>` entry is always a `String`, so there is no need to use the `<value>` element to differentiate between `String` values and non-`String` values:

```
<property name="barProps">
  <props>                                      The property key
    <prop key="key1">bar1</prop>
    <prop key="key2">bar2</prop>
  </props>
</property>

  The property value
```

You'll use <props> several places in Spring, including when you create URL mappings within Spring's Model/View/Controller (MVC) framework. We'll talk more about the details of URL mappings in chapter 8. But for now, here's an example showing how the <props> element is used to declare URL mappings:

```
<property name="mappings">
  <props>
    <prop key="/viewCourseDetails.htm">viewCourseController</prop>
  </props>
</property>
```

### Setting null values

So far we have talked about configuring the properties of our beans with primitive types, collections, or other beans within our application. But what if in order to satisfy a requirement you need to explicitly set a property to null? This is really just another kind of wiring, only in this case we are wiring null instead of a value or bean.

To set a property to null, you simply use the <null/> element. For example, to set a foo property to null, you'd use this:

```
<property name="foo"><null/><property>
```

Why would you ever need to do this? If you do not explicitly wire a property in Spring, you may assume that the property is left null. But that's not always true. For one thing, the bean itself may set the property to some default value. Or, if you're using autowiring, the property may be implicitly wired. In either case, you may need to use <null/> to explicitly set the property to null.

### An alternative to setter injection

Setter injection is a straightforward way to configure and wire bean properties. But one shortcoming of setter injection is that assumes that all mutable properties are available via a setter method. You may not want all of your beans to behave this way. For one thing, when this type of bean is instantiated, none of its properties have been set and it could possibly be in an invalid state. Second, you may want certain properties to be set just once—when the bean is created—and become immutable after that point. This is complicated, if not impossible, when exposing all properties through setters.

An alternative is to design your beans where some properties are set via constructors. This is a particularly good design if some properties are required *and* immutable, such as a DAO's DataSource. So if you choose to design some of your beans this way or are working with beans that are already designed this way, you still need a way to configure these objects through Spring. You're in luck.

Spring does offer another form of dependency injection: constructor injection. Let's see how to use constructor injection to set the minimal properties for a bean.

### 2.2.4  *Injecting dependencies via constructor*

In Java, a class can have one or more constructors, each taking a unique set of arguments. With that in mind, you can program your bean classes with constructors that take enough arguments to fully define the bean at instantiation. Using constructors this way, it is impossible to create a bean without it being ready to use.

Whereas the shortcoming of setter injection is that it is not clear which properties are required and which are optional, constructor injection's main strength is in the strong dependency contract imposed by constructors. That is, constructors make it virtually impossible to instantiate a bean that is not fully defined and ready to use.

With setter injection, we defined the property we were injecting with the <property> subelement. Constructor injection is similar, except in this case you'll use the <constructor-arg> subelement of <bean> to specify arguments to pass to a bean's constructor at instantiation. One difference between these two is that the <constructor-arg> does not contain a name attribute that the <property> subelement did (we will discuss why in a moment). An example of constructor injection configuration is demonstrated here:

```
<bean id="foo"                              <bean id="foo"
    class="com.springinaction.Foo">            class-"com.springinaction.Foo">
  <constructor-arg>                             <constructor-arg>
    <value>42</value>                             <ref bean="bar"/>
  </constructor-arg>                            </constructor-arg>
</bean                                        </bean>
```

Construct a Foo
through its constructor

Returning to our Spring Training application, both `CourseServiceImpl` and `StudentServiceImpl` require references to a DAO object (`CourseDaoImpl` and `StudentServiceImpl`, respectively). Because these service beans are useless without their DAO objects, each has a constructor that sets the DAO properties at bean creation time. To set the DAO properties on the `courseService` and `studentService` beans, use the following code:

```
<bean id="studentService"
    class="com.springinaction.training.service.StudentServiceImpl">
  <constructor-arg>
    <ref bean="studentDao"/>
  </constructor-arg>
</bean>

<bean id="courseService"
    class="com.springinaction.training.service.CourseServiceImpl">
  <constructor-arg>
    <ref bean="courseDao"/>
  </constructor-arg>
</bean>
```

Notice that `<constructor-arg>` can take a `<ref>` element just like `<property>` does. In fact, you can use any of the same subelements you used with `<property>` in the same way when setting constructor arguments with `<constructor-arg>`.

### Handling ambiguous constructor arguments

Single-argument constructors are easy to deal with. But what if your constructor has multiple arguments? Worse, what if the arguments are all the same type? How can you specify which values go to which arguments?

For example, what if your bean's constructor takes a `String` argument and an `java.net.URL` argument?

```
public class Foo {
  public Foo(String arg1, java.net.URL arg2) {
...
  }
}
```

Both the `java.net.URL` and `String` types can be converted from the `<value>` element.[1] So which one will be sent as `arg1` and which will be sent as `arg2`?

---

[1] We'll show you how Spring converts `String`s to URLs when we talk about `PropertyEditors` in section 2.4.3.

At first thought, this may seem to be a silly question. You may be thinking that the argument that looks like a URL will be sent as arg2. But suppose your bean is wired like this:

```
<bean id="foo"
    class="com.springinaction.Foo">
  <constructor-arg>
    <value>http://www.manning.com</value>
  </constructor-arg>
  <constructor-arg>
    <value>http://www.springinaction.com</value>
  </constructor-arg>
</bean>
```

Hmmm. Both <constructor-arg> elements have values that look like URLs. Okay, so maybe Spring will wire the arguments in the order that they appear—http:// www.manning.com will be wired to arg1 and http://www.springinaction.com will be wired to arg2. Is that how it works?

Good guess, but that's not how it works. Spring will not attempt to guess its way through your constructor arguments. Instead, it will throw an org.spring-framework.beans.factory.UnsatisfiedDependencyException, indicating that there is an ambiguity in the constructor arguments.

Fortunately, there are two ways you can deal with ambiguities among constructor arguments: by index and by type.

The <constructor-arg> element has an optional index attribute that specifies the ordering of the constructor arguments. For example, to send http:// www.manning.com as the URL argument and http://www.springinaction.com as the String argument, simply add the index attribute like this (index is zero-based):

```
<bean id="foo"
    class="com.springinaction.Foo">
  <constructor-arg index="1">
    <value>http://www.manning.com</value>
  </constructor-arg>
  <constructor-arg index="0">
    <value>http://www.springinaction.com</value>
  </constructor-arg>
</bean>
```

The other way to deal with <constructor-arg> ambiguity is to use the type attribute. The type attribute lets you specify exactly what type each <constructor-arg> is supposed to be so that Spring can make an informed decision as to which argument goes where. For example:

```
<bean id="foo"
    class="com.springinaction.Foo">
  <constructor-arg type="java.lang.String">
    <value>http://www.manning.com</value>
  </constructor-arg>
  <constructor-arg type="java.net.URL">
    <value>http://www.springinaction.com</value>
  </constructor-arg>
</bean>
```

Wired this way, `http://www.springinaction.com` will be the `URL` argument and `http://www.manning.com` will be the `String` argument.

Which should you use—`index` or `type`? In the example above, it didn't matter, because each argument had a distinct type. But what if both arguments were `Strings`? If that's the case, the `type` attribute won't help you much and you must opt for the more specific `index` attribute.

### How to choose: Constructor or setter?

There are certain things that most people can agree upon: The fact that the sky is blue, that Michael Jordan is the greatest player to touch a basketball, and that *Star Trek V* should have never happened. And then there are those things that stir up controversy, such as politics, religion, and the eternal "tastes great/less filling" debates.

Likewise, the choice between constructor injection and setter injection stirs up as much discourse as the arguments surrounding creamy versus crunchy peanut butter. Both have their merits and their weaknesses. Which should you choose?

Here are some arguments in favor of constructor injection:

- As we stated before, constructor injection enforces a strong dependency contract. In short, a bean cannot be instantiated without being given all of its dependencies. It is perfectly valid and ready to use upon instantiation. Of course, this assumes that the bean's constructor has all of the bean's dependencies in its parameter list.

- Because all of the bean's dependencies are set through its constructor, there's no need for superfluous setter methods. This helps keep the lines of code at a minimum.

- By only allowing properties to be set through the constructor, you are, in effect, making those properties immutable.

But there are also many arguments against constructor injection (and thus, in favor of setter injection):

- If a bean has several dependencies, the constructor's parameter list can be quite lengthy.
- If there are several ways to construct a valid object, it can be hard to come up with unique constructors since constructor signatures vary only by the number and type of parameters.
- If a constructor takes two or more parameters of the same type, it may be difficult to determine what each parameter's purpose is.
- Constructor injection does not lend itself readily to inheritance. A bean's constructor will have to pass parameters to super() in order to set private properties in the parent object.

Our approach to choosing between setter injection and constructor injection, for lack of a hard and fast rule, will be to do what works best in each situation. Quite simply, choose constructor injection when constructor injection makes sense and choose setter injection when setter injection makes sense. A good yardstick to go by is the clarity of your Spring configuration file. For instance, if you are creating a bean that has only one mandatory property (such as a DAO object as its Data-Source), constructor injection would probably be a good choice. On the other hand, if you have a bean that has multiple, optional properties (such as the Data-Source itself), setter injection would be more appropriate.

To put another way, sometimes you feel like a nut...sometimes you don't. Do what works for you.

Fortunately, Spring doesn't force you into any specific choice regarding dependency injection. You may inject a bean using either form of dependency injection. In fact, you are free to mix-'n'-match setter injection and constructor injection in the same context definition file—or even in the same bean.

Now that you've seen the basics of wiring beans in a Spring container using Spring's context definition file, let's look at ways to customize how Spring performs the wiring.

## 2.3 Autowiring

So far you've seen how to wire all of your bean's properties explicitly using the <property> element. Alternatively, you can have Spring wire them automatically by setting the autowire property on each <bean> that you want autowired:

```
<bean id="foo"
    class-"com.springinaction.Foo"
    autowire="autowire type"
/>
```

Auto-wire this bean's properties

There are four types of autowiring:

- `byName`—Attempts to find a bean in the container whose name (or ID) is the same as the name of the property being wired. If a matching bean is not found, then the property will remain unwired.

- `byType`—Attempts to find a single bean in the container whose type matches the type of the property being wired. If no matching bean is found, then the property will not be wired. If more than one bean matches, an `org.springrframework.beans.factory.UnsatisfiedDependencyExcpetion` will be thrown.

- `constructor`—Tries to match up one or more beans in the container with the parameters of one of the constructors of the bean being wired. In the event of ambiguous beans or ambiguous constructors, an `org.springframe-work.beans.factory.UnsatisfiedDependencyException` will be thrown.

- `autodetect`—Attempts to autowire by `constructor` first and then using `byType`. Ambiguity is handled the same way as with `constructor` and `byType` wiring.

For example, the declaration of the `courseService` bean when explicitly wired looks like this:

```
<bean id="courseService"
    class="com.springinaction.training.service.CourseServiceImpl">
  <property name="courseDao">
    <ref bean="courseDao"/>
  </property>
  <property name="studentService">
    <ref bean="studentService"/>
  </property>
</bean>
```

But when autowiring (by name), it looks like this:

```
<bean id="courseService"
    class="com.springinaction.training.service.CourseServiceImpl"
    autowire="byName"/>
```

By using `byName` autowiring, you are telling the container to consider all properties of the `CourseServiceImpl` and look for beans declared with the same name as the property. In this case, two properties, `courseDao` and `studentService`, are eligible for autowiring through setter injection. If beans are declared in the wiring file with the names `courseDao` and `studentService`, those beans will be wired to `courseDao` and `studentService`, respectively.

Autowiring using `byType` works in a similar way to `byName`, except that instead of considering a property's name, the property's type is examined. For example, if the `courseService` bean's `autowire` is set to `byType` instead of `byName`, the container will search itself for a bean whose type is `com.springinaction.training.CourseDao` and another bean whose type is `com.springinaction.training.StudentService`.

For an example of autowiring by `constructor` consider the `studentService` bean:

```
<bean id="studentService"
    class="com.springinaction.training.service.StudentServiceImpl"
    autowire="constructor"/>
```

The `StudentServiceImpl` class has a single-argument constructor that takes a `StudentDao` as an argument. If the container can find a bean whose type is `com.springinaction.training.StudentDao`, it will construct `StudentServiceImpl` by passing that bean to the constructor.

As you recall, `StudentServiceImpl` also has a `setStudentDao()` method that can be used to set the `studentDao` property. So, in addition to `constructor` autowiring, you could also apply `byType` or `byName`. Or if you'd like the flexibility of letting the container decide, you could use `autodetect`:

```
<bean id="studentService"
    class="com.springinaction.training.service.StudentServiceImpl"
    autowire="autodetect"/>
```

By setting `autowire` to `autodetect`, you instruct the Spring container to attempt to autowire by `constructor` first. If it can't find a suitable match between constructor arguments and beans, it will then try to autowire using `byType`.

### 2.3.1 *Handling ambiguities of autowiring*

When autowiring using `byType` or `constructor`, it's possible that the container may find two or more beans whose type matches the property's type or the types of the constructor arguments. What happens when there are ambiguous beans suitable for autowiring?

Unfortunately, Spring isn't capable of sorting out ambiguities and chooses to throw an exception rather than guess which bean you meant to wire in. If you encounter such ambiguities when autowiring, the best solution is often to simply not autowire the bean.

### 2.3.2 *Mixing auto and explicit wiring*

Just because you choose to autowire a bean, that doesn't mean you can't explicitly wire some properties. You can still use the `<property>` element on any property as if you hadn't set `autowire`.

For example, to explicitly wire the `courseDao` property of `CourseServiceImpl`, but still autowire the `studentService` property, you'd use this code:

```
<bean id="courseService"
    class="com.springinaction.training.service.CourseServiceImpl"
    autowire="byName">
  <property name="courseDao">
    <ref bean="someOtherCourseDao"/>
  </property>
</bean>
```

Mixing automatic and explicit wiring is also a great way to deal with ambiguous autowiring that may occur when autowiring using `byType`.

### 2.3.3 *Autowiring by default*

By default, beans will not be autowired unless you set the `autowire` attribute. However, you can set a default autowiring for all beans within the Spring configuration wiring file by setting `default-autowire` on the root `<beans>` element:

```
<beans default-autowire="byName">
```

Set this way, all beans will be autowired using `byName` unless specified otherwise.

### 2.3.4 *To autowire or not to autowire*

Although autowiring seems to be a powerful way to cut down on the amount of manual configuration required when writing the bean wiring file, it may lead to some problems.

For example, suppose that the `studentService` bean is set to be autowired using `byName`. As a result, its `studentDao` property will automatically be set to the bean in the container whose name is `studentDao`. Let's say that you decide that you want to refactor the `studentDao` property, renaming it as `studentData`. After refactoring, the container will try to autowire by looking for a bean named `studentData`. Unless you have changed the bean XML file, it won't find a bean by that name and will leave the property unwired. When the `studentService` bean tries to use the `studentData` property, you'll get a `NullPointerException`.

Worse still, what if there *is* a bean named `studentData` but it isn't the bean you want wired to the `studentData` property? Depending on the type of the `student-Data` bean, Spring may quietly wire in the unwanted bean, resulting in unexpected application behavior.

Autowiring is a powerful tool feature. But, as you may have heard, with great power comes great responsibility. If you choose to autowire, do so with caution.

Because autowiring hides so much of what is going on and because we want our examples to be abundantly clear, most of the examples in this book will not use autowiring. We'll leave it up to you whether or not you will autowire in your own applications.

You now know how to use Spring to wire your beans. But these aren't the only beans you can put to use in the container. Spring also comes with its own beans that can be wired into the container to do some additional work for you.

## 2.4 *Working with Spring's special beans*

Most beans configured in a Spring container are treated equally. Spring configures them, wires them together, and makes them available for use within an application. Nothing special.

But some beans have a higher purpose. By implementing certain interfaces, you can cause Spring to treat beans as being special—as being part of the Spring framework itself. By taking advantage of these special beans, you can configure beans that

- Become involved in the bean's and the bean factory's life cycles by postprocessing bean configuration
- Load configuration information from external property files
- Alter Spring's dependency injection to automatically convert `String` values to another type when setting bean properties—for example, being able to inject a `String` value into a `java.util.Date` field and have the date automatically converted
- Load textual messages from property files, including internationalized messages
- Listen for and respond to application events that are published by other beans and by the Spring container itself
- Are aware of their identity within the Spring container

In some cases, these special beans already have useful implementations that come packaged with Spring. In other cases, you'll probably want to implement the interfaces yourself.

Let's start the exploration of Spring's special beans by looking at beans that perform postprocessing of other beans and of the bean factory itself.

### 2.4.1 Postprocessing beans

Earlier in this chapter, you learned how to define beans within the Spring container and how to wire them together. For the most part, you have no reason to expect beans to be wired in any way different than how you define them in the bean definition XML file. The XML file is perceived as the source of truth regarding how your application's objects are configured.

But as you saw in figures 2.1 and 2.2, Spring offers two opportunities for you to cut into a bean's life cycle and review or alter its configuration. This is called postprocessing. From the name, you probably deduced that this processing done *after* some event has occurred. The event this postprocessing follows is the instantiation and configuring of a bean. The BeanPostProcessor interface gives you two opportunities to alter a bean after it has been created and wired:

```
public interface BeanPostProcessor {
   Object postProcessBeforeInitialization(
       Object bean, String name) throws BeansException;

   Object postProcessAfterInitialization(
       Object bean, String name) throws BeansException;
}
```

The postProcessBeforeInitialization() method is called immediately prior to bean initialization (the call to afterPropertiesSet() and the bean's custom init-method). Likewise, the postProcessAfterInitialization() method is called immediately after initialization.

#### Writing a bean post processor

For example, suppose that you wanted to alter all String properties of your application beans to translate them into Elmer Fudd-speak. The Fuddifier class in listing 2.5 is a BeanPostProcessor that does just that.

> **Listing 2.5  Fudd-ify your String properties with this BeanPostProcessor.**

```
public class Fuddifier implements BeanPostProcessor {
   public Object postProcessAfterInitialization(
       Object bean, String name) throws BeansException {
```

```
    Field[] fields = bean.getClass().getDeclaredFields();

    try {
      for(int i=0; i < fields.length; i++) {
        if(fields[i].getType().equals(
            java.lang.String.class)) {
          fields[i].setAccessible(true);
          String original = (String) fields[i].get(bean);
          fields[i].set(bean, fuddify(original));
        }
      }
    } catch (IllegalAccessException e) {
      e.printStackTrace();
    }

    return bean;
  }

  private String fuddify(String orig) {
    if(orig == null) return orig;
    return orig.replaceAll("(r|l)", "w")
        .replaceAll(" (R|L) ", "W");
  }

  public Object postProcessBeforeInitialization(
      Object bean, String name) throws BeansException {
    return bean;
  }
}
```

The postProcessAfterInitialization() method cycles through all of the bean's properties, looking for those that are of type java.lang.String. For each String property, it passes it off to the fuddify() method, which translates the String into Fudd-speak. Finally, the property is changed to the fudd-ified text. (You'll also notice a call to each property's setAccessible() method to get around the private visibilityof a property. We realize that this breaks encapsulation, but how else could we pull this off?)

The postProcessBeforeInitialization() method is left purposefully unexciting; it simply returns the bean unaltered. Actually, the fudd-ification process could have occurred just as well in this method.

Now that we have a Fudd-ifying BeanPostProcessor, let's look at how to tell the container to apply it to all beans.

### Registering bean post processors

If your application is running within a bean factory, you'll need to programmatically register each BeanPostProcessor using the factory's addBeanPostProcessor() method:

```
BeanPostProcessor fuddifier = new Fuddifier();
factory.addBeanPostProcessor(fuddifier);
```

If you're using an application context, you'll only need to register the post processor as a bean within the context.

```
<bean id=" fuddifier"
    class="com.springinaction.chapter02.Fuddifier"/>
```

The container will recognize the fuddifier bean as a BeanPostProcessor and call its postprocessing methods before and after each bean is initialized.

As a result of the fuddifier bean, all String properties of all beans will be Fudd-ified. For example, suppose you had the following bean defined in XML:

```
<bean id="bugs" class="com.springinaction.chapter02.Rabbit">
  <property name="description">
    <value>That rascally rabbit!</value>
  </property>
</bean>
```

When the "fuddifier" processor is finished, the description property will hold "That wascawwy wabbit!"

### Spring's own bean postprocessors

The Spring framework itself uses several implementations of BeanPostProcessor under the covers. For example, ApplicationContextAwareProcessor is a Bean-PostProcessor that sets the application context on beans that implement the ApplicationContextAware interface (see section 2.4.6). You do not need to register ApplicationContextAwareProcessor yourself. It is preregistered by the application context itself.

In the next chapter, you'll learn of another implementation of BeanPost-Processor. You'll also learn how to automatically apply aspects to application beans using DefaultAdvisorAutoProxyCreator, which is a BeanPostProcessor that creates AOP proxies based on all candidate advisors in the container.

### 2.4.2   Postprocessing the bean factory

While a BeanPostProcessor performs postprocessing on a bean after it has been loaded, a BeanFactoryPostProcessor performs postprocessing on a bean factory after the bean factory has loaded its bean definitions but before any of the beans have been instantiated. The `BeanFactoryPostProcessor` interface is defined as follows:

```
public interface BeanFactoryPostProcessor {
  public void postProcessBeanFactory(
      ConfigurableListableBeanFactory beanFactory)
      throws BeansException;
}
```

The `postProcessBeanFactory()` method is called by the Spring container after all bean definitions have been loaded but before any beans are instantiated (including `BeanPostProcessor` beans).

For example, the `BeanFactoryPostProcessor` implementation in listing 2.6 gives a whole new meaning to the term "bean counter." `BeanCounter` is a `BeanFactoryPostProcessor` that simply logs the number of bean definitions that have been loaded into the bean factory.

**Listing 2.6   Creating a BeanFactoryPostProcessor to count how many beans are created within the factory**

```
public class BeanCounter implements BeanFactoryPostProcessor {
  private Logger LOGGER = Logger.getLogger(BeanCounter.class);

  public void postProcessBeanFactory(
      ConfigurableListableBeanFactory factory)
      throws BeansException {

    LOGGER.debug("BEAN COUNT:  " +
        factory.getBeanDefinitionCount());
  }
}
```

If you're using an application context container, you won't need to do anything to register a `BeanFactoryPostProcessor` as a postprocessor in Spring other than register it as a regular bean:

```
<bean id="beanCounter"
      class="com.springinaction.chapter02.BeanCounter"/>
```

When the container sees that `beanCounter` is a `BeanFactoryPostProcessor`, it will automatically register it as a bean factory postprocessor. You cannot use `BeanFactoryPostProcessor`s with bean factory containers.

`BeanCounter` is a naïve use of `BeanFactoryPostProcessor`. To find more meaningful examples of `BeanFactoryPostProcessor`, we have to look no further than the Spring framework itself. Two very useful implementations of `BeanFactoryPostProcessor` are `PropertyPlaceholderConfigurer` and `CustomEditorConfigurer`.

`PropertyPlaceholderConfigurer` loads properties from one or more external property files and uses those properties to fill in placeholder variables in the bean wiring XML file. `CustomEditorConfigurer` lets you register custom implementations of `java.beans.PropertyEditor` to translate property wired values to other property types.

Let's take a look at how you can use the `PropertyPlaceholderConfigurer` implementation of `BeanFactoryPostProcessor`.

### 2.4.3  *Externalizing the configuration*

For the most part, it is possible to configure your entire application in a single bean wiring file. But sometimes you may find it beneficial to extract certain pieces of that configuration into a separate property file. For example, a configuration concern that is common to many applications is configuring a data source. In Spring, you could configure a data source with the following XML in the bean wiring file:

```
<bean id="dataSource" class=
    "org.springframework.jdbc.datasource.DriverManagerDataSource">
  <property name="url">
    <valuejdbc:hsqldb:Training</value>
  </property>
  <property name="driverClassName">
    <value>org.hsqldb.jdbcDriver</value>
  </property>
  <property name="username">
    <value>appUser</value>
  </property>
  <property name="password">
    <value>password</value>
  </property>
</bean>
```

Configuring the data source directly in the bean wiring file may not be appropriate. The database specifics are a deployment detail. Conversely, the purpose of the bean wiring file is mainly oriented toward defining how components within your application are put together. That's not to say that you cannot configure your application components within the bean wiring file. In fact, when the configuration is application-specific (as opposed to deployment-specific) it makes perfect sense to configure components in the bean wiring file. But deployment details should be separated.

Fortunately, externalizing properties in Spring is easy if you are using an `ApplicationContext` as your Spring container. You use Spring's `PropertyPlaceholderConfigurer` to tell Spring to load certain configuration from an external property file. To enable this feature, configure the following bean in your bean wiring file:

```
<bean id="propertyConfigurer" class="org.springframework.beans.
    ➡  factory.config.PropertyPlaceholderConfigurer">
  <property name="location">
    <value>jdbc.properties</value>
  </property>
</bean>
```

The `location` property tells Spring where to find the property file. In this case, the jdbc.properties file contains the following JDBC information:

```
database.url=jdbc:hsqldb:Training
database.driver=org.hsqldb.jdbcDriver
database.user=appUser
database.password=password
```

The `location` property allows you to work with a single property file. If you want to break down your configuration into multiple property files, use `Property-PlaceholderConfigurer`'s `locations` property to set a `List` of property files:

```
<bean id="propertyConfigurer" class="org.springframework.beans.
    ➡  factory.config.PropertyPlaceholderConfigurer">
  <property name="locations">
    <list>
      <value>jdbc.properties</value>
      <value>security.properties</value>
      <value>application.properties</value>
    </list>
  </property>
</bean>
```

Now you are able to replace the hard-coded configuration in the bean wiring file with placeholder variables. Syntactically, the placeholder variables take the form ${variable}, resembling Ant properties or the JavaServer Pages (JSP) expression language.

Applying the placeholder variables to the data source configuration yields the following:

```
<bean id="dataSource" class="org.springframework.
    ➡  jdbc.datasource.DriverManagerDataSource">
  <property name="url">
    <value>${database.url}</value>
  </property>
  <property name="driverClassName">
    <value>${database.driver}</value>
  </property>
  <property name="username">
```

```
    <value>${database.user}</value>
  </property>
  <property name="password">
    <value>${database.password}</value>
  </property>
</bean>
```

The placeholder variables will be replaced with properties from jdbc.properties when the context is loaded.

### 2.4.4 *Customizing property editors*

In section 2.2.4, you saw that it is possible to wire a String value to a property whose type is java.net.URL. Did you wonder how that works?

Actually, the magic behind this trick isn't something Spring provides, but rather comes from a little-known feature of the original JavaBeans API. The java.beans.PropertyEditor interface provides a means to customize how String values are mapped to non-String types. There is a convenience implementation of this interface—java.beans.PropertyEditorSupport—that has two methods of interest to us:

- getAsText() returns the String representation of a property's value.
- setAsText(String value) sets a bean property value from the String value passed in.

If an attempt is made to set a non-String property to a String value, the setAsText() method is called to perform the conversion. Likewise, the getAsText() method is called to return a textual representation of the property's value.

Spring comes with several custom editors based on PropertyEditorSupport, including org.springframework.beans.propertyeditors.URLEditor, which is the custom editor used to convert Strings to and from java.net.URL objects.

Some other custom editors that come with Spring include

- ClassEditor—Sets a java.lang.Class property from a String value that contain the fully qualified class name
- CustomDateEditor—Sets a java.util.Date property from a String using a custom java.text.DateFormat object
- FileEditor—Sets a java.io.File property from a String value that contains a file's path
- LocaleEditor—Sets a java.util.Locale property from a String value that contains a textual representation of the locale (i.e., "en_US")

- StringArrayPropertyEditor—Converts a comma-delimited String to a String array property
- StringTrimmerEditor—Automatically trims String properties with an option to convert empty String values to null

You can also write your own custom editor by extending the PropertyEditor-Support class. For example, suppose that your application has a Contact bean that conveniently carries contact information about the people in your organization. Among other things, the Contact bean has a phoneNumber property that holds the contact phone number:

```
public Contact {
  ...
  private PhoneNumber phoneNumber;

  public void setPhoneNumber(PhoneNumber phoneNumber) {
    this.phoneNumber = phoneNumber;
  }
}
```

The phone property is of type PhoneNumber and is defined as follows:

```
public PhoneNumber {
  private String areaCode;
  private String prefix;
  private String number;

  public PhoneNumber() { }

  public PhoneNumber(String areaCode, String prefix,
                     String number) {
    this.areaCode = areaCode;
    this.prefix = prefix;
    this.number = number;
  }
  ...
}
```

Using basic wiring techniques learned in section 2.2, you could wire a Phone-Number object into the Contact bean's phoneNumber property as follows:

```
<beans>
  <bean id="infoPhone"
        class="com.springinaction.chapter02.PhoneNumber">
    <constructor-arg index="0">
      <value>888</value>
    </constructor-arg>
    <constructor-arg index="1">
      <value>555</value>
```

```
        </constructor-arg>
        <constructor-arg index="2">
            <value>1212</value>
        </constructor-arg>
    </bean>
    <bean id="contact"
        class="com.springinaction.chapter02.Contact">
        <property name="phoneNumber">
          <ref bean="infoPhone"/>
        </property>
    </bean>
</beans>
```

Notice that you had to define a separate infoPhone bean to configure the Phone-Number object and then wire it into the phoneNumber property of the Contact bean.

But suppose you were to write a custom PhoneEditor like this:

```
public class PhoneEditor
    extends java.beans.PropertyEditorSupport {
  public void setAsText(String textValue) {
    String stripped = stripNonNumeric(textValue);

    String areaCode = stripped.substring(0,3);
    String prefix = stripped.substring(3,6);
    String number = stripped.substring(6);
    PhoneNumber phone = new PhoneNumber(areaCode, prefix, number);
    setValue(phone);
  }

  private String stripNonNumeric(String original) {
    StringBuffer allNumeric = new StringBuffer();

    for(int i=0; i<original.length(); i++) {
      char c = original.charAt(i);
      if(Character.isDigit(c)) {
        allNumeric.append(c);
      }
    }

    return allNumeric.toString();
  }
}
```

Now the only thing left is to get Spring to recognize your custom property editor when wiring bean properties. For that, you'll need to use Spring's CustomEditor-Configurer. CustomEditorConfigurer is a BeanFactoryPostProcessor that loads custom editors into the BeanFactory by calling the registerCustomEditor() method. (Optionally, you can call the registerCustomEditor() method in your own code after you have an instance of the bean factory.)

By adding the following piece of XML to the bean configuration file, you'll tell Spring to register the `PhoneEditor` as a custom editor:

```
<bean id="customEditorConfigurer" class="org.springframework.
      beans.factory.config.CustomEditorConfigurer">
  <property name="customEditors">
    <map>
      <entry key="com.springinaction.chapter02.Phone">
        <bean id="phoneEditor"
            class="com.springinaction.02.PhoneEditor">
        </bean>
      </entry>
    </map>
  </property>
</bean>
```

And you'll now be able to configure the `Contact` object's `phoneNumber` property using a simple `String` value and without creating a separate `Phone` bean:

```
<bean id="contact"
    class="com.springinaction.chapter02.Contact">
  <property name="phoneNumber">
    <value>888-555-1212</value>
  </property>
</bean>
```

Note that many of the custom editors that come with Spring (such as `URLEditor` and `LocaleEditor`) are already registered with the bean factory upon container startup. You do not need to register them yourself using `CustomEditorConfigurer`.

### 2.4.5 *Resolving text messages*

Oftentimes you may not want to hard-code certain text that will be displayed to the user of your application. This may be because the text is subject to change or perhaps your application will be internationalized and you will display text in the user's native language.

Java's support for parameterization and internationalization (I18N)[2] of messages enables you to define one or more properties files that contain the text that is to be displayed in your application. There should always be a default message file along with optional language-specific message files. For example, if the name of your application's message bundle is "trainingtext," you may have the following set of message property files:

---

[2] Internationalization is often referred to as "I18N" for short. It gets this name because there are 18 letters between the I and the N in "Internationalization."

- *trainingtext.properties*—Default messages when a locale cannot be determined or when a locale-specific properties file is not available
- *trainingtext_en_US.properties*—Text for English-speaking users in the United States
- *trainingtext_es_MX.properties*—Text for Spanish-speaking users in Mexico
- *trainingtext_de_DE.properties*—Text for German-speaking users in Germany

For example, both the default and English properties files may contain entries such as

```
course=class
student=student
computer=computer
```

while the Spanish message file would look like this:

```
course=clase
student=estudiante
computer=computadora
```

Spring's `ApplicationContext` supports parameterized messages by making them available to the container through the `MessageSource` interface:

```
public interface MessageSource {
  public String getMessage(
      MessageSourceResolvable resolvable, Locale locale)
      throws NoSuchMessageException;
  public String getMessage(
      String code, Object[] args, Locale locale)
      throws NoSuchMessageException;
  public String getMessage(
      String code, Object[] args, String defaultMessage,
      Locale locale);
}
```

Spring comes with a ready-to-use implementation of `MessageSource`. `Resource-BundleMessageSource` simply uses Java's own `java.util.ResourceBundle` to resolve messages. To use `ResourceBundleMessageSource`, add the following to the bean wiring file:

```
<bean id="messageSource" class="org.springframework.
      context.support.ResourceBundleMessageSource">
  <property name="basename">
    <value>trainingtext</value>
  </property>
</bean>
```

It is very important that this bean be named `messageSource` because the `ApplicationContext` will look for a bean specifically by that name when setting up its internal message source. You'll never need to inject the `messageSource` bean into your application beans, but will instead access messages via `ApplicationContext`'s own `getMessage()` methods. For example, to retrieve the message whose name is `computer`, use this code:

```
Locale locale = … ; //determine locale
String text =
    context.getMessage("computer", new Object[0], locale);
```

You'll likely be using parameterized messages in the context of a web application, displaying the text on a web page. In that case, you'll want to use Spring's `<spring:message>` JSP tag to retrieve messages and will not need to directly access the `ApplicationContext`:

```
<spring:message code="computer"/>
```

But if you need your beans, not a JSP, to retrieve the messages, how can you write them to access the `ApplicationContext`? Well, you're going to have to wait a bit for that. Or you can skip ahead to section 2.4.8 where we discuss making your beans aware of their container.

Right now, we are going to move on to examine the events that occur during an application context's life cycle, how to handle these events, and how to publish our own events.

### 2.4.6  *Listening for events*

In the course of an application's lifetime, the `ApplicationContext` will publish a handful of events that tell interested listeners what's going on. These events are all subclasses of the abstract class `org.springframework.context.Application-Event`. Three such application events are

- `ContextClosedEvent`—Published when the application context is closed
- `ContextRefreshedEvent`—Published when the application context is initialized or refreshed
- `RequestHandledEvent`—Published within a web application context when a request is handled

For the most part, these events are published rather…uh…well, uneventfully. Most beans will never know or care that they were published. But what if you want to be notified of application events?

If you want a bean to respond to application events, all you need to do is implement the `org.springframework.context.ApplicationListener` interface.

This interface forces your bean to implement the `onApplicationEvent()` method, which is responsible for reacting to the application event:

```
public class RefreshListener implements ApplicationListener {
  public void onApplicationEvent(ApplicationEvent event) {
  ...
  }
}
```

The only thing you need to do to tell Spring about an application event listener is to simply register it as a bean within the context:

```
<bean id="refreshListener"
    class="com.springinaction.foo.RefreshListener"/>
```

When the container loads the bean within the application context, it will notice that it implements `ApplicationListener` and will remember to call its `onApplicationEvent()` method when an event is published.

### 2.4.7  *Publishing events*

While it may be handy for your beans to respond to events published by the container itself, it's also possible for your application to publish its own events. These events are handled by implementations of `ApplicationListener` in the same way that any events are handled.

Imagine that you want to alert one or more application objects any time that a student signs up for a course and, as a result, the course is full. Maybe you want to fire off a routine to automatically schedule another course to handle the overflow.

First, define a custom event, such as the one in listing 2.7.

**Listing 2.7  A custom event indicating a course has reached capacity**

```
public class CourseFullEvent extends ApplicationEvent {
  private Course course;

  public CourseFullEvent(Object source, Course course) {
    super(source);
    this.course = course;
  }

  public Course getCourse() {
    return course;
  }
}
```

Next you'll need to publish the event. The `ApplicationContext` interface has a `publishEvent()` method that enables you to publish `ApplicationEvents`. Any `ApplicationListener` that is registered in the application context will receive the event in a call to its `onApplicationEvent()` method:

```
ApplicationContext context = …;
Course course = …;
context.publishEvent(new CourseFullEvent(this, course));
```

Finally, you'll need to make sure that the objects interested in handling the `CourseFullEvent` implement the `ApplicationListener` interface as described above. One thing to keep in mind is that these events are handled synchronously. So, you want to take care that any events handled in this fashion are handled quickly. Otherwise, you application's performance could be negatively impacted.

Unfortunately, in order to publish events, your beans will need to have access to the `ApplicationContext`. This means that beans will have to be made aware of the container that they're running in. And that's the next type of special bean we're going to talk about.

### 2.4.8 *Making beans aware*

Have you seen *The Matrix*? In the movie, humans have been unwittingly enslaved by machines, living their everyday lives in a virtual world while their life essence is being farmed to power the machines. Thomas Anderson, the main character, is given a choice between taking a red pill and learning the truth of his existence or taking a blue pill and continuing his life ignorant of the truth. He chooses the red pill, becoming aware his real-world identity and the truth about the virtual world.

For the most part, beans running in the Spring container are like the humans in *The Matrix*. For these beans, ignorance is bliss. They don't know (or even need to know) their names or even that they are running within a Spring container. This is usually a good thing because if a bean is aware of the container, then it becomes coupled with Spring and may not be able to exist outside of the container.

But sometimes, beans need to know more. Sometimes they need to know the truth who they are and where they are running. Sometimes they need to take the red pill.

The red pill, in the case of Spring beans, comes in the form of the `Bean-NameAware`, `BeanFactoryAware`, and `ApplicationContextAware` interfaces. By implementing these three interfaces, beans can be made aware of their name, their `BeanFactory`, and their `ApplicationContext`, respectively.

Be warned, however, that by implementing these interfaces, a bean becomes coupled with Spring. And, depending on how your bean uses this knowledge, you may not be able to use it outside of Spring.

### Knowing who you are

The Spring container tells a bean what its name is through the `BeanNameAware` interface. This interface has a single `setBeanName()` interface that takes a `String` containing the bean's name, which is set through either the `id` or the `name` attribute of `<bean>` in the bean wiring file:

```
public interface BeanNameAware {
  void setBeanName(String name);
}
```

It may be useful for a bean to know its name for bookkeeping purposes. For example, if a bean may have more than one instance within the application context, it may be beneficial for that bean to identify itself by both name and type when logging its actions.

Within the Spring framework itself, `BeanNameAware` is used several times. One notable use is with beans that perform scheduling. `CronTriggerBean`, for example, implements `BeanNameAware` to set the name of its Quartz `CronTrigger`[3] job. The following code snippet from `CronTriggerBean` illustrates this:

```
package org.springframework.scheduling.quartz;
public class CronTriggerBean extends CronTrigger
    implements ..., BeanNameAware, ... {
...
  private String beanName;
...
  public void setBeanName(String beanName) {
    this.beanName = beanName;
  }
...
  public void afterPropertiesSet() ... {
    if (getName() == null){
      setBeanName(this.beanName);
    }
...
  }
...
}
```

---

[3] The `CronTriggerBean` class allows you to schedule jobs within the Spring container using Quartz, an open source scheduling system. We will cover Quartz in detail in chapter 7.

You don't need to do anything special for a Spring container to call `setBean-Name()` on a `BeanNameAware` class. When the bean is loaded, the container will see that the bean implements `BeanNameAware` and will automatically call `setBean-Name()`, passing the name of the bean as defined by either the `id` or the `name` attribute of the `<bean>` element in the bean wiring XML file.

Here `CronTriggerBean` extends `CronTrigger`. After the Spring context has set all properties on the bean, the bean name is sent to `setBeanName()` (defined in `CronTrigger`) to set the name of the scheduled job.

This example showed you how to use `BeanNameAware` by showing how it is used in Spring's own scheduling support. We'll talk more about scheduling in chapter 7. For now, let's see how a bean can be made aware of its own container.

### Knowing where you live

As you've seen in this section, sometimes it's helpful for a bean to be able to access the application context. Perhaps your bean needs access to parameterized text messages in a message source. Or maybe it needs to be able to publish application events for application event listeners to respond to. Whatever the case, your bean should be aware of the container in which it lives.

Spring's `ApplicationContextAware` and `BeanFactoryAware` interfaces enable a bean to be aware of its container. These interfaces declare a `setApplication-Context()` method and a `setBeanFactory()` method, respectively. The Spring container will detect whether any of your beans implement either of these interfaces and provide the `BeanFactory` or `ApplicationContext`.

Going back to our event publishing example earlier, we would finish out that example like this:

```
public class StudentServiceImpl
    implements StudentService, ApplicationContextAware {

  private ApplicationContext context;

  public void setApplicationContext(ApplicationContext context) {
    this.context = context;
  }

  public void enrollStudentInCourse(Course course, Student student)
      throws CourseException;
    ...
    context.publishEvent(new CourseFullEvent(this, course));
    ...
  }
  ...
}
```

Being aware of the application container is both a blessing and a curse for a bean. On the one hand, access to the application context affords the bean a lot of power. On the other hand, being aware of the container couples the bean to Spring and is something that should be avoided if possible.

## 2.5 *Summary*

At the core of the Spring framework is the Spring container. Spring comes with several implementations of its container, but they all fall into one of two categories. A BeanFactory is the simplest form of container, providing basic dependency injection and bean wiring services. But when more advanced framework services are needed, Spring's ApplicationContext is the container to use.

In this chapter, you've seen how to wire beans together within the Spring container. Wiring is typically performed within a Spring container using an XML file. This XML file contains configuration information for all of the components of an application along with information that helps the container perform dependency injection to associate beans with other beans that they depend on.

You've also seen how to instruct Spring to automatically wire beans together by using reflection and making some guesses about which beans should be associated with each other.

Finally, you learned how to write and use special beans that become directly involved in Spring's wiring process. These special beans may alter how Spring performs wiring by changing how String values are interpreted (as is the case with CustomEditorConfigurer and PropertyPlaceholderConfigurer). Special beans can also be made aware of who they are and what container they are running in so that they can interact directly with their environment. Or a special bean may simply listen for and respond to application events as they are published.

Everything you learned in this chapter is the basis for what is to come. You'll continue working with Spring's bean definition XML file as you add more functionality to the Spring Training application. You'll also start recognizing practical uses of Spring's special beans and how they are used throughout Spring.

In the next chapter, you'll learn about Spring's aspect-oriented programming support. You'll find that dependency injection and AOP are complementary ways to extract common logic into loosely coupled modules. Spring's AOP support is important, not only because it enables you to modularize application concerns, but also because it is the basis for Spring's support for declarative transactions, which we'll cover in chapter 5.

# Creating aspects

91

In chapter 2 you learned how Spring can help manage and configure your application objects. You can follow sound object-oriented design, write loosely coupled code, and use Spring's inversion of control to make connecting your collaborators painless. But sometimes you have functionality that is used throughout your application that does not fit nicely into a single object hierarchy. This is where aspect-oriented programming (AOP) comes in.

Spring's AOP framework allows you to code functionality that is sprinkled throughout your application in one place—an aspect. Using Spring's powerful pointcut mechanism, you have a wide range of choices of how and where to apply your aspects in your application. This allows you to add powerful services, such as declarative transaction management, to simple JavaBeans.

## 3.1 *Introducing AOP*

Before we get started on how Spring implements AOP, we'll first cover the basics of AOP. It is important to understand AOP fundamentals and how AOP can help you write cleaner applications.

Most definitions of AOP say something about the modularization of *cross-cutting* concerns. Unfortunately, the term cross-cutting is not used often outside of an AOP context, so it doesn't have much meaning for most developers. Figure 3.1 gives a visual depiction of cross-cutting concerns.

This figure represents a typical application that is broken down into modules. Each module's main concern is to provide services for its particular domain. However, each of these modules also requires similar ancillary functionalities, such as security and transaction management. The common object-oriented technique for reusing common functionality is through inheritance or delegation. But inheritance can lead to a brittle object hierarchy if the same base class is

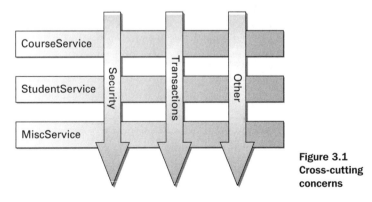

**Figure 3.1**
**Cross-cutting**
**concerns**

used throughout an application, and delegation can be cumbersome and still requires duplicated calls to the delegate object.

AOP presents an alternative that can be cleaner in many circumstances. With AOP, you still define the common functionality in one place, but you can declaratively define how and where this functionality is applied without having to modify the class to which you are applying the new feature. Cross-cutting concerns can now be modularized into special objects called *aspects*. This has two benefits. First, the logic for each concern is now in one place, as opposed to being scattered all over the code base. Second, our service modules are now cleaner since they only contain code for their core functionality and secondary concerns have been moved to aspects.

### 3.1.1 Defining AOP terminology

Like most technologies, AOP has a jargon unto itself. Unfortunately, many of the terms used to describe AOP features are not intuitive. But they are now part of the AOP language and, in order to understand AOP, you must know this language. In other words, before you walk the walk, you have to learn to talk the talk.

#### Aspect

An aspect *is* the cross-cutting functionality you are implementing. It is the *aspect*, or area, of your application you are modularizing. The most common (albeit simple) example of an aspect is logging. Logging is something that is required throughout an application. However, because applications tend to be broken down into layers based on functionality, reusing a logging module through inheritance does not make sense. However, you can create a logging aspect and apply it throughout your application using AOP.

#### Joinpoint

A joinpoint is a point in the execution of the application where an aspect can be plugged in. This point could be a method being called, an exception being thrown, or even a field being modified. These are the points where your aspect's code can be inserted into the normal flow of your application to add new behavior.

#### Advice

Advice is the actual implementation of our aspect. It is *advising* your application of new behavior. In our logging example, the logging advice would contain the code that implements the actual logging, such as writing to a log file. Advice is inserted into our application at joinpoints.

### Pointcut

A pointcut defines at what joinpoints advice should be applied. Advice *can* be applied at any joinpoint supported by the AOP framework. Of course, you don't want to apply all of your aspects at all of the possible joinpoints. Pointcuts allow you to specify where you want your advice to be applied. Often you specify these pointcuts using explicit class and method names or through regular expressions that define matching class and method name patterns. Some AOP frameworks allow you to create dynamic pointcuts that determine whether to apply advice based on runtime decisions, such as the value of method parameters.

### Introduction

An introduction allows you to add new methods or attributes to existing classes (kind of mind-blowing, huh?). For example, you could create an `Auditable` advice class that keeps the state of when an object was last modified. This could be as simple as having one method, `setLastModified(Date)`, and an instance variable to hold this state. This can then be *introduced* to existing classes without having to change them, giving them new behavior and state.

### Target

A target is the class that is being advised. This can be either a class you write or a third-party class to which you want to add custom behavior. Without AOP, this class would have to contain its primary logic *plus* the logic for any cross-cutting concerns. With AOP, the target class is free to focus on its primary concern, oblivious to any advice being applied.

### Proxy

A proxy is the object created after applying advice to the target object. As far as the client objects are concerned, the target object (pre-AOP) and the proxy object (post-AOP) are the same—as it should be. That is, the rest of your application will not have to change to support the proxy class.

### Weaving

Weaving is the process of applying aspects to a target object to create a new, proxied object. The aspects are *woven* into the target object at the specified joinpoints. The weaving can take place at several points in the target class's lifetime:

- *Compile time*—Aspects are woven in when the target class is compiled. This requires a special compiler.

- *Classload time*—Aspects are woven in when the target class is loaded into the JVM. This requires a special `ClassLoader` that enhances that target class's bytecode before the class is introduced into the application.

- *Runtime*—Aspects are woven in sometime during the execution of the application. Typically, an AOP container will dynamically generate a proxy class that will delegate to the target class while weaving in the aspects.

That's a lot of new terms to get to know. Figure 3.2 illustrates the key AOP concepts in action.

The advice contains the cross-cutting behavior that needs to be applied. The joinpoints are all the points within the execution flow of the application that are candidates to have advice applied. The point-cut defines at what joinpoints that advice is applied. The key concept you should take from this? Pointcuts define which joinpoints get advised.

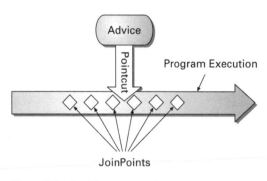

**Figure 3.2    Applying an aspect**

### 3.1.2 *Spring's AOP implementation*

Not all AOP frameworks are created equal. They may differ on how rich of a join-point model they offer. Some may allow you to apply advice at the field modification level, while others only expose the joinpoints related to method invocations. They may also differ on how and when they weave the aspects. Whatever the case, the ability to create pointcuts that define the joinpoints at which aspects should be woven is what makes it an AOP framework.

Although there are several implementations of AOP, right now we are concerned with how Spring implements AOP. So let's take a look at the key points of Spring's AOP framework.

#### *Spring advice is written in Java*

All of the advice you create within Spring will be written in a standard Java class. This means you will get the benefit of developing your aspects in the same integrated development environment (IDE) you would use for your normal Java development. What's more, the pointcuts that define where advice should be applied are typically written in XML in your Spring configuration file. This means both the aspect's code and configuration syntax will be familiar to Java developers.

Other frameworks out there, specifically AspectJ, require a special syntax to write the aspect and define pointcuts. There are benefits and drawbacks to this approach. By having an AOP-specific language, you get more power and fine-grained control, as well as a richer AOP toolset. However, you are required to learn a new tool and syntax to accomplish this.

### Spring's advises objects at runtime

Spring does not create a proxied object until that proxied bean is needed by the application. If you are using an `ApplicationContext`, the proxied objects will be created when it loads all of the beans from the `BeanFactory`. Because Spring creates proxies at runtime, you do not need a special compiler to use Spring's AOP.

Spring generates proxied classes in two ways. If your target object implements an interface(s) that exposes the required methods, Spring will use the JDK's `java.lang.reflect.Proxy` class. This class allows Spring to dynamically generate a new class that implements the necessary interfaces, weave in any advice, and proxy any calls to these interfaces to your target class.

If your target class does not implement an interface, Spring uses the CGLIB[1] library to generate a subclass to your target class. When creating this subclass, Spring weaves in advice and delegates calls to the subclass to your target class. When using this type of proxy generation, you need to deploy all of the JAR files in the `lib/cglib` directory of your Spring distribution with your application. There are two important things to take note of when using this approach:

- Creating a proxy with interfaces is favored over proxying classes, since this leads to a more loosely coupled application. The ability to proxy classes is provided so that legacy or third-party classes that do not implement interfaces can still be advised. This approach should be taken as the exception, not the rule.

- Methods marked as `final` cannot be advised. Remember, Spring generates a subclass to your target class. Any method that needs to be advised is over-ridden and advice is woven in. This is not possible with `final` methods.

---

[1] CGLIB is an open source, high-performance code generation library. You can find more information about CGLIB at http://cglib.sourceforge.net.

### Spring implements AOP Alliance interfaces

The AOP Alliance is a joint project between several parties interested in implementing AOP in Java. The AOP Alliance shares the same belief as Spring that AOP can provide cleaner and easier solutions for Java enterprise applications than what is currently offered by EJB. Their goal is to standardize Java's AOP interface to provide interoperability between various Java AOP implementations. This means that AOP advice that implements their interfaces (as do some of Spring's implementations) will be reusable in any other AOP Alliance–compatible framework.

### Spring only supports method joinpoints

As mentioned earlier, multiple joinpoint models are available through various AOP implementations. Spring only supports method joinpoints. This is in contrast to some other AOP frameworks, such as AspectJ and JBoss, which provide field joinpoints as well. This prevents you from creating very fine-grained advice, such as intercepting updates to an object's field.

However, as Spring focuses on providing a framework for implementing J2EE services, method interception should suit most, if not all, of your needs. Plus, Spring's philosophy is that field interception violates encapsulation. A fundamental object-oriented concept is that objects initiate operations on themselves and other objects through method calls. Having advice fired on field modification as opposed to method invocation arguably violates this concept.

Now you have a general idea of what AOP does and how it is supported by Spring. Let's take a look at how to create the different advice types in Spring.

## 3.2 Creating advice

If you recall from the previous section, advice contains the logic of your aspect. So when you create an advice object, you are writing the code that implements the cross-cutting functionality. Also, remember that Spring's joinpoint model is built around method interception. This means that the Spring advice you write will be woven into your application at different points around a method's invocation. Because there are several points during the execution of a method that Spring can weave in advice, there are several different advice types. Table 3.1 lists the types of advice offered by Spring and where they are woven into your code.[2]

---

[2] Actually, there is another advice type that is omitted: introduction advice. Since this advice type is handled so differently than the others, we devoted a section specifically to introduction advice later in this chapter.

**Table 3.1   Advice types in Spring**

| Advice type | Interface | Description |
|---|---|---|
| Around | `org.aopalliance.intercept.MethodInterceptor` | Intercepts calls to the target method |
| Before | `org.springframework.aop.BeforeAdvice` | Called before the target method is invoked |
| After | `org.springframework.aop.AfterReturningAdvice` | Called after the target method returns |
| Throws | `org.springframework.aop.ThrowsAdvice` | Called when target method throws an exception |

As you can see, these different advice types give you opportunities to add behavior before and after a method invocation, as well as when a method throws an exception. In addition, you can put advice around a method and optionally prevent the target method from even being called. So now that you know what advice types are at your disposal, exactly how do you go about implementing them?

To demonstrate this, we are going to create a running example. This example is meant to serve as a simple illustration of Spring AOP at work and not as a working J2EE application (don't worry, we'll get to that). To do so, let's take a trip to Springfield and visit Apu's KwikEMart (see http://www.thesimpsons.com for more information). We will start off with the KwikEMart interface where a Customer can purchase a Squishee:

```
public interface KwikEMart {
  Squishee buySquishee(Customer customer) throws KwikEMartException;
}
```

We also have an implementation of this interface: ApuKwikEMart. As listing 3.1 illustrates, our implementation is quite simple, but it does what we need.

**Listing 3.1   ApuKwikEMart.java**

```
public class ApuKwikEMart implements KwikEMart {

  private boolean squisheeMachineEmpty;

  public Squishee buySquishee(Customer customer)
      throws KwikEMartException {
    if (customer.isBroke()) {
      throw new CustomerIsBrokeException();
    }
```

```
    if (squisheeMachineEmpty) {
      throw new NoMoreSquisheesException();
    }
    return new Squishee();
  }
}
```

Without much effort we have a working KwikEMart implementation, including test cases. Now we want to add some additional behavior to this class. However, the class is working just fine doing its fundamental duty—serving Squishees. So instead of cracking open this class and adding more code, we are going to create some advice instead.

### 3.2.1 *Before advice*

As any convenience store owner knows, friendly customer service is key. So before our customers purchase their Squishee, we want to give them a warm greeting. To do this, we need to add some functionality before the buySquishee() method is executed. To accomplish this, we extend the MethodBeforeAdvice interface:

```
public interface MethodBeforeAdvice {
  void before(Method method, Object[] args, Object target)
    throws Throwable
}
```

This interface provides you with access to the target method, the arguments passed to this method, and the target object of the method invocation. Since you have access to the method arguments, you have the opportunity to implement advice using the runtime parameters. However, you cannot change the identity of these values. That is, you cannot substitute different argument objects or a different target object. You *can* alter these objects; just use caution when doing so.

Now let's take a look at our implementation of MethodBeforeAdvice, shown in listing 3.2.

**Listing 3.2   WelcomeAdvice.java**

```
package com.springinaction.chapter03.store;

import java.lang.reflect.Method;
import org.springframework.aop.MethodBeforeAdvice;

public class WelcomeAdvice implements MethodBeforeAdvice {
  public void before(Method method, Object[] args, Object target) {
    Customer customer = (Customer) args[0];   <-- Cast first argument to Customer
```

```
      System.out.println("Hello " + customer.getName() +      Say hello to
          ". How are you doing?");                             Customer
   }
}
```

Because the buySquishee() method we will be advising has only one argument, we cast the first element in the argument array to a Customer. Then all we have do to is give the Customer a nice, warm greeting.

Notice that we do not return anything at the end of the method. This is because the return type is void. It is void because the target method will *always* be called after the MethodBeforeAdvice returns and it is the target method that is responsible for returning any values. The only way MethodBeforeAdvice can prevent the target method from being invoked is to throw an exception (or call System.exit(), but we don't want to do that!). The results of throwing an exception depend on the type of exception thrown. If the exception is a RuntimeException or if it is in the throws clause of the target method, it will propagate to the calling method. Otherwise, Spring's framework will catch the exception and rethrow it wrapped in a RuntimeException.

Now that we have our advice, we need to apply it to our KwikEMart object. We do this through our Spring configuration file (kwikemart.xml), shown in listing 3.3.

**Listing 3.3  Wiring MethodBeforeAdvice to a bean**

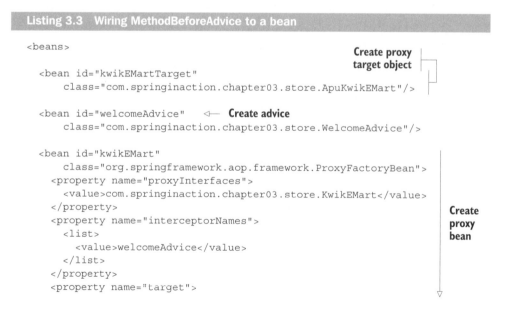

```
<beans>
                                                       Create proxy
                                                       target object
  <bean id="kwikEMartTarget"
      class="com.springinaction.chapter03.store.ApuKwikEMart"/>

  <bean id="welcomeAdvice"      <⎯  Create advice
      class="com.springinaction.chapter03.store.WelcomeAdvice"/>

  <bean id="kwikEMart"
      class="org.springframework.aop.framework.ProxyFactoryBean">
    <property name="proxyInterfaces">
      <value>com.springinaction.chapter03.store.KwikEMart</value>
    </property>                                                Create
    <property name="interceptorNames">                         proxy
      <list>                                                   bean
        <value>welcomeAdvice</value>
      </list>
    </property>
    <property name="target">
```

```
        <ref bean="kwikEMartTarget"/>    ⌁  Create
      </property>                            proxy
    </bean>                                  bean

  </beans>
```

We now have a KwikEMart bean that has the WelcomeAdvice applied to it. And if you notice, we created this bean using Spring's ProxyFactoryBean class. This is also your introduction to this very important class in Spring's AOP framework. The ProxyFactoryBean class is used by BeanFactory and ApplicationContext objects to generate proxies. In the above example, we configure a ProxyFactory-Bean using several of that bean's properties. Going down the list of properties in the example above, we tell Spring to create a bean that does the following:

- Implements the KwikEMart interface
- Applies the WelcomeAdvice (id welcomeAdvice) advice object to all incoming calls
- Uses the ApuKwikEMart bean (id kwikEMartTarget) as the target object

The ProxyFactoryBean class is a central class for explicitly creating proxied objects within a BeanFactory. As demonstrated, you can give it an interface to implement, a target object to proxy, and advice to weave in, and it will create a brand-new proxied object. And as in the example above, you will typically configure the ProxyFactoryBean to implement the same interface as your target object. We will explore this class in more detail in section 3.5. For now, assume we are going to configure all KwikEMart advice as illustrated in listing 3.3 unless otherwise noted.

### 3.2.2  *After advice*

Staying with the courteous store owner theme, we want to make sure we thank our patrons after they make their purchase. To do this, we implement AfterReturning-Advice:

```
public interface AfterReturningAdvice {
  void afterReturning(Object returnValue, Method method,
     Object[] args, Object target) throws Throwable
  }
}
```

Like MethodBeforeAdvice, this advice gives you access to the method that was called, the arguments that were passed, and the target object. You also have access to the return value of the advised method. Again, this interface returns `void`. While you have access to the return value of the target method, you cannot substitute a different return value. And as with `MethodBeforeAdvice`, the only way you can alter the flow of execution is by throwing an exception. The behavior for handling thrown exceptions is the same as `MethodBeforeAdvice`, as well.

Listing 3.4 shows what our advice would look like in our example.

**Listing 3.4    ThankYouAdvice.java**

```
package com.springinaction.chapter03.store;

import java.lang.reflect.Method;
import org.springframework.aop.AfterReturningAdvice;

public class ThankYouAdvice implements AfterReturningAdvice {

  public void afterReturning(Object returnValue, Method method,
      Object[] arg2, Object target) throws Throwable {
    System.out.println("Thank you. Come again!");
  }
}
```

With this advice, any normal method exit (i.e., no exception is thrown) of our proxied method will result in our customer being thanked.

### 3.2.3  *Around advice*

So far we have seen how to weave advice before and after a method. `MethodInterceptor` provides the ability to do both in one advice object:

```
public interface MethodInterceptor extends Interceptor {
  Object invoke(MethodInvocation invocation) throws Throwable;
}
```

There are two important differences between the `MethodInterceptor` interface and the previous two types of advice. First, the `MethodInterceptor` implementation controls whether the target method is actually invoked. Invoking the target method is done by calling `MethodInvocation.proceed()`. This is in contrast to `MethodBeforeAdvice`, where the target method is always called unless you throw an exception.

Second, `MethodInterceptor` gives you control over what object is returned. This means you can return a completely different object than the one returned by `proceed()`. Remember, with `AfterReturningAdvice` you had access to the object being returned, but you could not return a different object. While MethodInterceptor provides this added flexibility, you should use caution when returning a different object than the one returned by the target method and only do so when necessary.

Let's take a look at MethodInterceptor in use. Suppose we have a rule that a customer can order only one Squishee. OnePerCustomerInterceptor is shown in listing 3.5.

**Listing 3.5   OnePerCustomerInterceptor.java**

```java
package com.springinaction.chapter03.store;

import java.util.HashSet;
import java.util.Set;

import org.aopalliance.intercept.MethodInterceptor;
import org.aopalliance.intercept.MethodInvocation;

public class OnePerCustomerInterceptor implements MethodInterceptor {

  private Set customers = new HashSet();          ◁─┘ Define Set containing
                                                       previous customers

  public Object invoke(MethodInvocation invocation)          Get current
      throws Throwable {                                      customer
    Customer customer = (Customer) invocation.getArguments()[0];   ◁─┘
    if (customers.contains(customer)) {
      throw new KwikEMartException("One per customer.");    Throw exception if
    }                                                       repeat customer
    Object squishee = invocation.proceed();    ◁─ Invoke target method
    customers.add(customer);    ◁─ Add customer to Set
    return squishee;        ◁─┐ Return result of
  }                            target method

}
```

Notice that we have logic before and after the target method being invoked. Before we call the target method, we want to make sure the customer has not already purchased a Squishee. If they have not, we continue. After our target method has executed, we "remember" the customer so they cannot purchase another Squishee.

This example serves as a demonstration of when you should use this type of advice. You should only use a MethodInterceptor when you require cross-cutting aspect logic on both sides of the method invocation. Since you have to remember to explicitly call invocation.proceed(), it is better to use MethodBeforeAdvice or AfterReturningAdvice if this will satisfy your needs.

There is one more thing you should notice about `MethodInterceptor`. If you remember from table 3.1, `MethodInterceptor` in an AOP Alliance interface. This means that any advice you implement using this interface is compatible with any other AOP framework that is compliant with the AOP Alliance. You may want to make special note of this if you are planning to work with multiple AOP frameworks.

### 3.2.4 *Throws advice*

So what happens if something goes wrong during the method invocation and an exception is thrown? `ThrowsAdvice` lets you define behavior should an exception occur. Unlike the previous advice types, `ThrowsAdvice` is a marker interface and contains no methods that need to be implemented. Instead, a class that implements this interface must have at least one method with either of the following two signatures:

```
void afterThrowing(Throwable throwable)
```

```
void afterThrowing(Method method, Object[] args, Object target,
  Throwable throwable)
```

The first of these methods receives only one argument: the exception that was thrown. The second of these receives the exception and the invoked method, its argument, and the target object. Unless you need these additional arguments, you will only need to implement the one-argument variety. The type of exception handled by your `ThrowsAdvice` is determined by the type in your method signature. For example, `void afterThrowing(KwikEMartException e)` will catch any `KwikEMartException`, but `void afterThrowing(NoMoreSquisheesException e)` would only catch that specific subclass of `KwikEMartException`.

You can also have more than one `afterThrowing` method in the same class. Listing 3.6 gives an example of `ThrowsAdvice` in action.

#### Listing 3.6   KwikEMartExceptionAdvice.java

```
package com.springinaction.chapter03.store;

import org.springframework.aop.ThrowsAdvice;

public class KwikEMartExceptionAdvice implements ThrowsAdvice {

  public void afterThrowing(NoMoreSquisheesException e) {
    orderMoreSquishees();
  }
```

```
public void afterThrowing(CustomerIsBrokeException e) {
    showCustomerAtmMachine();
}
}
```

The correct method will be called depending on what type of exception is thrown. Notice that both of these methods add additional behavior to the application, but neither catches and handles the exception. This is because you cannot do this. The proxy object is catching the exception and calling the appropriate `ThrowsAdvice` method, if there is one. After the `ThrowsAdvice` is executed, the original exception will still be thrown and will propagate up the stack like any other exception. The only way your `ThrowsAdvice` can change this is to throw another exception.

### 3.2.5 *Introduction advice*

Introduction advice is a little different from the other types of advice we just covered. All the other types are woven in at some point surrounding a target object's method invocation. Introduction advice *adds* new methods (and attributes) to the target object. This is probably the most complex advice type to understand. And to understand Spring's introduction advice, you need to understand its pointcuts as well. So we will discuss pointcuts in the next section and revisit introduction advice in more detail in section 3.4.

## 3.3 *Defining pointcuts*

So far we have only discussed how to write advice. This is not very useful if we cannot expressively define where this advice should be applied in our application. This is where pointcuts come in. Pointcuts determine if a particular method on a particular class matches a particular criterion. If the method is indeed a match, then advice will be applied to this method. Spring's pointcuts allow us to define where our advice is woven into our classes in a very flexible manner.

### 3.3.1 *Defining a pointcut in Spring*

Spring defines pointcuts in terms of the class and method that is being advised. Advice is woven into the target class and its methods are based on their characteristics, such as class name and method signature. The core interface for Spring's pointcut framework is, naturally, the `Pointcut` interface.

```
public interface Pointcut {
    ClassFilter getClassFilter();
```

```
    MethodMatcher getMethodMatcher();
  }
```

This is logical since we just said a `Pointcut` decides where to weave our advice based on our method and classes. The `ClassFilter` interface determines if a class is eligible for advising:

```
public interface ClassFilter {
  boolean matches(Class clazz);
}
```

Classes implementing this interface determine if the `Class` that is passed in as an argument should be advised. Typical implementations of this interface make this decision based on the name of the class, but this does not always have to be the case. This interface also contains a simple implementation of the `ClassFilter` interface, `ClassFilter.TRUE`. This is the canonical instance of `ClassFilter` that matches any class, which can be useful for creating a `Pointcut` that only considers methods when matching.

While `ClassFilter` lets you filter your aspects by class, you are more likely interested in filtering by method. This feature is provided by the `MethodMatcher` interface:

```
public interface MethodMatcher {
  boolean matches(Method m, Class targetClass);
  public boolean isRuntime();
  public boolean matches(Method m, Class target, Object[] args);
}
```

As you can see, there are three methods in this interface, but each one is used in a certain point in a proxied object's life cycle. The `matches(Method, Class)` method determines whether a method is a candidate to be advised based on the target `Class` and `Method`. Since this can be determined statically, this method is only called once—when the AOP proxy is created. The result of this method determines if the advice is woven in at all.

If `matches(Method, Class)` returns `true`, `isRuntime()` is called to determine what type of `MethodMatcher` this is. There are two types: *static* and *dynamic*. Static pointcuts define advice that is *always* executed. If a pointcut is static, `isRuntime()` should return `false`. Dynamic pointcuts determine if advice should be executed by examining the runtime method arguments. If a pointcut is dynamic, `isRuntime()` should return `true`. Like `matches(Method, Class)`, `isRuntime()` is only called once—when the proxy class is created.

If a pointcut is static, `matches(Method, Class, Object[])` is never called, since runtime arguments are not necessary for determining whether advice should be applied. For dynamic pointcuts, the `matches(Method, Class, Object[])` method is called at runtime for *every* invocation of the target method. This adds runtime overhead for every time this method is invoked. To avoid this, use static pointcuts wherever possible.

Now you know how to define pointcuts in Spring. Although you can implement the `Pointcut` interface yourself, you will most likely use one of Spring's predefined `Pointcut` implementations. This is what we will explore next. Well, not exactly next. We need to cover advisors first.

### 3.3.2 *Understanding advisors*

Before we cover Spring's built-in pointcuts, you must understand another Spring concept: an *advisor*. Most aspects are a combination of advice that defines the aspect's behavior and a pointcut defining where the aspect should be executed. Spring recognizes this and offers advisors, which combine advice and pointcuts into one object. More specifically, the `PointcutAdvisor` does this.

```
public interface PointcutAdvisor {
    Pointcut getPointcut();
    Advice getAdvice();
}
```

Most of Spring's built-in pointcuts also have a corresponding `PointcutAdvisor`. This is convenient if you want to define a pointcut and the advice it is managing in one place. As we discuss pointcuts in depth, we will use `PointcutAdvisors` in of our examples where it makes sense.

### 3.3.3 *Using Spring's static pointcuts*

As discussed earlier, static pointcuts are preferred because they perform better than dynamic pointcuts since they are evaluated once (when the proxy is created) rather than at each runtime invocation. Spring provides a convenience superclass for creating static pointcuts: `StaticMethodMatcherPointcut`. So if you want to create a custom static pointcut, you can override this class and implement the `isMatch` method.

But for most of your needs, you will use a static pointcut provided by Spring.

#### *NameMatchMethodPointcut*

The most basic of these is the `NameMatchMethodPointcut`. This class has two methods you should be interested in:

```
public void setMappedName(String)
public void setMappedNames(String[])
```

As you might have guessed, this pointcut matches when the invoked method's name matches one of the given mapped names. You can provide explicit method names or use the wildcard character * at the beginning or end of the name. For instance, setting the mappedName property to set* will match all setter methods. Note that this matching only applies to the method name itself, not the fully qualified name that includes that class name as well. The two methods above behave exactly the same, except that the former matches against one name, while the latter looks at an array of Strings for a match. If any one of the mapped Strings matches, then the method is considered a match.

For example, let's say instead of a Spring Training service, we are running a Spring Cleaning maid service. For this application, we have a MaidService interface that has several methods for ordering services, such orderFurniturePolishing and orderWindowCleaning. For each of these methods, we want to add an aspect that adds points to the orderer's account so they can earn free services offered to frequent customers. Listing 3.7 illustrates how we would map this using a NameMatchMethodPointcut.

**Listing 3.7   Configuring a NameMatchMethodPointcutAdvisor**

```xml
<beans>

    <bean id="maidServiceTarget" class="com.springinaction.
        ➡ chapter03.cleaning.MaidServiceImpl"/>

    <bean id="frequentCustomerAdvice" class="com.springinaction.
        ➡ chapter03.cleaning.FrequentCustomerAdvice"/>

    <bean id="frequentCustomerPointcutAdvisor"
        class="org.springframework.aop.support.
            ➡ NameMatchMethodPointcutAdvisor">
      <property name="mappedName">
        <value>order*</value>
      </property>
      <property name="advice">
        <ref bean="frequentCustomerAdvice"/>
      </property>
    </bean>

    <bean id="maidService"
        class="org.springframework.aop.framework.ProxyFactoryBean">
      <property name="proxyInterfaces">
        <value>com.springinaction.chapter03.
            ➡ cleaning.MaidService</value>
      </property>
      <property name="interceptorNames">
```

```
      <list>
        <value>frequentCustomerAdvisor</value>
      </list>
    </property>
    <property name="target">
      <value ref="maidServiceTarget">
    </property>
  </bean>

</beans>
```

When our proxy is created, invocations of any method on our `MaidService` object that begins with `order` will be advised by our `FrequentCustomerAdvice`. And instead of supplying the wildcard characters, we just as easily explicitly name each of these methods:

```
<property name="mappedNames">
  <list>
    <value>orderFurniturePolishing</name>
    <value>orderWindowCleaning</name>
  </list>
</property>
```

Using a `NamedMethodMatcherPointcut` works well for clearly expressing exactly which methods you want advised. However, listing *every* method name you want advised could become quite verbose for a large application. Using the wildcard can help this, but its usefulness is limited if you want fine-grained control over your pointcuts. That is where regular expressions come in.

### Regular expression pointcuts

Spring's `RegexpMethodPointcut` lets you leverage the power of regular expressions to define your pointcuts. This enables you to use Perl-style regular expressions to define the pattern that should match your intended methods. If you are unfamiliar with regular expressions, table 3.2 lists the symbols you will most likely use when defining pointcuts.

**Table 3.2   Common regular expression symbols used in pointcuts**

| Symbol | Description | Example |
|--------|-------------|---------|
| . | Matches any single character | `setFoo.` matches `setFooB`, but not `setFoo` or `setFooBar` |
| + | Matches the preceding character one or more times | `setFoo.+` matches `setFooBar` and `setFooB`, but not `setFoo` |

*continued on next page*

**Table 3.2 Common regular expression symbols used in pointcuts** *(continued)*

| Symbol | Description | Example |
|--------|-------------|---------|
| * | Matches the preceding character zero or more times | `setFoo.*` matches `setFoo`, `setFooB` and `setFooBar` |
| \ | Escapes any regular expression symbol | `\.setFoo.` matches `bar.setFoo`, but not and `setFoo` |

Unlike the `NameMethodMatcherPointcut`, these patterns include the *class* name as well as the method name. That means if we want to match all `setXxx` methods, we need to use the pattern `.*set.*` (the first wildcard will match any preceding class name). Also, when you are using the `RegexpMethodPointcut`, you need to include the Jakarta Commons ORO[3] library in your application.

Continuing with our Spring Cleaning business, our `MaidService` interface also offers clients different methods for querying our cleaning packages, such as `getPackagesByPrice()` and `getSpecialsByDay()`. We decide we want to capture the details of our customers' queries so we know what they are looking for most frequently. So, we create a `QueryInterceptor` to do just that. We would apply this interceptor to our query methods as illustrated in listing 3.8.

**Listing 3.8 Configuring a RegexpMethodPointutAdvisor**

```xml
<beans>

  <bean id="maidServiceTarget"
      class="com.springinaction.chapter03.cleaning.MaidService"/>

  <bean id="queryInterceptor" class="com.springinaction.
      chapter03.cleaning.QueryInterceptor"/>

  <bean id="queryPointcutAdvisor"
      class="org.springframework.aop.support.RegExpPointcutAdvisor">
    <property name="pattern">
      <value>.*get.+By.+</value>
    </property>
    <property name="advice">
      <ref bean="queryInterceptor"/>
    </property>
  </bean>
```

---

[3] Jakarta Commons ORO is an open source utility for text-processing using Perl and Awk regular expressions. Its name comes from the company that donated the original libraries, ORO Inc. You can learn more about ORO at http://jakarta.apache.org/oro/.

```
<bean id="maidService"
    class="org.springframework.aop.framework.ProxyFactoryBean">
  <property name="proxyInterfaces">
    <value>com.springinaction.chapter03.
       ➡ cleaning.MaidService</value>
  </property>
  <property name="interceptorNames">
    <list>
      <value>queryPointcutAdvisor</value>
    </list>
  </property>
  <property name="target">
    <value ref="maidServiceTarget">
  </property>
</bean>

</beans>
```

Interpreting the regular expression, this means our pointcut should match any method on any class that begins with get and then contains at least one character, followed by By, followed by at least one character. As you can see, regular expressions offer you a way to define pointcuts in a way that is more expressive than a NameMatchMethodPointcut.

### 3.3.4 *Using dynamic pointcuts*

So far the only Spring-provided pointcuts we have discussed have been static pointcuts. They will be the type of pointcuts you will use most often. However, there may be some cases where your pointcuts will need to evaluate runtime attributes. Spring provides one built-in dynamic pointcut: ControlFlowPointcut. This pointcut matches based on information about the current thread's call stack. That is, it can be configured to return true only if a particular method or class is found in the current thread's stack of execution.

For example, let's say we have a service method that can be called from a variety of clients. If this method is initiated from a web application, we want to add some additional logic in the form of a MethodBeforeAdvice (the content of this advice is not important for this example). We can do so by creating a pointcut that matches if our call stack contains a call from javax.servlet.http.HttpServlet. Listing 3.9 illustrates how we would configure this.

**Listing 3.9  Configuring a ControlFlowPointcut**

```xml
<beans>

  <bean id="myServiceTarget" class="MyServiceImpl"/>

  <bean id="servletInterceptor" class="MyServletInterceptor"/>

  <bean id="servletPointcut"
      class="org.springframework.aop.support.
            ControlFlowPointcut">
    <constructor-arg>
      <value>javax.servlet.http.HttpServlet</value>
    </constructor-arg>
  </bean>

  <bean id="servletAdvisor"
    class="org.springframework.aop.support.DefaultPointcutAdvisor">
      <property name="advice">
        <ref bean="servletInterceptor"/>
      </property>
      <property name="pointcut">
        <ref bean="servletPointcut"/>
      </property>
  </bean>

  <bean id="service"
      class="org.springframework.aop.framework.ProxyFactoryBean">
    <property name="proxyInterfaces">
      <value>MyService</value></property>
    <property name="interceptorNames">
      <list>
        <value>servletAdvisor</value>
      </list>
    </property>
    <property name="target">
      <value ref="myServiceTarget">
    </property>
  </bean>
</beans>
```

Now any call to a method in our service object that comes from an `HttpServlet` will have the `ServletAdvice` applied. One important thing to point out about this class is the performance penalty it imposes. You should use the `ControlFlow-Pointcut` class only as needed because it is significantly slower than other dynamic pointcuts. For Java 1.4, they may be 5 times slower, and for Java 1.3 they could be more than 10 times slower.

As stated earlier, the `ControlFlowPointcut` is the only dynamic pointcut implementation provided by Spring. But remember, you can create your own dynamic pointcut by implementing `MethodMatcher` and have the `isRuntime()` method return `true`. This effectively makes the pointcut dynamic and the `matches(Method m, Class target, Object[] args)` method will be called for every method invocation this pointcut evaluates. Again, keep in mind that this approach can have significant performance penalties. And since a vast majority of your pointcut needs can be resolved statically, we feel you will rarely have the occasion to create a dynamic pointcut.

### 3.3.5 *Pointcut operations*

You can now create reusable pointcuts for your applications. Adding to this reusability, Spring supports operations on these pointcuts—namely unions and intersections—to create new pointcuts. Intersections match when both pointcuts match; unions match when either pointcut matches. Spring provides two classes for creating these types of pointcuts.

The first of these classes is `ComposablePointcut`. You assemble `ComposablePointcut` objects by creating unions and intersections with existing `ComposablePointcut` objects and `Pointcut`, `MethodMatcher`, and `ClassFilter` objects. You do this by calling one of the `intersection()` or `union()` methods on an instance of `ComposablePointcut`. Each `intersection()` and `union()` returns the resulting `ComposablePointcut` object, which can be useful for chaining method calls like so:

```
ComposablePointcut p = new ComposablePointcut();
p = p.intersection (myPointcut).union(myMethodMatcher);
```

You can combine any number of `Pointcut`, `ClassFilter`, and `MethodMatcher` objects in this manner. The only method not available in this class is a `union(Pointcut)` method. To create a union between two `Pointcut` objects, you must use the `Pointcuts` class. `Pointcuts` is a utility class that contains static methods that operate on `Pointcut` objects. Creating a union between two `Pointcut` objects would look like this:

```
Pointcut union = Pointcuts.union(pointcut1, pointcut2);
```

You would create an intersection between two `Pointcut` objects in a similar fashion. The one drawback to this approach is that it is done programmatically. It would be nice if we could do the same thing in a declarative fashion. But since Spring works so well configuring JavaBeans, there is no reason we could not construct our own class that creates `Pointcut` unions in a configurable fashion. Listing 3.10 is an example of how this might be done.

**Listing 3.10   UnionPointcut.java**

```java
package com.springinaction.chapter03.aop;

import java.util.List;

import org.springframework.aop.ClassFilter;
import org.springframework.aop.MethodMatcher;
import org.springframework.aop.Pointcut;
import org.springframework.aop.framework.AopConfigException;
import org.springframework.aop.support.Pointcuts;

public class UnionPointcut implements Pointcut {

  private Pointcut delegate;        ◁— Declare unioned Pointcut instance

  public ClassFilter getClassFilter() {
    return getDelegate().getClassFilter();
  }

  public MethodMatcher getMethodMatcher() {
    return getDelegate().getMethodMatcher();
  }

  private Pointcut getDelegate() {
    if (delegate == null) {
        throw new AopConfigException(
            "No pointcuts have been configured.");
    }
    return delegate;
  }

  public void setPointcuts(List pointcuts) {

    if (pointcuts == null || pointcuts.size() == 0) {
      throw new AopConfigException(
            "Must have at least one Pointcut.");
    }

    delegate = (Pointcut) pointcuts.get(0);

    for (int i = 1; i < pointcuts.size(); i++) {
      Pointcut pointcut = (Pointcut) pointcuts.get(i);
      delegate = Pointcuts.union(delegate, pointcut);
    }
  }
}
```

Annotations (right margin):
- **Delegate Pointcut interface methods** — pointing to `getClassFilter()` and `getMethodMatcher()` methods
- **Throw exception if not configured** — pointing to `getDelegate()` method
- **Create unioned Pointcut** — pointing to `setPointcuts()` method

We now have a bean that allows us to declaratively create a `Pointcut` made up of two or more existing `Pointcut` beans, freeing us from having to do this programmatically.

## 3.4 *Creating introductions*

As we mentioned earlier, introductions are a little different than the other types of Spring advice. The other advice types are woven in at different joinpoints surrounding a method invocation. Introductions affect an entire class. They do so by adding new methods and attributes to the advised class. This means you can take an existing class and have it implement additional interfaces and maintain additional state (this is also known as a *mix-in*). In other words, introductions allow you to build composite objects dynamically, affording you the same benefits as multiple inheritance.

### 3.4.1 *Implementing IntroductionInterceptor*

Spring implements introductions through a special subinterface of `Method-Interceptor`: `IntroductionMethodInterceptor`. This interface adds one additional method:

```
boolean implementsInterface (Class intf);
```

This method is critical to how introduction works. `implementsInterface` returns `true` if the `IntroductionMethodInterceptor` is responsible for implementing the given interface. This means that any invocation of a method that is declared by this interface will be delegated to the `invoke()` method of the `Introduction-MethodInterceptor`. The `invoke()` method is now responsible for implementing this method—it cannot call `MethodInvocation.proceed()`. It is introducing the new interface; proceeding to the target object doesn't make sense.

To better explain this, let's return to our Spring Training application for an example. We now have a new requirement where we have to track the time of the most recent modification to any of our domain objects. Currently, none of these objects (`Course`, `Student`, etc.) support this functionality. Instead of altering each one of these classes to add this new method and state, we decide to introduce this feature through, what else, an introduction.

First, let's take a look at the interface we are introducing in listing 3.11.

**Listing 3.11  Auditable.java**

```
package com.springinaction.training.advice;

import java.util.Date;

public interface Auditable {
  void setLastModifiedDate(Date date);
  Date getLastModifiedDate();
}
```

Pretty straightforward, right? Now we need to implement an Introduction-
MethodInterceptor, as shown in listing 3.12.

**Listing 3.12  AuditableMixin.java subclassing IntroductionInterceptor**

```
package com.springinaction.training.advice;

import java.util.Date;

import org.aopalliance.intercept.MethodInvocation;
import org.springframework.aop.IntroductionInterceptor;

public class AuditableMixin
    implements IntroductionInterceptor, Auditable {

  public boolean implementsInterface(Class intf) {          Implement
    return intf.isAssignableFrom(Auditable.class);          Auditable
  }

  public Object invoke(MethodInvocation m) throws Throwable {
    if (implementsInterface(m.getMethod().getDeclaringClass())) {
      return m.getMethod().invoke(this, m.getArguments());
    }                                                         Invoke introduced method
    else {              Delegate
      return m.proceed();   other
    }                       method
  }

  private Date lastModifiedDate;

  public Date getLastModifiedDate() {
    return lastModifiedDate;                                 Implement
  }                                                          mix-in
                                                             logic
  public void setLastModifiedDate(Date lastModifiedDate) {
    this.lastModifiedDate = lastModifiedDate;
  }

}
```

There are a couple things worth noting in this example. First, our class implements not only the Spring interface `IntroductionInterceptor` but also our business interface `Auditable`. This is because this class is responsible for the actual implementation of this interface. This is evident by the two `Auditable` methods and the `lastModifiedDate` attribute that is used to keep track of the state.

Second, `implementsInterface` returns `true` if the class declaring the invoked method is of type `Auditable`. This means that for either of the two `Auditable` methods, our interceptor must provide an implementation. And that is exactly what we are doing in our invoke method; for any invocation of an `Auditable` interface method, we invoke that method on our interceptor; for all others we allow the method invocation to proceed.

This is a typical introduction scenario—so typical, in fact, that Spring provides a convenience class that handles most of this for us: `DelegatingIntroduction-Interceptor`. Listing 3.13 shows how by using this class, our previous example becomes much simpler.

> **Listing 3.13   AuditableMixin.java subclassing** `DelegatingIntroduction-Interceptor`

```
package com.springinaction.training.advice.AuditableMixin;

import java.util.Date;

import org.springframework.aop.support.
       DelegatingIntroductionInterceptor;

public class AuditableMixin
    extends DelegatingIntroductionInterceptor implements Auditable {

  private Date lastModifiedDate;

  public Date getLastModifiedDate() {
    return lastModifiedDate;
  }

  public void setLastModifiedDate(Date lastModifiedDate) {
    this.lastModifiedDate = lastModifiedDate;
  }

}
```

Notice how we don't have to implement `invoke()`—`DelegatingIntroductionInterceptor` handles that for us. `DelegatingIntroductionInterceptor` will also implement any interface exposed on your mix-in class and delegate any calls to these methods to this mix-in. Since our class implements `Auditable`, all invocations for methods on this interface will be called on our interceptor. Any other methods are delegated to the target object. If your interceptor class implements an interface you do *not* want exposed as a mix-in, simply pass the interface to the `suppressInterface()` method of the `DelegatingIntroductionInterceptor` class.

Now we said that you do not have to implement `invoke()`, but you can if your mix-in alters the behavior of any target method. For instance, suppose you have an `Immutable` interface with a single method that you want to introduce. This interface should provide the ability to make an object immutable—its internal state cannot be changed. Listing 3.14 illustrates how we might do this.

**Listing 3.14   ImmutableMixin.java**

```
package com.springinaction.chapter03.aop;

import org.aopalliance.intercept.MethodInvocation;
import org.springframework.aop.support.
       DelegatingIntroductionInterceptor;

public class ImmutableMixin
    extends DelegatingIntroductionInterceptor implements Immutable {

  private boolean immutable;

  public void setImmutable(boolean immutable) {       Keep track of
    this.immutable = immutable;                        immutable
  }

  public Object invoke(MethodInvocation mi) throws Throwable {
    String name = mi.getMethod().getName();            Throw
    if (immutable && name.indexOf("set") == 0) {       exception
      throw new IllegalModificationException();        if setter is
    }                                                  invoked
    return super.invoke(mi);
  }
}
```

Our mix-in now overrides `invoke()` so that it intercepts all method invocations. We do this so any call to a method with the signature `set*` will throw an exception if `immutable` is set to `true`. Notice how we call `super.invoke()` if we do not throw an exception, as opposed to calling `mi.proceed()`. We do this so that the `Delegating-IntroductionInterceptor` superclass can determine what class is responsible for handling the method invocation (it may not be our target object). It is important that whenever you override the `invoke()` method you also call `super.invoke()` to ensure the method invocation proceeds correctly.

### 3.4.2  *Creating an IntroductionAdvisor*

Now that we have our introduction advice, we need to create an advisor. Since introduction advice is applied only at the class level, introductions have their own advisor: `IntroductionAdvisor`. Spring also provides a default implementation that is suitable most of the time. It is aptly named `DefaultIntroductionAdvisor` and takes an `IntroductionInterceptor` as a constructor argument. So, when we integrate an `IntroductionAdvisor` into our `AuditableMixin` example, listing 3.15 gives an example of what our configuration might look like.

**Listing 3.15   Configuring an introduction**

```
<beans>

  <bean id="courseTarget"
      class="com.springinaction.training.model.Course"
      singleton="false"/>

  <bean id="auditableMixin"
      class="com.springinaction.training.advice.AuditableMixin"
      singleton="false"/>

  <bean id="auditableAdvisor" class="org.springframework.
          aop.support.DefaultIntroductionAdvisor"
      singleton="false">
    <constructor-arg>
        <ref bean="auditableMixin"/>
    </constructor-arg>
  </bean>

  <bean id="course"
      class="org.springframework.aop.framework.ProxyFactoryBean">
    <property name="proxyTargetClass">
      <value>true</value>
    </property>
    <property name="singleton">
      <value>false</value>
    </property>
    <property name="proxyInterfaces">
      <value>com.springinaction.training.advice.Auditable</value>
    </property>
    <property name="auditableAdvisor">
      <list>
        <value>servletAdvisor</value>
```

```
      </list>
    </property>
    <property name="target">
      <value ref="courseTarget">
    </property>
  </bean>

</beans>
```

One important thing to notice is all three of our AOP-related beans (`auditable-Mixin`, `auditableAdvisor`, and `course`) have their `singleton` property set to `false`. This is because we are introducing a *stateful* mixin. Therefore, we need to have a new instance of each of these created every time we request a course bean from the `BeanFactory`. If we did not set the singleton property to `false`, we would have one introduction object holding the state for all of our advised objects. Clearly we do not want this.

### 3.4.3 *Using introduction advice carefully*

Most other types of advice, such as before and after advice, typically introduce new behavior. Introduction advice, on the other hand, adds new interfaces and often new state to objects. This is a very powerful concept, but it must be used with caution.

In our earlier example, we are introducing the `Auditable` interface to our `Course` class. However, this advice in woven into a `Course` object *only* when that object is obtained from a Spring `BeanFactory`. Remember, Spring advice is woven into your objects at runtime, as opposed to other AOP frameworks that may weave the advice into the class's bytecode. This means that a `Course` object that is created or obtained by any other means will *not* have the introduced advice. This applies to `Course` instances created by your code via a `Course` constructor, instances created by another framework (e.g., a persistence framework such as Hibernate), and instances that are deserialized.

This means you cannot use introductions for objects that are created with your code. It is possible to instantiate an object somewhere in your code but still have the introduction advice applied. The way to do this is to acquire your object from a factory. For example, you could create a `CourseFactory` interface that is used to obtain new instance of `Course` objects:

```java
public interface CourseFactory {
  Course getCourse();
}
```

Since you don't want your classes to depend on any Spring-specific classes, any class that needs to obtain a new instance of a Course object can be wired with an instance of a CourseFactory. You can then create an implementation that delegates to the Spring BeanFactory, as shown in listing 3.16.

**Listing 3.16   BeanFactoryCourseFactory.java**

```
package com.springinaction.training.model;

import org.springframework.beans.factory.BeanFactory;
import org.springframework.beans.factory.BeanFactoryAware;

public BeanFactoryCourseFactory
    implements CourseFactory, BeanFactoryAware {

  private BeanFactory beanFactory;

  public void setBeanFactory(BeanFactory beanFactory) {
    this.beanFactory = beanFactory;
  }

  public Course getCourse() {
    return (Course) beanFactory.getBean("course");
  }
}
```

Now, instead of instantiating a Course object via a constructor, your code can obtain new Course instances through a CourseFactory:

```
...
private CourseFactory courseFactory;

public void setCourseFactory(CourseFactory courseFactory) {
  this.courseFactory = courseFactory;
}

public void someMethod() {
  Course course = CourseFactory.getCourse();
  ...
}
```

Your class now receives the advised version of the Course object, which was our goal. This is one solution for getting new instances of objects that have introduction. However, if you rely on frameworks that also instantiate these same objects, you may still have some problems. You should just be aware of this issue when dealing with introduction advice.

## 3.5 *Using ProxyFactoryBean*

Throughout this chapter we demonstrated how to create an advised class using a `ProxyFactoryBean`. When you want to explicitly control how your advising classes are assembled, this is your best and most flexible choice.

As you learned in the previous chapter, `BeanFactory` objects are JavaBeans that are responsible for creating other JavaBeans. In this case, our `ProxyFactoryBean` creates proxied objects. And like other JavaBeans, it has properties that control its behavior. We touched on a couple of these earlier, but we are going to cover them all in more detail right now. Table 3.3 explains each property on `ProxyFactoryBean`.

**Table 3.3** `ProxyFactoryBean` **properties**

| Property | Use |
|---|---|
| target | The target bean of the proxy. |
| proxyInterfaces | A list of interfaces that should be implemented by the proxy. |
| interceptorNames | The bean names of the advice to be applied to the target. These can be names of interceptors, advisors, or any other advice type. This property must be set in order to use this bean in a `BeanFactory`. |
| singleton | Whether the factory should return the same instance of the proxy for each `get-Bean` invocation. If you're using stateful advice, this should be set to `false`. |
| aopProxyFactory | The implementation of the `ProxyFactoryBean` interface to be used. Spring comes with two implementations (JDK dynamic proxies and CGLIB). You probably won't need to use this property. |
| exposeProxy | Whether the target class should have access to the current proxy. This is done by calling `AopContext.getCurrentProxy`. Keep in mind that doing so introduces Spring-specific AOP code into your code base, so this should be avoided unless necessary. |
| frozen | Whether changes can be made to the proxy's advice once the factory is created. When set to `true`, this disables runtime `ProxyFactoryBean` changes. You will probably not need this property, |
| optimize | Whether to aggressively optimize generated proxies (only applies to CGLIB proxies). This can add slight performance gains, but should be used judiciously. |
| proxyTargetClass | Whether to proxy the target class, rather than implementing an interface. You must use CGLIB for this (i.e., the CGLIB JAR files must be deployed). |

In most `ProxyFactoryBean` configurations, you will need to be concerned with only a few of these properties. The three properties you will probably use most often are `target`, `proxyInterfaces`, and `interceptorNames`.

The `target` property defines what bean should be the target object of the generated proxy object. This is the object that is being advised. In this example:

```
<bean id="courseServiceTarget" class="com.springinaction.
    training.service.CourseServiceImpl"/>

<bean id="courseService"
    class="org.springframework.aop.framework.ProxyFactoryBean">
  <property name="target">
    <ref bean="courseServiceTarget"/>
  </property>
  ...
</bean>
```

As you can see, an instance of `CourseServiceImpl` is the target object of our `ProxyFactoryBean`. However, in this configuration, both beans can be obtained from our `BeanFactory` with a call to `getBean()`. Both beans can also be wired to other beans with your application. If you want to avoid exposing the target class to other beans in your application, you can declare it as an inner bean of the `ProxyFactoryBean`:

```
<bean id="courseService"
    class="org.springframework.aop.framework.ProxyFactoryBean">
  <property name="target">
    <bean class"com.springinaction.training.
                service.CourseServiceImpl"/>
  </property>
  ...
</bean>
```

Now the `ProxyFactoryBean` is the only `CourseService` bean that can be obtained from the `BeanFactory`. This can help prevent you from accidentally wiring an unadvised `CourseService` object to one of your beans.

The `proxyInterfaces` property is a list of interfaces that should be implemented by the beans created by the factory. For example, suppose you set this property as follows:

```
<property name="proxyInterfaces">
  <value>com.springinaction.training.service.CourseService</value>
</property>
```

This would let the `ProxyBeanFactory` know that any bean it creates should also implement the `CourseService` interface. You can supply a single interface as above or multiple interfaces with a `<list>` element.

The `interceptorNames` property is a list of advisor or advice bean names that should be applied to the target bean. The ordering of the list is important as this dictates the order in which the advice will be applied. Returning to our `Course-Service` example, here is how we would apply a series of advice beans to our `CourseServiceTarget` bean:

```
<property name="proxyInterfaces">
  <list>
    <value>securityAdvice</value>
    <value>transactionAdvice</value>
  </list>
</property>
```

In this example, `securityAdvice` will be applied first, followed by `transaction-Advice`. You can also include the bean name of your *target* bean in this list, but it must the last one in the list.

```
<property name="proxyInterfaces">
  <list>
    <value>securityAdvice</value>
    <value>transactionAdvice</value>
    <value>courseServiceTarget</value>
  </list>
</property>
```

In this case, both advice beans will be applied, followed by an invocation of the target bean. Although this configuration is possible, it is better to configure the target bean using the `target` property, simply because it is clearer.

## 3.6 Autoproxying

So far we have created our proxy objects using the `ProxyFactoryBean` class. This works fine for small applications since there are not that many classes we want to advise. But when we have several, sometimes dozens of classes we want to advise, it becomes cumbersome to explicitly create every proxy.

Luckily, Spring has an autoproxy facility that enables the container to generate proxies for us. We do so in a very Springy way—we configure a bean to do the dirty work for us. Specifically, we create autoproxy creator beans. Spring comes with two classes that provide this support: `BeanNameAutoProxyCreator` and `DefaultAdvisorAutoProxyCreator`.

### 3.6.1 BeanNameAutoProxyCreator

`BeanNameAutoProxyCreator` generates proxies for beans that match a set of names. This name matching is similar to the `NameMethodMatcherPointcut` discussed earlier, as it allows for wildcard matching on both ends of the name. This is typically used to apply an aspect or a group of aspects uniformly across a set of beans that follow a similar naming convention. For example, we may want to add a `Perfor-manceThresholdInterceptor` to all of our service beans. This interceptor would track how long each service method invocation lasts, and take action if this time exceeds a given threshold. Listing 3.17 provides a sample of what this class would look like.

**Listing 3.17   PerformanceThresholdInterceptor**

```
package com.springinaction.training.advice;

import org.aopalliance.intercept.MethodInterceptor;
import org.aopalliance.intercept.MethodInvocation;

public class PerformanceThresholdInterceptor
    implements MethodInterceptor {

  private final long thresholdInMillis;

  public PerformanceThresholdInterceptor(long thresholdInMillis) {
    this.thresholdInMillis = thresholdInMillis;
  }

  public Object invoke(MethodInvocation invocation)
      throws Throwable {
    long t = System.currentTimeMillis();
    Object o = invocation.proceed();
    t = System.currentTimeMillis() - t;
    if (t > thresholdInMillis) {
      warnThresholdExceeded();
    }
    return o;
  }

  private void warnThresholdExceeded() {
    System.out.println("Danger! Danger!");
  }
}
```

**Configure threshold**

**Track invocation duration**

**Take action if threshold exceeded**

Now we want to configure a `BeanNameAutoProxyCreator` that will apply this interceptor to all of our beans that end with `Service`. Listing 3.18 demonstrates how we would do this.

**Listing 3.18   Configuring a BeanNameAutoProxyCreator**

```
...
    <bean id="performanceThresholdInterceptor"
        class="com.springinaction.training.advice.
                ➡ PerformanceThresholdInterceptor">
      <constructor-arg>
        <value>5000</value>
      </constructor-arg>
    </bean>

    <bean id="preformanceThresholdProxyCreator"
        class="org.springframework.aop.framework.
                autoproxy.BeanNameAutoProxyProxyCreator">

    <bean>
      <property name="beanNames">
        <list>
          <value>*Service</value>
        </list>
      </property>
      <property name="interceptorNames">
        <value>performanceThresholdInterceptor</value>
      </property>
    </bean>
    ...
```

The code in listing 3.17 will apply our interceptor to every method on every bean with a name that ends in `Service`. Like `ProxyFactoryBean`, the `interceptorNames` property can contain the bean names of interceptors, advice, or advisors. Keep in mind that if the bean is an advisor or an interceptor, it will be applied to all methods in the proxied class. If it is an advisor, the advisor's pointcut may cause the advice to be applied differently to different beans.

So when the proxy is created, what does it look like? The autoproxy framework makes some assumptions about what interfaces the proxy should expose. Any interfaces implemented by the target class will be exposed by the proxy object. If the target class does not implement an interface, the same rules apply as when we discussed `ProxyFactoryBean`—a subclass will be created dynamically.

### 3.6.2 *DefaultAdvisorAutoProxyCreator*

The more powerful autoproxy creator is the `DefaultAdvisorAutoProxyCreator`. All you need to do to make use of this class is to include it as a bean in your `Bean-Factory` configuration. The magic of this class lies within its implementation of the `BeanPostProcessor` interface. After your beans' definitions have been read in by the `ApplicationContext`, the `DefaultAdvisorAutoProxyCreator` scours the context for any advisors. It then applies these advisors to any beans that match the advisor's pointcut.

It is important to point out this proxy creator only works with advisors. If you remember, an advisor is a construct that combines a pointcut and advice. The `DefaultAdvisorAutoProxyCreator` needs the advisors to let it know what beans it should advise.

Let's take a look at a practical example of this approach. In the previous example we applied a performance interceptor to all of our service objects. Listing 3.19 shows the same thing, only with a `DefaultAdvisorAutoProxyCreator`.

**Listing 3.19   Configuring a BeanNameAutoProxyCreator**

```
...
    <bean id="performanceThresholdInterceptor"
        class="com.springinaction.training.advice.
                ➡ PerformanceThresholdInterceptor">
      <constructor-arg>
        <value>5000</value>
      </constructor-arg>
    </bean>

    <bean id="advisor" class="org.springframework.aop.support.
                            ➡ RegexpMethodPointcutAdvisor">
        <property name="advice">
          <bean class="performanceThresholdInterceptor"/>
        </property>
        <property name="pattern">
          <value>.+Service\..+</value>
        </property>
    </bean>


    <bean id="autoProxyCreator"
        class="org.springframework.aop.framework.
                ➡ autoproxy.DefaultAdvisorAutoProxyCreator"/>
...
```

When all of the bean definitions are read in, all the advisors in the `BeanFactory` will be cut loose so they can apply their advice to any beans that match their pointcuts. (Remember the scene in *Minority Report* where the robotic spiders where unleashed to find Tom Cruise? Well, the advisors are kind of like those spiders, only much less creepy.) This allows you to really flex the power of pointcuts.

Instead of having to explicitly associate your advisors with anything, you can simply define them and have them automatically applied to any bean they are configured to match. This is where the loose coupling of beans and their advice is really achieved; you write your beans, you write your advice, and the container plays matchmaker.

But in the words of Peter Parker, with great power comes great responsibility. When using the `DefaultAdvisorAutoProxyCreator`, you *are* giving up control of explicitly wiring your advice. Because it is happening "automagically," you must make sure that your advisor's pointcuts are as fine-grained as possible. This will ensure your advice is applied precisely where you want it. The last thing you want happening is to have advice applied to classes and methods where it was never intended. This would lead to strange application behavior indeed. So when using this class, make should you first have a sound understanding of Spring's AOP framework.

### 3.6.3 *Metadata autoproxying*

Spring also supports auto proxying driven by metadata. In this type of autoproxying, the proxy configuration is determined by source-level attributes as opposed to external configuration (e.g., an XML file). This is quite powerful since it keeps the AOP metadata with the source code that is being advised, letting you keep your code and configuration metadata in one place.

The most common use for metadata autoproxying is for declarative transaction support. Spring provides a powerful framework for declarative transactions via its AOP framework. This offers the same capabilities as EJB's declarative transactions. Because this is such an important feature for enterprise development, we cover this topic in depth in chapter 5.

## 3.7 *Summary*

AOP is a powerful complement to object-oriented programming. With aspects, you can now group application behavior that was once spread throughout your applications into reusable modules. You can then declaratively or programmatically define exactly where and how this behavior is applied. This reduces code duplication and lets your classes focus on their main functionality.

Spring provides an AOP framework that lets you insert aspects around method executions. You have learned how you can weave advice before, after, and around a method invocation, as well as add custom behavior for handling exceptions.

You also discovered that with Spring's pointcut mechanism, you have several choices of how to define where this advice is woven into your application. Typically you will use one of Spring's predefined static pointcuts. With these, you define your pointcuts based on your bean's class and method names. If this does not suit your needs, you are free to implement your own static or dynamic pointcuts.

And on top of adding advice around method invocations, you also discovered introductions. Using an introduction enables you to add new methods *and* state to your application objects. You learned that introductions allow you to create composite objects dynamically, giving you the same power as multiple inheritance.

Finally, you saw that Spring provides several convenient ways to create your proxied objects. With the `ProxyFactoryBean`, you have complete control over how your proxies are created. You also have more flexible means at your disposal when you use autoproxying. Specifically, the `DefaultAdvisorAutoProxyCreator` lets you create advice throughout your application with minimal configurations.

So now you know how to wire your beans and apply advice. In the coming chapters, you will learn how you can apply these tools to help you more easily develop enterprise applications.

# Part 2

# Spring in the business layer

In part 1, you learned about Spring's core container and its support for inversion of control (IoC) and aspect-oriented programming (AOP). In part 2, you'll learn how to apply IoC and AOP to implement business layer functionality for your application.

Most applications ultimately persist business information in a relational database. Chapter 4, "Hitting the database," will guide you in using Spring's support for data persistence. You'll be introduced to Spring's JDBC support, which helps you remove much of the boilerplate code associated with JDBC. You'll also see how Spring integrates with several popular object-relational mapping frameworks, such as Hibernate, JDO, and iBATIS.

Once you are persisting your data, you'll want to ensure that its integrity is preserved. In chapter 5, "Managing transactions," you'll learn how Spring enables you to declaratively apply transactional policies to your application objects using AOP. You'll see that Spring affords EJB-like transaction support to plain Java objects and even goes beyond EJB's transactional capabilities.

In chapter 6, "Remoting," you'll learn how to expose your application objects as remote services. You'll also see how to transparently access remote services as though they are any other object in your application. Remoting technologies explored will include RMI, Hessian/Burlap, EJB, web services, and Spring's own `HttpInvoker`.

Chapter 7, "Accessing enterprise services," will wrap up the discussion of Spring in the business layer by showcasing some of Spring's support for common enterprise services. In this chapter, you'll learn how to use Spring to send messages using JMS, to access objects in JNDI, to send e-mails, and to schedule tasks.

# Hitting the database

**This chapter covers**
- Defining Spring's overall persistence support
- Configuring database resources in your application
- Simplifying JDBC code using Spring's JDBC framework
- Integrating with third-party ORM frameworks

With the core of the Spring container now under your belt, it's time to put it to work in real applications. A perfect place to start is with a requirement of nearly any enterprise application: persisting data. Each and every one of us has probably dealt with database access in an application in the past. In doing so, you know that data access has lots of pitfalls. We have to initialize our data access framework, manage resources, and handle various exceptions. If we get any of this wrong, we could potentially corrupt or delete valuable company data. For those who don't know yet, that is a Bad Thing.

Since we strive for Good Things, we turn to Spring. Spring comes with a family of data access frameworks that integrate with a variety of data access technologies. Whether you are persisting your data via direct JDBC, Java Data Objects (JDO), or an object/relational mapping (ORM) tool like Hibernate, Spring removes the tedium of data access from your persistence code. Instead, you can lean on Spring to handle the low-level data-access work for you so that you can turn your attention to managing your application's data.

## 4.1 *Learning Spring's DAO philosophy*

Before we jump into Spring's different DAO frameworks, let's talk about Spring's DAO support in general. From the first section, you know that one of Spring's goals is to allow you to develop applications following the sound object-oriented (OO) principle of coding to interfaces. Well, Spring's data access support is no exception.

DAO stands for data access object, which perfectly describes a DAO's role in an application. DAOs exist to provide a means to read and write data to the database. They should expose this functionality through an interface by which the rest of the application will access them. Figure 4.1 shows the proper approach to designing your data access tier.

As you can see, the service objects are accessing the DAOs through interfaces. This has a couple of advantages. First, it makes your service objects easily testable since they are not coupled to a specific data access implementation. In fact, you can create mock implementations of these data access interfaces. That would allow you to test your service object without ever having to connect to the database, which would significantly speed up your unit tests.

In addition, the data access tier is accessed in a persistence technology-agnostic manner. That is, the data access interface does not expose what technology it is using to access data. Instead, only the relevant data access methods are exposed. This makes for a flexible application design. If the implementation

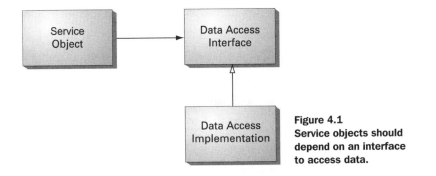

**Figure 4.1
Service objects should
depend on an interface
to access data.**

details of the data access tier were to leak into other parts of the application, the entire application becomes coupled with the data access tier, leading to a rigid application design.

One way Spring helps you insulate your data access ties from the rest of your application is by providing you with a consistent exception hierarchy that is used across all of its DAO frameworks.

### 4.1.1 *Understanding Spring's DataAccessException*

Spring's DAO frameworks do not throw technology-specific exceptions, such as `SQLException` or `HibernateException`. Instead, all exceptions thrown are subclasses of the technology-agnostic `org.springframework.dao.DataAccess-Exception`. This enables your data access interfaces to throw Spring's general `DataAccessException` instead of implementation-specific exceptions that would force other application layers to catch them and thus become coupled to a particular persistence implementation. In fact, you can intermingle multiple persistence technologies within the same application without your service objects even knowing it.

Since `DataAccessException` is the root of all Spring DAO exceptions, there are a couple of important things to know.

#### *You are not forced to handle DataAccessExceptions*

`DataAccessException` is a `RuntimeException`, so it is an unchecked exception. This means that your code will not be required to handle these exceptions when they are thrown by the data access tier. This follows the general Spring philosophy that checked exceptions can lead to extraneous `catch` or `throws` clauses throughout your code, cluttering things up. This is especially true for data access exceptions. Since these are quite often unrecoverable (e.g., unable to connect to a database, invalid column name, etc.), you are not forced to try to handle these.

Instead, you can catch the exceptions if recovery is possible and let others bubble up the call stack.

Also, `DataAccessException` is not only a `RuntimeException`, but it subclasses Spring's `NestedRuntimeException`. This means that the root `Exception` is always available via `NestedRuntimeException`'s `getCause()` method. So even though you do not have to handle technology-specific exceptions, they are always available if you need them, so no information is ever lost.

### Spring classifies exceptions for you

In a perfect world, our data access APIs would always throw very meaningful exceptions. We don't know about you, but most of us are a *long* way from utopia. If you are using JDBC, there is a greater than zero chance you will eventually get a generic `SQLException` with a vendor-specific error. JDO has its own exception hierarchy, as do all of the other persistence technologies that Spring supports. As we said before, we do not want to expose these to the rest of our application.

Fortunately, Spring understands each of these technology-specific exceptions. It even understands database vendors' error codes. Because Spring can interpret the meaning of many of these exception, it can rethrow one of the more specific exceptions in its own exception hierarchy. As table 4.1 illustrates, Spring's DAO framework comes with a rich hierarchy exception.

**Table 4.1  Spring's DAO exception hierarchy**

| Exception | Is thrown when... |
|---|---|
| `CleanupFailureDataAccessException` | An operation completes successfully, but an exception occurs while cleaning up database resources (e.g., closing a `Connection`). |
| `DataAccessResourceFailureException` | A data access resource fails completely, such as not being able to connect to a database. |
| `DataIntegrityViolationException` | An insert or update results in an integrity violation, such as a violation of a unique constraint. |
| `DataRetrievalFailureException` | Certain data could not be retrieved, such as not finding a row by primary key. |
| `DeadlockLoserDataAccessException` | The current process was a deadlock loser. |
| `IncorrectUpdateSemanticsData-AccessException` | When something unintended happens on an update, such as updating more rows than expected. When this exception is thrown, the operation's transaction has not been rolled back. |

*continued on next page*

**Table 4.1   Spring's DAO exception hierarchy** *(continued)*

| Exception | Is thrown when... |
|-----------|-------------------|
| `InvalidDataAccessApiUsageException` | A data access Java API is used incorrectly, such as failing to compile a query that must be compiled before execution. |
| `InvalidDataAccessResourceUsage-Exception` | A data access resource is used incorrectly, such as using bad SQL grammar to access a relational database. |
| `OptimisticLockingFailureException` | There is an optimistic locking failure. This will be thrown by ORM tools or by custom DAO implementations. |
| `TypeMismatchDataAccessException` | There is a mismatch between Java type and data type, such as trying to insert a `String` into a numeric database column. |
| `UncategorizedDataAccessException` | Something goes wrong, but a more specific exception cannot be determined. |

Since Spring's DAO exception hierarchy is so fine-grained, your service objects can select exactly what kind of exceptions they want to catch and which ones they want to let continue up the call stack. For example, a `DataAccessResourceFailure-Exception` signals a critical problem—your application cannot connect to its data store. You probably want to catch this and start ringing some alarms (metaphorically speaking). On the other hand, a `DataRetrievalFailureException` is not as critical and might possibly be a user error. Catching this exception would allow you to possibly give the user a helpful message.

So we can now properly handle exceptions thrown by our data access tools. Now let's see how to actually connect to the database.

### 4.1.2   *Working with DataSources*

In order to execute any JDBC operation on a database, you need a `Connection`. In Spring's DAO frameworks, `Connection` objects are obtained through a `Data-Source`. Spring provides several options for making a `DataSource` available to your application.

#### *Getting a DataSource from JNDI*

Quite often Spring applications will be running within a J2EE application server or even a web server like Tomcat. One thing these servers can provide is a `Data-Source` via JNDI. With Spring, we treat this we would any other service object in our application—as a Spring bean. In this case, we use the `JndiObjectFactoryBean`. All we need to do is configure it with the JNDI name of our `DataSource`:

```
<bean id="dataSource"
      class="org.springframework.jndi.JndiObjectFactoryBean">
  <property name="jndiName">
    <value>java:comp/env/jdbc/myDatasource</value>
  </property>
</bean>
```

We have now wired in our server's `DataSource` and its connection pooling facility. But what if we are not running within a server that provides this?

### Creating a DataSource connection pool

If we are running our Spring container in an environment where a `DataSource` is not already present and we want the benefits of connection pooling, we can still provide this. All we need is a connection pooling bean that implements `DataSource`. A good example of this would be the `BasicDataSource` class from the Jakarta Commons DBCP[1] project. Since all of its properties are exposed through setter methods, we would configure it like we would any other Spring bean:

```
<bean id="dataSource"
      class="org.apache.commons.dbcp.BasicDataSource">
  <property name="driver">
    <value>${db.driver}</value>
  </property>
  <property name="url">
    <value>${db.url}</value>
  </property>
  <property name="username">
    <value>${db.username}</value>
  </property>
  <property name="password">
    <value>${db.password}</value>
  </property>
</bean>
```

We now have a `DataSource` with connection pooling independent of an application server.

### Using a DataSource while testing

Since making code easily testable is central to Spring's philosophy, it would be a shame if we could not unit-test our data access code. Fortunately, Spring comes

---

[1] Jakarta Commons DBCP is an open source database connection pool. You can learn more about this project and download it at http://jakarta.apache.org/commons/dbcp/.

with a very lightweight `DataSource` implementation specifically for this: `Driver-ManagerDataSource`. This class can easily be configured and used with a unit test or suite of unit tests.

```
DriverManagerDataSource dataSource = new DriverManagerDataSource();
dataSource.setDriverClassName(driver);
dataSource.setUrl(url);
dataSource.setUsername(username);
dataSource.setPassword(password);
```

You now have a `DataSource` to use when testing your data access code.

We can connect to the database. Now let's take a look at the overall design of Spring's DAO frameworks and how they make using persistence technologies easier.

### 4.1.3 *Consistent DAO support*

You have probably traveled by plane before. If so, you will surely agree that one of the most important parts of traveling is getting your luggage from point A to point B. There are lots of steps to this process. You have to drop it off at the counter. Then it has to go through security and then be placed on the plane. If you need to catch a connecting flight, your luggage needs to be moved as well. When you arrive at your final destination, the luggage has to be removed from the plane and placed on the carousel. Finally, you go down to the baggage claim area and pick it up.

As we said, there are many steps to this process. But you are only actively involved in a couple of those steps. The carrier itself is responsible for driving the process. You are only involved when you need to be; the rest is just "taken care of." And believe or not, this mirrors a very powerful design pattern: the template method pattern.

A template method defines the skeleton of a process. In our example, the process is moving luggage from departure city to arrival city. The process itself is fixed; it never changes. The overall sequence of events for handling luggage occurs the same way every time: luggage is checked in, luggage is loaded on the plane, etc. Some steps of the process are fixed as well. That is, some steps happen the same way every time. When the plane arrives at its destination, every piece of luggage is unloaded one at a time and placed on a carousel to be taken to baggage claim.

But at certain points, the process delegates to other collaborators to fill in some implementation-specific details. This is the part of the process that is variable. For example, the handling of luggage starts with a passenger checking in the luggage at the counter. This part of the process always has to happen at the beginning, so its sequence in the process is fixed. But each passenger's luggage check-in is different. The implementation of this process is determined by the passenger. In software terms, a template method delegates the implementation-specific portions of the process to an interface. Different implementations of this interface define specific implementations of this portion of the process.

Spring applies this pattern to data access. No matter what technology we are using, certain data access steps are required. For example, we always need to obtain a connection to our data store and clean up resources when we are done. These are the fixed steps in a data access process. But each data access implementation we write is slightly different. We query for different objects and update the data in different ways. These are the variable steps in a data access process.

Spring separates the fixed and variant parts of the data access process into two distinct classes: templates and callbacks. Templates manage the fixed part of the process while callbacks are where you fill in the implementation details. Figure 4.2 shows the responsibilities of both of these classes.

As you can see in figure 4.2, Spring's template classes handle the invariant parts of data access—controlling transactions, managing resources, and handling exceptions. Implementations of the callback interfaces define what is specific to *your* application—creating statements, binding parameters, and marshalling result sets. In practice, this makes for a very elegant framework because all you have to worry about is your data access logic.

But that is not where these frameworks end. On top of the template-callback design, each framework provides a support class meant to be subclassed by your own data access classes. The relationship between your class, the support class, and the template class is illustrated in figure 4.3.

The support classes already have a property for holding a template class, so you will not have to create this property for each of your DAO classes. Plus, each support class allows you to get direct access to whatever class is used to communicate

**Figure 4.2**   Relationship between persistence APIs, template class, DAO support class, and your DAO class

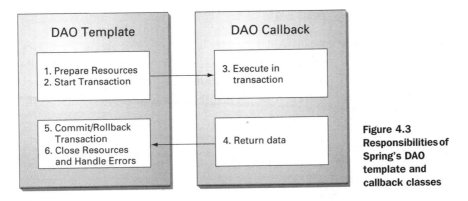

**Figure 4.3**
**Responsibilities of Spring's DAO template and callback classes**

with the database. For instance, the JdbcDaoSupport class contains a getConnection() method for obtaining a Connection object. You would do this if you needed to execute an operation independent of Spring's JDBC framework.

One other benefit you get by subclassing these support classes is that they each implement the InitializingBean interface. This means that the Spring container notifies them after they have been configured. If any of your DAO classes require special initialization after they have been configured, all you have to do is override the initDao() method.

As we cover each technology separately, we will go over each of these template and support classes in depth. And what better technology to start with than the granddaddy of them all, JDBC.

## 4.2 Using JDBC with Spring

There are a lot of persistence technologies out there. Entity beans. Hibernate. JDO. Despite this, there is a wealth of applications out there that are writing Java objects to a database the old-fashioned way: they *earn* it. No, wait—that's how people make money. The tried-and-true method for persisting data is with good old JDBC.

And why not? JDBC does not require learning another framework's query language to master. It is built on top of SQL, which is *the* data access language. Plus, you can more finely tune the performance of your data access when you use JDBC than practically any other technology. And JDBC allows you to take advantage of your database's proprietary features where other frameworks may discourage or flat-out prohibit this.

But, all is not sunny in the world of JDBC. With its power, flexibility, and other niceties also comes, well, some not-so-niceties.

### 4.2.1 The problem with JDBC code

While JDBC gives you an API that works closely with your database, you are responsible for handling *everything* related to accessing the database. This includes managing database resources and handling exceptions.

If you have ever written JDBC that inserts data into the database, the code in listing 4.1 should look familiar.

---

**Listing 4.1   Inserting data with JDBC**

```
public void insertPerson(Person person) throws SQLException {
    Connection conn = null;                       Declare
    PreparedStatement stmt = null;                resources

    try {                                                  Open
        conn = dataSource.getConnection();          ⤴     connection
        stmt = conn.prepareStatement("insert into person (" +    Create
            "id, firstName, lastName) values (?, ?, ?)");        statement
        stmt.setInt(0, person.getId().intValue());
        stmt.setString(1, person.getFirstName());     Set
        stmt.setString(2, person.getLastName());      parameters
        stmt.executeUpdate();           ⟵  Execute statement
    }
    catch(SQLException e) {
        LOGGER.error(e);              Handle
    }                                 exceptions
    finally {
        try { if (stmt != null) stmt.close(); }
        catch(SQLException e) { LOGGER.warn(e); }    Clean up
                                                     resources
        try { if (conn != null) conn.close(); }
        catch(SQLException e) { LOGGER.warn(e); }
    }
}
```

---

Holy runaway code, Batman! That is roughly a 25-line method to insert a simple object into a database. As far as database operations go, this is about as simple as it gets. So why does it take this many lines to execute this? Actually, it doesn't, but to properly handle errors and resources, it does. It's too bad that of these 25 lines, only four are unique to our particular use case: inserting a `Person` object. Listing 4.2 shows how updating a `Person` object would look strikingly similar.

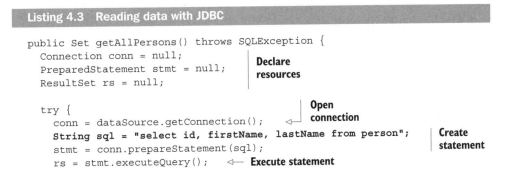

**Listing 4.2  Updating data with JDBC**

```
public void updatePerson(Person person) throws SQLException {
  Connection conn = null;          Declare
  PreparedStatement stmt = null;   resources

  try {                                        Open
    conn = dataSource.getConnection();     ◁┘ connection
    stmt = conn.prepareStatement("update person " +          Create
        "set firstName = ?, lastName = ? where id = ?");     statement
    stmt.setString(0, person.getFirstName());
    stmt.setString(1, person.getLastName());      Set
    stmt.setInt(2, person.getId().intValue());    parameters
    stmt.executeUpdate();    ◁┐ Execute statement
  }
  catch(SQLException e) {           Handle
    LOGGER.error(e);               exceptions
  }
  finally {
    try { if (stmt != null) stmt.close(); }
    catch(SQLException e) { LOGGER.warn(e); }      Clean up
                                                   resources
    try { if (conn != null) conn.close(); }
    catch(SQLException e) { LOGGER.warn(e); }
  }
}
```

At first glance, listing 4.1 and listing 4.2 appear to be identical. They practically are, except for those four critical lines where we create the statement and set the parameters. Ideally, all we would have to write are these four lines and the rest would be handled for us. After all, those four lines are the only distinguishing lines of the method. The rest is just boilerplate code.

What about getting data out of the database? That's not too pretty either, as listing 4.3 shows us.

**Listing 4.3  Reading data with JDBC**

```
public Set getAllPersons() throws SQLException {
  Connection conn = null;
  PreparedStatement stmt = null;    Declare
  ResultSet rs = null;              resources

  try {                                        Open
    conn = dataSource.getConnection();     ◁┘ connection
    String sql = "select id, firstName, lastName from person";    Create
    stmt = conn.prepareStatement(sql);                            statement
    rs = stmt.executeQuery();    ◁─ Execute statement
```

```
Set persons = new HashSet();
while (rs.next()) {
  persons.add(new Person(rs.getInt("id"),
      rs.getString("firstName"), rs.getString("lastName")));
}                                               Iterate over ResultSet
return persons;    <─  Return results
}
catch(SQLException e) {
  LOGGER.error(e);        Handle
  throw e;                exceptions
}
finally {
  try { if (rs != null) rs.close(); }
  catch(SQLException e) { LOGGER.warn(e); }

  try { if (stmt != null) stmt.close(); }    Clean up
  catch(SQLException e) { LOGGER.warn(e); }  resources

  try { if (conn != null) conn.close(); }
  catch(SQLException e) { LOGGER.warn(e); }
}
}
```

That's about as verbose as our previous example, maybe more. It's like Pareto's Principle flipped on its head; 20 percent of the code is needed for this particular method while 80 percent is boilerplate code. With our point made, we will end the torture here and not make you look at any more of this nasty, nasty code.

But the fact is that this boilerplate code *is* important. Cleaning up resources and handling errors is what makes data access robust. Without it, errors would go undetected and resources would be left open, leading to unpredictable code and resource leaks. So not only do we need this code, we also need to make sure this code is correct. This is all the more reason to use a framework where this code is written right and written once.

That is what Spring's JDBC framework brings to the table.

### 4.2.2 Using JdbcTemplate

Spring's JDBC framework will clean up your JDBC code by shouldering the burden of resource management and error handling. This leaves you free to write the statements and queries to get your data to and from the database.

As we explained before, all of Spring's data access frameworks incorporate a template class. In this case, it is the JdbcTemplate class. All a JdbcTemplate needs to do its work is a Datasource, which makes creating an instance simple enough:

```
JdbcTemplate template = new JdbcTemplate(myDataSource);
```

And since all of Spring's DAO template classes are thread-safe, we only need one `JdbcTemplate` instance for each `DataSource` in our application. To make use of the `JdbcTemplate`, each of your DAO classes needs to be configured with a `Jdbc-Template` instance like so:

```
public class StudentDaoJdbc implements StudentDao {
  private JdbcTemplate jdbcTemplate;

  public void setJdbcTemplate(JdbcTemplate jdbcTemplate) {
    this.jdbcTemplate = jdbcTemplate;
  }
  ...
}
```

This makes for easy configuration since each of your DAO classes can be configured with the same `JdbcTemplate`, as listing 4.4 demonstrates.

**Listing 4.4   Wiring a `JdbcTemplate` to DAO beans**

```
<bean id="jdbcTemplate"
      class="org.springframework.jdbc.core.JdbcTemplate">
  <property name="dataSource"><ref bean="dataSource"/></property>
</bean>

<bean id="studentDao" class="StudentDaoJdbc">
  <property name="jdbcTemplate"><ref bean="jdbcTemplate"/></property>
</bean>

<bean id="courseDao" class="CourseDaoJdbc">
  <property name="jdbcTemplate"><ref bean="jdbcTemplate"/></property>
</bean>
```

Now we are ready to start accessing the database. To start off, let's take a look at how to execute database writes using the `JbdcTemplate` class.

### Writing data

Earlier we discussed how each of Spring's DAO template classes works in concert with callback interfaces. The `JdbcTemplate` uses several of these callbacks when writing data to the database. The usefulness you will find in each of these interfaces will vary. We will first introduce two of the simpler interfaces, and then we will show you some shortcuts provided by the `JdbcTemplate` class.

The first callback we will explore is `PreparedStatementCreator`. As the name suggests, implementers of this interface are responsible for creating a `Prepared-Statement`. This interface provides one method:

```
PreparedStatement createPreparedStatement(Connection conn)
    throws SQLException;
```

When you implement this interface, you are responsible for creating and returning a `PreparedStatement` from the `Connection` argument, but you don't have to worry about exception handling. An implementation that inserts a `Person` object might look like the example in listing 4.5.

**Listing 4.5  Creating a `PreparedStatement` with a `PreparedStatementCreator`**

```
public class InsertPersonStatementCreator
    implements PreparedStatementCreator {

  public PreparedStatement createPreparedStatement(
      Connection conn) throws SQLException {
    String sql = "insert into person (id, first_name, last_name) " +
                 "values (?, ?, ?)";
    return conn.prepareStatement(sql);
  }
}
```

Implementers of this interface will often implement another interface as well: `SqlProvider`. By implementing this interface's one method—`getSql()`—you enable your class to provide SQL strings to the `JdbcTemplate` class. This is very useful since the `JdbcTemplate` class can log every SQL statement it executes. Listing 4.6 illustrates what this would look like.

**Listing 4.6  Implementing `SqlProvider` in a `PreparedStatementCreator`**

```
public class InsertPersonStatementCreator
    implements PreparedStatementCreator, SqlProvider {

  private final String sql =
      "insert into person (id, firstName, lastName) " +
      "values (?, ?, ?)";

  public PreparedStatement createPreparedStatement(
      Connection conn) throws SQLException {
    return conn.prepareStatement(sql);
  }

  public String getSql() { return sql; }
}
```

Now whenever the `JdbcTempate` calls on this class to create a `PreparedStatment`, it will also be able to log the executed SQL. This can prove invaluable during development and debugging.

The complement to `PreparedStatementCreator` is `PreparedStatementSetter`. Classes that implement this interface receive a `PreparedStatement` and are responsible for setting any of the parameters, as the single method's signature indicate:

```
void setValues(PreparedStatement ps) throws SQLException;
```

Continuing with the example above, setting parameters to insert a `Person` object would look like this:

```
...
private Person person;

public void setValues(PreparedStatement ps) throws SQLException {
  ps.setInt(0, person.getId().intValue());
  ps.setString(1, person.getFirstName());
  ps.setString(2, person.getLastName());
}
...
```

Again, all you have to worry about is setting the parameters. Any exceptions will be handled by the `JdbcTemplate` class. Notice a pattern here? You are only doing what is necessary to define how to insert a `Person` object; the framework is doing the rest.

As we mentioned earlier, these are fairly simple callbacks. The former creates a `PreparedStatement` and the latter sets the parameters. It almost seems like overkill to create a class for something so trivial. Fortunately the `JdbcTemplate` class provides some convenience methods to simplify this.

Since many updates consist of creating a `PreparedStatement` from a SQL string and then binding parameters, `JdbcTemplate` provides an `execute(String sql, Object[] params)` method that facilitates just that. You would use this method in this way:

```
String sql = "insert into person (id, firstName, lastName) " +
             "values (?, ?, ?)";
Object[] params = new Object[] { person.getId(),
                                 person.getFirstName(),
                                 person.getLastName() };
return jdbcTemplate.update(sql, params);
```

Ahhh! Now we are getting to some nice, concise code! Behind the scenes, the `JdbcTemplate` class creates a `PreparedStatementCreator` and `PreparedStatement-Setter`. But now we don't have to worry about that. We just supply the SQL and the parameters.

One improvement we can make is to use the `JdbcTemplate` method that also accepts the JDBC types of our parameters, `update(String sql, Object[] args, int[] argTypes)`. This provides type safety, which allows for better support when setting parameters to `null`. Let's take a look at how we would use this method. This time, listing 4.7 will examine the `execute()` of our method in the context of one our DAO methods.

**Listing 4.7  Inserting data using the `JdbcTemple.execute` method**

```
public int insertPerson(Person person) {

    String sql = "insert into person (id, firstName, lastName) " +     Create
                    "values (?, ?, ?)";                                SQL
    Object[] params = new Object[] { person.getId(),
                                    person.getFirstName(),             Set
                                    person.getLastName() };            parameters
    int[] types =                                                      Set
        new int[] { Types.INTEGER, Types.VARCHAR, Types.VARCHAR };     datatypes
    return jdbcTemplate.update(sql, params, types);         ◄─┐ Execute
}                                                                  statement
```

Now we have the simplicity for which we have been searching. Four statements: declare the SQL, declare the parameters, declare the types, execute the operation. Spring does the rest. That's leverage. For the vast majority of your database writes, the method in listing 4.7 will serve as a perfect template.

But what if we want to update more than one row? Suppose we also have a method that supports adding multiple `Person` objects en masse. In that case, we would use the `BatchPreparedStatementSetter`. This interface has two methods:

```
setValues(PreparedStatement ps, int i) throws SQLException;
int getBatchSize();
```

`getBatchSize()` tells the `JdbcTemplate` class how many statements to create. This also determines how many times `setValues()` will be called. Listing 4.8 shows how you would use this in conjunction with the `JdbcTemplate.batch-Update()` method.

**Listing 4.8  Using a `BatchPreparedStatementCreator` to insert multiple objects**

```
public int[] updatePersons(final List persons) {
    String sql = "insert into person (id, firstName, lastName) " +    Create
                "values (?, ?, ?)";                                   SQL
    BatchPreparedStatementSetter setter = null;
    setter = new BatchPreparedStatementSetter() {
```

```
    public int getBatchSize() {          Define number of
      return persons.size();             batch statements
    }

    public void setValues(PreparedStatement ps, int index)
        throws SQLException {
      Person person = (Person) persons.get(index);         Set
      ps.setInt(0, person.getId().intValue());             parameters
      ps.setString(1, person.getFirstName());
      ps.setString(2, person.getLastName());
    }

  };
  return jdbcTemplate.batchUpdate(sql, setter);     ◁─  Execute batch
}                                                        statement
```

So if your JDBC driver supports batching, the updates will be batched, creating more efficient database access. If not, Spring will simulate batching, but the statements will be executed individually.

So now you have seen how to write data to the database. Let's take a look at how we can use Spring to help get data *out* of the database.

### Reading data

As we saw in our JDBC code without Spring, when we queried the database we had to iterate through the ResultSet. Spring recognizes that this is a step that is always required for queries, so it handles that for us. Instead, we simply need to tell Spring what to do with each row in the ResultSet. We do so through the Row-CallbackHandler interface by implementing its only method:

```
void processRow(java.sql.ResultSet rs)
```

This method is called for each row in our ResultSet. Going back to our Person-Dao, we are likely to have method to retrieve a Person object by its id. Listing 4.9 shows how we would do so using a RowCallbackHandler.

**Listing 4.9  Executing a query using RowCallbackHandler**

```
public Person getPerson(final Integer id) {
  String sql = "select id, first_name, last_name from person " +    Create
            "where id = ?";                                          SQL
  final Person person = new Person();      ◁─  Create object being queried
  final Object[] params = new Object[] { id };   ◁─  Create query parameters
  jdbcTemplate.query(sql, params, new RowCallbackHandler() {
```

```
  public void processRow(ResultSet rs) throws SQLException {
    person.setId(new Integer(rs.getInt("id")));
    person.setFirstName(rs.getString("first_name"));
    person.setLastName(rs.getString("last_name"));
  }
});
return person;
}
```

Process query results

return person;    ◁— **Return queried object**

As you can see, we define our SQL and parameters as we did before. And since we are now getting data from the database, we also supply a RowCallbackHandler that knows how to extract the data from the ResultSet.

There is also a subinterface you can implement that is useful for retrieving multiple objects through a query. Suppose we want a method that retrieves all of our Person objects. To do this we would implement ResultReader. Spring provides an implementation of this interface that does exactly what we need: RowMapperResultReader. But in order to use this class, we must discuss the RowMapper interface first.

The RowMapper interface is responsible for mapping a ResultSet row to an object. To map a row to Person object, we would create a RowMapper like this:

```
class PersonRowMapper implements RowMapper {
  public Object mapRow(ResultSet rs, int index)
      throws SQLException {
    Person person = new Person();
    person.setId(new Integer(rs.getInt("id")));
    person.setFirstName(rs.getString("first_name"));
    person.setLastName(rs.getString("last_name"));
    return person;
  }
}
```

We now have a reusable class that can take a ResultSet row and create a Person object. This can now be used in any Person query, as long as id, first_name, and last_name columns are being selected as part of the query. Now let's go back and see how we would use this in our getAllPersons() method:

```
public List getAllPersons() {
  String sql = "select id, first_name, last_name from person";
  return jdbcTemplate.query(
      sql, new RowMapperResultReader(new PersonRowMapper()));
}
```

Nice and tidy. Now that we have our reusable RowMapper object, listing 4.10 illustrates how we can clean up our getPerson() method from earlier.

**Listing 4.10  Executing a query using a** `RowMapper`

```
public Person getPerson(final Integer id) {
   String sql = "select id, first_name, last_name from person " +
               "where id = ?";
   final Person person = new Person();
   final Object[] params = new Object[] { id };
   List list = jdbcTemplate.query(sql, params,
      new RowMapperResultReader(new PersonRowMapper()));
   return (Person) list.get(0);
}
```

See, we told you that you would get great reuse from the `RowMapper` interface. In fact, there is really no reason you should not encapsulate the extraction of `ResultSet` data in exactly one `RowMapper` for each of your classes. You could conceivably have dozens of query methods for a particular object, but you should never need more than one `RowMapper` object.

So far we have covered queries that pull data to create domain objects. But what about queries that just return simple types, like `int` or `String`? `JdbcTemplate` also contains some convenience methods for precisely this. For instance, here's how you would write a query to get the count of all `Person` objects:

```
public int getNumberOfPersons() {
   return jdbcTemplate.queryForInt("select count(*) from person");
}
```

Similarly, to execute a query to find the last name for a particular person id, we would write a method like this:

```
public String getLastNameForId(Integer id) {
   String sql = "select last_name from person where id = ?";
   return (String) jdbcTemplate.queryForObject(
      sql, new Object[] { id },  String.class);
}
```

By now you must be enjoying seeing JDBC query methods that are not littered with `try-catch-finally` blocks and `ResultSet` iterations. Now we are going to turn our attention to one more area where Spring's JDBC framework can help. Let's look at how to call stored procedures using `JdbcTemplate`.

### Calling stored procedures

Sometimes we choose to execute our persistence operations as stored procedures in the database rather than SQL in our application. This may be due to performance reasons, company policy, or just a matter of taste. Whatever the case,

Spring provides the same support for calling stored procedures as it does for executing statements and queries. This time get the support by implementing `CallableStatementCallback`.

Let's say we have a stored procedure in our application that is responsible for moving all old student data to archive tables. Assuming this procedure is named `ARCHIVE_STUDENTS`, listing 4.11 shows how we would access it.

**Listing 4.11  Executing a stored procedure with `CallableStatementCallback`**

```
public void archiveStudentData() {
  CallableStatementCallback cb = new CallableStatementCallback() {
    public Object doInCallableStatement(CallableStatement cs)
        throws SQLException{
      cs.execute();
      return null;
    }
  };
  jdbcTemplate.execute("{ ARCHIVE_STUDENTS }", cb);
}
```

Once again, we have all the benefits of resource management and exception handling. All we have to do is define the name of our stored procedure and execute it.

You should now have a good idea of how to put the `JdbcTemplate` class to work for you. Now let's take a look at how we can represent database operations as objects themselves.

### 4.2.3  *Creating operations as objects*

In the examples we just covered, you learned how you write JDBC code in a much cleaner fashion. But the code was still tightly coupled to SQL. This is not necessarily a bad thing. But what if we want to write JDBC code in a more OO fashion? Spring provides a way to actually model database operations as objects. This adds another layer of insulation between your code and straight JDBC.

Spring provides classes for both reading and writing data. As we work through some examples of these, there are a couple of things you should know. First, these database operation objects are thread-safe, meaning you need to create only one instance per database operation. Second, any database operation object must be compiled before being used. This lets the object know when to prepare the statement so that it can be executed later. Not surprisingly, you compile a database operation object by calling the `compile()` method. We will demonstrate this practice in our examples. To start off, let's see how we would create an object to write data to the database.

### Creating an SqlUpdate object

To create a reusable object for executing inserts or updates, you subclass the SqlUpdate class. An object for inserting a Person object would look like this:

```
public class InsertPerson extends SqlUpdate {

  public InsertPerson(DataSource ds) {
    setDataSource(ds);
    setSql("insert into person (id, firstName, lastName) " +
        "values (?, ?, ?)";
    declareParameter(new SqlParameter(Types.NUMERIC));
    declareParameter(new SqlParameter(Types.VARCHAR));
    declareParameter(new SqlParameter(Types.VARCHAR));
    compile();
  }

  public int insert(Person person) {
    Object[] params = new Object[] {
        person.getId(),
        person.getFirstName(),
        person.getLastName()
    };
    return update(params);
  }
}
```

There are a couple of things you should notice in this example. First, we have to supply our SqlUpdate object with a DataSource. It uses this to create a JdbcTemplate (it uses a JdbcTemplate to do its work). Second, notice the three declareParameter() calls after we configure the SQL. We need to call this method for each of the parameters in our statement. Note that the order in which we issue these statements is important; they must be issued in the same order that they appear in the SQL.

Finally, notice that we call compile() at the end of our constructor. As we mentioned, every database operation object must be compiled before it can be used. By calling compile() in the constructor, we ensure that it will always be called when an instance is created. Speaking of constructing these objects, you can keep an instance of this class as an instance variable in your DAO class since all of these objects are thread-safe.

We would actually call this object like this:

```
private InsertPerson insertPerson;

public int insertPerson(Person person) {
  return updatePerson.insert(person);
}
```

Notice that we did not use a single JDBC API in either the InsertPerson object or our insertPerson() method. There is no reference to a PreparedStatement or Connection object to be found. This is the extra layer of abstraction we referred to earlier. Now let's take a look at how to create a query object.

### Querying the database with a MappingSqlQuery

To model a query as an object, we subclass the MappingSqlQuery class like so:

```
private class PersonByIdQuery extends MappingSqlQuery {

  public PersonByIdQuery(DataSource ds) {
    super(ds, "select id, first_name, last_name from person " +
            "where id = ?");
    declareParameter(new SqlParameter("id", Types.INTEGER));
    compile();
  }

  public Object mapRow(ResultSet rs, int rowNumber)
      throws SQLException {
    Person person = new Person();
    person.setId( (Integer) rs.getObject("id"));
    person.setFirstName(rs.getString("first_name"));
    person.setLastName(rs.getString("last_name"));
    return person;
  }
}
```

Again, we supply a DataSource to the constructor and we compile at the end of the constructor. We use this object like this:

```
private PersonByIdQuery personByIdQuery;
...
public Person getPerson(Integer id) {
  Object[] params = new Object[] { id };
  return (Person) personByIdQuery.execute(params).get(0);
}
```

Once again, we interact very little with the JDBC APIs. If this type of design is attractive to you, you may prefer modeling your database operations as objects. But deciding to take this approach or to access the JdbcTemplate directly is more of matter of taste. One approach is not inherently better than the other.

### 4.2.4 *Auto-incrementing keys*

When you insert a row in the database, you typically assign it a primary key that uniquely identifies that row. It is good practice to use a surrogate key for your primary key. That is, the primary key should have no business meaning but is instead generated within your application. Spring provides a means to do this via the `DataFieldMaxValueIncrementer` interface. This interface has three different methods for obtaining the next value to be used as a key: `nextIntValue()`, `nextLongValue()`, and `nextStringValue()`.

We would use a `DataFieldMaxValueIncrementer` like this:

```
...
private DataFieldMaxValueIncrementer incrementer;

public void setIncrementer(
    DataFieldMaxValueIncrementer incrementer) {
  this.incrementer = incrementer;
}

public void insertPerson(Person person) {
  Integer id = new Integer(incrementer.nextIntValue());
  JdbcTemplate jdbcTemplate = new JdbcTemplate(dataSource);
  String sql = "insert into person (id, firstName, lastName) " +
               "values (?, ?, ?)";
  Object[] params = new Object[] { id,
                                   person.getFirstName(),
                                   person.getLastName() };
  jdbcTemplate.update(sql, params);

  // everything was successful
  person.setId(id);
}
...
```

We can then wire in an implementation of this interface. Spring comes with implementations that hook into the sequence mechanism for Oracle, Postgre-SQL, MySQL, and Hypersonic databases. You are free to write your own implementation as well.

We have now covered the multitude of ways Spring's JDBC framework can help you write cleaner JDBC code. But as your applications grow larger and more complex, JDBC can still become cumbersome even with this framework. To help manage the persistence complexities of large applications, you will need a persistence tool. And as you will see, Spring provides great support for these tools as well.

## *4.3 Introducing Spring's ORM framework support*

When we were kids, riding a bike was fun, wasn't it? We would ride to school in the mornings. When school let out we would cruise to our best friend's house. When it got late and our parents were yelling at us for staying out past dark, we would peddle home for the night. Gee, those days were fun.

But then we grew up—and we needed more than a bike. Sometimes we have to travel quite a distance to work. Groceries have to be hauled and ours kids need to get to soccer practice. And if you live in Texas, air conditioning is a must! Our needs have simply outgrown our bike.

JDBC is the bike of the persistence world. It is great for what it does, and for some jobs it works just fine. But as our applications become more complex, so do our persistence requirements. We need to be able to map object properties to database columns and have our statements and queries created for us, freeing us from typing an endless string of question marks. We also need more sophisticated features such as the following:

- *Lazy loading*—As our object graphs become more complex, we sometimes don't want to fetch entire relationships immediately. To use a typical example, suppose we are selecting a collection of PurchaseOrder objects, and each of these objects contains a collection of LineItem objects. If we are only interested in PurchaseOrder attributes, it makes no sense to grab the LineItem data. This could be quite expensive. Lazy loading allows us to grab data only as it is needed.

- *Eager fetching*—This is the opposite of lazy loading. Eager fetching allows you to grab an entire object graph in one query. So if we know we need a PurchaseOrder object and its associated LineItems, eager fetching lets us get this from the database in one operation, saving us from costly round-trips.

- *Caching*—For data that is read-mostly (used often but changed infrequently), we don't want to fetch this from the database every time it is used. Caching can add a significant performance boost.

- *Cascading*—Sometimes changes to a database table should result in changes to other tables as well. Going back to our purchase order example, it is reasonable that a LineItem object has an association with a Product object. In the database, this is most likely represented as a many-to-many relationship. So when a LineItem object is deleted, we also want to disassociate this LineItem from its Product object in the database.

Fortunately, there are frameworks out there that already provide these services. The general term for these services is object/relational mapping (ORM). Using an ORM tool for your persistence layer can save you literally thousands of lines of code and hours of development time. This lets you switch your focus from writing error-prone SQL code to addressing your application requirements.

Spring provides integration for Sun's standard persistence API JDO, as well as the open source ORM frameworks Hibernate, Apache OJB, and iBATIS SQL Maps. Spring's support for each of these technologies is not as extensive as its JDBC support. This is not a poor reflection on Spring's APIs, but rather a testament to how much work each of these ORM frameworks does. With the ORM tool doing most of the actual persistence, Spring provides integration points to these frameworks, as well as some additional services:

- Integrated transaction management
- Exception handling
- Thread-safe, lightweight template classes
- Convenience support classes
- Resource management

While we are going to cover Spring's integration with all four of these ORM frameworks, we will not go into the details of each specific framework. We will give an explanation of their general behavior and some example configurations. If you want to explore any of these frameworks in detail, a wealth of resources is available.

## 4.4 *Integrating Hibernate with Spring*

Hibernate is a high-performance, open source persistence framework that has gained significant popularity recently. It provides not only basic object/relational mapping but also all the other sophisticated features you would expect from a full-featured ORM tool, such as caching, lazy loading, eager fetching, and distributed caching. You can learn more about it in *Hibernate in Action* from Manning or at the Hibernate web site http://www.hibernate.org.

### 4.4.1 *Hibernate overview*

You configure how Hibernate maps your objects to a relational database through XML configuration files. For an example of how this is done, let's examine how we would map the Student class from our Spring Training application. First, let's examine the Student class, shown in listing 4.12.

**Listing 4.12    Student.java**

```java
import java.util.Set;

public class Student {

  private Integer id;
  private String firstName;
  private String lastName;
  private Set courses;

  public Integer getId() { return id; }
  public void setId(Integer id) { this.id = id; }

  public String getFirstName() { return firstName; }
  public void setFirstName(String firstName) {
    this.firstName = firstName;
  }

  public String getLastName() { return lastName; }
    public void setLastName(String lastName) {
    this.lastName = lastName;
  }

  public Set getCourses() { return courses; }
  public void setCourses(Set courses) { this.courses = courses; }
}
```

Typically, each persistent class will have a corresponding XML mapping file that
ends with the extension ".hbm.xml." Let's take a look at the mapping file for the
Student class. By convention, we would name this file Student.hbm.xml, which is
shown in listing 4.13.

**Listing 4.13    Student.hbm.xml Hibernate mapping file**

```xml
<?xml version="1.0"?>
<!DOCTYPE hibernate-mapping
    PUBLIC "-//Hibernate/Hibernate Mapping DTD//EN"
    "http://hibernate.sourceforge.net/hibernate-mapping-2.0.dtd">

<hibernate-mapping>

  <class name="org.springinaction.training.model.Student">

    <id name="id">
      <generator class="assigned"/>
    </id>
```

**Define
class being
mapped**

**Map primary key**

```
  <property name="sex"/>          |  Map
  <property name="weight"/>       |  properties

  <set name="courses" table="transcript">
    <key column="student_id"/>
    <many-to-many column="course_id"
        class="org.springinaction.training.model.Course"/>
  </set>

  </class>

</hibernate-mapping>
```

Map relationships

In a typical application, you will have several of these files. These configuration files are then read in to create a SessionFactory. A SessionFactory will last the lifetime of your application and you will use it to obtain (what else?) Session objects. It is with these Session objects that you will access the database. So assuming that we have a configured SessionFactory, here is how we would get a Student object by its primary key:

```
public Student getStudent(Integer id) throw HibernateException {
    Session session = sessionFactory.openSession();
    Student student = (Student) session.load(Student.class, id);
    session.close();
    return student;
}
```

This is a trivial example of using Hibernate that excludes exception handling. But there is one thing you should take from this: Very little code is required to execute this operation. In fact, we actually load the Student object in one line of code. This is because Hibernate is doing all the work based on your mappings. Since Hibernate is taking care of making persistence easier, Spring focuses on making it easier to integrate with Hibernate. Let's look at some of the ways Spring does this.

### 4.4.2 *Managing Hibernate resources*

As we said, you will keep a single instance of a SessionFactory throughout the life of your application. So it makes sense to configure this object through your Spring configuration file. You do so using the Spring class LocalSessionFactoryBean:

```
<bean id="sessionFactory"class="org.springframework.
        orm.hibernate.LocalSessionFactoryBean">
```

Of course the `SessionFactory` needs to know to which database to connect. The preferred way to do this is to wire a `DataSource` to the `LocalSessionFactoryBean`:

```
<bean id="dataSource"
      class="org.springframework.jndi.JndiObjectFactoryBean">
  <property name="jndiName">
    <value>java:comp/env/jdbc/trainingDatasource</value>
  </property>
</bean>

<bean id="sessionFactory" class="org.springframework.
    orm.hibernate.LocalSessionFactoryBean">
  <property name="dataSource">
    <ref bean="dataSource"/>
  </property>
</bean>
```

You also manage how Hibernate is configured through the same `LocalSession-FactoryBean` bean. Hibernate itself has dozens of properties by which you can tweak its behavior. When used outside of Spring, Hibernate looks for a file named `hibernate.properties` somewhere on the application class path for its configurations. However, with Spring you do not have to manage these configurations in a separate properties file. Instead, you can wire them to the `hibernateProperties` property of the `LocalSessionFactoryBean`:

```
<bean id="sessionFactory" class="org.springframework.
    orm.hibernate.LocalSessionFactoryBean">
  <property name="hibernateProperties">
    <props>
      <prop key="hibernate.dialect">net.sf.hibernate.
          dialect.MySQLDialect</prop>
    </props>
  </property>
  ...
</bean>
```

One last thing you must configure is which mapping files Hibernate should read in. Remember when we created a Student.hbm.xml file? Well, we actually have to tell Hibernate it needs to use this file. Otherwise it will not know how to map the `Student` class to the database. Again, we can configure this through a property of the `LocalSessionFactoryBean` bean. In this case, we use the `mapping-Resources` property:

```
<bean id="sessionFactory" class="org.springframework.
    orm.hibernate.LocalSessionFactoryBean">
  <property name="mappingResources">
```

```
      <list>
        <value>Student.hbm.xml</value>
        <value>Course.hbm.xml</value>
        ...
      </list>
    </property>
    ...
  </bean>
```

This example works just fine for our small Spring Training application. But what happens if your application grows and you have dozens, if not hundreds, of persistent classes? It would be cumbersome to configure them all in this fashion. Fortunately, Spring offers you an alternative. You can also configure the mapping-DirectoryLocations property with a path that is a subset of your application's class path, and Spring will configure the SessionFactory with *every* *.hbm.xml it finds in this path. For example, assuming that all the persistent classes we want to configure are contained in the com.springinaction.training.model package, we would configure our SessionFactory like this:

```
<bean id="sessionFactory" class="org.springframework.
       ➡ orm.hibernate.LocalSessionFactoryBean">
  <property name="mappingDirectoryLocations">
    <list>
      <value>classpath:/com/springinaction/training/model</value>
    </list>
  </property>
  ...
</bean>
```

Now we have a fully configured SessionFactory and we didn't even need to create a second configuration file. Now all we need to do is create an object through which we will access Hibernate. Like all of Spring's DAO frameworks, this will be a template class. In this case, it is the HibernateTemplate class. And because the HibernateTemplate class is thread-safe, we can share this template class with multiple DAO objects:

```
<bean id="hibernateTemplate"
       class="org.springframework.orm.hibernate.HibernateTemplate">
  <property name="sessionFactory">
    <ref bean="sessionFactory"/>
  </property>
</bean>

<bean id="studentDao" class="com.springinaction.
       ➡ training.dao.hibernate.StudentDaoHibernate">
  <property name="hibernateTemplate">
    <ref bean="hibernateTemplate"/>
```

```
    </property>
  </bean>

  <bean id="courseDao" class="com.springinaction.
      ➡ training.dao.hibernate.CourseDaoHibernate">
    <property name="hibernateTemplate">
      <ref bean="hibernateTemplate"/>
    </property>
  </bean>
```

And remember, if it becomes cumbersome to wire the template into each of your DAO beans, you can always use Spring's autowire facility to implicitly wire your DAO beans. Now that you know how to wire a `HibernateTemplate` to your DAO objects, we are ready to start using Hibernate.

### 4.4.3 Accessing Hibernate through HibernateTemplate

The template-callback mechanism in Hibernate is pretty simple. There is the `HibernateTemplate` and one callback interface: `HibernateCallback`. And the `HibernateCallback` interface has just one method:

```
Object doInHibernate(Session session)
    throws HibernateException, SQLException;
```

As you can see, the `HibernateCallback` interface is pretty straightforward. Now, let's put the `HibernateTemplate` to use. We'll begin by getting an object from the database:

```
public Student getStudent(final Integer id) {
  return (Student) hibernateTemplate.execute(
    new HibernateCallback() {
      public Object doInHibernate(Session session)
          throws HibernateException {
        return session.load(Student.class, id);
      }
    });
}
```

Since we are using an inner class, a little more code is required and is not quite as clean as when we were not using Spring's Hibernate support. But we can have it both ways—clean code and Spring Hibernate support. The `HibernateTemplate` class provides some convenience methods that implicitly create a `HibernateCall-back` instance for you. All you have to do is call one of the convenience methods and Spring's framework does the rest. For example, here is how you would take advantage of one of these methods to accomplish the exact same thing as we did earlier—get an object from the database:

```
public Student getStudent(Integer id) {
  return (Student) hibernateTemplate.load(Student.class, id);
}
```

Now we are getting somewhere! We now have the benefits of having Spring managing our resources, converting proprietary exceptions, and, if we choose, adding transactions. The previous example is how you will access Hibernate through the Hibernate template the majority of the time. The HibernateTemplate class contains a wealth of convenience methods for you to use. For example, to update a Student object, this is all that would be required:

```
public void updateStudent(Student student) {
  hibernateTemplate.update(student);
}
```

Executing queries is not that much different. All we need to do is specify the query (usually in Hibernate's query language, HQL). Querying for students by last name would look something like this:

```
public List findStudentsByLastName(String lastName) {
  return hibernateTemplate.find("from Student student " +
                                "where student.lastName = ?",
                                lastName, Hibernate.STRING);
}
```

Pretty straightforward, right? Even if you have never seen HQL before, this code should be easy to follow. As we said before, Spring's framework makes for easy integration.

### 4.4.4 *Subclassing HibernateDaoSupport*

Spring's Hibernate ORM framework also comes with the convenience class HibernateDaoSupport that your DAO classes can subclass:

```
public class StudentDaoHibernate extends HibernateDaoSupport
    implements StudentDao {
  ...
}
```

If you opt for this design, you need to wire in a SessionFactory—the HibernateDaoSupport class comes with this property. This class provides you with a convenience method, getHibernateTemplate(), to easily get an instance of a HibernateTemplate. It also has a getSession() and a closeSessionIfNecessary() method if, for some reason, you need to perform a Hibernate operation without using a HibernateTemplate. We are sure you will find these cases will be the exception (no pun intended). So now you can see how easily you can integrate an ORM tool like Hibernate. We think you will find the JDO integration just as easy.

## 4.5 *Spring and JDO*

JDO is Sun's standard persistence specification. The important words from that sentence are *standard specification*. Like EJB, JDO is a specification developed by Sun that is implemented by different vendors. Currently there are more than ten different vendor implementations. To learn more about JDO, you can visit Sun's site at http://java.sun.com/products/jdo.

### 4.5.1 *Configuring JDO*

Similar to Hibernate's `SessionFactory`, JDO has a long-lived object that holds the persistence configurations. This is the `PersistenceManagerFactory`. Since JDO is a specification, `PersistenceManagerFactory` is the interface that vendors must implement. Without using Spring, we would get an instance using the `javax.jdo.JDOHelper` like so:

```
Properties props = new Properties();
// set JDO properties
PersistenceManagerFactory factory =
    JDOHelper.getPersistenceManagerFactory(props);
```

Some of these properties are defined by the JDO specification. For example, `javax.jdo.option.PersistenceManagerFactoryClass` defines the class that is implementing the `PersistenceManagerFactory` interface. Vendors are free to define other properties as well.

We configure a `PersistenceManagerFactory` in Spring using the `LocalPersistenceManagerFactoryBean`. If your data store is a relational database, you can also wire in your `DataSource`. Let's take a look at listing 4.14 to see who you wire in a `LocalPersistenceManagerFactoryBean`.

**Listing 4.14   Wiring a `LocalPersistenceManagerFactoryBean`**

```
<bean id="dataSource"
      class="org.springframework.jndi.JndiObjectFactoryBean">     Create
  <property name="jndiName">                                       DataSource
    <value>java:comp/env/jdbc/trainingDatasource</value>          bean
  </property>
</bean>

<bean id="persistenceManagerFactory" class="org.springframework.
      orm.jdo.LocalPersistenceManagerFactoryBean">             Create
  <property name="dataSource">               Wire              LocalPersistence-
    <ref bean="dataSource"/>                 DataSource        ManagerFactory-
  </property>                                                  Bean
```

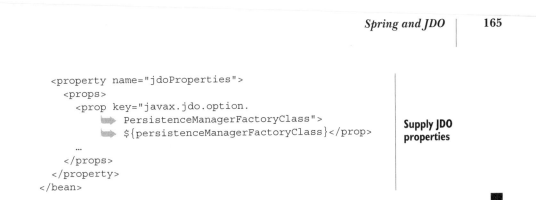

```
    <property name="jdoProperties">
      <props>
        <prop key="javax.jdo.option.
            PersistenceManagerFactoryClass">
            ${persistenceManagerFactoryClass}</prop>
        ...
      </props>
    </property>
  </bean>
```

**Supply JDO properties**

Now we have a JDO `PersistenceManagerFactory`. The next step is to wire this into a JdoTemplate:

```
<bean id="jdoTemplate"
    class="org.springframework.orm.jdo.JdoTemplate">
  <property name="persistenceManagerFactory">
    <ref bean="persistenceManagerFactory"/>
  </property>
</bean>
```

Since this has been drilled into your head by now, we will be brief. JdoTemplate is the Spring's JDO framework's central class. It is the class we will use to access the JDO framework. And this is the object we will wire into all of our DAO classes.

```
<bean id="studentDao" class="com.springinaction.
        training.dao.hibernate.StudentDaoJdo">
  <property name="jdoTemplate">
    <ref bean="jdoTemplate"/>
  </property>
</bean>
```

Of course, all of our JDO DAO classes must have a JdoTemplate property. We are now up and running with JDO. It's time to do some readin' and writin'.

### 4.5.2 *Accessing data with JdoTemplate*

In Spring's JDO framework, the template and callback classes are pretty easy to master. There is only one method on the JdoTemplate class that you will you use for accessing data: execute(JdoCallback). And the JdoCallback is likewise simple, having just one method:

```
Object doInJdo(PersistenceManager pm) throws JDOException;
```

So if we want to find a Student object by last name, we would use the following:

```
public Collection findPersonByLastName(final String lastName) {
  Collection persons = (Collection)
      jdoTemplate.execute(new JdoCallback() {
```

```
    public Object doInJdo(PersistenceManager pm) {
      Query q = pm.newQuery(
          Person.class, "lastName == " + lastName);
      return (Collection) q.execute();
    }
  });
  List list = new ArrayList();
  list.addAll(persons);
  return list;
}
```

As you can see, all of the JDO work is done within a simple inner class implementation of `JdoCallback`. You then pass this callback object to the `execute()` method of your `JdoTemplate` instance, and Spring's JDO framework does the rest. And like the previous template classes, `JdoTemplate` also has a handful of convenience methods. For example, you would retrieve a `Student` object by its id using the `getObjectById()` method:

```
public Student getStudent(Integer id) {
  return (Student) jdoTemplate.getObjectById(Student.class, id);
}
```

We don't want to disappoint you, but this is really about it. You execute your JDO code within a callback object or take advantage of a `JdoTemplate` convenience method and lean on Spring for resource management and exception handling.

## 4.6 *Spring and iBATIS*

Like Hibernate, iBATIS SQL Maps is an open source persistence framework. It provides the standard ORM features like mapping complex objects and caching, but is not quite as feature-rich as Hibernate. To learn more about SQL Maps, visit the iBATIS web site at http://www.ibatis.com/sqlmaps.

Spring actually supports two versions of SQL Maps: version 1.3 and the most recent version, 2.0. It is easy to distinguish between which Spring classes are meant for which version. All of the Spring classes that are meant for version 1.3 are named `SqlMapXxx`, and the classes to be used with version 2.0 are named `SqlMapClientXxx`. For example, you would use the `SqlMapTemplate` class with 1.3 and `SqlMapClientTemplate` with 2.0. In all of our examples we will be using version 2.0.

Speaking of examples, let's take a peek at how to configure SQL Maps.

### 4.6.1 Setting up SQL Maps

Similar to how you would with Hibernate, you configure SQL Maps with an XML configuration file. Listing 4.15 shows how to configure the Student class.

**Listing 4.15  Configuring the Student class in iBATIS SQL Maps**

```
<sql-map name="Student">                          Define Student mappings
  <result-map name="result"
              class="org.springinaction.training.model.Student">
    <property name="id" column="id" columnIndex="1"/>
    <property name="firstName" column=" first_name"
              columnIndex="2"/>
    <property name="lastName" column=" last_name"
              columnIndex="3"/>
  </result-map>

  <mapped-statement name="getStudentById" result-map="result">
    select student.id, student.first_name, student.last_name    Define
    from student                                                 select
    where student.id = #value#                                   statement
  </mapped-statement>

  <mapped-statement name="insertAccount">
    insert into student (id, first_name, last_name)        Define insert
    values (#id#, #firstName#, #lastName#)                 statement
  </mapped-statement>
</sql-map>
```

Give this file a meaningful name, like Student.xml. The next step is to create an iBATIS SQL Maps configuration file called sql-map-config.xml. Within this file, we configure our Student.xml file:

```
<sql-map-config>
  <sql-map resource="Student.xml"/>
</sql-map-config>
```

Now that our configuration files are in place, we need to configure a SQLMapClient:

```
<bean id="sqlMapClient"
      class="org.springframework.orm.ibatis.SqlMapClientFactoryBean">
  <property name="configLocation">
    <value>sql-map-config.xml</value>
  </property>
  <property name="dataSource">
    <ref bean="dataSource"/>
  </property>
</bean>
```

By now you should know the drill: create a template class and wire it to our DAO objects:

```
<bean id="sqlMapClientTemplate"
      class=" org.springframework.orm.ibatis.SqlMapClientTemplate">
  <property name="sqlMapClient">
    <ref bean="sqlMapClient"/>
  </property>
</bean>

<bean id="studentDao"
      class="org.springinaction.training.model.StudentDaoSqlMap">
  <property name="sqlMapClientTemplate">
    <ref bean="sqlMapClientTemplate"/>
  </property>
</bean>
```

We have our DAO objects configured and ready to go. Now we need to use the `SqlMapClientTemplate` to hit the database.

### 4.6.2  Using SqlMapClientTemplate

Like the previous ORM frameworks, using the template class and its callback is pretty straightforward. In this case, we need to implement the `SqlMapClient-Callback`'s method:

```
Object doInSqlMapClient(SqlMapExecutor  executor)
   throws SQLException;
```

And just like all of the other template-callback pairs, the template manages the nasty stuff and we worry about operating on the data. Here is an example of how we would query for a `Student` using `SqlMapClientCallback`:

```
public Student getStudent(Integer id) throws DataAccessException {
  return getSqlMapClientTemplate().execute(
     new SqlMapClientCallback() {
   public Object doInSqlMapClient(SqlMapExecutor executor)
      throws SQLException {
     return (Student) executor.queryForObject("getPerson", id);
   }
  });
}
```

Once again, we end up with a method that is short and sweet. And believe it or not, it can be even shorter and sweeter, because `SqlMapClientTemplate` comes with a handful of convenience methods for common data access operations. Using one of these methods, we would rewrite the above method as so:

```
public Student getStudent(Integer id) throws DataAccessException {
  return (Student) getSqlMapTemplate().executeQueryForObject(
    "getStudentById", id);
}
```

Writing data to the database is just as simple:

```
public void insertStudent(Student student)
    throws DataAccessException {
  getSqlMapTemplate().executeUpdate("insertStudent", student);
}
```

By now you should have noticed a theme in Spring's ORM frameworks. Since these persistence frameworks focus on their job (O/R mapping), the Spring integration points are simple. Once we have configured our ORM tool through Spring's XML files, accessing and using the tool become quite straightforward.

## 4.7 Spring and OJB

ObJectRelationalBridge, or OJB, is another open source ORM framework from Apache. Like Hibernate, is has nearly every feature you would want in an ORM tool, including lazy loading and distributed caching. You can learn more about OJB at the OJB web site at http://db.apache.org/ojb.

OJB supports several persistence APIs, including two standard APIs—JDO and ODMG—as well as its own proprietary API. Spring integrates with OJB's proprietary API, which is based around a `PersistenceBroker` class. Let's see how we can configure a `PersistenceBroker` using Spring.

### 4.7.1 Setting up OJB's PersistenceBroker

Like the other two open source ORM frameworks we have already discussed, OJB defines its mapping in an XML file. Typically, you will do this in a file named `OJB-repository.xml`. This is also the file in which you tell OJB which `DataSource` to use. Listing 4.16 illustrates how you would configure the `Student` class in OJB.

**Listing 4.16  Configuring the `Student` class in OJB**

```
<descriptor-repository version="1.0">

  <jdbc-connection-descriptor jcd-alias="dataSource"         Configure
                              default-connection="true"      DataSource
                              useAutoCommit="1"/>
  <class-descriptor                                          Configure
      class="org.springinaction.training.model.Student"      Student
      table="Student">                                       mapping
```

```
<field-descriptor name="id" column="id"
                   primarykey="true"
                   autoincrement="true"/>

<field-descriptor name="firstName" column="first_name"/>
<field-descriptor name="lastName" column="last_name"/>
...
  </class-descriptor>
</descriptor-repository>
```

Configure
Student
mapping

When the Spring OJB framework tries to access the database, it will use the Data-
Source whose bean name is the same as the jcd-alias property above. For example, in the above OJB-repository.xml file, you would need to wire a DataSource
with the name dataSource.

OJB also requires a properties file named OJB.properties for OJB-specific
properties. When you download OJB, you get an OJB.properties file with the
default values set. This file has a *lot* of properties with which you can configure
OJB. The only property you need to change to integrate Spring with OJB is the
ConnectionFactoryClass:

```
ConnectionFactoryClass=org.springframework.orm.ojb.
                support.LocalDataSourceConnectionFactory
```

To see how to configure the multitude of other OJB properties, see the OJB documentation. Now we are ready to wire our Spring beans. To integrate OJB, all we
need to do is wire a DataSource as described above:

```
<beans>
  <bean id="dataSource" .../>

  <bean id="studentDao"
        class="com.springinaction.training.dao.ojb.StudentDaoOjb">
  </bean>

  <bean id="ojbConfigurer" class="org.springframework.orm
                ojb.support.LocalOjbConfigurer"/>
</beans>
```

Notice that we did not wire a template class this time. This is because the Persis-
tenceBrokerTemplate class configures itself upon instantiation, so there is nothing
to configure. Listing 4.17 shows how StudentDao would be implemented using
OJB and the PersistenceBrokerDaoSupport class.

**Listing 4.17  Implementing `PersistenceBrokerDaoSupport`**

```
public class StudentDaoOjb extends PersistenceBrokerDaoSupport
    implements StudentDao {

  public Student getStudent(final Integer id) {
    Criteria criteria = new Criteria();
    criteria.addLike("id", Integer.toString(id));      Query
    return (Student)                                   data
        getPersistenceBrokerTemplate().getObjectByQuery(
        new QueryByCriteria(Student.class, criteria));
}

  public void create(Student student) {               Write
    getPersistenceBrokerTemplate().store(student);     data
  }

}
```

As you see, we still get a template class to access the OJB framework. Since we sub-classed the `PersistenceBrokerDaoSupport` class, the `PersistenceBrokerTemplate` class is already available to us. Also, notice that we take advantage of some of the convenience methods available in the `PersistenceBrokerTemplate` class, such as `getObjectByQuery()` and `store()`. Like Spring's other ORM integration frameworks, its OJB support comes with a wealth of convenience methods that make integration as painless as possible.

## 4.8  Summary

As you discovered, no matter what persistence technology you are using, Spring aims to make this transparent to the rest of your application. The key way it does this is by providing a consistent exception hierarchy across all of its DAO frameworks. By interpreting technology-specific exceptions and vendor-specific error codes, Spring allows you to throw generic `DataAccessException` subclasses so that your persistence tier does not leak into the rest of your application.

Of all the persistence technologies available, straight JDBC requires the most work from your code. And as you learned, Spring provides a wealth of support to help write better JDBC code. By providing a clean callback design, you are able to write your JDBC statement and queries without the hassle of resource management and exception handling. It also provides you with other support facilities such as a framework for generating primary keys and custom error code interpretation.

Beyond plain JDBC, many applications use an ORM tool to handle more complex persistence needs. You discovered that Spring has very capable support for several of these frameworks: Hibernate, JDO, iBATIS SQL Maps, and Apache OJB. By integrating Spring with your ORM tool, you can have a more unified configuration, as well as take advantage of Spring's resource management and exception handling.

One thing noticeably missing from this chapter is transaction management. That is because transaction management is so complex it warrants its own chapter. In chapter 5, you will learn how you can integrate Spring's rich transaction support into each of these persistence technologies.

# Managing transactions

**This chapter covers**

- Integrating Spring with different transaction managers
- Managing transaction programmically
- Using Spring's declarative transactions
- Describing transactions using annotations

Take a moment to recall your younger days. If you were like many children, you spent more than a few carefree moments on the playground swinging on the swings, traversing the monkey bars, getting dizzy while spinning on the merry-go-round, and going up and down on the teeter-totter.

The problem with the teeter-totter is that it is practically impossible to enjoy on your own. You see, to truly enjoy a teeter-totter, you need another person. You and a friend both have to agree to play on the teeter-totter. This agreement is an all-or-nothing proposition. Both of you will either teeter-totter or you will not. If either of you fails to take your respective seat on each end of the teeter-totter, then there will be no teeter-tottering—there'll just be a sad little kid sitting motionless on the end of a slanted board.[1]

In software, all-or-nothing operations are called *transactions*. Transactions allow you to group several operations into a single unit-of-work that either fully happens or fully doesn't happen. If everything goes well, then the transaction is a success. But if anything goes wrong, then the slate is wiped clean and it's as if nothing ever happened.

Probably the most common example of a real-world transaction is a money transfer. Imagine that you were to transfer $100 from your savings account to your checking account. The transfer involves two operations: $100 is deducted from the savings account and $100 is added to the checking account. The money transfer must be performed completely or not at all. If the deduction from the savings account works, but the deposit into the checking account fails, you'll be out $100 (good for the bank, bad for you). On the other hand, if the deduction fails but the deposit succeeds, you'll be ahead $100 (good for you, bad for the bank). It's best for both parties involved if the entire transfer is rolled back if either operation fails.

Spring has rich support for transaction management, both programmatic and declarative. In this chapter, you'll learn how to place application code in transactions to ensure that when things go right they are made permanent—and when things go wrong nobody needs to know.

## 5.1 *Understanding transactions*

To illustrate transactions, consider the purchase of a movie ticket. Purchasing a ticket typically involves the following actions:

---

[1] We're still checking into it, but this may qualify as a record for the most uses of the word "teeter-totter" in a programming book.

- The number of available seats will be examined to verify that there are enough seats available for your purchase.
- The number of available seats is decremented by one for each ticket purchased.
- You provide payment for the ticket.
- The ticket is issued to you.

If everything goes well, you'll be enjoying a blockbuster movie and the theater will be a few dollars richer. But what if something goes wrong? For instance, what if you paid with a credit card that had reached its limit? Certainly, you would not receive a ticket and the theater wouldn't receive payment. But if the number of seats isn't reset to its value before the purchase, then the movie may artificially run out of seats (and thus lose sales). Or consider what would happen if everything else works fine, but the ticket issue fails. You'd be short a few dollars and be stuck at home watching cable TV.

In order to ensure that neither you nor the theater loses out, the actions above should be wrapped in a transaction. As a transaction, they're all treated as a single action, guaranteeing that they'll either all fully succeed or they'll all be rolled back as if it never happened. Figure 5.1 illustrates how this transaction plays out.

Transactions play an important role in software, ensuring that data and resources are never left in an inconsistent state. Without them, there is potential for data to be corrupted or inconsistent with the business rules of the application.

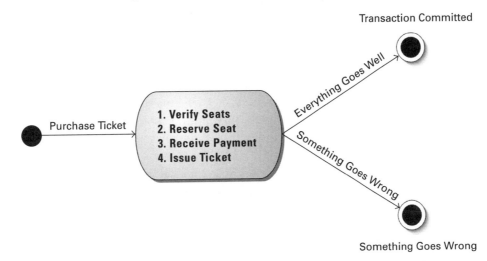

**Figure 5.1 Purchasing a movie ticket as a transaction**

Let's take a quick look at the four factors that guide transactions and how they work.

### 5.1.1 Explaining transactions in only four words

In the grand tradition of software development, an acronym has been created to describe transactions: ACID. In short, ACID stands for

- *Atomic*—Transactions are made up of one or more activities bundled together as a single unit of work. Atomicity ensures that all of the operations in the transaction happen or that none of them happen. If all of the activities succeed, then the transaction is a success. If any of the activities fail, then the entire transaction fails and is rolled back.

- *Consistent*—Once a transaction ends (whether successful or not), the system is left in a state that is consistent with the business that it models. The data should not be corrupted with respect to reality.

- *Isolated*—Transactions should allow multiple users to work with the same data, without each user's work getting tangled up with the others. Therefore, transactions should be isolated from each other, preventing concurrent reads and writes to the same data from occurring. (Note that isolation typically involves locking rows and/or tables in a database.)

- *Durable*—Once the transaction has completed, the results of the transaction should be made permanent so that they will survive any sort of system crash. This typically involves storing the results in a database or some other form of persistent storage.

In the movie ticket example, a transaction could ensure atomicity by undoing the result of all of the steps if any step fails. Atomicity supports consistency by ensuring that the system's data is never left in an inconsistent, partially done state. Isolation also supports consistency by preventing another concurrent transaction from stealing seats out from under you while you are still in the process of purchasing them.

Finally, the effects are durable because they will have been committed to some persistent storage. In the event of a system crash or other catastrophic event, you shouldn't have to worry about results of the transaction being lost.

For a more detailed explanation of transactions, we suggest that you read *Patterns of Enterprise Application Architecture* by Martin Fowler. Specifically, chapter 5 discusses concurrency and transactions.

### 5.1.2 *Understanding Spring's transaction management support*

Spring, like EJB, provides support for both programmatic and declarative transaction management support. But Spring's transaction management capabilities exceed those of EJB.

Spring's support for programmatic transaction management differs greatly from that of EJB. Unlike EJB, which is coupled with a Java Transaction API (JTA) implementation, Spring employs a callback mechanism that abstracts away the actual transaction implementation from the transactional code. In fact, Spring's transaction management support doesn't even require a JTA implementation. If your application uses only a single persistent resource, Spring can use the transactional support afforded by the persistence mechanism. This includes JDBC, Hibernate, Java Data Objects (JDO), and Apache's Object Relational Bridge (OJB). However, if your application has transaction requirements that span multiple resources, Spring can support distributed (XA) transactions using a third-party JTA implementation. We'll discuss Spring's support for programmatic transactions in section 5.2.

While programmatic transaction management affords you flexibility in precisely defining transaction boundaries in your code, declarative transactions help you decouple an operation from its transaction rules. Spring's support for declarative transactions is reminiscent of EJB's container-managed transactions (CMT). Both allow you to define transaction boundaries declaratively. But Spring's declarative transaction go beyond CMT by allowing you to declare additional attributes such as isolation level and timeouts.[2] We'll begin working with Spring's declarative transaction support in section 5.3.

Choosing between programmatic and declarative transaction management is largely a decision of fine-grained control versus convenience. When you program transactions into your code, you gain precise control over transaction boundaries, beginning and ending them precisely where you want. Typically, you will not require the fine-grained control offered by programmatic transactions and will choose to declare your transactions in the context definition file.

Regardless of whether you choose to program transactions into your beans or to declare them as aspects, you'll be using a Spring transaction manager to interface with a platform-specific transaction implementation. Let's take a look at how

---

[2] Although the EJB specification doesn't provide for transaction isolation levels and timeouts in CMT, several EJB containers provide these capabilities.

Spring's transaction managers free you from dealing directly with platform-specific transaction implementations.

### 5.1.3 Introducing Spring's transaction manager

Spring does not directly manage transactions. Instead, it comes with a selection of transaction managers that delegate responsibility for transaction management to a platform-specific transaction implementation provided by either JTA or the persistence mechanism. Spring's transaction managers are listed in table 5.1.

**Table 5.1** Spring's selection of transaction managers for many different transaction implementations

| Transaction manager implementation | Purpose |
|---|---|
| `org.springframework.jdbc.datasource.DataSourceTransactionManager` | Manages transactions on a single JDBC `DataSource`. |
| `org.springframework.orm.hibernate.HibernateTransactionManager` | Used to manage transactions when Hibernate is the persistence mechanism. |
| `org.springframework.orm.jdo.JdoTransactionManager` | Used to manage transactions when JDO is used for persistence. |
| `org.springframework.transaction.jta.JtaTransactionManager` | Manages transactions using a Java Transaction API (JTA) implementation. Must be used when a transaction spans multiple resources. |
| `org.springframework.orm.ojb.PersistenceBrokerTransactionManager` | Manages transactions when Apache's Object Relational Bridge (OJB) is used for persistence. |

Each of these transaction managers acts as a façade to a platform-specific transaction implementation (figure 5.2). This makes it possible for you to work with a transaction in Spring with little regard to what the actual transaction implementation is.

To use a transaction manager, you'll need to declare it in your application context. Let's look at how to declare each of these transaction managers, starting with `DataSourceTransactionManager`.

#### JDBC transactions

If you're using straight JDBC for your application's persistence, `DataSourceTransactionManager` will handle transactional boundaries for you. To use `DataSourceTransactionManager`, wire it into your application's context definition using the following XML:

```
<bean id="transactionManager" class="org.springframework.jdbc.
    datasource.DataSourceTransactionManager">
```

```
    <property name="dataSource">
      <ref bean="dataSource"/>
    </property>
  </bean>
```

Notice that the `dataSource` property is set with a reference to a bean named `data-Source`. Presumably, the `dataSource` bean is a `javax.sql.DataSource` bean defined elsewhere in your context definition file.

Behind the scenes, `DataSourceTransactionManager` manages transactions by making calls on the `java.sql.Connection` object retrieved from the `DataSource`. For instance, a successful transaction is committed by calling the `commit()` method on the connection. Likewise, a failed transaction is rolled back by calling the `rollback()` method.

### Hibernate transactions

If your application's persistence is handled by Hibernate, then you'll want to use `HibernateTransactionManager`. Declare it in your application using the XML on the following page.

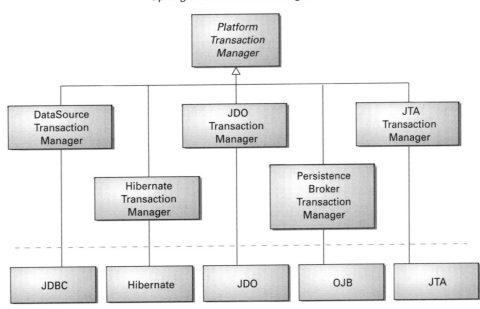

*Spring's Transaction Managers*

*Platform-Specific Transaction Implementations*

**Figure 5.2**  Spring's transaction managers delegate transaction-management responsibility to platform-specific transaction implementations.

```
<bean id="transactionManager" class="org.springframework.
    orm.hibernate.HibernateTransactionManager">
  <property name="sessionFactory">
    <ref bean="sessionFactory"/>
  </property>
</bean>
```

The `sessionFactory` property should be wired with a Hibernate `SessionFactory`, here cleverly named `sessionFactory`. See chapter 4 for details on setting up a Hibernate session factory.

`HibernateTransactionManager` delegates responsibility for transaction management to a `net.sf.hibernate.Transaction` object that it retrieves from the Hibernate session. When a transaction successfully completes, `HibernateTransactionManager` will call the `commit()` method on the `Transaction` object. Similarly, when a transaction fails, the `rollback()` method will be called on the `Transaction` object.

### Java Data Objects transactions

Perhaps JDBC and Hibernate aren't for you and you've decided to implement your application's persistence layer using Java Data Objects (JDO). In that case, the transaction manager of choice will be `JdoTransactionManager`. It can be declared into your application's context like this:

```
<bean id="transactionManager"
    class="org.springframework.orm.jdo.JdoTransactionManager">
  <property name="persistenceManagerFactory">
    <ref bean="persistenceManagerFactory"/>
  </property>
</bean>
```

With `JdoTransactionManager`, you need to wire in a `javax.jdo.PersistenceManagerFactory` instance to the `persistenceManagerFactory` property. See chapter 4 for more information on how to set up a JDO persistence manager factory.

Under the covers, `JdoTransactionManager` works with the transaction object retrieved from the JDO persistence manager, calling `commit()` at the end of a successful transaction and `rollback()` if the transaction fails.

### Object Relational Bridge transactions

Yet another persistence framework available to use within a Spring application is Apache's Object Relational Bridge (OJB). If you've chosen to use OJB for persistence, you can use the `PersistenceBrokerTransactionManager` to manage transactions:

```
<bean id="transactionManager" class="org.springframework.orm.
    ➥ ojb.PersistenceBrokerTransactionManager">
...
</bean>
```

PersistenceBrokerTransactionManager starts a transaction by retrieving an org.apache.ojb.broker.PersistenceBroker. When a transaction completes successfully, the PersistenceBrokerTransactionManager calls the commitTransaction() method on the PersistenceBroker. When a transaction fails, it is rolled back by a call to the setRollbackOnly() method.

### Java Transaction API transactions

If none of the aforementioned transaction managers meet your needs or if your transactions span multiple transaction sources (e.g., two or more different databases), you'll need to use JtaTransactionManager:

```
<bean id="transactionManager" class="org.springframework.
    ➥ transaction.jta.JtaTransactionManager">
  <property name="transactionManagerName">
    <value>java:/TransactionManager</value>
  </property>
</bean>
```

JtaTransactionManager delegates transaction management responsibility to a JTA implementation. JTA specifies a standard API to coordinate transactions between an application and one or more data sources. The transactionManagerName property specifies a JTA transaction manager to be looked up via JNDI.

JtaTransactionManager works with javax.transaction.UserTransaction and javax.transaction.TransactionManager objects, delegating responsibility for transaction manager to those objects. A successful transaction will be committed with a call to the UserTransaction.commit() method. Likewise, if the transaction fails, the UserTransaction's rollback() method will be called.

By now, we hope you've found a Spring transaction manager suitable for your application's needs and have wired it into your Spring configuration file. Now it's time to put that transaction manager to work. We'll start by employing the transaction manager to program transactions manually.

## 5.2 Programming transactions in Spring

The enrollStudentInCourse() method of CourseService has multiple actions that are taken during the course of enrolling a student in a course. If any of these actions go sour, then all actions should be rolled back as if nothing happened. In other words, enrollStudentInCourse() needs to be wrapped in a transaction.

One approach to adding transactions to your code is to programmatically add transactional boundaries using Spring's `TransactionTemplate` class. Like other template classes in Spring (such as `JdbcTemplate` discussed in chapter 4), `TransactionTemplate` utilizes a callback mechanism. Listing 5.1 shows how to wrap your code within a `TransactionTemplate`.

**Listing 5.1  Programmatic transaction in the `enrollStudentInCourse()` method**

```
public void enrollStudentInCourse() {
  transactionTemplate.execute(
    new TransactionCallback() {
      public Object doInTransaction(TransactionStatus ts) {
        try {
          // do stuff      <--  Runs within doInTransaction()
        } catch (Exception e) {
          ts.setRollbackOnly();    <--  Calls setRollbackOnly() to roll back
        }

        return null;    <--  If successful, transaction is committed
      }
    }
  );
}
```

You start by implementing the `TransactionCallback` interface. Because `TransactionCallback` has only one method to implement, it is often easiest to implement it as an anonymous inner-class, as shown in listing 5.1. Place the code you want to run within a transactional context in the `doInTransaction()` method.

Calling the `execute()` method on the `TransactionTemplate` instance will execute the code contained within the `TransactionCallback` instance. If your code encounters a problem, calling `setRollbackOnly()` on the `TransactionStatus` object will roll back the transaction. Otherwise, if the `doInTransaction()` method returns successfully, the transaction will be committed.

Where does the `TransactionTemplate` instance come from? Good question. It should be injected into `CourseServiceImpl`, as follows:

```
<bean id="transactionTemplate" class="org.springframework.
       transaction.support.TransactionTemplate">
  <property name="transactionManager">
    <ref bean="transactionManager"/>
  </property>
</bean>

<bean id="courseService"
    class="com.springinaction.training.service.CourseServiceImpl">
```

```
...
    <property name=" transactionTemplate">
      <ref bean=" transactionTemplate"/>
    </property>
  </bean>
```

Notice that the `transactionTemplate` bean has a `transactionManager` property. Under the hood, `TransactionTemplate` uses an implementation of `Platform-TransactionManager` to handle the platform-specific details of transaction management. Here we've wired in a reference to a bean named `transactionManager`, which could be any of the implementations of the `PlatformTransactionManager` interface discussed in section 5.1.3.

Programmatic transactions are good when you want complete control over transactional boundaries. But, as you can see from listing 5.1, they are a bit intrusive. You had to alter the implementation of `enrollStudentInCourse()`—using Spring-specific classes—to employ Spring's programmatic transaction support.

Usually your transactional needs won't require such precise control over transactional boundaries. That's why you'll typically choose to declare your transactions outside of your application code (in the Spring configuration file, for instance). The rest of this chapter will cover Spring's declarative transaction management.

## 5.3 *Declaring transactions*

At one time not too long ago, declarative transaction management was a capability only available in EJB containers. But now Spring offers support for declarative transactions to POJOs. This is a significant feature of Spring because your applications will no longer require complex and heavyweight EJBs just to achieve atomic operations declaratively.

Spring's support for declarative transaction management is implemented through Spring's AOP framework. This is a natural fit because transactions are a system-level service above an application's primary functionality. You can think of a Spring transaction as an aspect that "wraps" a method.

To employ declarative transactions in your Spring application, you use `TransactionProxyFactoryBean`. This proxy factory bean is similar to `ProxyFactoryBean` that you learned about in chapter 3, except that it has the specific purpose of wrapping methods in transactional contexts. (You could achieve the same results by creating your own `ProxyFactoryBean` to handle transactions, but it is much easier to use a `TransactionProxyFactoryBean` since it is specifically designed for declarative transactions.) Listing 5.2 shows how you can declare a `TransactionProxyFactoryBean`.

**Listing 5.2  Proxying a service for transactional processing**

```
<bean id="courseService" class="org.springframework.transaction.
      interceptor.TransactionProxyFactoryBean">
  <property name="proxyInterfaces">
    <list>
      <value>
        com.springinaction.training.service.CourseService          <--- Interface
      </value>                                                           implemented
    </list>                                                             by proxy
  </property>

  <property name="target">
    <ref bean="courseServiceTarget"/>     <--- Bean being proxied
  </property>

  <property name="transactionManager">
    <ref bean="transactionManager"/>   <--- Transaction manager
  </property>

  <property name="transactionAttributeSource">
    <ref bean="attributeSource"/>    <--- Transaction attribute source
  </property>
</bean>
```

Notice that this bean has an id of courseService. This is so that when the application asks for a courseService from the application context, it will retrieve an instance that is wrapped by this TransactionProxyFactoryBean. The original courseService bean should be renamed so that there is no conflict in bean ids. Any name will work, but it is a recognized convention to derive the name of the target bean by appending "Target" to the name of the target bean's proxy. In this case, courseServiceTarget is appropriate:

```
<bean id="courseServiceTarget"
    class="com.springinaction.training.service.CourseServiceImpl">
  ...
</bean>
```

The TransactionProxyFactoryBean has two collaborators in addition to its target bean. The transactionManager property indicates an instance of PlatformTransactionManager to use when realizing the transactional context. This can be any one of the PlatformTransactionManagers covered in section 5.1.3.

The transactionAttributeSource property takes a reference to a TransactionAttributeSource bean. To understand how transaction attribute sources work, you must first understand transaction attributes. So, let's take a detailed look at how transaction attributes are defined.

### 5.3.1 *Understanding transaction attributes*

In Spring, a transaction attribute is a description of how transaction policies should be applied to a method. This description could include one or more of the following parameters:

- Propagation behavior
- Isolation level
- Read-only hints
- The transaction timeout period

We'll see how to piece these transaction attribute parameters together to declare a transaction policy soon. But let's first take a look at how each of these parameters impacts how a transaction is applied.

#### *Propagation behavior*

Propagation behavior defines the boundaries of the transaction with respect to the client and to the method being called. Spring defines seven distinct propagation behaviors, as cataloged in table 5.2.

Table 5.2   Spring's transactional propagation rules[3]

| Propagation behavior | What it means |
| --- | --- |
| PROPAGATION_MANDATORY | Indicates that the method must run within a transaction. If no existing transaction is in progress, an exception will be thrown. |
| PROPAGATION_NESTED | Indicates that the method should be run within a nested transaction if an existing transaction is in progress. The nested transaction can be committed and rolled back individually from the enclosing transaction. If no enclosing transaction exists, behaves like PROPAGATION_REQUIRED. Beware that vendor support for this propagation behavior is spotty at best. Consult the documentation for your resource manager to determine if nested transactions are supported. |
| PROPAGATION_NEVER | Indicates that the current method should not run within a transactional context. If there is an existing transaction in progress, an exception will be thrown. |

*continued on next page*

[3] The propagation behaviors described in table 5.3 are defined as constants in the org.springframework.transaction.TransactionDefinition interface.

**Table 5.2** Spring's transactional propagation rules *(continued)*

| Propagation behavior | What it means |
| --- | --- |
| `PROPAGATION_NOT_SUPPORTED` | Indicates that the method should not run within a transaction. If an existing transaction is in progress, it will be suspended for the duration of the method. If using `JTATransactionManager`, access to `TransactionManager` is required. |
| `PROPAGATION_REQUIRED` | Indicates that the current method must run within a transaction. If an existing transaction is in progress, the method will run within that transaction. Otherwise, a new transaction will be started. |
| `PROPAGATION_REQUIRES_NEW` | Indicates that the current method must run within its own transaction. A new transaction is started and if an existing transaction is in progress, it will be suspended for the duration of the method. If using `JTATransactionManager`, access to `Transaction-Manager` is required. |
| `PROPAGATION_SUPPORTS` | Indicates that the current method does not require a transactional context, but may run within a transaction if one is already in progress. |

Most of the propagation behaviors in table 5.2 may look familiar. That's because they mirror the propagation rules available in EJB's container-managed transactions (CMT). For instance, Spring's `PROPAGATION_REQUIRES_NEW` is equivalent to CMT's requiresNew. Spring adds an additional propagation behavior not available in CMT, `PROPAGATION_NESTED`, to support nested transactions.

Propagation rules answer the question of whether or not a new transaction should be started or suspended, or if a method should even be executed within a transactional context at all.

For example, if a method is declared to be transactional with `PROPAGATION_REQUIRES_NEW` behavior, it means that the transactional boundaries are the same as the method's own boundaries: A new transaction is started when the method begins and the transaction ends with the method returns or throws an exception. If the method has `PROPAGATION_REQUIRED` behavior, then the transactional boundaries depend on whether a transaction is already under way.

### *Isolation levels*

In a typical application, multiple transactions run concurrently, often working with the same data to get their job done. Concurrency, while necessary, can lead to the following problems:

- *Dirty read*—Dirty reads occur when one transaction reads data that has been written but not yet committed by another transaction. If the changes are later rolled back, the data obtained by the first transaction will be invalid.

- *Nonrepeatable read*—Nonrepeatable reads happen when a transaction performs the same query two or more times and each time the data is different. This is usually due to another concurrent transaction updating the data between the queries.
- *Phantom reads*—Phantom reads are similar to nonrepeatable reads. These occur when a transaction (T1) reads several rows, then a concurrent transaction (T2) inserts rows. Upon subsequent queries, the first transaction (T1) finds additional rows that were not there before.

In an ideal situation, transactions would be completely isolated from each other, preventing these problems. However, perfect isolation can affect performance because it often involves locking rows (and sometimes complete tables) in the datastore. Aggressive locking can hinder concurrency, requiring transactions to wait on each other to do their work.

Realizing that perfect isolation can impact performance and because not all applications will require perfect isolation, sometimes it is desirable to be flexible with regard to transaction isolation. Therefore, there are several levels of isolation, as described in table 5.3.

**Table 5.3  Spring's transaction isolation levels[4]**

| Isolation level | What it means |
|---|---|
| ISOLATION_DEFAULT | Use the default isolation level of the underlying datastore. |
| ISOLATION_READ_UNCOMMITTED | Allows you to read changes that have not yet been committed. May result in dirty reads, phantom reads, and nonrepeatable reads. |
| ISOLATION_READ_COMMITTED | Allows reads from concurrent transactions that have been committed. Dirty reads are prevented, but phantom and nonrepeatable reads may still occur. |
| ISOLATION_REPEATABLE_READ | Multiple reads of the same field will yield the same results, unless changed by the transaction itself. Dirty reads and nonrepeatable reads are prevented by phantom reads may still occur. |
| ISOLATION_SERIALIZABLE | This fully ACID-compliant isolation level ensures that dirty reads, nonrepeatable reads, and phantom reads are all prevented. This is the slowest of all isolation levels because it is typically accomplished by doing full table locks on the tables involved in the transaction. |

---

[4] The isolation levels described in table 5.3 are defined as constants in the `org.springframework.transaction.TransactionDefinition` interface.

ISOLATION_READ_UNCOMMITTED is the most efficient isolation level, but isolates the transaction the least, leaving the transaction open to dirty, nonrepeatable, and phantom reads. At the other extreme, ISOLATION_SERIALIZABLE prevents all forms of isolation problems but is the least efficient.

Be aware that not all resource managers support all of the isolation levels listed in table 5.3. Consult the documentation for your resource manager to determine what isolation levels are available.

### Read-only

If a transaction performs only read operations against the underlying datastore, the datastore may be able to apply certain optimizations that take advantage of the read-only nature of the transaction. By declaring a transaction as read-only, you give the underlying datastore the opportunity to apply those optimizations as it sees fit.

Because read-only optimizations are applied by the underlying datastore when a transaction begins, it only makes sense to declare a transaction as read-only on methods with propagation behaviors that may start a new transaction (PROPAGATION_REQUIRED, PROPAGATION_REQUIRES_NEW, and PROPAGATION_NESTED).

Furthermore, if you are using Hibernate as your persistence mechanism, declaring a transaction as read-only will result in Hibernate's flush mode being set to FLUSH_NEVER. This tells Hibernate to avoid unnecessary synchronization of objects with the database, delaying all updates until the end of the transaction.

### Transaction timeout

Finally, one other attribute you may choose to set on a transaction is a timeout. Suppose that your transaction becomes unexpectedly long-running. Because transactions may involve locks on the underlying datastore, long-running transactions may tie up database resources unnecessarily. Instead of waiting it out, you can declare a transaction to automatically roll back after a certain number of seconds.

Because the timeout clock begins ticking when a transaction starts, it only makes sense to declare a transaction timeout on methods with propagation behaviors that may start a new transaction (PROPAGATION_REQUIRED, PROPAGATION_REQUIRES_NEW, and PROPAGATION_NESTED).

### 5.3.2 *Declaring a simple transaction policy*

TransactionProxyFactoryBean consults a method's transaction attributes to determine how to administer transaction policies on that method. But from where does TransactionProxyFactoryBean get a method's transaction attributes?

As you saw in listing 5.2, TransactionProxyFactoryBean has a transactionAttributeSource property. This property is wired to an instance of TransactionAttributeSource. A TransactionAttributeSource is used as a reference for looking up transaction attributes on a method.

A TransactionAttributeSource is defined by the following interface:

```
public interface TransactionAttributeSource {
  public TransactionAttribute getTransactionAttribute(
    java.lang.reflect.Method method,
    java.lang.Class targetClass
  );
}
```

The getTransactionAttribute() method is called to find the transaction attributes for a particular method, given the target class and method. The TransactionAttribute returned indicates the transactional policies that should be applied to the method.

Now let's define the transactionAttributeSource bean in the application context definition XML file as follows:

```
<bean id="transactionAttributeSource"
    class="org.springframework.transaction.interceptor.
          MatchAlwaysTransactionAttributeSource">

  ...
</bean>
```

Voilà! With the transactionAttributeSource bean declared, all the methods proxied by the target class of TransactionProxyFactoryBean are now performed within a transactional context. But notice that you didn't specify which methods are to be transactional or even what transaction policy to apply. That's because here we've decided to use MatchAlwaysTransactionAttributeSource.

MatchAlwaysTransactionAttributeSource is probably the simplest implementation of TransactionAttributeSource. When its getTransactionAttribute() method is called, it naively returns the same TransactionAttribute every time, regardless of which method is being wrapped in the transaction (by default, PROPAGATION_REQUIRED and ISOLATION_DEFAULT). That's the "MatchAlways" part of MatchAlwaysTransactionAttributeSource in play.

### *Changing the default TransactionAttribute*

As mentioned earlier, `MatchAlwaysTransactionAttributeSource`'s `getTransactionAttribute()` method will always return a transaction attribute with a policy of `PROPAGATION_REQUIRED/ISOLATION_DEFAULT`. If you'd like `MatchAlwaysTransactionAttributeSource` to return a different `TransactionAttribute` than the default, you can wire in another `TransactionAttribute` to the `transactionAttribute` property.

For example, to have `MatchAlwaysTransactionAttributeSource` always return a `TransactionAttribute` with a policy of `PROPAGATION_REQUIRES_NEW` and of `ISOLATION_REPEATABLE_READ`, place this snippet of XML into the context definition file:

```
<bean id="myTransactionAttribute"
    class="org.springframework.transaction.interceptor.
          ➥ DefaultTransactionAttribute">
  <property name="propagationBehaviorName">
    <value>PROPAGATION_REQUIRES_NEW</value>
  </property>
  <property name="isolationLevelName">
    <value>ISOLATION_REPEATABLE_READ</value>
  </property>
</bean>

<bean id="transactionAttributeSource"
    class="org.springframework.transaction.interceptor.
          ➥ MatchAlwaysTransactionAttributeSource">
  <property name="transactionAttribute">
    <ref bean="myTransactionAttribute"/>
  </property>
</bean>
```

The `myTransactionAttribute` bean defines a custom transaction attribute. The `propagationBehaviorName` property sets the propagation behavior and the `isolationLevelName` sets the isolation level. This bean is then wired into `MatchAlwaysTransactionAttributeSource`'s `transactionAttribute` property to override the default transaction attribute.

Be aware, however, that while you may change the parameters of the transaction attribute applied by `MatchAlwaysTransactionAttributeSource`, it will always return the same transaction attribute, regardless of the method being transacted.

Using `MatchAlwaysTransactionAttributeSource` is great when you have a relatively simple application and it's okay to apply the same transaction policies to all methods. But in more complex applications, you'll likely need to apply different transaction policies to different methods. In that case, you'll need more fine-grained control over what policies are applied. So, let's take a look at another

`TransactionAttributeSource` that allows you to declare transactional policies on a method-by-method basis.

## 5.4 Declaring transactions by method name

One of the key features of the EJB specification has always been container-managed transactions (CMT). Using CMT, it is possible to declare transaction policies in the EJB's deployment descriptor. For example, suppose that we've rewritten the Spring Training application using EJB instead of Spring. We have declared a `CourseServiceBean`'s `enrollStudentInCourse()` method to be transactional using the following declaration in the ejb-jar.xml file:

```
<ejb-jar>
...
  <assembly-descriptor>
    <container-transaction>
      <method>
        <ejb-name>CourseServiceBean</ejb-name>
        <method-name>enrollStudentInCourse</method-name>
      </method>
      <trans-attribute>RequiresNew</trans-attribute>
    </container-transaction>
  </assembly-descriptor>
</ejb-jar>
```

Spring took a page from EJB's declarative transaction model, providing several transaction attribute sources that let you declare transaction policies on POJOs. We'll start by looking at `NameMatchTransactionAttributeSource`, a transaction attribute source that lets you declare transactions on POJOs in a way that is reminiscent of EJB's CMT.

### 5.4.1 Using NameMatchTransactionAttributeSource

The Spring-equivalent of CMT is the `NameMatchAttributeSource`. This transaction attribute source lets you declare transaction attributes on a method name–by–method name basis. For example, to declare the `enrollStudentInCourse()` method to have a propagation behavior of "requires new", replace the declaration of the `transactionAttributeSource` bean (from section 5.3.2) as follows:

```
<bean id="transactionAttributeSource"
    class="org.springframework.transaction.interceptor.
           NameMatchTransactionAttributeSource">
  <property name="properties">
    <props>
      <prop key="enrollStudentInCourse">
```

```
       PROPAGATION_REQUIRES_NEW
    </prop>
  </props>
 </property>
</bean>
```

Because this bean is named `transactionAttributeSource`, it will be wired into `TransactionProxyFactoryBean`'s `transactionAttributeSource` property just as `MatchAlwaysTransactionAttributeSource` was in section 5.3.2. `TransactionProxy-FactoryBean` will consult this transaction attribute source when it needs to know how to administer transactions on a method.

The `properties` property of `NameMatchTransactionAttributeSource` maps method names to a transaction property descriptor. The transaction property descriptor takes the following form:

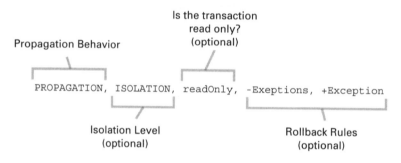

In the example above, only the propagation behavior was specified. But as you can see, many other parameters of a transaction attribute can be defined in the transaction attribute descriptor. Let's take a look at the other components of a transaction attribute descriptor.

### Specifying the transaction isolation level

Up until this point, you've only seen how to use `NameMatchTransactionAttribute-Source` to declare transaction propagation behavior. If this were EJB CMT, that's where the story would end. But with Spring, you can declare more.

For example, suppose that, in addition to "requires new" propagation behavior you want the `enrollStudentInCourse()` method to have an isolation level of "repeatable read". All you need to do is add `ISOLATION_REPEATABLE_READ` to the transaction property, separating it from the propagation behavior with a comma:

```
<bean id="transactionAttributeSource"
    class="org.springframework.transaction.interceptor.
        ➥ NameMatchTransactionAttributeSource">
```

```
    <property name="properties">
      <props>
        <prop key="enrollStudentInCourse">
          PROPAGATION_REQUIRES_NEW,ISOLATION_REPEATABLE_READ
        </prop>
      </props>
    </property>
  </bean>
```

### Using read-only transactions

But wait, there's more. You can also declare transactions to be read-only by adding readOnly to the list of transaction attributes. For example, to declare that the getCompletedCourses method be wrapped in a transaction that is optimized for read-only access, use the following:

```
<bean id="transactionAttributeSource"
    class="org.springframework.transaction.interceptor.
          ⮕ NameMatchTransactionAttributeSource">
  <property name="properties">
    <props>
      <prop key="getCompletedCourses">
        PROPAGATION_REQUIRED,ISOLATION_REPEATABLE_READ,readOnly
      </prop>
    </props>
  </property>
</bean>
```

### Specifying rollback rules

Finally, transactions can be declared to roll back or not roll back based on exceptions that are thrown during the course of the transaction. By default, transactions are rolled back only on runtime exceptions and not on checked exceptions. (For those familiar with EJB, you may recognize that this is EJB's behavior as well.) However, you can specify that a transaction be rolled back on specific checked exceptions as well.

For example, to have the transaction always roll back when a CourseException (or any subclass of CourseException) is thrown, alter the transaction attribute to appear as follows:

```
<bean id="transactionAttributeSource"
    class="org.springframework.transaction.interceptor.
          ⮕ NameMatchTransactionAttributeSource">
  <property name="properties">
    <props>
      <prop key="enrollStudentInCourse">
        PROPAGATION_REQUIRES_NEW,ISOLATION_REPEATABLE_READ,
        -CourseException
```

```
         </prop>
        </props>
      </property>
    </bean>
```

Notice that the `CourseException` is marked with a negation sign (-). Exceptions can be marked as being either negative (-) or positive (+). Negative exceptions will trigger a rollback if the exception (or any subclass thereof) is thrown. Positive exceptions, on the other hand, indicate that the transaction should be committed even if the exception is thrown. You can even mark runtime exceptions as positive to prevent rollbacks (but carefully consider if this is what you want to do).

### Using wildcard matches

Just as with EJB, you can also use wildcards to declare transaction policies for multiple methods that match a pattern. For example, to apply "supports" propagation behavior to all methods whose name start with "get", use the following:

```
<bean id="transactionAttributeSource"
    class="org.springframework.transaction.interceptor.
            NameMatchTransactionAttributeSource">
  <property name="properties">
    <props>
      <prop key="get*">
        PROPAGATION_SUPPORTS
      </prop>
    </props>
  </property>
</bean>
```

`NameMatchTransactionAttributeSource` is a great way to mimic EJB's CMT, only with POJOs and with even more power. We'll pick up the discussion of Spring's other transaction attribute sources in section 5.5. First, let's look at how you can declare name-matched transactions directly with `TransactionProxyFactoryBean`, without declaring a `NameMatchTransactionAttributeSource`.

### 5.4.2 Shortcutting name-matched transactions

So far, we've shown you how to use `NameMatchTransactionAttributeSource` by defining a bean instance and naming it `transactionAttributeSource`. Done this way, the `transactionAttributeSource` bean will be wired into `TransactionProxyFactoryBean`'s `transactionAttributeSource` property. This way will work fine, but there is a slightly easier way.

As it turns out, `TransactionProxyFactoryBean` also has a `transactionAttributes` property. Instead of wiring a `NameMatchTransactionAttributeSource` into this property, you can directly wire the transaction properties into `Transaction-ProxyFactoryBean`'s `transactionAttributes` property as follows:

```
<bean id="courseService" class="org.springframework.transaction.
    interceptor.TransactionProxyFactoryBean">
...
  <property name="transactionProperties">
    <props>
      <prop key="enrollStudentInCourse">
        PROPAGATION_REQUIRES_NEW
      </prop>
    </props>
  </property>
</bean>
```

Wiring transaction properties into the `transactionProperties` property is functionally identical to wiring the `NameMatchTransactionAttributeSource` to the `transactionAttributeSource` property. Under the covers, `TransactionProxy-FactoryBean` instantiates its own `NameMatchTransactionAttributeSource` and passes the properties wired into its `transactionProperties` property into the `NameMatchTransactionAttributeSource`'s `setProperties()` method. As a result, you don't need to create a separate `transactionAttributeSource` bean.

## 5.5 *Declaring transactions with metadata*

So far, you've seen how to declare transactions in Spring's context definition file using XML. This has proved to be less intrusive than programmatically defining transactions in your code. In doing so, however, you were forced to declare the method's transaction policy in a file separate from the method's definition. Wouldn't it be great if you could declare the transaction attributes along with the method definition in the code itself (without resorting to programmatic transactions)?

An exciting and relatively new approach to adding information to code is to tag classes and methods with metadata attributes. This capability has been available in C# since the beginning of the Microsoft .NET platform, but has only recently been added to Java.

By themselves, metadata attributes do not directly alter the behavior of your code. Instead, they provide hints and suggestions to the application's underlying platform to guide the platform on how it can apply additional behavior to the application.

Transaction attributes are a natural use of metadata. As you've seen, transaction attributes do not directly alter the execution of your methods, but when a method is proxied by a `TransactionProxyFactoryBean`, it may be wrapped in a transaction.

Currently two implementations of metadata are available to Java developers: Jakarta Commons Attributes and JSR-175 (the metadata specification for Java). JSR-175's metadata support was released as part of Java 5 and is probably the most highly anticipated feature for Java in a long time. Without doubt, it will become the standard approach to tagging code with metadata in the future. However, many developers grew impatient waiting for a standard approach to metadata in Java. As a result, the Jakarta Commons Attributes project was born.

At the time that this book was written, Java 5 had just been released and Spring only supported the Jakarta Commons Attributes implementation for metadata. We anticipate that support for JSR-175 metadata will soon be available in a future release of Spring. If so, we recommend that you choose JSR-175 metadata over Jakarta Commons Attributes, primarily because JSR-175 is a standard feature of Java 5 and requires no additional compilation step. However, if support for JSR-175 is not yet available (in either Spring or in the version of Java that your application is targeting), then your only choice will be to use Jakarta Commons Attributes.

Regardless of which implementation you use, you'll need to give `Transaction-ProxyFactoryBean` a transaction attribute source suitable for retrieving transaction attributes from metadata.

### 5.5.1 *Sourcing transaction attributes from metadata*

For `TransactionProxyFactoryBean` to retrieve transaction attributes from metadata, it will need its `transactionAttributeSource` to be an `AttributesTransactionAttributeSource`, as follows:

```
<bean id="transactionAttributeSource"
    class="org.springframework.transaction.interceptor.
         AttributesTransactionAttributeSource">

  <constructor-arg>
    <ref bean="attributesImpl"/>
  </constructor-arg>
</bean>
```

Notice that we wired in a constructor argument to this transaction attribute source with a reference to a bean named `attributesImpl`. The `attributesImpl` bean (which we'll define soon) will be used by the transaction attribute source to interact with the underlying metadata implementation. This way, `AttributesTransactionAttributeSource` is kept generic with regard to which metadata implementation is used, whether it is Jakarta Commons Attributes or JSR-175 annotations.

Let's start our exploration of metadata using the Jakarta Commons Attributes implementation.

### 5.5.2 *Declaring transactions with Commons Attributes*

Jakarta Commons Attributes was one of the first metadata implementations available for Java. The good thing about Commons Attributes is that it doesn't require that you make the jump to Java 5 to use it. So, if you are still deploying to an older version of Java and want to declare transactions with metadata, your only option is to use Commons Attributes.

#### *Declaring an attributes implementation*

When we declared the `AttributesTransactionAttributeSource` bean in section 5.5.1, we passed a reference to the `attributesImpl` bean to the constructor. Now we'll define that bean to use Commons Attributes as the metadata implementation for retrieving transaction attributes:

```
<bean id="attributesImpl" class="org.springframework.
    metadata.commons.CommonsAttributes">
...
</bean>
```

With `CommonsAttributes` wired in as the metadata implementation for `Attributes-TransactionAttributeSource`, Spring will look for transaction attributes as metadata tagged on transactional methods. Therefore, the next thing to do is to tag those methods with transaction attributes.

#### *Tagging transactional methods*

Jakarta Commons Attributes are applied to a class or method by placing doclet tags in comments preceding the class/method. These doclet tags take the following form:

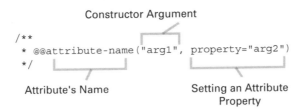

In Jakarta Commons Attributes, metadata can be defined using any form of Java-Bean. As it turns out, the classes that implement Spring's transaction attributes are perfectly suitable to be used as metadata with Jakarta Commons Attributes. This includes `DefaultTransactionAttribute` and `RuleBasedTransactionAttribute`.

The `enrollStudentInCourse()` method needs to be executed within the context of a transaction (although, not necessarily a new transaction). Tagging it with the `DefaultTransactionAttribute` class and setting the `propagationBehaviorName` property to `PROPAGATION_REQUIRED` will do the trick:

```
/**
 * @@org.springframework.transaction.interceptor.
 ➡ DefaultTransactionAttribute(propagationBehaviorName=
 ➡ "PROPAGATION_REQUIRED")
 */
public void enrollStudentInCourse() {
 …
 }
```

Notice that you had to use the fully qualified class name of `DefaultTransaction-Attribute` when using it as an attribute. This is important because after the Jakarta Commons Attributes precompiler is finished with `CourseServiceImpl`, it will have rewritten `CourseServiceImpl` to reference an instance of `DefaultTransactionAttribute`. Unless you specify the package, you'll get compilation errors when trying to compile the generated `CourseServiceImpl` class. Optionally, you may choose to import the package so that you can use the class name by itself.

The choice between using the fully qualified class name or importing the package is really a matter of taste. As you can see, including the fully qualified class name is quite verbose. However, if you choose to avoid this by importing the package, be careful that your IDE does not remove this package automatically. Since the attribute class name is within doclet comments, your IDE may not recognize the attribute's package as a necessary import and remove it. For our examples, we are going to use the qualified class name.

Now the `enrollStudentInCourse()` method is tagged to require a transactional context. As for all of the other methods of `CourseServiceImpl`, you'd like them to support transactional contexts, but they do not require a transaction. One way to accomplish this is to tag each of the other methods with `DefaultTransaction-Attribute`, setting `propagationBehaviorName` to `PROPAGATION_SUPPORTS`. But there's a better way.

By placing transaction tags at the class level, you can specify the transaction attributes that are to apply to all methods in the class that aren't already tagged otherwise. So, to specify that all methods of `CourseServiceImpl` support transactions:

```
/**
 * @@org.springframework.transaction.interceptor.
```

```
 ➡  DefaultTransactionAttribute(
 ➡  propagationBehaviorName="PROPAGATION_SUPPORTS")
 */
public class CourseServiceImpl implements CourseService {
 …
 }
```

Now you've tagged the service methods and classes with transactional metadata. But how does that metadata get out of the comment block and into the code so that `AttributesTransactionAttributeSource` can find it and apply the transactional policies? That's where the Commons Attributes precompiler comes in.

### Setting up the build for Commons Attributes

The magic behind Jakarta Commons Attributes is a precompiler that parses the doclet tags in your code and then rewrites your class, embedding the metadata in its code. It's not important to fully understand how the precompilation step works to be able to use it to declare transactions in Spring, but it is important that you add the precompiler to the build file so that the transaction metadata is set in the code.

If you're using Ant to do your build, you'll need to download the following files and place them in your $ANT_HOME/lib directory:

- http://cvs.apache.org/~leosutic/commons-attributes-api-SNAPSHOT.jar
- http://cvs.apache.org/~leosutic/commons-attributes-compiler-SNAPSHOT.jar
- http://www.ibiblio.org/maven/commons-collections/jars/commons-collections-2.1.jar
- http://www.ibiblio.org/maven/xjavadoc/jars/xjavadoc-1.0.jar

Next, you'll need to add the following line to your build.xml file to load the precompiler task into Ant:

```
<taskdef
    resource="org/apache/commons/attributes/anttasks.properties"/>
```

The precompiler task is named `attribute-compiler`. To use it, add the following target to your build.xml file:

```
<target name="compile-attributes">
  <attribute-compiler destdir=".">
    <fileset dir="." includes="*.java"/>
  </attribute-compiler>
</target>
```

Finally, change your `compile` target to depend on the `compile-attributes` target:

```
<target name="compile"
    depends="compile-attributes">
  <javac
      srcdir="."
      destdir="${basedir}"
      deprecation="true"
      debug="true"
      classpath="${ant.home}/lib/
                    commons-attributes-api-SNAPSHOT.jar;."
      optimize="false">
  </javac>
</target>
```

Notice that you'll also need to add the commons-attributes-api-SNAPSHOT.jar file to `<javac>`'s class path. This is so that `<javac>` can find the Commons Attributes classes when it compiles your code.

If you're using Maven to do your build, then setting up the precompiler is a bit easier. First, download these two JAR files and place them in the commons-attributes/jars directory in your local Maven repository (.maven/repository/commons-attributes/jars):

- http://cvs.apache.org/~leosutic/commons-attributes-api-SNAPSHOT.jar
- http://cvs.apache.org/~leosutic/commons-attributes-compiler-SNAPSHOT.jar

Then download the following JAR file and place it in the Maven plugins directory (.maven/plugins):

- http://cvs.apache.org/~leosutic/commons-attributes-plugin-2.0alpha.jar

That's it! The plug-in sets up the attributes precompiler as a prerequisite to the `java:compile` goal. This means that you won't be able to compile Java source code without first passing it through the attributes precompiler.

Now the application is set up to apply transactions based on transaction metadata. We've gone through several steps to get here, so let's review: When you run your build, the transaction attributes will be compiled directly into your service classes. When `AttributesTransactionAttributeSource` attempts to look up the transaction attributes for any method in `CourseServiceImpl`, it will find the attributes that were tagged on the method and `TransactionProxyFactoryBean` will use them when determining the transaction policy for the method.

## 5.6 *Trimming down transaction declarations*

By now you've chosen a `TransactionAttributeSource`, declared your service layer methods to be transactional, and wired in a transaction manager suited for your persistence layer. Everything works as expected. But there's still one thing that nags at you.

Looking through the bean wiring file, you find several service/target pairs. That is, you find several declarations of beans whose name implies that they are service beans, but in fact, they are instances of `TransactionProxyFactoryBean`. The real service bean is named with a `Target` suffix and wired into the `Transaction-ProxyFactoryBean`'s `target` property.

For example, the course service is defined by the following two `<bean>` declarations:

```
<bean id="courseService"
    class="org.springframework.transaction.interceptor.
          TransactionProxyFactoryBean">

  <property name="target">
    <ref bean="courseServiceTarget"/>
  </property>

  <property name="transactionManager">
    <ref bean="transactionManager"/>
  </property>

  <property name="transactionAttributeSource">
    <ref bean="attributeSource"/>
  </property>
</bean>

<bean id="courseServiceTarget"
    class="com.springinaction.training.service.CourseServiceImpl">
</bean>
```

What's more, you notice that all of your service beans are defined the same way and wired with the same transaction manager and the same transaction attribute source. This seems like a lot of redundant XML. Auto-wiring some of `TransactionProxyFactoryBean`'s properties would go a long way toward cleaning up the XML, but you'd still be left with a target/service pair. Wouldn't it be great if you could eliminate the redundant instances of `TransactionProxyFactory-Bean` altogether?

Fortunately, you can. Spring offers two ways to combat the redundant XML:

- Bean inheritance
- AOP autoproxying

Let's take a look at each of these approaches, starting with bean inheritance.

### 5.6.1 *Inheriting from a parent TransactionProxyFactoryBean*

One way to simplify declaration of transactions and service beans is to use Spring's support for parent beans. Using the `parent` attribute of the `<bean>` element, you can specify that a bean be a child of some other bean, inheriting the parent bean's properties. The concept is similar to one class subclassing another class, except that it happens at the bean declaration level. Think of it as "sub-beaning."

To use bean inheritance to reduce XML that results from multiple declarations of `TransactionProxyFactoryBean`, start by adding an `abstract` declaration of `TransactionProxyFactoryBean` to the context definition:

```
<bean id="abstractTxDefinition"
    class="org.springframework.transaction.interceptor.
            ➡ TransactionProxyFactoryBean"
    lazy-init="true">

  <property name="transactionManager">
    <ref bean="transactionManager"/>
  </property>

  <property name="transactionAttributeSource">
    <ref bean="attributeSource"/>
  </property>
</bean>
```

This declaration is similar to the declaration of `courseService` from earlier, except for two things:

- First, its `lazy-init` property is set to `true`. Application contexts will usually instantiate all singleton beans at startup. Since our application will only use sub-beans of `abstractTxDefinition` and never use `abstractTxDefinition` directly, we don't want the container to attempt to instantiate a bean we'll never use. The `lazy-init` property tells the container to not create the bean unless we ask for it (which we won't do). In effect, `lazy-init` is what makes this bean abstract.

- The `target` property is curiously missing. We'll set that property in the sub-beans.

The next thing to do is to create the sub-bean. Consider the following declaration of the `courseService` bean:

```
<bean id="courseService"
    parent="abstractTxDefinition">
  <property name="target">
    <bean class="com.springinaction.training.
                   service.CourseServiceImpl">
  </property>
</bean>
```

The `parent` attribute indicates that this bean should inherit its definition from the `abstractTxDefinition` bean. The only thing that this bean adds is to wire in a value for the `target` property. In this case, we're taking advantage of inner-beans to declare the target bean right where we're using it. This keeps the XML tidy by not declaring a separate `CourseServiceImpl` bean (knowing that you'll never use a `CourseServiceImpl` outside the scope of a transaction).

So far, this technique hasn't saved us much XML. But think about what you'll need to do to make another bean transactional. You'll only have to add another sub-bean of `abstractTxDefinition`. For example:

```
<bean id="studentService"
    parent="abstractTxDefinition">
  <property name="target">
    <bean class="com.springinaction.training.
                   service.StudentServiceImpl"/>
  </property>
</bean>
```

But notice you didn't have to completely declare another `TransactionProxy-FactoryBean` again. Now imagine if your application had dozens (or hundreds) of service beans that need to be transactional. Bean inheritance really pays off when you have many transactional beans.

Now let's look at how to use AOP auto-proxying to completely eliminate the need for `TransactionProxyFactoryBean`.

### 5.6.2 *Autoproxying transactions*

As you learned in chapter 3, you can eliminate instances of `ProxyFactoryBean` by employing autoproxying. Since transactions in Spring are based on AOP, you can also use auto-proxying to get rid of redundant instances of `TransactionProxy-FactoryBean`. Here's how.

First, just as you would do any auto-advising, you need to declare a bean that is an instance of `DefaultAdvisorAutoProxyCreator`:

```
<bean id="autoproxy"
    class="org.springframework.aop.framework.autoproxy.
        ➡ DefaultAdvisorAutoProxyCreator">
    ...
</bean>
```

DefaultAdvisorAutoProxyCreator will scour the application context for advisors, automatically using them to proxy all beans that match the advisor's pointcut. For transactions, the advisor to use is TransactionAttributeSourceAdvisor:

```
<bean id="transactionAdvisor"
    class="org.springframework.transaction.interceptor.
        ➡ TransactionAttributeSourceAdvisor">
    <constructor-arg>
      <ref bean="transactionInterceptor"/>
    </constructor-arg>
</bean>
```

TransactionAttributeSourceAdvisor is a full-fledged AOP advisor just like those you read about in chapter 3. And just like any advisor, it is made up of a pointcut and an interceptor. The pointcut is a static method pointcut that consults a transaction attribute source to determine if a method has any transaction attributes associated with it. If a method has transaction attributes, then the method will be proxied to be contained within a transaction.

As for the interceptor, it is wired into TransactionAttributeSourceAdvisor via a constructor argument. It's implemented by the TransactionInterceptor class and wired into the application as follows:

```
<bean id="transactionInterceptor"
    class="org.springframework.transaction.interceptor.
        ➡ TransactionInterceptor">
    <property name="transactionManager">
      <ref bean="transactionManager"/>
    </property>
    <property name="transactionAttributeSource">
      <ref bean="transactionAttributeSource"/>
    </property>
</bean>
```

TransactionInterceptor has two collaborators that it uses to do its job. It uses a PlatformTransactionManager, wired into the transactionManager property, to coordinate transactions with the underlying transaction implementation. And it uses the transaction attribute source wired into the transactionAttributeSource property to determine the transaction policies to be applied to the methods it will intercept. As it turns out, you've already defined transactionManager and

transactionAttributeSource beans when you were using TransactionProxy-
FactoryBean—they'll do just fine for the transaction interceptor, too.

The final thing to do is to remove all instances of TransactionProxyFactory-
Bean and rename the service layer beans back to their rightful name (e.g., course-
ServiceTarget becomes courseService).

### Choosing an attribute source for autoproxying

When autoproxying transactions, the transaction attribute source is the key to
whether or not a method is proxied. This fact may prompt you to choose a different transaction attribute source. For example, consider the consequences of using
the following transaction attribute source with autoproxying:

```
<bean id="transactionAttributeSource"
    class="org.springframework.transaction.interceptor.
        NameMatchTransactionAttributeSource">
  <property name="properties">
    <props>
      <prop key="get*v>PROPAGATION_SUPPORTS</prop>
    </props>
  </property>
</bean>
```

Used this way, all methods (regardless of which class they are in) whose name
starts with "get" will be proxied with a transaction propagation behavior of "supports". Maybe this is what you desire, but probably not. Keep in mind that
DefaultAdvisorAutoProxyCreator will attempt to proxy all methods on all beans
within the application context. If any method on any bean has a name that starts
with "get", it will be proxied.

When auto-proxying, a better choice for the transaction attribute source is
MethodMapTransactionAttributeSource. This transaction attribute source is similar to NameMatchTransactionAttributeSource, but lets you specify the fully qualified class and method name to be transactional. For example:

```
<bean id="transactionAttributeSource"
    class="org.springframework.transaction.interceptor.
        MethodMapTransactionAttributeSource">
  <property name="methodMap">
    <map>
      <entry key="com.springinaction.training.service.
              CourseServiceImpl.get*">
        <value>PROPAGATION_SUPPORTS</value>
      </entry>
    </map>
  </property>
</bean>
```

Using `MethodMapTransactionAttributeSource` this way, you have specified that only "get" methods of `CourseServiceImpl` are to have a transaction propagation behavior of "supports". To add transactional behavior to other methods in other classes, you'll need to add `<entry>` elements to the method map.

Now, here's the cool part. An even better choice for transaction attribute source when you are auto-proxying is `AttributesTransactionAttributeSource`. Recall that `AttributesTransactionAttributeSource` pulls transaction attributes from metadata placed directly in the code of the methods that are to be transactional. This means that if you are using `AttributesTransactionAttributeSource` as the attribute source and you are also using auto-proxying, making a method transactional or not is simply a matter of adding the appropriate metadata to the method.

## 5.7  *Summary*

Transactions are an important part of enterprise application development that leads to more robust software. They ensure an all-or-nothing behavior, preventing data from being inconsistent should the unexpected occur. They also support concurrency by preventing concurrent application threads from getting in each other's way as they work with the same data.

Spring supports both programmatic and declarative transaction management. In either case, Spring shields you from having to work directly with a specific transaction management implementation by abstracting the transaction management platform behind a common transaction manager façade.

Spring employs its own AOP framework to support declarative transaction management. Spring's declarative transaction support rivals that of EJB's CMT, enabling you to declare more than just propagation behavior on POJOs, including isolation levels, read-only optimizations, and rollback rules for specific exceptions.

Finally, when used with metadata and autoproxying, making a method transactional is often simply a matter of tagging it with the appropriate transaction attribute.

In the next chapter, we're going to look at how Spring supports remoting and see how you can expose your application beans to remote clients via RMI and web services.

# Remoting

6

207

Imagine for a moment that you are stranded on a deserted island. This may sound like a dream come true. After all, who wouldn't want to get some solitude on a beach, blissfully ignorant of the goings-on of the outside world?

But on a deserted island, it's not piña coladas and sunbathing all of the time. Even if you enjoy the peaceful seclusion, it won't be long before you'll get hungry, bored, and lonely. You can only live on coconuts and spear-caught fish for so long. You'll eventually need food, fresh clothing, and other supplies. And if you don't get in contact with another human soon, you may end up talking to a volleyball!

Many applications that you'll develop are like island castaways. On the surface they may seem self-sufficient, but in reality, they may collaborate with other systems, both within your organization and external.

For example, consider a procurement system that needs to communicate with a vendor's supply chain system. Maybe your company's human resources system needs to integrate with the payroll system. Or even the payroll system may need to communicate with an external system that prints and mails paychecks. No matter the circumstance, your application will need to communicate with the other system to access services *remotely*.

Several remoting technologies are available to you, as a Java developer, including

- Remote Method Invocation (RMI)
- Caucho's Hessian and Burlap
- Spring's own HTTP invoker
- Enterprise JavaBeans (EJB)
- Web services

Regardless of which remoting technology you choose, Spring provides rich support for accessing and creating remote services. In this chapter, you'll learn how Spring both simplifies and complements these remoting services. But first, let's set the stage for this chapter with an overview of how remoting works in Spring.

## 6.1 Spring remoting overview

*Remoting* is a conversation between a client application and a service. On the client side, some functionality is required that isn't within the scope of the application. So, the application reaches out to another system that can provide the functionality. The remote application exposes the functionality through a *remote service*.

For example, when a student registers for a course in the Spring Training application, you'd like to be able to take payment from the customer for the course (Spring Training is a business, after all). Therefore, the Spring Training application needs to perform credit card authorization and payment settlement. This is functionality that is outside the scope of the Spring Training application itself. There's no way that Spring Training can directly debit a student's credit card or even know if the credit card is good for the funds. Only the bank that issued the card can perform authorization and settlement. Therefore, it makes sense for the Spring Training application to make a remote call to a payment service exposed by the bank (as illustrated in figure 6.1).

The conversation between Spring Training and the bank begins with a *remote procedure call (RPC)* from the Spring Training application to the bank's payment service. On the surface, an RPC is similar to a call to a method on a local object. Both are synchronous operations, blocking execution in the calling code until the called procedure is complete.

The difference is a matter of proximity, with an analogy in human communication. If you are at the proverbial watercooler at work discussing the outcome of the weekend's football game, you are conducting a local conversation—that is, the conversation takes place between two people in the same room. Likewise, a local method call is when execution flow is exchanged between two blocks of code within the same application.

On the other hand, if you were to pick up the phone to call a client in another city, your conversation would be conducted remotely over the telephone network. Similarly, RPC is when execution flow is handed off from one application to another application, theoretically on a different machine in a remote location over the network.

Spring supports remoting for six different RPC models: Remote Method Invocation (RMI), Caucho's Hessian and Burlap, Spring's own HTTP invoker, EJB, and web services using JAX-RPC. Table 6.1 outlines each of these models and briefly discusses their usefulness in various situations.

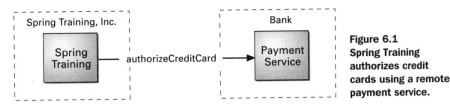

**Figure 6.1**
**Spring Training authorizes credit cards using a remote payment service.**

**Table 6.1  The RPC models supported by Spring remoting**

| RPC Model | Useful when... |
|---|---|
| Remote Method Invocation (RMI) | Accessing/exposing Java-based services when network constraints such as firewalls aren't a factor |
| Hessian or Burlap | Accessing/exposing Java-based services over HTTP when network constraints are a factor |
| HTTP Invoker | Accessing/exposing Spring-based services when network constraints are a factor |
| EJB | Accessing legacy J2EE systems implemented as Enterprise Java-Beans |
| JAX-RPC | Accessing web services |

Regardless of which remoting model you choose, you'll find that a common theme runs through Spring's support for each of the models. This means that once you understand how to configure Spring to work with one of the models, you'll have a very low learning curve if you decide to use a different model.

In all models, services can be configured into your application as Spring-managed beans. This is accomplished using a proxy factory bean that enables you to wire remote services into properties of your other beans as if they were local objects. Figure 6.2 illustrates how this works.

The client makes calls to the proxy as if the proxy were providing the service functionality. The proxy communicates with the remote service on behalf

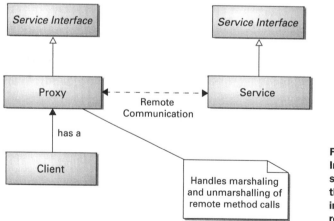

**Figure 6.2
In Spring, remote services are proxied so that they can be wired into client code as a regular bean.**

of the client. It handles the details of connecting and making remote calls to the remote service.

What's more, if the call to the remote service results in a `java.rmi.RemoteException`, the proxy handles that exception and rethrows it as an unchecked `org.springframework.remoting.RemoteAccessException`. Remote exceptions usually signal problems such as network or configuration issues that can't be gracefully recovered from. Since there's usually very little that a client can do to gracefully recover from a remote exception, rethrowing a `RemoteAccessException` makes it optional for the client to handle the exception.

On the service side, you are able to expose the functionality of any Spring-managed bean as a remote service using any of the models in listed in table 6.1 (except for EJB and JAX-RPC). Figure 6.3 illustrates how remote exporters expose bean methods as remote services.

Whether you'll be developing code that consumes remote services, implements those services, or both, working with remote services in Spring is purely a matter of configuration. You won't have to write any Java code to support remoting. Your service beans don't have to be aware that they are involved in an RPC (although any beans passed to or returned from remote calls may need to implement `java.io.Serializable`).

Let's start our exploration of Spring's remoting support by looking at RMI, the original remoting technology for Java.

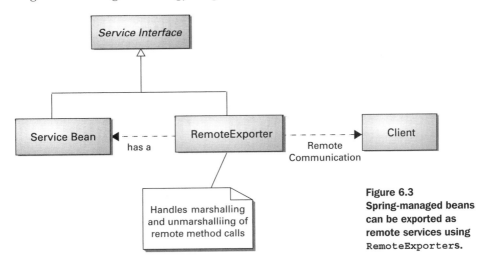

**Figure 6.3**
**Spring-managed beans can be exported as remote services using `RemoteExporters`.**

## 6.2 *Working with RMI*

If you've been working in Java for any length of time, you've no doubt heard of (and probably used) *Remote Method Invocation (RMI)*. RMI—first introduced into the Java platform in JDK 1.1—gives Java programmers a powerful way to conduct communication between Java programs. Before RMI, the only remoting options available to Java programmers were CORBA (which at the time required the purchase of a third-party Object Request Broker, or ORB) or hand-written socket programming.

But developing and accessing RMI services is tedious, involving several steps, both programmatic and manual. Spring simplifies the RMI model by providing a proxy factory bean that enables you to wire RMI services into your Spring application is if they were a local JavaBean. Spring also provides a remote exporter that makes short work of converting your Spring-managed beans into RMI services.

To get started with Spring's RMI, let's see how to wire an RMI service into the Spring Training application.

### 6.2.1 *Wiring RMI services*

As mentioned earlier, Spring Training, Inc. needs to be able to take payment via credit card when their students register for a course. Fortunately, a payment service is available that can handle this functionality on behalf of Spring Training. All you'll need to do is hook the Spring Training application into it. As it turns out, the payment service exposes its functionality as an RMI service.

One way to access the payment service is to write a factory method that retrieves a reference to the payment service in the traditional RMI way:

```
private String payServiceUrl = "rmi:/creditswitch/PaymentService";

public PaymentService lookupPaymentService()
    throws RemoteException, NotBoundException,
    MalformedURLException {

  PaymentService payService = (PaymentService)
    Naming.lookup(payServiceUrl);

  return payService;
}
```

The `payServiceUrl` property will need to be set to the address for the RMI service. Then, any time the Spring Training application needs a reference to the payment service, it would need to call the `lookupPaymentService()` method. While this would certainly work, it presents two problems:

1. Traditional RMI lookups could result in any one of three exceptions (`RemoteException`, `NotBoundException`, and `MalformedURLException`) that must be caught or rethrown.

2. Any code that needs the payment service is responsible for retrieving a reference to the service itself by calling `lookupPaymentService()`.

The exceptions thrown in the course of an RMI lookup are the kinds that typically signal a fatal and unrecoverable condition in the application. `MalformedUrl-Exception`, for instance, indicates that the address given for the service is not valid. To recover from this exception, the application will at least need to be reconfigured and may have to be recompiled. No try/catch block will be able to recover gracefully, so why should your code be forced to catch and handle it?

But perhaps even more sinister is the fact that `lookupPaymentService()` is a direct violation of inversion of control. This is bad because it means that the client of `lookupPaymentService()` is also aware of where the payment service is located and of the fact that it is an RMI service. Ideally, you should be able to inject a `PaymentService` object into any bean that needs one instead of having the bean look up the service itself. Using dependency injection, any client of `Payment-Service` can be ignorant of where the `PaymentService` comes from.

Spring's `RmiProxyFactoryBean` is a factory bean that creates a proxy to an RMI service. Using `RmiProxyFactoryBean` to reference an RMI `PaymentService` is as simple as declaring the following `<bean>` in the Spring configuration file:

```
<bean id="paymentService"
    class="org.springframework.remoting.rmi.RmiProxyFactoryBean">
  <property name="serviceUrl">
    <value>rmi://${paymenthost}/PayService</value>
  </property>
  <property name="serviceInterface">
    <value>com.springinaction.payment.PaymentService</value>
  </property>
</bean>
```

The URL of the RMI service is set through the `serviceUrl` property. Here, the service is named `PayService` and is hosted on a machine whose name is configured using a property placeholder (see section 2.4.3 in chapter 2). The `service-Interface` property specifies the interface that the service implements and through which the client invokes methods on the service.

With the payment service defined as a Spring-managed bean, you are able to wire it as a collaborator into another bean just as you would any other nonremote bean. For example, suppose that `StudentServiceImpl` needs to use the payment service to authorize a credit card payment. You'd use this code to wire the RMI service into `StudentServiceImpl`:

```
<bean id="studentService"
    class="com.springinaction.training.service.StudentServiceImpl">
...
  <property name="paymentService">
    <ref bean="paymentService"/>
  </property>
...
</bean>
```

What's great about accessing an RMI service in this way is that `StudentService-Impl` doesn't even know that it's dealing with an RMI service. It simply receives a `PaymentService` object via injection, without any concern for where it comes from. Furthermore, the proxy catches any `RemoteExceptions` that may be thrown by the service and rethrows them as runtime exceptions so that you may safely ignore them. This makes it possible to swap out the remote service bean with another implementation of the service—perhaps a different remote service or maybe a mock implementation used when unit-testing.

`RmiProxyFactoryBean` certainly simplifies the use of RMI services in a Spring application. But that's only half of an RMI conversation. Let's see how Spring supports the service side of RMI.

### 6.2.2 *Exporting RMI services*

Suppose that instead of working on the portion of the Spring Training application that accesses the payment service, you are responsible for writing the payment service itself. Again, the payment service should be exposed as an RMI service.

Taking a traditional approach to RMI, you might end up implementing the payment service shown in listing 6.1.

**Listing 6.1   Implementing the payment service as an RMI service in the traditional (non-Spring) way**

```
public class PaymentServiceImpl extends UnicastRemoteObject
    implements PaymentService {

  public PaymentServiceImpl() throws RemoteException {}

  public String authorizeCreditCard(String creditCardNumber,
      String cardHolderName, int expirationMonth,
      int expirationYear, float amount)
      throws AuthorizationException, RemoteException {
```

```
    String authCode = ...;

    // implement authorization

    return authCode;
  }

  public void settlePayment(String authCode, int accountNumber,
      float amount) throws SettlementException, RemoteException {
    // implement settlement
  }
}
```

As for the `PaymentService` interface that `PaymentServiceImpl` implements, you'll need to ensure that it extends `java.rmi.Remote` as follows:

```
public interface PaymentService extends Remote {
  public String authorizeCreditCard(String cardNumber,
      String cardHolderName, int expireMonth, int expireYear,
      float amount) throws AuthorizationException, RemoteException;

  public void settlePayment(String authCode, int merchantNumber,
      float amount) throws SettlementException, RemoteException;
}
```

But it isn't enough that you've written a service implementation class and interface. You also need to generate client stub and server skeleton classes using the RMI compiler:

```
% rmic -d PaymentServiceImpl
```

Finally, you'll need to start an RMI registry and bind the service in the registry. The following code handles this task:

```
try {
  PaymentService paymentService = new PaymentServiceImpl();

  Registry registry = LocateRegistry.createRegistry(1099);

  Naming.bind("PayService", paymentService);
} catch (RemoteException e) {
...
} catch (MalformedURLException e) {
...
}
```

Wow! That's a lot of work just to publish a simple RMI service. In addition to all the steps required, you may have noticed that `RemoteExceptions` and `Malformed-UrlExceptions` are thrown around quite a bit, even though these exceptions usually indicate a fatal error that can't be recovered from in a catch block. Clearly a lot of code and manual work is involved to publish an RMI service without Spring.

### Configuring an RMI service in Spring

Fortunately, Spring provides an easier way to publish RMI services using simple POJOs. To start, you'll need to write the service interface:

```
public interface PaymentService {
    public String authorizeCreditCard(String cardNumber,
        String cardHolderName, int expireMonth, int expireYear,
        float amount) throws AuthorizationException;

    public void settlePayment(String authCode, int merchantNumber,
        float amount) throws SettlementException;
}
```

Because the service interface doesn't extend `java.rmi.Remote` and none of its methods throw `java.rmi.RemoteException`, this trims the interface down a bit. But more importantly, a client accessing the payment service through this interface will not have to catch exceptions that they probably won't be able to deal with.

Next you'll need to define the service implementation class. Listing 6.2 shows how this service may be implemented.

**Listing 6.2   The payment service defined as a POJO**

```
public class PaymentServiceImpl implements PaymentService {

    public PaymentServiceImpl() {}

    public String authorizeCreditCard(String creditCardNumber,
        String cardHolderName, int expirationMonth,
        int expirationYear, float amount)
        throws AuthorizationException {

      String authCode = ...;

      // implement authorization

      return authCode;
    }

    public void settlePayment(String authCode, int accountNumber,
        float amount) throws SettlementException {
      // implement settlement
    }
}
```

The next thing you'll need to do is to configure `PaymentServiceImpl` as a `<bean>` in the Spring configuration file:

```
<bean id="paymentService"
    class="org.springframework.payment.PaymentServiceImpl">
...
</bean>
```

Notice that there's nothing about this version of `PaymentServiceImpl` that is intrinsically RMI. It's just a simple POJO suitable for declaration in a Spring configuration file. In fact, it's entirely possible to use this implementation in a non-remote manner by wiring it directly into a client.

But we're interested in using this service remotely. So, the last thing to do is to export `PaymentServiceImpl` as an RMI service. But instead of generating a server skeleton and client stub using `rmic` and manually adding it to the RMI registry (as you would in conventional RMI), you can use Spring's `RmiServiceExporter`.

`RmiServiceExporter` exports any Spring-managed bean as an RMI service. It works by wrapping the bean in an adapter class. The adapter class is then bound to the RMI registry and proxies requests to the service class—in this case `PaymentServiceImpl`:

```
<bean class="org.springframework.remoting.rmi.RmiServiceExporter">
  <property name="service">
    <ref bean="paymentService"/>
  </property>
  <property name="serviceName">
    <value>PayService</value>
  </property>
  <property name="serviceInterface">
    <value>com.springinaction.payment.PaymentService</value>
  </property>
</bean>
```

Here the `paymentService` bean is wired into the `service` property to indicate that `RmiServiceExporter` is going to export the payment service as an RMI service. Just as with `RmiProxyFactoryBean` described in section 6.2.1, the `serviceName` property names the RMI service and the `serviceInterface` property specifies the interface implemented by the service.

RMI is an excellent way to communicate with remote services, but it has its limitations. First, RMI has difficulty working across firewalls. That's because RMI uses arbitrary ports for communication—something firewalls typically will not allow. In an intranet environment, this usually isn't a concern, but if you are working on the "evil Internet," you'll probably run into trouble with RMI. Even though RMI has support for tunneling through HTTP (which is usually allowed by firewalls), setting up the tunneling can be tricky.

Another thing to consider is that RMI is Java-based. That means that both the client and the service must be written in Java. This may or may not be an issue for your application, but it is something to bear in mind when choosing RMI for remoting.

Caucho Technology (the same people behind the Resin application server) has developed a remoting solution that addresses the limitations of RMI. Actually, they have come up with two solutions: Hessian and Burlap. Let's see how to use Hessian and Burlap to work with remote services in Spring.

## 6.3 *Remoting with Hessian and Burlap*

Hessian and Burlap are two solutions provided by Caucho Technology (http://www.caucho.com) that enable lightweight remote services over HTTP. They each aim to simplify web services by keeping both their API and their communication protocols as simple as possible.

You may be wondering why Caucho has two solutions to the same problem. Indeed, Hessian and Burlap are two sides of the same coin, but each serves slightly different purposes. Hessian, like RMI, uses binary messages to communicate between client and service. But unlike other binary remoting technologies (such as RMI), the binary message is portable to languages other than Java. In fact, Caucho has developed an implementation of Hessian for the Python programming language.

Burlap is an XML-based remoting technology, which automatically makes it portable to any language that can parse XML. And because it's XML, it is more easily human-readable than Hessian's binary format. But unlike other XML-based remoting technologies (such as SOAP or XML-RPC), Burlap's message structure is as simple as possible and does not require an external definition language (e.g., WSDL or IDL).[1]

Both Hessian and Burlap are also lightweight with regard to their size. Each is fully contained in an 84K JAR file, with no external dependencies other than the Java runtime libraries. This makes them both ideal for use in environments that are constrained on memory, such as Java applets or handheld devices.

---

[1] Burlap's simplicity is evident even in its name. Caucho claims that they chose the name "Burlap" because of one simple reason: it's boring.

You may be wondering how to make a choice between Hessian and Burlap. For the most part, they are identical. The only difference is that Hessian messages are binary and Burlap messages are XML. Because Hessian messages are binary, they are more bandwidth-friendly. But if human-readability is important to you (for debugging purposes) or if your application will be communicating with a language for which there is no Hessian implementation (anything other than Java or Python), then Burlap's XML messages may be preferable.

To demonstrate Hessian and Burlap services in Spring, let's revisit the payment service problem that was solved with RMI in section 6.2. This time, however, we'll look at how to solve the problem using Hessian and Burlap as the remoting models.

### 6.3.1 *Accessing Hessian/Burlap services*

As you'll recall from section 6.2.1, StudentServiceImpl has no idea that the payment service is an RMI service. All of the RMI details were completely contained in the configuration of the beans in Spring's configuration file. The good news is that because of the client's ignorance of the service's implementation, switching from an RMI client to a Hessian client is extremely easy, requiring no changes to the client code.

The bad news is that if you really like writing code, then this section may be a bit of a letdown. That's because the only difference between wiring the client side of an RMI-based service and wiring the client side of a Hessian-based service is that you'll use Spring's HessianProxyFactoryBean instead of RmiProxyFactory-Bean. A Hessian-based payment service is declared in the client code like this:

```
<bean id="paymentService" class="org.springframework.
    remoting.caucho.HessianProxyFactoryBean">
  <property name="serviceUrl">
    <value>http://${serverName}/${contextPath}/pay.service</value>
  </property>
  <property name="serviceInterface">
    <value>com.springinaction.payment.PaymentService</value>
  </property>
</bean>
```

Just as with an RMI-based service, the serviceInterface property specifies the interface that the service implements. And, as with RmiProxyFactoryBean, service-Url indicates the URL of the service. Since Hessian is HTTP-based, it has been set to an HTTP URL here (you'll see how this URL is derived in the next section).

As it turns out, wiring a Burlap service is equally uninteresting. The only difference is that you'll use BurlapProxyFactoryBean instead of HessianProxyFactoryBean:

```
<bean id="paymentService" class="org.springframework.
    remoting.caucho.BurlapProxyFactoryBean">
  <property name="serviceUrl">
    <value>http://${serverName}/${contextPath}/pay.service</value>
  </property>
  <property name="serviceInterface">
    <value>com.springinaction.payment.PaymentService</value>
  </property>
</bean>
```

Although we've made light of how uninteresting the configuration differences are among RMI, Hessian, and Burlap services, this tedium is actually a benefit. It means that you'll be able to switch effortlessly between the various remoting technologies supported by Spring without having to learn a completely new model. Once you've configured a reference to an RMI service, it's short work to reconfigure it as a Hessian or Burlap service.

Now let's switch to the other side of the conversation and expose the functionality of a Spring-managed bean as either a Hessian or Burlap service.

### 6.3.2 *Exposing bean functionality with Hessian/Burlap*

Again, let's suppose that you are tasked with implementing the payment service and exposing its functionality as a remote service. This time, however, you're going to expose it as a Hessian-based service.

Even without Spring, writing a Hessian service is fairly trivial. You simply write your service class to extend com.caucho.hessian.server.HessianServlet and make sure that your service methods are public (all public methods are considered service methods in Hessian).

Because Hessian services are already quite easy to implement, Spring doesn't do much to simplify the Hessian model any further. However, when used with Spring, a Hessian service can take full advantage of the Spring framework in ways that a pure Hessian service cannot. This includes using Spring AOP to advise a Hessian service with systemwide services such as declarative transactions.

#### *Exporting a Hessian service*

Exporting a Hessian service in Spring is remarkably similar to implementing an RMI service in Spring. In fact, if you followed the RMI example in section 6.2.2, you've already done most of the work required to expose the payment service as a Hessian service.

To expose the payment service as an RMI service, you configured an Rmi-ServiceExporter bean in the Spring configuration file. In a very similar way, to expose the payment service as a Hessian service, you'll need to configure another exporter bean. This time, however, it will be a `HessianServiceExporter`:

```
<bean name="hessianPaymentService" class="org.springframework.
    remoting.caucho.HessianServiceExporter">
  <property name="service">
    <ref bean="paymentService"/>
  </property>
  <property name="serviceInterface">
    <value>com.springinaction.payment.PaymentService</value>
  </property>
</bean>
```

`HessianServiceExporter` performs the exact same function for a Hessian service as `RmiServiceExporter` does for an RMI service. That is, it exposes the public methods of a bean as methods of a Hessian service.

Just as with `RmiServiceExporter`, the `service` property is wired with a reference to the bean that implements the service. Here the `service` property is wired with a reference to the `paymentService` bean. The `serviceInterface` property is set to indicate that `PaymentService` is the interface that the service implements.

Unlike with `RmiServiceExporter`, however, you do not need to set a `serviceName` property. With RMI, the `serviceName` property is used to register a service in the RMI registry. Hessian doesn't have a registry and therefore there's no need to name a Hessian service.

### Configuring the Hessian controller

Another major difference between `RmiServiceExporter` and `HessianServiceExporter` is that because Hessian is HTTP-based, `HessianServiceExporter` is implemented as a Spring MVC `Controller`. This means that in order to use exported Hessian services, you'll need to perform two additional configuration steps:

1. Configure a URL handler in your Spring configuration file to dispatch Hessian service URLs to the appropriate Hessian service bean.
2. Configure a Spring `DispatcherServlet` in web.xml and deploy your application as a web application.

You'll learn the details of how Spring URL handlers and `DispatcherServlet` work in chapter 8. But for now we're only going to show you enough to expose the Hessian payment service.

In section 6.3.1, you configured the `serviceUrl` property on the client side to point to `http://${serverName}/${contextPath}/pay.service`. The `${serverName}` and `${contextPath}` are placeholders that are configured via `PropertyPlaceholderConfigurer`. The last part of the URL, `/pay.service`, is the part we're interested in here. This is the URL pattern that you'll map the Hessian payment service to.

A URL handler maps a URL pattern to a specific `Controller` that will handle requests. In the case of the Hessian payment service, you want to map `/pay.service` to the `hessianPaymentService` bean as follows using `SimpleUrlHandlerMapping`:

```
<bean id="urlMapping" class="org.springframework.web.
    ➥ servlet.handler.SimpleUrlHandlerMapping">
  <property name="mappings">
    <props>
      <prop key="/pay.service">hessianPaymentService</prop>
    </props>
  </property>
</bean>
```

You'll learn more about `SimpleUrlHandlerMapping` in chapter 8 (section 8.2.2). For now, suffice it to say that the `mappings` property takes a set of properties whose key is the URL pattern. Here it has been given a single property with a key of `/pay.service`, which is the URL pattern for the payment service. The value of the property is the name of a Spring `Controller` bean that will handle requests to the URL pattern—in this case, `hessianPaymentService`.

Because `HessianServiceExporter` is implemented as a controller in Spring MVC, you must also configure Spring's `DispatcherServlet` in web.xml:

```
<servlet>
  <servlet-name>credit</servlet-name>
  <servlet-class>
      org.springframework.web.servlet.DispatcherServlet
  </servlet-class>
  <load-on-startup>1</load-on-startup>
</servlet>
```

The name given to the servlet is significant because it is used by `Dispatcher-Servlet` to locate the Spring configuration file. In this case, because the servlet is named "credit", the configuration file must be named "credit-servlet.xml".

One final step required to expose the Hessian service is to set up a servlet mapping:

```
<servlet-mapping>
  <servlet-name>credit</servlet-name>
  <url-pattern>*.service</url-pattern>
</servlet-mapping>
```

Configured this way, any request whose URL ends with ".service" will be given to `DispatcherServlet`, which will in turn hand off the request to the `Controller` that is mapped to the URL. Thus requests to "/pay.service" will ultimately be handled by the `hessianPaymentService` bean (which is actually just a proxy to `Payment-ServiceImpl`).

### Exporting a Burlap service

As an anticlimactic conclusion to this section, we thought you might like to also see how to export a Spring-managed bean as a Burlap service. Spring's `Burlap-ServiceExporter` is used in place of `HessianServiceExporter` to perform this task. For example, the following bean definition shows how to expose the payment service as a Burlap service:

```
<bean name="burlapPaymentService"class="org.springframework.
       remoting.caucho.BurlapServiceExporter">
  <property name="service">
    <ref bean="paymentService"/>
  </property>
  <property name="serviceInterface">
    <value>com.springinaction.payment.PaymentService</value>
  </property>
</bean>
```

You'll notice that aside from the bean's name (which is purely arbitrary) and the use of `BurlapServiceExporter`, this bean is identical to the `hessianPayment-Service`. Configuring a Burlap service is otherwise the same as configuring a Hessian service. This includes the need to set up a URL handler and the `DispatcherServlet`.

Hessian and Burlap address the firewall problems that RMI suffers from. And both are lightweight enough to be used in constrained environments where memory and space are a premium, such as applets and wireless devices.

But RMI has both Hessian and Burlap beat when it comes to serializing objects that are sent in RPC messages. Whereas Hessian and Burlap both use a proprietary serialization mechanism, RMI uses Java's own serialization mechanism. If your data model is complex, the Hessian/Burlap serialization model may not be sufficient.

There is a best-of-both-worlds solution. Let's take a look at Spring's HTTP invoker, which offers RPC over HTTP (like Hessian/Burlap) while at the same time using Java serialization of objects (like RMI).

## 6.4  *Using Http invoker*

The Spring team recognized a void between RMI services and HTTP-based services like Hessian and Burlap. On one side, RMI uses Java's standard object serialization but is difficult to use across firewalls. On the other side, Hessian/Burlap work well across firewalls but use a proprietary object serialization mechanism.

Thus Spring's HTTP invoker was born. HTTP invoker is a new remoting model created as part of the Spring framework to perform remoting across HTTP (to make the firewalls happy) and using Java's serialization (to make programmers happy).

Working with HTTP invoker-based services is quite similar to working with Hessian/Burlap-based services. To get started with HTTP invoker, let's take another look at the payment service—this time implemented as an HTTP invoker payment service.

### 6.4.1 *Accessing services via HTTP*

To access an RMI service, you declared an `RmiProxyFactoryBean` that pointed to the service. To access a Hessian service, you declared a `HessianProxyFactoryBean`. And to access a Burlap service, you used `BurlapProxyFactoryBean`. Carrying this monotony over to HTTP invoker, it should be of little surprise to you that to access an HTTP invoker service, you'll need to use `HttpInvokerProxyFactoryBean`.

Had the payment service been exposed as an HTTP invoker-based service, you could configure a bean that proxies it using `HttpInvokerProxyFactoryBean` as follows:

```
<bean id="paymentService" class= "org.springframework.remoting.
    httpinvoker.HttpInvokerProxyFactoryBean">
  <property name="serviceUrl">
    <value>http://${serverName}/${contextPath}/pay.service</value>
  </property>
  <property name="serviceInterface">
    <value>com.springinaction.payment.PaymentService</value>
  </property>
</bean>
```

Comparing this bean definition to those in sections 6.2.1 and 6.3.1, you'll find that little has changed. The `serviceInterface` property is still used to indicate interface implemented by the payment service. And the `serviceUrl` property is still used to indicate the location of the remote payment service. Because HTTP invoker is HTTP-based like Hessian and Burlap, the `serviceUrl` can contain the same URL as with the Hessian and Burlap versions of the bean.

Moving on to the other side of an HTTP invoker conversation, let's now look at how to export a bean's functionality as an HTTP invoker-based service.

### 6.4.2 *Exposing beans as HTTP Services*

You've already seen how to expose the functionality of `PaymentServiceImpl` as an RMI service, as a Hessian service, and as a Burlap service. Next let's rework the payment service as an HTTP invoker service using Spring's `HttpInvokerService-Exporter` to export the payment service.

At the risk of sounding like a broken record, we must tell you that exporting a bean's methods as remote method using `HttpInvokerServiceExporter` is very much like what you've already seen with the other remote service exporters. In fact, it's virtually identical. For example, the following bean definition shows how to export the `paymentService` bean as a remote HTTP invoker-based service:

```
<bean id="httpPaymentService" class="org.springframework.remoting.
       httpinvoker.HttpInvokerServiceExporter">
  <property name="service">
    <ref bean="paymentService"/>
  </property>
  <property name="serviceInterface">
    <value>com.springinaction.payment.PaymentService</value>
  </property>
</bean>
```

Feeling a strange sense of déjà vu? You may be having a hard time finding the difference between this bean declaration and the ones in section 6.3.2. In case the bold text didn't help you spot it, the only difference is the use of `HttpInvoker-ServiceExporter`. Otherwise, this exporter is no different than the other remote service exporters.

HTTP invoker–based services, as their name suggests, are HTTP-based just like Hessian and Burlap services. And, just like `HessianServiceExporter` and `Burlap-ServiceExporter`, `HttpInvokerServiceExporter` is a Spring `Controller`. This means that you'll need to set up a URL handler to map an HTTP URL to the service:

```
<bean id="urlMapping" class="org.springframework.web.
       servlet.handler.SimpleUrlHandlerMapping">
  <property name="mappings">
    <props>
      <prop key="/pay.service">httpPaymentService</prop>
    </props>
  </property>
</bean>
```

And you'll also need to deploy the payment service in a web application with Spring's `DispatcherServlet` configured in web.xml:

```
<servlet>
  <servlet-name>credit</servlet-name>
```

```
    <servlet-class>
        org.springframework.web.servlet.DispatcherServlet
    </servlet-class>
    <load-on-startup>1</load-on-startup>
</servlet>

<servlet-mapping>
  <servlet-name>credit</servlet-name>
  <url-pattern>*.service</url-pattern>
</servlet-mapping>
```

Configured this way, the payment service will be available at `/pay.service`, the same URL as it was when exposed as either a Hessian or Burlap service.

Spring's HTTP invoker presents a best-of-both-worlds remoting solution combining the simplicity of HTTP communication with Java's built-in object serialization. This makes HTTP invoker services an appealing alternative to either RMI or Hessian/Burlap.

HTTP invoker has one significant limitation that you should keep in mind. HTTP invoker is a remoting solution offered by the Spring framework only. This means that both the client and the service must be Spring-enabled applications. And, at least for now, this also implies that both the client and the service must be Java-based.[2]

Of all of the remoting technologies discussed so far, none has received as much attention as Enterprise JavaBeans (EJBs). Indeed more words have probably been printed about EJB than any other Java technology. Let's take a look at how EJBs can fit into your Spring applications.

## 6.5 Working with EJBs

You may be surprised to find a section on how to use Spring with EJBs in this book. Much of this book so far has shown you how to implement enterprise-class applications without resorting to EJBs. A section on EJBs may seem a bit juxtaposed in this book. So why are we talking about EJBs now?

The fact is that although Spring provides a lot of functionality that gives POJOs the power of EJBs, you may not always have the luxury of working on a project that is completely EJB-free. On the one hand, you may have to interface

---

[2] The Java-only nature of HTTP invoker may soon not be an issue. The Spring team has started a new project to port the Spring framework to Microsoft .NET. This may open up HTTP invoker to be used with .NET languages such as C# and Visual Basic (although how serialized Java objects get deserialized in .NET is yet to be seen).

with other systems that expose their functionality through stateless session EJBs. On the other hand, you may be placed in a project where for legitimate technical (or perhaps political) reasons you must write EJB code.

Whether your application is the client of an EJB or if you must write the EJB itself, you don't have to completely abandon all of the benefits of Spring in order to work with EJBs. Spring provides support for EJBs in two ways:

- Spring enables you to declare EJBs as beans within your Spring configuration file. This makes it possible to wire EJB references into the properties of your other beans as though the EJB was just another POJO.

- Spring lets you write EJBs that act as a façade to Spring-configured beans.

Let's start exploring Spring's EJB abstraction features by looking at how to declare EJBs as beans within the Spring configuration file.

### 6.5.1 *Accessing EJBs*

To illustrate Spring's support for accessing EJBs, let's return to the payment service. This time, however, suppose that the payment service is implemented as a legacy system that exposes its functionality through a stateless session EJB.[3]

You may recall how to access EJBs in the traditional way. You know that you must look up the home interface through JNDI. Perhaps you'll write something like this to look up the payment service's home interface:

```
private PaymentServiceHome paymentServiceHome;
private PaymentServiceHome getPaymentServiceHome ()
    throws javax.naming.NamingException {

  if(paymentServiceHome != null)
     return paymentServiceHome;

  javax.naming.InitialContext ctx =
     new javax.naming.InitialContext();

  try {
    Object objHome = ctx.lookup("paymentService");

    PaymentServiceHome home =
        (PaymentServiceHome) javax.rmi.PortableRemoteObject.narrow(
         objHome, PaymentServiceHome.class);
```

---

[3] Isn't it interesting that we're referring to an EJB-based system as a legacy system? My, how times have changed!

```
        return home;
    } finally {
      ctx.close();
    }
  }
```

Once you've got a reference to the home interface, you'll then need to get a reference to the EJB's remote (or local) interface and call its business methods. For example, the following code shows how to call the payment service EJB's authorize-CreditCard() method:

```
try {
  PaymentServiceHome home = getPaymentServiceHome ();
  PaymentService paymentService = home.create();

  String authCode =
      paymentService.authorizeCreditCard(ccNumber, cardHolderName,
      expMonth, expYear, amount);
} catch (javax.rmi.RemoteException e) {
  throw new CreditException();
} catch (CreateException e) {
  throw new CreditException();
}
```

Wow, that's a lot of code! What's disturbing is that only a few lines have anything to do with authorizing a credit card. Most of it is there just to obtain a reference to the EJB. This seems like a lot of work just to make a single call to the EJB's authorize-CreditCard() method.

Hold on. Throughout this book, you've seen ways to inject your application beans with the services that they need. Beans don't look up other beans…beans are *given* to other beans. But this whole exercise of looking up an EJB via JNDI and its home interface doesn't seem to fit how the rest of the application is constructed. If you proceed to interact with the EJB in the traditional EJB way, it will muddy up your code with lookup code and will definitely couple your application with the EJB. Isn't there a better way?

### Proxying EJBs

As you've probably guessed from this lead-up, yes, there is a better way. Earlier in this chapter we showed you how to configure proxies to various remote services, including RMI, Hessian, Burlap, and HTTP invoker services. In much the same way, Spring provides two proxy factory beans that proxy access to EJBs:

- LocalStatelessSessionProxyFactoryBean—Used to access local EJBs (EJBs in the same container as their clients).

■ SimpleRemoteStatelessSessionProxyFactoryBean—Used to access remote EJBs (EJBs that are in a separate container from their clients).

To break the monotony of the first few sections of this chapter, you'll configure these proxy factory beans very differently than how you configured those for RMI, Hessian/Burlap, and HTTP invoker. Let's see how to use these beans to access the payment service EJB. Suppose, for simplicity's sake, that the EJB is a local EJB with a JNDI name of payService. The following XML shows how to declare the EJB within the Spring configuration file:

```
<bean id="paymentService" class="org.springframework.ejb.
    access.LocalStatelessSessionProxyFactoryBean"
    lazy-init="true">

  <property name="jndiName">
    <value>payService</value>
  </property>

  <property name="businessInterface">
    <value>com.springinaction.payment.PaymentService</value>
  </property>
</bean>
```

Because it is a local EJB, the LocalStatelessSessionProxyFactoryBean is the appropriate proxy factory bean class to use. You also set the jndiName property to paymentService so that the proxy factory bean can look up the EJB's home interface.

An important thing to notice about this declaration is the lazy-init attribute on the <bean> element. This is important when either of the EJB-loading proxy factory beans is used in an ApplicationContext. This is because ApplicationContext-style bean factories pre-instantiate singleton beans once the Spring configuration file is loaded. This is usually a good thing, but it may result in the EJB proxy factory beans attempting to look up the EJB's home interface before the EJB is bound in the naming service. Setting lazy-init to true ensures that the "paymentService" will not attempt to look up the home interface until it is first used—which should be plenty of time for the EJB to be bound in the naming service.

The businessInterface property is equivalent to the serviceInterface property used with the other remote service proxy factory beans. Again it is set to com.springinaction.payment.PaymentService to indicate that the service adheres to the PaymentService interface.

### Wiring the EJB

Now let's wire the payment service EJB into the studentService bean:

```
<bean id="studentService"
    class="com.springinaction.training.service.StudentServiceImpl">
...
  <property name="paymentService">
    <ref bean="paymentService"/>
  </property>
...
</bean>
```

Did you see that? Wiring the payment service EJB into the studentService bean was no different than wiring a POJO. The paymentService bean (which just happens to be a proxy to the EJB) is simply injected into the paymentService property of studentService.

The wonderful thing about using a proxy factory bean to access the payment service EJB is that you don't have to write your own service locator or business delegate code. In fact, you don't have to write any JNDI code of any sort. Nor must you deal with the EJB's home interface (or local home interface in this case).

Furthermore, by hiding it all behind the PaymentService business interface, the studentService bean isn't even aware that it's dealing with an EJB. As far as it knows, it's collaborating with a POJO. This is significant because it means that you are free to swap out the EJB implementation of PaymentService with any other implementation (perhaps even a mock implementation that's used when unit-testing StudentServiceImpl).

### What's going on?

You may be wondering how all this magic works. How were you able to wire in an EJB as if it were just any other bean? Well, there's a lot of stuff going on under the covers of LocalStatelessSessionProxyFactoryBean that makes this possible.

First, during startup, LocalStatelessSessionProxyFactoryBean uses the JNDI name specified by the jndiName property to look up the EJB's local home interface via JNDI. It then caches this interface for later use so that it won't have to do any more JNDI calls.

Then, every time a method is called on the PaymentService interface, the proxy calls the create() method on the local home interface to retrieve a reference to the EJB. Finally, the proxy invokes the corresponding method on the EJB.

All of this skullduggery gives the illusion that the payment service is a simple POJO, when in fact there is interaction with an EJB. (Pretty sneaky, huh?)

### Accessing a remote EJB

Now you've seen how to wire a local EJB into your Spring application. But if this were a real-world application, the payment service EJB would more likely be a remote EJB. In that case, you'd declare it in the Spring configuration file using SimpleRemoteStatelessSessionProxyFactoryBean as follows:

```
<bean id="paymentService" class="org.springframework.ejb.
    ➡ access.SimpleRemoteStatelessSessionProxyFactoryBean"
    lazy-init="true">

  <property name="jndiName">
    <value>payService</value>
  </property>

  <property name="businessInterface">
    <value>com.springinaction.payment.PaymentService</value>
  </property>
</bean>
```

Notice that the only difference here is the choice of SimpleRemoteStateless-SessionProxyFactoryBean. Other than that, Spring makes the choice between local and remote EJBs transparent in the code that uses the EJB.

But you're probably wondering about java.rmi.RemoteException. How can the choice between local and remote EJBs be completely transparent if invoking a remote EJB method could throw a RemoteException? Doesn't someone need to catch that exception?

This is one more benefit of using Spring's EJB support to access EJBs. As with RMI services, any RemoteExceptions thrown from EJBs are caught and then rethrown as org.springframework.remoting.RemoteAccessException (which is an unchecked exception). This makes catching the exception optional for the EJB client.

Now that you've seen how to wire EJBs into your Spring application, let's look at how Spring supports EJB development.

## 6.5.2 Developing Spring-enabled EJBs

Although Spring provides many capabilities that make it possible to implement enterprise applications without EJBs, you may still find yourself needing to develop your components as EJBs.

Up until this point, you've seen how Spring supports remoting by providing service exporter classes that magically export POJOs into remote services. We hate to disappoint you, but unfortunately Spring doesn't provide an `EjbService-Exporter` class that exports POJOs as EJBs. (But we do agree that such an exporter would be really cool.)

Nevertheless, Spring provides four abstract support classes to make developing EJBs a little bit easier:

- `AbstractMessageDrivenBean`—Useful for developing message-driven beans that accept messages from sources other than JMS (as allowed by the EJB 2.1 specification)

- `AbstractJmsMessageDrivenBean`—Useful for developing message-driven beans that accept messages from JMS sources

- `AbstractStatefulSessionBean`—Useful for developing stateful session EJBs

- `AbstractStatelessSessionBean`—Useful for developing stateless session EJBs

These abstract classes simplify EJB development in two ways:

- They provide default empty implementations of EJB life-cycle methods (e.g., `ejbActivate()`, `ejbPassivate()`, `ejbRemove()`). These methods are required per the EJB specification, but are typically implemented as empty methods.

- They provide access to a Spring bean factory. This makes it possible for you to implement an EJB as a façade that delegates responsibility for the business logic to Spring-configured POJOs.

For example, suppose that you were to expose the functionality of the course service bean as a stateless session EJB. Listing 6.3 shows how you might implement this EJB.

**Listing 6.3    A stateless session EJB delegates responsibility for business logic to a POJO.**

```
public class CourseServiceEjb extends AbstractStatelessSessionBean
    implements CourseService {

  private CourseService courseService;    <— Declare the POJO

  protected void onEjbCreate() {              Look up the course service
    courseService =
        (CourseService) getBeanFactory().getBean("courseService");
  }

  public Course getCourse(Integer id) {
    return courseService.getCourse(id);    <— Delegate to the POJO
  }
```

```
public void createCourse(Course course) {
  courseService.createCourse(course);                ◁──┐
}                                                        │   Delegate to
                                                         │   the POJO
public Set getAllCourses() {                             │
  return courseService.getAllCourses();            ◁──┘
}

public void enrollStudentInCourse(Course course, Student student)
    throws CourseException {
  courseService.enrollStudentInCourse(course, student);   ◁──┐  Delegate to
}                                                              │  the POJO
}
```

When the `CourseServiceEjb` is created, its `onEjbCreate()` method retrieves the `courseService` bean from the Spring bean factory. Then, when any of its methods are invoked, they delegate responsibility to the bean `courseService` bean.

The big unanswered question regarding the EJB in listing 6.3 is where the bean factory comes from. In typical J2EE fashion, the abstract EJB classes retrieve the bean factory from JNDI. By default, they will look up the bean factory using `java:comp/env/ejb/BeanFactoryPath` as the JNDI name. To look up the bean factory by another JNDI name, set the `beanFactoryLocatorKey` property before the bean factory is loaded (in either the constructor or in the `setSessionContext()` method). For example:

```
public void setSessionContext(SessionContext sessionContext) {
  super.setSessionContext(sessionContext);

  setBeanFactoryLocatorKey("java:comp/env/ejb/MyBeanFactory");
}
```

For good or bad, EJBs have certainly been the talk of the Java development community for several years. But web services are a remoting technology that have generated buzz that transcends language and platform boundaries. To wrap up this chapter, let's see how Spring supports web services via JAX-RPC.

## 6.6 *Using JAX-RPC web services*

JAX-RPC is short for "Java APIs for XML-based remote procedure call." That's a mouthful of words that simply means that JAX-RPC is a means for Java programs to access remote services using XML. In particular, the services are web services that expose their functionality using the Simple Object Access Protocol (SOAP).

The ins and outs of JAX-RPC and SOAP-based web services are outside the scope of this book. We're going to assume that you are already familiar with the basics of SOAP and JAX-RPC. If you need a primer or a refresher on JAX-RPC and SOAP, take a look at *J2EE Web Services* by Richard Monson-Haefel (Addison-Wesley, 2003).

To illustrate Spring's support for web service access through JAX-RPC, we could revisit the payment service again, but you're probably growing quite weary of the monotony (we know that we are). So, for JAX-RPC, we thought you'd appreciate a break from the payment service example. Instead we're going to work with a Babel Fish service.

If you've ever read *The Hitchhiker's Guide to the Galaxy*, you probably already know what a Babel Fish is. For those of you who don't know what we're talking about, a Babel Fish is a small yellow fish that, when placed in the ear, translates one spoken language to another. In short, it enables anyone with the fish placed in their ear to understand anything that is spoken, regardless of what language it is spoken in.

We recognize that most readers probably don't have access to a real Babel Fish (and even if you did, you might find it creepy to put a fish in your ear). But there is a web service that performs a similar function. In fact, it is appropriately named "BabelFishService." You can find the Web Service Definition Language (WSDL) file for the Babel Fish web service at the following URL: http://www.xmethods.com/sd/2001/BabelFishService.wsdl.

### 6.6.1 *Referencing a web service with JAX-RPC*

To use the Babel Fish web service, you'll need to create an interface that defines the service. Looking at the WSDL, you'll find that the Babel Fish web service has a single operation called `BabelFish`. This operation takes two arguments: A `String` that indicates the translation mode (see SIDEBAR) and another `String` that is the original untranslated text. It returns a `String` that contains the translated text. `BabelFishRemote.java` (listing 6.4) shows the remote interface that defines this service.

**Listing 6.4  The remote interface for the Babel Fish web service**

```
package com.springinaction.chapter06.babelfish;

import java.rmi.Remote;
import java.rmi.RemoteException;
```

```
public interface BabelFishRemote extends Remote {
  public String BabelFish(String translationMode,
     String sourceData) throws RemoteException;
}
```

**SIDEBAR** The translation mode is made up of two language codes separated by an underscore (_). Some valid language codes are "en" for English, "fr" for French, "dr" for German, and "es" for Spanish. The language code that precedes the underscore is the language that the source text is in. The language code that is after the underscore is the language that you want to the source text to be translated to. For example, a translation mode of "de_en" will translate German text into English text.

The `BabelFishRemote` interface contains the single `BabelFish()` method. This method name comes from the operation name in the WSDL. Unfortunately this web service begins with a capital "B," unlike Java conventions where method names begin with lowercase letters. The following code shows how you might obtain a reference to the Babel Fish service using conventional JAX-RPC (that is, without Spring's help):

```
String wsdlDocumentUrl =
    "http://www.xmethods.com/sd/2001/BabelFishService.wsdl";
String namespaceUri =
    "http://www.xmethods.net/sd/BabelFishService.wsdl";
String serviceName = "BabelFishService";
String portName = "BabelFishPort";
QName serviceQN = new QName(namespaceUri, serviceName);
QName portQN = new QName(namespaceUri, portName);

ServiceFactory sf = ServiceFactory.newInstance();
Service service =
    sf.createService(new URL(wsdlDocumentUrl), serviceQN);

BabelFishRemote babelFish = (BabelFishRemote)
    service.getPort(BabelFishRemote.class, portQN);
```

With a reference to the service in hand, you can use it to translate any text you want. For example, to translate "Hello world" from English (en) to Spanish (es):

```
String translated = babelFish.BabelFish("en_es", "Hello World");
```

Likewise, you could translate from Spanish (es) to French (fr) using the following:

```
String translated = babelFish.BabelFish("es_fr", "Hola Mundo");
```

Or from French (fr) to German (de):

```
String translated = babelFish.BabelFish("fr_de", "Bonjour Monde");
```

The Babel Fish service is a lot of fun, but one problem with the standard JAX-RPC approach is that it results in a lot of code just to be able to look up the payment service. To make it a bit briefer, you could take the approach recommended by JSR-109 (Implementing Enterprise Web Services) and use JNDI to retrieve the web service:

```
Context ic = new InitialContext();
BabelFishService babelFishService =
    (BabelFishService) ic.lookup("java:comp/env/service/BabelFish");
BabelFishRemote babelFish =
    (BabelFishRemote) babelFishService.getBabelFishPort();
```

But, even though the JNDI version is more concise, it still leaves the client responsible for obtaining its own reference to the service. In doing that, it doesn't embrace the spirit of inversion of control. What's more, it places the burden of handling `RemoteExceptions` on the client.

Now that you've seen the conventional way to access a web service using JAX-RPC, let's see the Spring way to do it.

### 6.6.2 *Wiring a web service in Spring*

Just as with the other remoting technologies discussed in this chapter, Spring provides a proxy factory bean, `JaxRpcPortProxyFactoryBean`, that enables you to seamlessly wire a web service in as a collaborator of another bean in the application. Under the hood, `JaxRpcPortProxyFactoryBean` uses JAX-RPC to access the remote web service.

The XML in listing 6.5 shows how to declare the Babel Fish service as a bean in the Spring configuration file.

**Listing 6.5  The Babel Fish service as a bean in the Spring application context**

```
<bean id="babelFish" class="org.springframework.remoting.
       jaxrpc.JaxRpcPortProxyFactoryBean">

   <property name="wsdlDocumentUrl">
     <value>http://www.xmethods.com/sd/2001/
        BabelFishService.wsdl</value>                    ❶
   </property>
```

```
<property name="serviceInterface">
  <value>com.springinaction.chapter06.babelfish.
     ➥ BabelFishService</value>                           ❷
</property>

<property name="portInterface">
  <value>com.habuma.remoting.client.BabelFishRemote</value>    ❸
</property>

<property name="namespaceUri">
  <value>http://www.xmethods.net/sd/BabelFishService.wsdl</value>   ❹
</property>

<property name="serviceName">
  <value>BabelFishService</value>      ❺
</property>

<property name="portName">
  <value>BabelFishPort</value>     ❻
</property>

<property name="serviceFactoryClass">
  <value>org.apache.axis.client.ServiceFactory</value>      ❼
</property>
</bean>
```

The first property set on this `JaxRpcPortProxyFactoryBean` is `wsdlDocumentUrl` ❶.
This tells the proxy where the web service's WSDL document is.

The `serviceInterface` property ❷ defines the interface that the client of the
Babel Fish service uses to access the service. Here it has been set to use the
`BabelFishService` interface, which is defined as follows:

```
public interface BabelFishService {
  public String BabelFish(String translationMode,
                          String sourceData);
}
```

The `BabelFishService` interface closely resembles the remote interface, which is
set to the `portInterface` property ❸. The difference is that the remote interface
is considered an RMI interface in that it extends `javax.rmi.Remote` and the
`BabelFish()` method throws `javax.rmi.RemoteException`. `JaxRpcPortProxy-`
`FactoryBean` uses the `BabelFishRemote` interface when it accesses the remote service. But if any `RemoteExceptions` are thrown, the proxy will catch them and
rethrow them as (runtime) `RemoteAccessExceptions` so that the client won't have
to deal with them.

The next three properties are used to construct qualified names (QNames) for the Babel Fish service and its port. The namespaceUri property ❹ is used with the serviceName property ❺ to construct the QName for the service and is also used with the portName property ❻ to construct a QName for the port. The values of all three of these fields can be found by examining in the WSDL definition for the Babel Fish service.

By default, JaxRpcPortProxyFactoryBean uses javax.xml.rpc.ServiceFactory as its service factory. But you may choose to use another service factory, such as Apache Axis's service factory, by setting the serviceFactoryClass property ❼.

With the Babel Fish service configured in the Spring configuration file in this way, you can use it just like you would any other bean in the application context. This includes retrieving it from the application context directly or wiring it as a collaborator into a property on another bean. For example, use this to pull the bean out of the application context directly:

```
ApplicationContext context =
    new FileSystemXmlApplicationContext("babelFish.xml");
BabelFishService babelFish =
    (BabelFishService) context.getBean(babelFish);
String translated = babelFish.BabelFish("en_es", "Hello World");
```

When the previous snippet of code is complete, the translated variable will contain the text "Hola Mundo," which is the Spanish way of saying "Hello World."

**FUN WITH A BABEL FISH** For fun, here are some other phrases you might try to translate using the Babel Fish service:

- "Qui a couple le fromage" using "fr_en" as the translation mode
- "Mi perro is muy feo" using "es_en" as the translation mode
- "Ich habe eine socke voll der Zehen" using "de_en" as the translation mode
- "No me gusto a comer los cocos" using "es_en" as the translation mode
- "Mon volleyball est mon meilleur ami" using "fr_en" as the translation mode

## 6.7 *Summary*

Working with remote services is typically a tedious chore. But Spring provides remoting support that makes working with remote services as simple as working with any regular JavaBean.

On the client side, Spring provides proxy factory beans that enable you to configure remote services in your Spring application. Regardless of whether you are using RMI, Hessian, Burlap, HTTP invoker, EJB, or web services, you can wire remote services into your application as if they were POJOs. Spring even catches any `RemoteExceptions` that are thrown and rethrows runtime `RemoteAccessExceptions` in their place, freeing your code from having to deal with an exception that it probably can't recover from.

Spring's support for the service side is varied. For RMI, Hessian, Burlap, and HTTP invoker services, Spring provides remote exporters that expose the functionality of your Spring-managed beans as remote services to be consumed by another application. Although Spring doesn't enable you to export POJOs as EJB, it does provide support classes that make it possible for your EJBs to access a Spring application context.

Even though Spring hides many of the details of remote services, making them appear as though they are local JavaBeans, you should bear in mind the consequences of remote services. Remote services, by their nature, are typically less efficient than local services. You should take this into consideration when writing code that accesses remote services, limiting remote calls to avoid performance bottlenecks.

In the next chapter, you'll learn how to use Spring's support for several enterprise services, including JNDI, e-mail, scheduling, and messaging.

# Accessing enterprise services    7

There are several enterprise services that Spring doesn't support directly. Instead Spring relies on other APIs to provide the services, but then places them under an abstraction layer so that they're easier to use.

You've already seen a few of Spring's abstraction layers. In chapter 4, you saw how Spring abstracts JDBC and Hibernate. In addition to eliminating the need to write certain boilerplate code, these abstractions eliminated the need for you to catch checked exceptions.

In this chapter, we're going to take a whirlwind tour of the abstraction layers that Spring provides for several enterprise services, including Spring's support for

- Java Naming and Directory Interface (JNDI)
- E-mail
- Scheduling
- Java Message Service (JMS)

We'll begin by looking at Spring's support for JNDI, since this provides the basis for several of the other abstraction layers.

## 7.1  *Retrieving objects from JNDI*

JNDI affords Java applications a central repository to store application objects. For example, a typical J2EE application uses JNDI to store and retrieve such things as JDBC data sources and JTA transaction managers.

But why would you want to configure these objects in JNDI instead of in Spring? Certainly, you could configure a `DataSource` object in Spring's configuration file, but you may prefer to configure it in an application server to take advantage of the server's connection pooling. Likewise, if your transactional requirements demand JTA transaction support, you'll need to retrieve a JTA transaction manager from the application server's JNDI repository.

Spring's JNDI abstraction makes it possible to declare JNDI lookups in your application's configuration file. Then you can wire those objects into the properties of other beans as though the JNDI object were just another POJO. Let's take a look at how to use Spring's JNDI abstraction to simplify lookup of objects in JNDI.

### 7.1.1  *Working with conventional JNDI*

Looking up objects in JNDI can be a tedious chore. For example, suppose you need to retrieve a `javax.sql.DataSource` from JNDI. Using the conventional JNDI APIs, your might write some code that looks like this:

```
InitialContext ctx = null;

try {

  ctx = new InitialContext();

  DataSource ds =
      (DataSource)ctx.lookup("java:comp/env/jdbc/myDatasource");

} catch (NamingException ne) {

  // handle naming exception

  ...

} finally {

  if(ctx != null) {

    try {

      ctx.close();

    } catch (NamingException ne) {}

  }
}
```

At first glance, this may not look like a big deal. But take a closer look. There are a few things about this code that make it a bit clumsy:

- You must create and close an initial context for no other reason than to look up a DataSource. This may not seem like a lot of extra code, but it is extra plumbing code that is not directly in line with the goals of your application code.

- You must catch or, at very least, rethrow a javax.naming.NamingException. If you choose to catch it, you must deal with it appropriately. If you choose to rethrow it, then the calling code will be forced to deal with it. Ultimately, someone somewhere will have to deal with the exception.

- You code is tightly coupled with a JNDI lookup. All your code needs is a DataSource. It doesn't matter whether or not it comes from JNDI. But if your code contains code like that shown earlier, you're stuck retrieving the DataSource from JNDI.

- Your code is tightly coupled with a specific JNDI name—in this case java:comp/env/jdbc/myDatasource. Sure, you could extract that name into a properties file, but then you'll have to add even more plumbing code to look up the JNDI name from the properties file.

The overall problem with the conventional approach to looking up objects in JNDI is that it is the antithesis of dependency injection. Instead of your code being given an object, your code must go get the object itself. This means that your code is doing stuff that isn't really its job. It also means that your code is unnecessarily coupled to JNDI.

Regardless, this doesn't change the fact that sometimes you need to be able to look up objects in JNDI. DataSources are often configured in an application server, to take advantage of the application server's connection pooling, and then retrieved by the application code to access the database. How can you get all the benefits of JNDI along with all of the benefits of dependency injection?

### 7.1.2 *Proxying JNDI objects*

Spring's JndiObjectFactoryBean gives you the best of both worlds. It is a factory bean, which means that when it is wired into a property, it will actually create some other type of object that will wire into that property. In the case of JndiObjectFactoryBean, it will wire an object retrieved from JNDI.

To illustrate how this works, let's revisit an example from chapter 4 (section 4.1.2). There you used JndiObjectFactoryBean to retrieve a DataSource from JNDI:

```
<bean id="dataSource"
    class="org.springframework.jndi.JndiObjectFactoryBean"
    singleton="true">
  <property name="jndiName">
    <value>java:comp/env/jdbc/myDatasource</value>
  </property>
</bean>
```

The jndiName property specifies the name of the object in JNDI. Here the full JNDI name of java:comp/env/jdbc/myDatasource is specified. However, if the object is a Java resource, you may choose to leave off java:comp/env/ to specify the name more concisely. For example, the following declaration of the jndiName property is equivalent to the previous declaration:

```
<property name="jndiName">
  <value>jdbc/myDatasource</value>
</property>
```

With the dataSource bean declared, you may now inject it into a DataSource property. For instance, you may use it to configure a Hibernate session factory as follows:

```
<bean id="sessionFactory" class="org.springframework.orm.
      hibernate.LocalSessionFactoryBean">
  <property name="dataSource">
```

```
        <ref bean="dataSource"/>
    </property>
  ...
  </bean>
```

When Spring wires the `sessionFactory` bean, it will inject the `DataSource` object retrieved from JNDI into the session factory's `dataSource` property.

The great thing about using `JndiObjectFactoryBean` to look up an object in JNDI is that the only part of the code that knows that the `DataSource` is retrieved from JNDI is the XML declaration of the `dataSource` bean. The `session-Factory` bean doesn't know (or care) where the `DataSource` came from. This means that if you decide that you would rather get your `DataSource` from a JDBC driver manager, all you need to do is redefine the `dataSource` bean to be a `DriverManagerDataSource`.

We'll see even more uses of JNDI later in this chapter. But first, let's switch gears a bit and look at another abstraction provided by the Spring framework— Spring's e-mail abstraction layer.

## 7.2 *Sending e-mail*

Suppose that the course director of Spring Training has asked you to send her a daily e-mail outlining all of the upcoming courses, including a seat count and how many students have enrolled in the course. She'd like this report to be e-mailed at 6:00 a.m. every day so that she can see it when she first gets to work. Using this report, she'll schedule additional offerings of popular courses and cancel courses that aren't filling up very quickly.

As laziness is a great attribute of any programmer,[1] you decide to automate the e-mail so that you don't have to pull together the report every day yourself.

The first thing to do is to write the code that sends the e-mail (you'll schedule it for daily delivery in section 7.3).

To get started, you'll need a mail sender, defined by Spring's `MailSender` interface. A mail sender is an abstraction around a specific mail implementation. This decouples the application code from the actual mail implementation being used. Spring comes with two implementations of this interface:

---

[1] The other two attributes of a programmer are impatience and hubris. See *Programming Perl, 3rd Edition*, by Larry Wall et al. (O'Reilly & Associates, 2000).

- CosMailSenderImpl—Simple implementation of an SMTP mail sender based on Jason Hunter's COS (com.oreilly.servlet) implementation from his *Java Servlet Programming* book (O'Rielly, 1998).

- JavaMailSenderImpl—A JavaMail API-based implementation of a mail sender. Allows for sending of MIME messages as well as non-SMTP mail (such as Lotus Notes).

Either MailSender implementation is sufficient for the purposes of sending the report to the course director. But we'll choose JavaMailSenderImpl since it is the more versatile of the two. You'll declare it in your Spring configuration file as follows:

```
<bean id="mailSender"
    class="org.springframework.mail.javamail.JavaMailSenderImpl">
  <property name="host">
    <value>mail.springtraining.com</value>
  </property>
</bean>
```

The host property specifies the host name of the mail server, in this case Spring Training's SMTP server. By default, the mail sender assumes that the port is listening on port 25 (the standard SMTP port), but if your SMTP server is listening on a different port, you can set it using the port property of JavaMailSenderImpl.

The mailSender declaration above explicitly names the mail server that will send the e-mails. However, if you have a javax.mail.MailSession in JNDI (perhaps placed there by your application server) you have the option to retrieve it from JNDI instead. Simply use JndiObjectFactoryBean (as described in section 7.1) to retrieve the mail session and then wire it into the mailSession property as follows:

```
<bean id="mailSession"
    class="org.springframework.jndi.JndiObjectFactoryBean">
  <property name="jndiName">
    <value>java:comp/env/mail/Session</value>
  </property>
</bean>

<bean id="mailSender"
    class="org.springrframework.mail.javamail.JavaMailSenderImpl">
  <property name="session"><ref bean="mailSession"/></property>
</bean>
```

Now that the mail sender is set up, it's ready to send e-mails. But you might want to declare a template e-mail message:

```
<bean id="enrollmentMailMessage"
    class="org.springframework.mail.SimpleMailMessage">
  <property name="to">
    <value>coursedirector@springtraining.com</value>
  </property>
  <property name="from">
    <value>system@springtraining.com</value>
  </property>
  <property name="subject">
    <value>Course enrollment report</value>
  </property>
</bean>
```

Declaring a template e-mail message is optional. You could also create a new instance of `SimpleMailMessage` each time you send the e-mail. But by declaring a template in the Spring configuration file, you won't hard-code the e-mail addresses or subject in Java code.

The next step is to add a `mailSender` property to `CourseServiceImpl` so that `CourseServiceImpl` can use it to send the e-mail. Likewise, if you declared an e-mail template you should add a `message` property that will hold the message template bean:

```
public class CourseServiceImpl implements CourseService {
  ...
  private MailSender mailSender;
  public void setMailSender(MailSender mailSender) {
    this.mailSender = mailSender;
  }

  private SimpleMailMessage mailMessage;
  public void setMailMessage(SimpleMailMessage mailMessage) {
    this.mailMessage = mailMessage;
  }
  ...
}
```

Now that `CourseServiceImpl` has a `MailSender` and a copy of the e-mail template, you can write the `sendCourseEnrollmentReport()` method (listing 7.1) that sends the e-mail to the course director. (Don't forget to add a declaration of `sendCourse-EnrollmentReport()` to the `CourseService` interface.)

**Listing 7.1  Sending the enrollment report e-mail**

```
public void sendCourseEnrollmentReport() {
  Set courseList = courseDao.findAll();

  SimpleMailMessage message =                       Copy mail
      new SimpleMailMessage(this.mailMessage);      template
```

```
StringBuffer messageText = new StringBuffer();
messageText.append(
    "Current enrollment data is as follows:\n\n");

for(Iterator iter = courseList.iterator(); iter.hasNext(); ) {
  Course course = (Course) iter.next();
  messageText.append(course.getId() + "     ");
  messageText.append(course.getName() + "     ");
  int enrollment = courseDao.getEnrollment(course);
  messageText.append(enrollment);
}

message.setText(messageText.toString());    <-- Set mail text

try {
  mailSender.send(message);    <-- Send e-mail
} catch (MailException e) {
  LOGGER.error(e.getMessage());
}
}
```

The `sendCourseEnrollmentReport()` starts by retrieving all courses using the `CourseDao`. Then, it creates a working copy of the e-mail template so that the original will remain untouched. It then constructs the message body and sets the message text. Finally, the e-mail is sent using the `mailSender` property.

The final step is to wire the `mailSender` and `enrollmentMailMessage` beans into the `courseService` bean:

```
<bean id="courseService"
    class="com.springinaction.training.service.CourseServiceImpl">
...
  <property name="mailMessage">
    <ref bean="enrollmentMailMessage"/>
  </property>

  <property name="mailSender">
    <ref bean="mailSender"/>
  </property>
</bean>
```

Now that the `courseService` bean has everything it needs to send the enrollment report, the job is half done. Now the only thing left is to set it up on a schedule to send to the course director on a daily basis. Gee, it would be great if Spring had a way to help us schedule tasks...

## 7.3 *Scheduling tasks*

Not everything that happens in an application is the result of a user action. Sometimes the software itself initiates an action.

The enrollment report e-mail, for example, should be sent to the course director every day. To make this happen, you have two choices: You can either come in early every morning to e-mail the report manually or you can have the application perform the e-mail on a predefined schedule. (We think we know which one you would choose.)

Two popular scheduling APIs are Java's `Timer` class and OpenSymphony's Quartz scheduler.[2] Spring provides an abstraction layer for both of these schedulers to make working with them much easier. Let's look at both abstractions, starting with the simpler one, Java's `Timer`.

### 7.3.1 *Scheduling with Java's Timer*

Starting with Java 1.3, the Java SDK has included rudimentary scheduling functionality through its `java.util.Timer` class. This class lets you schedule a task (defined by a subclass `java.util.TimerTask`) to occur every so often.

#### *Creating a timer task*

The first step in scheduling the enrollment report e-mail using Java's `Timer` is to create the e-mail task by subclassing `java.util.TimerTask`, as shown in listing 7.2.

**Listing 7.2  A timer task to e-mail the enrollment report**

```
public class EmailReportTask extends TimerTask {
  public EmailReportTask() {}

  public void run() {
    courseService.sendCourseEnrollmentReport();    <—  Send the report
  }

  private CourseService courseService;
  public void setCourseService(CourseService courseService) {
    this.courseService = courseService;                Inject the
  }                                                     CourseService
}
```

---

[2]  Quartz is an open source job scheduling system from the OpenSymphony project. You can learn more about Quartz at http://www.opensymphony.com/quartz/.

The run() method defines what to do when the task is run. In this case, it calls the sendCourseEnrollmentReport() of the CourseService (see listing 7.1) to send the enrollment e-mail. As for the CourseService, it will be supplied to EmailReport-Task via dependency injection.

Declare the EmailReportTask in the Spring configuration file like this:

```
<bean id="reportTimerTask"
    class="com.springinaction.training.schedule.EmailReportTask">
  <property name="courseService">
    <ref bean="courseService"/>
  </property>
</bean>
```

By itself, this declaration simply places the EmailReportTask into the application context and wires the courseService bean into the courseService property. It won't do anything useful until you schedule it.

### Scheduling the timer task

Spring's ScheduledTimerTask defines how often a timer task is to be run. Since the course director wants the enrollment report e-mailed to her every day, a ScheduledTimerTask should be wired as follows:

```
<bean id="scheduledReportTask"
    class="org.springframework.scheduling.timer.ScheduledTimerTask">
  <property name="timerTask">
    <ref bean="reportTimerTask"/>
  </property>
  <property name="period">
    <value>86400000</value>
  </property>
</bean>
```

The timerTask property tells the ScheduledTimerTask which TimerTask to run. Here it is wired with a reference to the reportTimerTask bean, which is the Email-ReportTask. The period property is what tells the ScheduledTimerTask how often the TimerTask's run() method should be called. This property, specified in milliseconds, is set to 86400000 to indicate that the task should be kicked off every 24 hours.

### Starting the timer

The final step is to start the timer. Spring's TimerFactoryBean is responsible for starting timer tasks. Declare it in the Spring configuration file like this:

```
<bean class="org.springframework.scheduling.timer.TimerFactoryBean">
  <property name="scheduledTimerTasks">
```

```
    <list>
      <ref bean="scheduledReportTask"/>
    </list>
  </property>
</bean>
```

The `scheduledTimerTasks` property takes an array of timer tasks that it should start. Since you only have one timer task right now, the list contains a single reference to the `scheduledReportTask` bean.

Unfortunately, even though the task will be run every 24 hours, there is no way to specify what time of the day it should be run. `ScheduledTimerTask` does have a `delay` property that lets you specify how long to wait before the task is first run. For example, to delay the first run of `EmailReportTask` by an hour:

```
<bean id="scheduledReportTask"
    class="org.springframework.scheduling.timer.ScheduledTimerTask">
  <property name="timerTask">
    <ref bean="reportTimerTask"/>
  </property>
  <property name="period">
    <value>86400000</value>
  </property>
  <property name="delay">
    <value>3600000</value>
  </property>
</bean>
```

Even with the delay, however, the time that the `EmailReportTask` will run will be relative to when the application starts. How can you have it sent at 6:00 a.m. every morning as requested by the course director (aside from starting the application at 5:00 a.m.)?

Unfortunately, that's a limitation of using Java's `Timer`. You can specify how often a task runs, but you can't specify exactly when it will be run. In order to specify precisely when the e-mail is sent, you'll need to use the Quartz scheduler instead.

### 7.3.2 *Using the Quartz scheduler*

The Quartz scheduler provides richer support for scheduling jobs. Just as with Java's `Timer`, you can use Quartz to run a job every so many milliseconds. But Quartz goes beyond Java's `Timer` by enabling you to schedule a job to run at a particular time and/or day.

For more information about Quartz, visit the Quartz home page at http://www.opensymphony.com/quartz.

Let's start working with Quartz by defining a job that sends the report e-mail.

### Creating a job

The first step in defining a Quartz job is to create the class that defines the job. For that, you'll subclass Spring's `QuartzJobBean`, as shown in listing 7.3.

**Listing 7.3 Defining a Quartz job**

```
public class EmailReportJob extends QuartzJobBean {

  public EmailReportJob() {}

  protected void executeInternal(JobExecutionContext context)
      throws JobExecutionException {

    courseService.sendCourseEnrollmentReport();    ←— Send enrollment report
  }

  private CourseService courseService;
  public void setCourseService(CourseService courseService) {
    this.courseService = courseService;             Inject
  }                                                  CourseService
}
```

A `QuartzJobBean` is the Quartz equivalent of a Java `TimerTask`. It is an implementation of the `org.quartz.Job` interface. The `executeInternal()` method defines the actions that the job does when its time comes. Here, just as with `EmailReportTask`, you simply call the `sendCourseEnrollmentReport()` method on the `courseService` property.

Declare the job in the Spring configuration file as follows:

```
<bean id="reportJob"
    class="org.springframework.scheduling.quartz.JobDetailBean">
  <property name="jobClass">
    <value>com.springinaction.training.
        ➡ schedule.EmailReportJob</value>
  </property>
  <property name="jobDataAsMap">
    <map>
      <entry key="courseService">
        <ref bean="courseService"/>
      </entry>
    </map>
  </property>
</bean>
```

Notice that you don't declare an `EmailReportJob` bean directly. Instead you declare a `JobDetailBean`. This is an idiosyncrasy of working with Quartz.

JobDetailBean is a subclass of Quartz's org.quartz.JobDetail, which requires that the Job object be set through the jobClass property.

Another quirk of working with Quartz's JobDetail is that the courseService property of EmailReportJob is set indirectly. JobDetail's jobDataAsMap takes a java.util.Map that contains properties that are to be set on the jobClass. Here, the map contains a reference to the courseService bean with a key of course-Service. When the JobDetailBean is instantiated, it will inject the courseService bean into the courseService property of EmailReportJob.

### Scheduling the job

Now that the job is defined, you'll need to schedule the job. Quartz's org.quartz.Trigger class decides when and how often a Quartz job should run. Spring comes with two triggers, SimpleTriggerBean and CronTriggerBean. Which trigger should you use? Let's take a look at both of them, starting with SimpleTriggerBean.

SimpleTriggerBean is similar to ScheduledTimerTask. Using it, you can specify how often a job should run and (optionally) how long to wait before running the job for the first time. For example, to schedule the report job to run every 24 hours, with the first run starting after one hour, declare it as follows:

```
<bean id="simpleReportTrigger"
    class="org.springframework.scheduling.quartz.SimpleTriggerBean">
  <property name="jobDetail">
    <ref bean="reportJob"/>
  </property>
  <property name="startDelay">
    <value>3600000</value>
  </property>
  <property name="repeatInterval">
    <value>86400000</value>
  </property>
</bean>
```

The jobDetail property is wired to the job that is to be scheduled, here the reportJob bean. The repeatInterval property tells the trigger how often to run the job (in milliseconds). Here, we've set it to 86400000 so that it gets triggered every 24 hours. And the startDelay property can be used (optionally) to delay the first run of the job. We've set it to 3600000 so that it waits an hour before firing off for the first time.

### Scheduling a *cron* job

Although you can probably think of many applications for which `SimpleTrigger-Bean` is perfectly suitable, it isn't sufficient for e-mailing the enrollment report. Just as with `ScheduledTimerTask`, you can only specify how often the job is run—not exactly when it is run. Therefore, you can't use `SimpleTriggerBean` to send the enrollment report to the course directory at 6:00 a.m. every day.

`CronTriggerBean`, however, gives you more precise control over when your job is run. If you're familiar with the Unix `cron` tool, then you'll feel right at home with `CronTriggerBean`. Instead of declaring how often a job is run you get to specify exact times (and days) for the job to run. For example, to run the report job every day at 6:00 a.m., declare a `CronTriggerBean` as follows:

```
<bean id="cronReportTrigger"
    class="org.springframework.scheduling.quartz.CronTriggerBean">
  <property name="jobDetail">
    <ref bean="reportJob"/>
  </property>
  <property name="cronExpression">
    <value>0 0 6 * * ?</value>
  </property>
</bean>
```

As with `SimpleTriggerBean`, the `jobDetail` property tells the trigger which job to schedule. Again, we've wired it with a reference to the `reportJob` bean. The `cronExpression` property tells the trigger when to fire. If you're not familiar with `cron`, this property may seem a bit cryptic, so let's examine this property a bit closer.

A `cron` expression has at least 6 (and optionally 7) time elements, separated by spaces. In order from left to right, the elements are defined as follows:

1. Seconds (0–59)
2. Minutes (0–59)
3. Hours (0–23)
4. Day of month (1–31)
5. Month (1–12 or JAN–DEC)
6. Day of week (1–7 or SUN–SAT)
7. Year (1970–2099)

Each of these elements can be specified with an explicit value (e.g., 6), a range (e.g., 9–12), a list (e.g., 9,11,13), or a wildcard (e.g., *). The day of the month and day of the week elements are mutually exclusive, so you should also indicate which one of these fields you don't want to set by specifying it with a question mark (?). Table 7.1 shows some example `cron` expressions and what they mean.

**Table 7.1  Some sample `cron` expressions**

| Expression | What it means |
|---|---|
| 0 0 10,14,16 * * ? | Every day at 10 a.m., 2 p.m., and 4 p.m. |
| 0 0,15,30,45 * 1–10 * ? | Every 15 minutes on the first 10 days of every month |
| 30 0 0 1 1 ? 2012 | 30 seconds after midnight on January 1, 2012 |
| 0 0 8-5 ? * MON–FRI | Every working hour of every business day |

In the case of `cronReportTrigger`, we've set `cronExpression` to 0 0 6 * * ? You can read this as "at the zero second of the zero minute of the sixth hour on any day of the month of any month (regardless of the day of the week), fire the trigger." In other words, the trigger is fired at 6:00 a.m. every day.

Using `CronTriggerBean`, you are able to adequately meet the course director's expectations. Now all that's left is to start the job.

### Starting the job

Spring's `SchedulerFactoryBean` is the Quartz equivalent to `TimerFactoryBean`. Declare it in the Spring configuration file as follows:

```
<bean class="org.springframework.scheduling.
     ➡ quartz.SchedulerFactoryBean">
  <property name="triggers">
    <list>
      <ref bean="cronReportTrigger"/>
    </list>
  </property>
</bean>
```

The `triggers` property takes an array of triggers. Since you only have a single trigger at this time, you simply need to wire it with a list containing a single reference to the `cronReportTrigger` bean.

At this point, you've satisfied the requirements for scheduling the enrollment report e-mail. But in doing so, you've done a bit of extra work. Before we move on, let's take a look at a slightly easier way to schedule the report e-mail.

### 7.3.3  Invoking methods on a schedule

In order to schedule the report e-mail you had to write the `EmailReportJob` bean (or the `EmailReportTask` bean in the case of timer tasks). But this bean does little more than make a simple call to the `sendCourseEnrollmentReport()` method of `CourseService`. In this light, `EmailReportTask` and `EmailReportJob` both seem a bit superfluous. Wouldn't it be great if you could specify that the `sendCourse-EnrollmentReport()` method be called without writing the extra class?

Good news! You can schedule single method calls without writing a separate `TimerTask` or `QuartzJobBean` class. To accomplish this, Spring has provided `MethodInvokingTimerTaskFactoryBean` and `MethodInvokingJobDetailFactoryBean` to schedule method calls with Java's timer support and the Quartz scheduler, respectively.

For example, to schedule a call to `sendCourseEnrollmentReport()` using Java's timer service, re-declare the `scheduledReportTask` bean as follows:

```
<bean id="scheduledReportTask">
    class="org.springframework.scheduling.timer.
        MethodInvokingTimerTaskFactoryBean">
  <property name="targetObject">
    <ref bean="courseService"/>
  </property>
  <property name="targetMethod">
    <value>sendCourseEnrollmentReport</value>
  </property>
</bean>
```

Behind the scenes, `MethodInvokingTimerTaskFactoryBean` creates a `TimerTask` that calls the method specified by the `targetMethod` property on the object specified by the `targetObject` property. This is effectively the same as the `EmailReportTask`.

With `scheduledReportTask` declared this way, you can now eliminate the `EmailReportTask` class and its declaration in the `reportTimerTask` bean.

`MethodInvokingTimerTaskFactoryBean` is good for making simple one-method calls when you are using a `ScheduledTimerTask`. But you're using Quartz's `CronTriggerBean` so that the report will be sent every morning at 6:00 a.m. So instead of using `MethodInvokingTimerTaskFactoryBean`, you'll want to re-declare the `reportJob` bean as follows:

```
<bean id="courseServiceInvokingJobDetail">
    class="org.springframework.scheduling.quartz.
        MethodInvokingJobDetailFactoryBean">
  <property name="targetObject">
    <ref bean="courseService"/>
  </property>
  <property name="targetMethod">
    <value>sendCourseEnrollmentReport</value>
  </property>
</bean>
```

`MethodInvokingJobDetailFactoryBean` is the Quartz equivalent of `MethodInvokingTimerTaskFactoryBean`. Under the covers, it creates a Quartz `JobDetail` object that makes a single method call to the object and method specified in the targetObject and targetMethod properties. Using MethodInvokingJobDetail-FactoryBean this way, you can eliminate the superfluous EmailReportJob class.

## 7.4 *Sending messages with JMS*

Most operations that take place in software are performed synchronously. In other words, when a routine is called the program flow is handed off to that routine to perform its functionality. Upon completion, control is returned to the calling routine and the program proceeds. Figure 7.1 illustrates this.

But sometimes, it's not necessary (or even desirable) to wait for the called routine to complete. For example, if the routine is slow, it may be preferable to send a message to a routine and then just assume that the routine will process the message or to check on its progress sometime later.

When you send a message to a routine and do not wait for a result, it is said to be *asynchronous*. Asynchronous program flow is illustrated in figure 7.2.

The Java Messaging Service (JMS) is a Java API for asynchronous processing. JMS supports two types of messaging: point-to-point and publish-subscribe.

A point-to-point message is placed into a message *queue* by the message producer and later pulled off the queue by the message consumer. Once the message is pulled from the queue, it is no longer available to any other message consumer that is watching the queue. This means that even though several consumers may observe a queue, a single consumer will consume each point-to-point message.

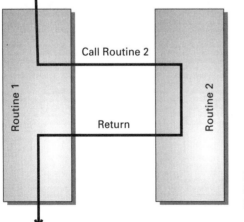

**Figure 7.1
Synchronous
program flow**

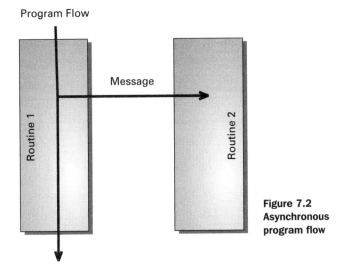

Program Flow

Message

Routine 1

Routine 2

**Figure 7.2
Asynchronous
program flow**

The publish-subscribe model invokes images of a magazine publisher who sends out copies of its publication to multiple subscribers. This is, in fact, a good analogy of how publish-subscribe messaging works. Multiple consumers subscribe to a message *topic*. When a message producer publishes a message to the topic, all subscribers will receive the message and have an opportunity to process it.

Spring provides an abstraction for JMS that makes it simple to access a message queue or topic (abstractly referred to as a *destination*) and publish messages to the destination. Moreover, Spring frees your application from dealing with `javax.jms.JMSException` by rethrowing any JMS exceptions as unchecked `org.springframework.jms.JmsExceptions`.

Let's see how to apply Spring's JMS abstraction.

### 7.4.1 *Sending messages with JMS templates*

In chapter 6 you learned to use Spring's remoting support to perform credit card authorization against the Spring Training payment service. Now you're ready to settle the account and receive payment.

When authorizing payment, it was necessary to wait for a response from the credit card processor, because you needed to know whether or not the credit card's issuing bank would authorize payment. But now that authorization has been granted, payment settlement can be performed asynchronously. There's no need to wait for a response—you can safely assume that the payment will be settled.

The credit card processing system accepts an asynchronous message, sent via JMS, for the purposes of payment settlement. The message it accepts is a `javax.jms.MapMessage` containing the following fields:

- `authCode`—The authorization code received from the credit card processor
- `creditCardNumber`—The credit card number
- `customerName`—The card holder's name
- `expirationMonth`—The month that the credit card expires
- `expirationYear`—The year that the credit card expires

Spring employs a callback mechanism to coordinate JMS messaging. This callback is reminiscent of the JDBC callback described in chapter 4. The callback is made up of two parts: a message creator that constructs a JMS message (`javax.jms.Message`) and a JMS template that actually sends the message.

### Using the template

The first thing to do is to equip the `PaymentServiceImpl` class with a `JmsTemplate` property:

```
private JmsTemplate jmsTemplate;
public void setJmsTemplate(JmsTemplate jmsTemplate) {
  this.jmsTemplate = jmsTemplate;
}
```

The `jmsTemplate` property will be wired with an instance of `org.springframework.jms.core.JmsTemplate` using setter injection. We'll show you how to wire this a little bit later. First, however, let's implement the service-level method that sends the settlement message.

`PaymentServiceImpl` will need a `sendSettlementMessage()` method to send the settlement message to the credit card processor. Listing 7.4 shows how `sendSettlementMessage()` uses the `JmsTemplate` to send the message. (The `PaySettlement` argument is a simple JavaBean containing the fields needed for the message.)

---

**Listing 7.4   Sending a payment settlement via the JMS callback**

```
public void sendSettlementMessage(final PaySettlement settlement) {
    jmsTemplate.send(     <-- Send message

      new MessageCreator() {    <-- Define message creator
        public Message createMessage(Session session)
            throws JMSException {
```

```
            MapMessage message = session.createMapMessage();
            message.setString("authCode",
                settlement.getAuthCode());
            message.setString("customerName",
                settlement.getCustomerName());
            message.setString("creditCardNumber",
                settlement.getCreditCardNumber());
            message.setInt("expirationMonth",
                settlement.getExpirationMonth());
            message.setInt("expirationYear",
                settlement.getExpirationYear());

            return message;
          }
        }
    );
  }
```

Construct
message

The `sendSettlementMessage()` method uses the `JmsTemplate`'s `send()` method to
send the message. This method takes an instance of `org.springframework.`
`jms.core.MessageCreator`, here defined as an anonymous inner class, which constructs the `Message` to be sent. In this case, the message is a `javax.jms.Map-`
`Message`. To construct the message, the `MessageCreator` retrieves values from the
`PaySettlement` bean's properties and uses them to set fields on the `MapMessage`.

### Wiring the template

Now you must wire a `JmsTemplate` into the `PaymentServiceImpl`. The following
XML from the Spring configuration file will do just that:

```
<bean id="paymentService"
    class="com.springinaction.training.service.PaymentServiceImpl">
...
  <property name="jmsTemplate">
    <ref bean="jmsTemplate"/>
  </property>
<bean>
```

The declaration of the `jmsTemplate` bean is as follows:

```
<bean id="jmsTemplate"
    class="org.springframework.jms.core.JmsTemplate">
  <property name="connectionFactory">
    <ref bean="jmsConnectionFactory"/>
  </property>
  <property name="defaultDestination">
    <ref bean="destination"/>
```

```
      </property>
    </bean>
```

Notice that the `jmsTemplate` bean is wired with a JMS connection factory and a default destination. The `connectionFactory` property is mandatory because it is how `JmsTemplate` gets a connection to a JMS provider. In the case of the Spring Training application, the connection factory is retrieved from JNDI, as shown in the following declaration of the `connectionFactory` bean:

```
<bean id="jmsConnectionFactory"
    class="org.springframework.jndi.JndiObjectFactoryBean">
  <property name="jndiName">
    <value>connectionFactory</value>
  </property>
</bean>
```

Wired this way, Spring will use `JndiObjectFactoryBean` (see section 7.1) to look up the connection factory in JNDI using the name `java:comp/env/connection-Factory`. (Of course, this assumes that you have a JMS implementation with an instance of `JMSConnectionFactory` registered in JNDI.)

The `defaultDestination` property defines the default JMS destination (an instance of `javax.jms.Destination`) that the message will be published to. Here it is wired with a reference to the `destination` bean. Just as with the `connection-Factory` bean, the `destination` bean will be retrieved from JNDI using a `Jndi-ObjectFactoryBean`:

```
<bean id="destination"
    class="org.springframework.jndi.JndiObjectFactoryBean">
  <property name="jndiName">
    <value>creditCardQueue</value>
  </property>
</bean>
```

The `defaultDestination` property is optional. But because there's only one JMS destination for credit card messages, it is set here for convenience. If you do not set a default destination, then you must pass a `Destination` instance or the JNDI name of a `Destination` when you call `JmsTemplate`'s `send()` method. For example, you'd use this to specify the JNDI name of the JMS destination in the call to `send()`:

```
jmsTemplate.send(
    "creditCardQueue", new MessageCreator() { … });
```

### Working with JMS 1.0.2

Until now, the `jmsTemplate` bean has been declared to be an instance of `JmsTemplate`. Although it isn't very apparent, this implies that the JMS provider implementation adheres to version 1.1 of the JMS specification. If your JMS provider is 1.0.2-compliant and not 1.1-compliant, then you'll want to use `JmsTemplate102` instead of `JmsTemplate`.

The big difference between `JmsTemplate` and `JmsTemplate102` is that `JmsTemplate102` needs to know whether you're using point-to-point or publish-subscribe messaging. By default, `JmsTemplate102` assumes that you'll be using point-to-point messaging, but you can specify publish-subscribe by setting the `pubSubDomain` property to `true`:

```
<bean id="jmsTemplate"
    class="org.springframework.jms.core.JmsTemplate">
...
  <property name="pubSubDomain">
    <value>true</value>
  </property>
</bean>
```

Other than that, you use `JmsTemplate102` the same as you would `JmsTemplate`.

### Handling JMS exceptions

An important thing to notice about using `JmsTemplate` is that you weren't forced to catch a `javax.jms.JMSException`. Many of `JmsTemplate`'s methods (including `send()`) catch any `JMSException` that is thrown and converts it to an unchecked runtime `org.springframework.jms.JmsException`.

## 7.4.2 Consuming messages

Now suppose that you are writing the code for the receiving end of the settlement process. You're going to need to receive the message, convert it to a `PaySettlement` object, and then pass it on to be processed. Fortunately, `JmsTemplate` can be used for receiving messages as well as sending messages.

Listing 7.5 demonstrates how you might use `JmsTemplate` to receive a settlement message.

> **Listing 7.5   Receiving a `PaySettlement` message**

```
public PaySettlement processSettlementMessages() {
  Message msg = jmsTemplate.receive("creditCardQueue");     ◁─┐  Receive
                                                              └  message
```

```
    try {
      MapMessage mapMessage = (MapMessage) msg;
      PaySettlement paySettlement = new PaySettlement();

      paySettlement.setAuthCode(mapMessage.getString("authCode"));
      paySettlement.setCreditCardNumber(
          mapMessage.getString("creditCardNumber"));
      paySettlement.setCustomerName(
          mapMessage.getString("customerName"));
      paySettlement.setExpirationMonth(
          mapMessage.getInt("expirationMonth"));
      paySettlement.setExpirationYear(                    Map message to
          mapMessage.getInt("expirationYear"));           PaySettlement

      return paySettlement;
    } catch (JMSException e) {
      throw JmsUtils.convertJmsAccessException(e);
    }
  }
```

The `receive()` method of `JmsTemplate` attempts to receive a `Message` from the specified `Destination`. As used earlier, `receive()` will try to receive a message from the `Destination` that has a JNDI name of `creditCardQueue`.

Once the `Message` is received, it is cast to a `MapMessage` and a `PaySettlement` object is initialized with the values from the fields of the `MapMessage`.

By default, `receive()` will wait indefinitely for the message. However, it may not be desirable to have your application block while it waits to receive a message. It'd be nice if you could set a timeout period so that `receive()` will give up after a certain time.

Fortunately, you can specify a timeout by setting the `receiveTimeout` property on the `jmsTemplate` bean. For example:

```
<bean id="jmsTemplate"
    class="org.springframework.jms.core.JmsTemplate">
  <property name="receiveTimeout">
    <value>10000</value>
  </property>
</bean>
```

The `receiveTimeout` property takes a value that is the number of milliseconds to wait for a message. Setting it to `10000` specifies that the `receive()` method should give up after 10 seconds. If no message is received in 10 seconds, the `JmsTemplate` will throw an unchecked `JmsException` (which you may choose to catch or ignore).

### 7.4.3 *Converting messages*

In listing 7.4, the `MessageCreator` instance was responsible for mapping the properties of `PaySettlement` to fields in a `MapMessage`. The `processSettlement()` message in listing 7.5 performs the reverse mapping of a `Message` to a `PaySettlement` object. That'll work fine, but it does result in a lot of mapping code that may end up being repeated every time you need to send or receive a `PaySettlement` message.

To avoid repetition and to keep the send and receive code clean, it may be desirable to extract the mapping code to a separate utility object.

### Converting PaySettlement messages

Although you could write your own utility object to handle message conversion, Spring's `org.springframework.jms.support.converter.MessageConverter` interface defines a common mechanism for converting objects to and from JMS `Messages`.

To illustrate, `PaySettlementConverter` (listing 7.6) implements `Message-Converter` to accommodate the conversion of `PaySettlement` objects to and from JMS `Message` objects.

**Listing 7.6   Convert a `PaySettlement` to and from a JMS `Message`**

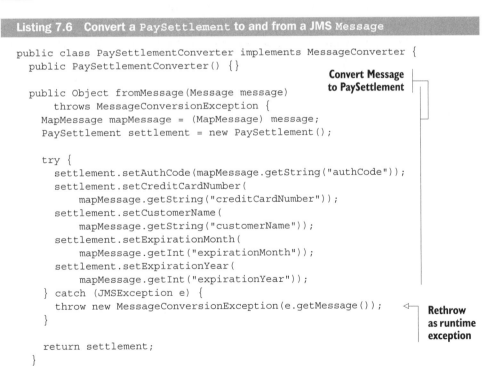

```java
public class PaySettlementConverter implements MessageConverter {
  public PaySettlementConverter() {}
                                                    Convert Message
                                                    to PaySettlement
  public Object fromMessage(Message message)
      throws MessageConversionException {
    MapMessage mapMessage = (MapMessage) message;
    PaySettlement settlement = new PaySettlement();

    try {
      settlement.setAuthCode(mapMessage.getString("authCode"));
      settlement.setCreditCardNumber(
          mapMessage.getString("creditCardNumber"));
      settlement.setCustomerName(
          mapMessage.getString("customerName"));
      settlement.setExpirationMonth(
          mapMessage.getInt("expirationMonth"));
      settlement.setExpirationYear(
          mapMessage.getInt("expirationYear"));
    } catch (JMSException e) {
      throw new MessageConversionException(e.getMessage());    ⟵ Rethrow
    }                                                              as runtime
                                                                   exception
    return settlement;
  }
```

```
public Message toMessage(Object object, Session session)
   throws JMSException, MessageConversionException {

   PaySettlement settlement = (PaySettlement) object;
   MapMessage message = session.createMapMessage();
   message.setString("authCode", settlement.getAuthCode());
   message.setString("customerName",
      settlement.getCustomerName());
   message.setString("creditCardNumber",
      settlement.getCreditCardNumber());
   message.setInt("expirationMonth",
      settlement.getExpirationMonth());           Convert
   message.setInt("expirationYear",             PaySettlement
      settlement.getExpirationYear());             to Message

   return message;
   }
}
```

As its name implies, the `fromMessage()` method is intended to take a `Message` object and convert it to some other object. In this case, the `Message` is converted to a `PaySettlement` object by pulling the fields out of the `MapMessage` and setting properties on the `PaySettlement` object.

The conversion is performed in reverse by the `toMessage()` method. This method takes an `Object` (in this case, assumed to be a `PaySettlement` bean) and sets elements in the `MapMessage` from the properties of the `Object`.

### *Wiring a message converter*

To use the message converter, you first must declare it as a bean in the Spring configuration file:

```
<bean id="settlementConverter" class="com.springinaction.
   ▸ training.service.PaySettlementConverter">
...
</bean>
```

Next, the `JmsTemplate` needs to know about the message converter. You tell it about the `PaySettlementConverter` by wiring it into `JmsTemplate`'s message-Converter property:

```
<bean id="jmsTemplate"
   class="org.springframework.jms.core.JmsTemplate">
...
   <property name="messageConverter">
     <ref bean="settlementConverter"/>
   </property>
</bean>
```

Now that JmsTemplate knows about PaySettlementConverter, you're ready to send messages converted from PaySettlement objects.

### Sending and receiving converted messages

With a converted message wired into PayServiceImpl, the implementation of sendSettlementMessage() becomes significantly simpler:

```
public void sendSettlementMessage(PaySettlement settlement) {
    jmsTemplate.convertAndSend(settlement);
}
```

Instead of calling JmsTemplate's send() method and using a MessageCreator to construct the Message object, you simply call JmsTemplate's convertAndSend() method passing in the PaySettlement object. Under the covers, the convertAndSend() method creates its own MessageCreator instance that uses PaySettlement-Converter to create a Message object from a PaySettlement object.

Likewise, to receive converted messages, you call the JmsTemplate's receiveAndConvert() method (instead of the receive() method) passing the name of the JMS message queue:

```
PaySettlement settlement = (PaySettlement)
    jmsTemplate.receiveAndConvert("creditCardQueue");
```

Other than automatically converting Message objects to application objects, the semantics of receiveAndConvert() are the same as receive().

### Using SimpleMessageConverter

Spring comes with one prepackaged implementation of the MessageConverter interface. SimpleMessageConverter converts MapMessages, TextMessages, and ByteMessages to and from java.util.Map collections, Strings, and byte arrays, respectively.

To use SimpleMessageConverter to convert PaySettlement objects to and from JMS Messages, replace the settlementConverter bean declaration with the following declaration:

```
<bean id="settlementConverter" class="org.springframework.jms.
    support.converter.SimpleMessageConverter">
    ...
</bean>
```

Although this converter's function is quite simple, it may prove useful when your messages are simple and do not correspond directly to an object in your application's domain.

## 7.5 Summary

Even though Spring provides functionality that eliminates much of the need to work with EJBs, there are still many enterprise services that Spring doesn't provide direct replacements for. In those cases, Spring provides abstraction layers that make it easy to wire those services into your Spring-enabled applications.

In this chapter, you've seen how to obtain references to objects that are kept in JNDI. These references could then be wired into bean properties as though they were locally defined beans. This proved to be useful throughout the chapter as you used Spring's JNDI abstraction to look up such things as mail sessions and JMS connection factories.

You've also seen how to send e-mails using Spring's e-mail abstraction and how to schedule tasks using either Java's `Timer` or OpenSymphony's Quartz scheduler.

Finally, you saw how to send and receive asynchronous messages using Spring's JMS abstraction.

In the next chapter, we'll move our focus to the presentation layer of our application, learning how to use Spring's MVC framework to develop web applications.

# Part 3

# Spring in the web layer

Now that you've built the business layer of your application using Spring, it's time to put a face on it.

In chapter 8, "Building the web layer," you'll learn the basics of using Spring MVC, a web framework built within the Spring framework. You will discover how Spring can transparently bind web parameters to your business objects and provide validation and error handling at the same time. You will also see how easy it is to add functionality to your web applications using Spring's interceptors.

Building on the foundation of Spring MVC, chapter 9, "View layer alternatives," shows you how to move beyond JavaServer Pages and use other templating languages such as Velocity and FreeMarker. In addition, you'll see how to use Spring MVC to dynamically produce binary content such as PDF and Excel documents.

Although Spring MVC is a fantastic web framework, you may already have an investment in another framework. In chapter 10, "Working with other web frameworks," you'll see how to integrate Spring into several of the popular web frameworks, such as Struts, Tapestry, and JavaServer Faces.

After you have learned how to use Spring to develop a web application, it is time to secure that application. In chapter 11, "Securing Spring applications," you will learn how to use the Acegi Security System to provide authentication to your web applications. In addition, you will see how to integrate Acegi with your business objects to apply security at the method level as well.

# Building the web layer

As a J2EE developer, you have more than likely developed a web-based application. In fact, for many Java developers web-based applications are their primary focus. If you do have this type of experience, you are well aware of the challenges that come with these systems. Specifically, state management, workflow, and validation are all important features that need to be addressed. None of these are made any easier given the HTTP protocol's stateless nature.

Spring's web framework is designed to help you address these concerns. Using Spring, you can leverage its web framework to automatically populate your model objects from incoming request parameters while providing validation and error handling as well. You can also rely on the framework to help manage the state of the object that is being created by your users through web forms.

It addition to these features, you will find that the entire framework is very modular, with each set of components having specific roles and completely decoupled from the rest of the framework. This allows you to develop the front end of your web application in a very pluggable manner.

With that in mind, let's take a look at how Spring's web framework is put together.

## 8.1  *Getting started with Spring MVC*

Have you ever seen the children's game Mousetrap? It's a crazy game in which the goal is to send a small steel ball over a series of wacky contraptions in order to trigger a mousetrap. The ball goes over all kinds of intricate gadgets, from rolling down a curvy ramp to getting sprung off a teeter-totter[1] to spinning on a miniature Ferris wheel to being kicked out of a bucket by a rubber boot. It goes through of all of this to spring a trap on a poor, unsuspecting mouse.

At first glance, you may think that Spring's MVC framework is a lot like Mousetrap. Instead of moving a ball around through various ramps, teeter-totters, and wheels, Spring moves requests around between a dispatcher servlet, handler mappings, controllers, and view resolvers.

But don't draw too strong of a comparison between Spring MVC and the Rube Goldberg-esque game of Mousetrap. Each of the components in Spring MVC performs a specific purpose. Let's start the exploration of Spring MVC by examining the life cycle of a typical request.

---

[1]  We really felt this book needed *one* more teeter-totter reference (see chapter 5).

### 8.1.1 *A day in the life of a request*

From the time that a request is received by Spring until the time that a response is returned to the client, many pieces of the Spring MVC framework are involved. Figure 8.1 shows the life cycle of a request from start to finish.

The process starts when a client (typically a web browser) sends a request ①. The first component to receive the request is Spring's `DispatcherServlet`. Like most Java-based MVC frameworks, Spring MVC funnels requests through a single *front controller* servlet. A front controller is a common web-application pattern where a single servlet delegates responsibility for a request to other components of an application to perform the actual processing. In the case of Spring MVC, `DispatcherServlet` is the front controller.

The Spring MVC component that is responsible for handling the request is a `Controller`. To figure out which controller should handle the request, `DispatcherServlet` starts by querying one or more `HandlerMappings` ②. A `HandlerMapping` typically performs its job by mapping URL patterns to `Controller` objects.

Once the `DispatcherServlet` has a `Controller` object, it dispatches the request to the `Controller` to perform whatever business logic it was designed to do ③. (Actually, a well-designed `Controller` performs little or no business logic itself and instead delegates responsibility for the business logic to one or more service objects.)

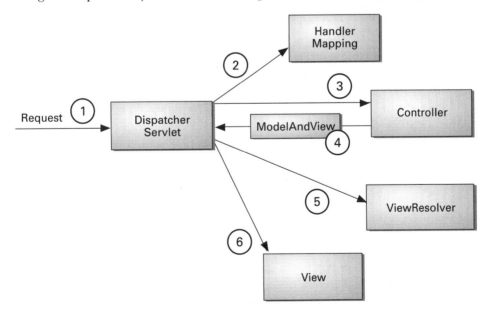

**Figure 8.1   The life cycle of a request in Spring MVC**

Upon completion of business logic, the Controller returns a ModelAndView object ④ to the DispatcherServlet. The ModelAndView can either contain a View object or a logical name of a View object.

If the ModelAndView object contains the logical name of a View, the Dispatcher-Servlet queries a ViewResolver ⑤ to look up the View object that will render the response. Finally, the DispatcherServlet dispatches the request to the View object ⑥ indicated by the ModelAndView object. The View object is responsible for rendering a response back to the client.

We'll discuss each of these steps in detail throughout this chapter. But first things first—you'll need to configure DispatcherServlet to use Spring MVC.

### 8.1.2 Configuring DispatcherServlet

At the heart of Spring MVC is DispatcherServlet, a servlet that functions as Spring MVC's front controller. Like any servlet, DispatcherServlet must be configured in your web application's web.xml file. Place the following <servlet> declaration in your application's web.xml file:

```
<servlet>
  <servlet-name>training</servlet-name>
  <servlet-class>org.springframework.web.servlet.DispatcherServlet
  </servlet-class>
  <load-on-startup>1</load-on-startup>
</servlet>
```

The <servlet-name> given to the servlet is significant. By default, when Dispatcher-Servlet is loaded, it will load the Spring application context from an XML file whose name is based on the name of the servlet. In this case, because the servlet is named training, DispatcherServlet will try to load the application context from a file named training-servlet.xml.

Next you must indicate what URLs will be handled by the DispatcherServlet. Add the following <servlet-mapping> to web.xml to let DispatcherServlet handle all URLs that end in ".htm":

```
<servlet-mapping>
  <servlet-name>training</servlet-name>
  <url-pattern>*.htm</url-pattern>
</servlet-mapping>
```

So, you're probably wondering why we chose this particular URL pattern. It could be because all of the content produced by our application is HTML. It could also be because we want to fool our friends into thinking that our entire application is composed of static HTML files. And it could be that we think ".do" is a silly extension.

But the truth of the matter is that the URL pattern is somewhat arbitrary and we could've chosen any URL pattern for `DispatcherServlet`. Our main reason for choosing "*.htm" is that this pattern is the one used by convention in most Spring MVC applications that produce HTML content.

Now that `DispatcherServlet` is configured in web.xml and given a URL mapping, you are ready to start writing the web layer of your application. However, there's one more thing that we recommend you add to web.xml.

### Breaking up the application context

As we mentioned earlier, `DispatcherServlet` will load the Spring application context from a single XML file whose name is based on its `<servlet-name>`. But this doesn't mean that you can't split your application context across multiple XML files. In fact, we recommend that you split your application context across application layers, as shown in figure 8.2.

As configured, `DispatcherServlet` already loads training-servlet.xml. You could put all of your application's `<bean>` definitions in training-servlet.xml, but eventually that file would become quite unwieldy. Splitting it into logical pieces across application layers can make maintenance easier by keeping each of the Spring configuration files focused on a single layer of the application. It also makes it easy to swap out a layer configuration without affecting other layers (e.g., swapping out a training-data.xml file that uses Hibernate with one that uses iBATIS, for example).

Because `DispatcherServlet`'s configuration file is training-servlet.xml, it makes sense for this file to contain `<bean>` definitions pertaining to controllers and other Spring MVC components. As for beans in the service and data layers, we'd like those beans to be placed in training-service.xml and training-data.xml, respectively.

To ensure that all of these configuration files are loaded, you'll need to configure a context loader in your web.xml file. A context loader loads context

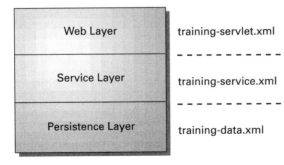

Figure 8.2
**Splitting Spring configuration files across application layers eases maintenance.**

configuration files in addition to the one that `DispatcherServlet` loads. Depending on how you'll be deploying your application, you have two context loaders to choose from: `ContextLoaderListener` and `ContextLoaderServlet`.

Most likely, you'll be deploying to a web container that supports the Servlet 2.3 specification (or higher) and initializes servlet listeners before servlets. If that's the case, you'll want to configure `ContextLoaderListener` in your web.xml file as follows:

```
<listener>
  <listener-class>org.springframework.
      ➡ web.context.ContextLoaderListener</listener-class>
</listener>
```

But if your application is going to be deployed to an older web container that adheres to Servlet 2.2 or if the web container is a Servlet 2.3 container that does *not* initialize listeners before servlets,[2] you'll need to configure `ContextLoader-Servlet` in web.xml like this:

```
<servlet>
  <servlet-name>context</servlet-name>
  <servlet-class>org.springframework.
      ➡ web.context.ContextLoaderServlet</servlet-class>
  <load-on-startup>1</load-on-startup>
</servlet>
```

Regardless of which context loader you end up using, you'll need to tell it the location of the Spring configuration file(s) to load. If not specified otherwise, the context loader will look for a Spring configuration file at /WEB-INF/application-Context.xml. But this location doesn't lend itself to breaking up the application context across application layers, so you'll need to override this default.

You can specify one or more Spring configuration files for the context loader to load by setting the `contextConfigLocation` parameter in the servlet context:

```
<context-param>
  <param-name>contextConfigLocation</param-name>
  <param-value>/WEB-INF/training-service.xml,
      ➡ /WEB-INF/training-data.xml</param-value>
</context-param>
```

---

[2] As far as we know, Oracle OC4J 9.0.3, BEA WebLogic containers up to version 8.1, and IBM WebSphere 5.x are the only Servlet 2.3 containers that do not initialize listeners before servlets. For any other container, `ContextLoaderListener` should work fine.

The `contextConfigLocation` parameter is specified as a comma-separated list of paths (relative to the web application root). As configured here, the context loader will use `contextConfigLocation` to load two context configuration files—one for the service layer and one for the data layer.

`DispatcherServlet` is now configured and ready to dispatch requests to the web layer of your application. But the web layer hasn't been built yet! No problem, though. That's what's up next. We'll start by building controller objects that perform the application logic.

### 8.1.3  Spring MVC in a nutshell

As a quick introduction to the nuts and bolts of Spring MVC, let's build the homepage for the Spring Training application. In order to maintain focus on Spring MVC, we'll keep the homepage as simple as possible. For now, it will do nothing more than display a simple greeting message.

The following list of steps defines the bare minimum that you must do to build the homepage in Spring MVC:

1　Write the controller class that performs the logic behind the homepage.

2　Configure the controller in the `DispatcherServlet`'s context configuration file (training-servlet.xml).

3　Configure a view resolver to tie the controller to the JSP.

4　Write the JSP that will render the homepage to the user.

#### Building the controller

The first step is to build a controller object that will handle the homepage request. `HomeController` (listing 8.1) shows such a controller.

**Listing 8.1　A simple controller to display the Spring Training homepage**

```
public class HomeController implements Controller {
  public ModelAndView handleRequest(HttpServletRequest request,
      HttpServletResponse response) throws Exception {
    return new ModelAndView("home", "message", greeting);
  }

  private String greeting;
  public void setGreeting(String greeting) {
    this.greeting = greeting;
  }
}
```

In Spring MVC, a controller is a class that is ultimately responsible for handling a request and performing some processing on it. In this respect a controller isn't much different than an `HttpServlet` or a Struts `Action`. In fact, you may find the signature of the `handleRequest()` somewhat familiar as it is very similar to the signature of a servlet's `service()` method.

Where a Spring MVC controller differs from a servlet or a Struts `Action` is that it is configured as just another JavaBean in the Spring application context. This means you can take full advantage of dependency injection and Spring AOP with a controller class just as you would any other bean. In the case of `HomeController`, dependency injection is used to configure the greeting that will be displayed on the homepage. In a more complex controller, you might wire service layer beans into the controller so that the controller can delegate responsibility for business logic to a service-layer bean.

The last thing that `handleRequest()` does (in fact, the only thing that it does in the case of `HomeController`) is to return a `ModelAndView` object. A `ModelAndView` object is an object that holds both view information and model data that will be used when rendering the output. All of Spring's controllers return a `ModelAndView` object from their execution methods. In this case, the `ModelAndView` returned tells `DispatcherServlet` to take the user to the view whose name is `home` and to place the greeting object into the "message" field of the model data.

### Configuring the controller bean

Now that the `HomeController` has been written, you must configure it in the `DispatcherServlet`'s context configuration file (which is training-servlet.xml for the Spring Training application). The following chunk of XML declares the `HomeController`:

```
<bean name="/home.htm"
    class="com.springinaction.training.mvc.HomeController">
  <property name="greeting">
    <value>Welcome to Spring Training!</value>
  </property>
</bean>
```

As mentioned before, the `greeting` property should be wired with a message that is to be displayed on the homepage. Here we've kept the greeting simple with "Welcome to Spring Training!"

One thing that may have struck you as odd is that instead of specifying a bean id for the `HomeController` bean, we've specified a `name`. And to make things even weirder, instead of giving it a real name, we've given it a URL pattern of "/ home.htm". Here the `name` attribute is serving double duty as both the name of the bean and a URL pattern for requests that should be handled by this controller. Because the URL pattern has special characters that are not valid in an XML `id` attribute—specifically, the slash (/) character—the `name` attribute had to be used instead of `id`.

When a request comes to `DispatcherServlet` with a URL that ends with "/home.htm", `DispatcherServlet` will dispatch the request to `HomeController` for handling. Note, however, that the only reason that the bean's name attribute is used as the URL pattern is because we haven't configured a handler mapping bean. The default handler mapping used by `DispatcherServlet` is `BeanNameUrlHandler-Mapping`, which uses the base name as the URL pattern. Later (in section 8.2) you'll see how to use some of Spring's other handler mappings that let you decouple a controller's bean name from its URL pattern.

### Declaring a view resolver

One other bean you'll need to declare in training-servlet.xml is a view resolver bean. A view resolver's job is to take the view name returned in the `ModelAndView` and map it to a view. In the case of `HomeController`, we need a view resolver to resolve "home" to a JSP file that renders the home page.

As you'll see in section 8.4, Spring MVC comes with several view resolvers to choose from. But for views that are rendered by JSP, there's none simpler than `InternalResourceViewResolver`:

```
<bean id="viewResolver" class="org.springframework.web.
       servlet.view.InternalResourceViewResolver">
  <property name="prefix">
    <value>/WEB-INF/jsp/</value>
  </property>
  <property name="suffix">
    <value>.jsp</value>
  </property>
</bean>
```

`InternalResourceViewResolver` prefixes the view name returned in the `Model-AndView` with the value of its `prefix` property and suffixed it with the value from its `suffix` property. Since `HomeController` returns a view name of `home` in the `ModelAndView`, `InternalResourceViewResolver` will find the view at /WEB-INF/jsp/home.jsp.

### Creating the JSP

The only thing left to do is create the JSP that renders the output. The simple JSP that follows is sufficient for now:

```
<html>
  <head><title>Spring Training, Inc.</title></head>
  <body>
    <h2>${message}</h2>
  </body>
</html>
```

Be sure to name this JSP "home.jsp" and to place it in the /WEB-INF/jsp folder within your web application. That's where `InternalResourceViewResolver` will try to find it.

### Putting it all together

The homepage is now complete. You've written a controller to handle requests for the homepage, configured it to rely on `BeanNameUrlHandlerMapping` to have a URL pattern of "/home.htm", written a simple JSP that represents the homepage, and configured a view resolver to find the JSP. Now, how does this all fit together?

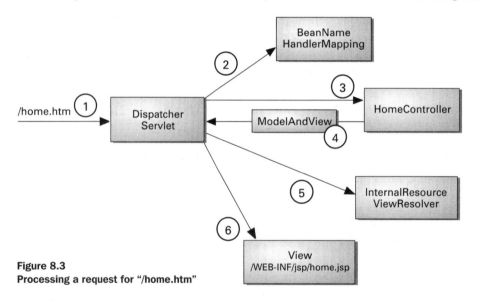

**Figure 8.3**
**Processing a request for "/home.htm"**

Figure 8.3 shows the steps that a request for "/home.htm" will go through given the work done so far.

To recap this process:

1  `DispatcherServlet` receives a request whose URL pattern is "/home.htm".

2  `DispatcherServlet` consults `BeanNameUrlHandlerMapping` to find a controller whose bean name is "/home.htm", finding the `HomeController` bean.

**3** `DispatcherServlet` dispatches the request to `HomeController` for processing.

**4** `HomeController` returns a `ModelAndView` object with a logical view name of home.

**5** `DispatcherServlet` consults its view resolver (configured as `InternalRe-sourceViewResolver`) to find a view whose logical name is home. `Internal-ResourceViewResolver` returns the path to /WEB-INF/jsp/home.jsp.

**6** `DispatcherServlet` forwards the request to the JSP at /WEB-INF/jsp/home.jsp to render the home page to the user.

Now that you've seen the big picture of Spring MVC, let's take a closer look at each of the moving parts involved in servicing a request. We'll start where it all begins—with handler mappings.

## 8.2 *Mapping requests to controllers*

When associating a request with a specific controller, `DispatcherServlet` consults a handler mapping bean. Handler mappings typically map a specific controller bean to a URL pattern.[3] This is similar to how URLs are mapped to servlets using a `<servlet-mapping>` in a web application's web.xml or how `Actions` in Jakarta Struts are mapped to URLs using the `path` attribute of `<action>` in struts-config.xml.

In the previous section, we relied on the fact that `DispatcherServlet` defaults to use `BeanNameUrlHandlerMapping`. `BeanNameUrlHandlerMapping` was fine to get started, but it may not be suitable in all cases. Fortunately, Spring MVC offers several handler mapping implementations to choose from.

All of Spring MVC's handler mappings implement the `org.springframe-work.web.servlet.HandlerMapping` interface. Spring comes prepackaged with three useful implementations of `HandlerMapping`:

- `BeanNameUrlHandlerMapping`—Maps controllers to URLs that are based on the controllers' bean name
- `SimpleUrlHandlerMapping`—Maps controllers to URLs using a property collection defined in the context configuration file

---

[3] Even though the prepackaged implementations of `HandlerMapping` map requests to controllers using URL patterns, the `HandlerMapping` interface is actually much more flexible than that. If you are so inclined, it is possible to write a custom implementation of `HandlerMapping` that chooses its mapping based on cookie values, session state, or other values contained within an `HttpServletRequest` object.

- CommonsPathMapHandlerMapping—Maps controllers to URLs using source-level metadata placed in the controller code

Let's look at how to use each of these handler mappings, starting with Bean-NameUrlHandlerMapping.

### 8.2.1 *Mapping URLs to bean names*

A simple approach for mapping a controller to a URL is to base the URL pattern on the controller's bean name. BeanNameUrlHandlerMapping performs this type of mapping.

For example, suppose that you want the ListCoursesController bean to handle requests to URLs of the form "http://*server-name*/training/listCourses.htm". To set up bean name mapping, you must declare a BeanNameUrlHandlerMapping bean in your context configuration file like this:

```
<bean id="beanNameUrlMapping" class="org.springframework.web.
    servlet.handler.BeanNameUrlHandlerMapping"/>
```

Then you'll need to name your controller beans with the URL pattern that they are to handle. The URL pattern for the ListCoursesController is "listCourses.htm", so you'll need to declare the controller in the context configuration file as follows:

```
<bean name="/listCourses.htm"
    class="com.springinaction.training.mvc.ListCoursesController">
  <property name="courseService">
    <ref bean="courseService"/>
  </property>
</bean>
```

Whenever BeanNameUrlHandlerMapping is asked to resolve a mapping to "/list-CoursesController.htm", it will scour the application context for a bean whose name matches the URL pattern, finding ListCoursesController.

BeanNameUrlHandlerMapping is the default handler mapping used by DispatcherServlet. You shouldn't have to declare it explicitly in your context configuration file, but you may choose to anyway so that it is clear which handler mapping is being used. You may also have to declare it explicitly if you are using multiple handler mappings and need to specify ordering (see section 8.3.4).

Although BeanNameUrlHandlerMapping is quite simple, it creates a coupling between presentation-layer URLs and your controller names. In doing so, it also makes your controller names look odd. As such, we don't recommend using Bean-NameUrlHandlerMapping except in extremely simple applications with only a handful of controllers. In most cases, you are encouraged to consider one of the other handler mappings, such as `SimpleUrlHandlerMapping`.

### 8.2.2 Using SimpleUrlHandlerMapping

`SimpleUrlHandlerMapping` is probably one of the most straightforward of Spring's handler mappings. It lets you map URL patterns directly to controllers without having to name your beans in a special way.

For example, consider the following declaration of `SimpleUrlHandlerMapping` that associates several of the Spring Training application's controllers with their URL patterns:

```
<bean id="simpleUrlMapping" class=
    "org.springframework.web.servlet.handler.SimpleUrlHandlerMapping">
  <property name="mappings">
    <props>
      <prop key="/listCourses.htm">listCoursesController</prop>
      <prop key="/register.htm">registerStudentController</prop>
      <prop key="/displayCourse.htm">displayCourseController</prop>
      <prop key="/login.htm">loginController</prop>
      <prop key="/enroll.htm">enrollController</prop>
    </props>
  </property>
</bean>
```

`SimpleUrlHandlerMapping`'s mappings property is wired with a `java.util.Proper-ties` using `<props>`. The `key` attribute of each `<prop>` element is a URL pattern. Just as with `BeanNameUrlHandlerMapping`, all URL patterns are relative to `Dis-patcherServlet`'s `<servlet-mapping>`. URL. The value of each `<prop>` is the bean name of a controller that will handle requests to the URL pattern.

### 8.2.3 Using metadata to map controllers

The final handler mapping we'll look at is `CommonsPathMapHandlerMapping`. This handler mapping considers source-level metadata placed in a controller's source code to determine the URL mapping. In particular the metadata is expected to be an `org.springframework.web.servlet.handler.commonsattributes.PathMap` attribute compiled into the controller using the Jakarta Commons Attributes compiler.

To use `CommonsPathMapHandlerMapping`, simply declare it as a `<bean>` in your context configuration file as follows:

```
<bean id="urlMapping" class="org.springframework.web.
         servlet.handler.metadata.CommonsPathMapHandlerMapping"/>
```

Then tag each of your controllers with a `PathMap` attribute to declare the URL pattern for the controller. For example, to map `DisplayCourseController` to "/displayCourse.htm", tag `DisplayCourseController` as follows:

```
/**
 * @@org.springframework.web.servlet.handler.
   ➥ commonsattributes.PathMap("/displayCourse.htm")
 */
public class DisplayCourseController
    extends AbstractCommandController {
…
}
```

Finally, you'll need to set up your build to include the Commons Attributes compiler so that the attributes will be compiled into your application code. See chapter 5, section 5.5.2 for details on how to add the attributes compiler to your build.

### 8.2.4 *Working with multiple handler mappings*

As you've seen, Spring comes with several useful handler mappings. But what if you can't (or don't want to) settle on a single handler mapping? For instance, suppose that your application has been simple and you've been using `BeanNameUrl-HandlerMapping`. But it is starting to grow and you'd like to start using `SimpleUrlHandlerMapping` going forward. How can you mix-'n'-match handler mappings during the transition?

As it turns out, all of the handler mapping classes implement Spring's `Ordered` interface. This means that you can declare multiple handler mappings in your application, and set their `order` property to indicate which has precedence with relation to the others.

For example, suppose that you want to use both `BeanNameUrlHandlerMapping` and `SimpleUrlHandlerMapping` alongside each other in the same application. You'd need to declare the handler mapping beans as follows:

```
<bean id="beanNameUrlMapping" class="org.springframework.web.
    ➥ servlet.handler.BeanNameUrlHandlerMapping">
  <property name="order"><value>1</value></property>
</bean>
<bean id="simpleUrlMapping" class="org.springframework.web.
    ➥ servlet.handler.SimpleUrlHandlerMapping">
  <property name="order"><value>0</value></property>
  <property name="mappings">
…
  </property>
</bean>
```

Note that the lower the value of the `order` property, the higher the priority. In this case, `SimpleUrlHandlerMapping`'s `order` is lower than that of `BeanNameUrlHandlerMapping`. This means that `DispatcherServlet` will consult `SimpleUrlHandlerMapping` first when trying to map a URL to a controller. `BeanNameUrlHandlerMapping` will only be consulted if `SimpleUrlHandlerMapping` turns up no results.

Handler mappings map requests to controllers based on the requests' URL patterns. But that's only the beginning of the story. Now let's see how to write controllers—the next step in the life of a request.

## 8.3 *Handling requests with controllers*

If `DispatcherServlet` is the heart of Spring MVC, then controllers are the brains. When implementing the behavior of your Spring MVC application, you extend one of Spring's controller classes. The controller receives requests from `DispatcherServlet` and performs some business functionality on behalf of the user.

If you're familiar with other web frameworks such as Struts or WebWork, you may recognize controllers as being roughly equivalent in purpose to a Struts or WebWork action. One huge difference between Spring controllers and Struts/ WebWork actions, however, is that Spring provides a rich controller hierarchy (as shown in figure 8.4) in contrast to the rather flat action hierarchy of Struts or WebWork.

At first glance, figure 8.4 may seem somewhat daunting. Indeed, when compared to other MVC frameworks such as Jakarta Struts or WebWork, there's a lot more to swallow with Spring's controller hierarchy. But in reality, this perceived complexity is actually quite simple and flexible.

At the top of the controller hierarchy is the `Controller` interface. Any class implementing this interface can be used to handle requests through the Spring MVC framework. To create your own controller all you must do is write a class that implements this interface.

While you could write a class that directly implements the `Controller` interface, you're more likely to extend one of the classes lower in the hierarchy. Whereas the `Controller` interface defines the basic contract between a controller and Spring MVC, the various controller classes provide additional functionality beyond the basics.

The wide selection of controller classes is both a blessing and a curse. Unlike other frameworks that force you to work with a single type of controller object (such as Struts' `Action` class), Spring lets you choose the controller that is most appropriate for your needs. However, with so many controller classes to

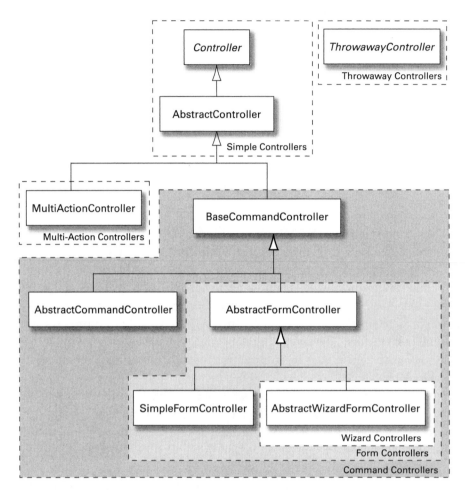

**Figure 8.4  Spring comes with several controllers to choose from.**

choose from, many developers find themselves overwhelmed and don't know how to decide.

To help you in deciding which controller class to extend for your application's controllers, consider table 8.1. As you can see, Spring's controller classes can be grouped into six categories that provide more functionality (and introduce more complexity) as you progress down the table. You may also notice from figure 8.4 that (with the exception of `ThrowawayController`) as you move down the controller hierarchy, each controller builds on the functionality of the controllers above it.

**Table 8.1  Spring MVC's selection of controller classes**

| Controller type | Classes | Useful when... |
|---|---|---|
| Simple | Controller (interface) AbstractController | Your controller is extremely simple, requiring little more functionality than is afforded by basic Java servlets. |
| Throwaway | ThrowawayController | You want a simple way to handle requests as commands (in a manner similar to WebWork Actions). |
| Multi-Action | MultiActionController | Your application has several actions that perform similar or related logic. |
| Command | BaseCommandController AbstractCommandController | Your controller will accept one or more parameters from the request and bind them to an object. Also capable of performing parameter validation. |
| Form | AbstractFormController SimpleFormController | You need to display an entry form to the user and also process the data entered into the form. |
| Wizard | AbstractWizardFormController | You want to walk your user through a complex, multipage entry form that ultimately gets processed as a single form. |

In the sections that follow, we're going to build several controllers that define the web layer of the Spring Training application by extending several of the Controller classes in figure 8.4. Let's start by writing a simple controller based on the `AbstractController` class.

### 8.3.1  *Writing a simple controller*

Many times you'll need to implement a simple controller class that takes no (or few) parameters and just performs some logic and provides model data to be displayed by the view. Consider a controller from the Spring Training application, for example, that lists all available courses being offered. Because this controller will always list all available courses, there's no need for it to take any input. It will simply retrieve a list of courses and make the course available for the view to display.

When controller requirements are this straightforward, you may consider implementing your controller as a subclass of `org.springframework.web.servlet.mvc.AbstractController`. Listing 8.2 shows `ListCoursesController`, a controller that is used to display the course listing.

**Listing 8.2  ListCoursesController is an extremely simple controller.**

```
public class ListCoursesController extends  AbstractController {
  public ModelAndView handleRequestInternal(                          Handle
      HttpServletRequest request, HttpServletResponse response)       request
      throws Exception {
                                                            Retrieve list
    Set courses = courseService.getAllCourses();       ◁┘ of courses

    return new ModelAndView("courseList", "courses", courses);  ◁┐
  }                                                         Return course
                                                            list to view
  private CourseService courseService;
  public void setCourseService(CourseService courseService) {
    this.courseService = courseService;                  Inject the
  }                                                     CourseService
}
```

The handleRequestInternal() method is the main method of execution in an AbstractController. Override this method to implement the functionality of the controller. As you can see, it takes only an HttpServletRequest and HttpServlet-Response as parameters, but you usually won't need to use them. In the case of ListCoursesController, the courses are retrieved using a CourseService (received via setter injection). The course list is then returned to the view wrapped nicely in a ModelAndView object.

### Introducing ModelAndView

The ModelAndView class represents an important concept in Spring MVC. In fact, every controller execution method must return a ModelAndView. So, let's take a moment to understand how this important class works.

A ModelAndView object, as its name implies, fully encapsulates the view and model data that is to be displayed by the view. In the case of ListCoursesController, the ModelAndView object is constructed as follows:

```
new ModelAndView("courseList", "courses", courses);
```

The first parameter of this ModelAndView constructor is the logical name of a view component that will be used to display the output from this controller. Here the logical name of the view is courseList. A view resolver will use this name to look up the actual View object (you'll learn more about Views and view resolvers later in section 8.4).

The next two parameters represent the model object that will be passed to the view. These two parameters act as a name-value pair. The second parameter is the name of the model object given as the third parameter. In this case, the list of courses in the `courses` variable will be passed to the view with a name of `courses`.

### Wiring the controller

Now that you've written `ListCoursesController`, you'll need to configure it in the context configuration file. Remember that since this is a Spring MVC component, you must place it in the training-servlet.xml file. `ListCoursesController` is configured using the following `<bean>` definition:

```
<bean id="ListCoursesController"
    class="com.springinaction.training.mvc.ListCoursesController">
  <property name="courseService">
    <ref bean="courseService"/>
  </property>
</bean>
```

Notice that the `courseService` property is injected with a reference to the `course-Service` object (which is declared in the training-service.xml file).

Basing your controller on `AbstractController` is fine when you don't need a lot of power. But most controllers are going to be more interesting, taking parameters and requiring validation of those parameters. For those circumstances, let's take a step down the controller hierarchy and look at how to work with command controllers.

### 8.3.2 *Processing commands*

It's not unusual for a web request to take one or more parameters that help determine the results. For instance, after viewing a list of available courses, you may want to view more details about that course. The controller that displays course information will need to take the ID of the course as a parameter.

Of course, you could extend `AbstractController` and retrieve the parameters your controller needs from the `HttpServletRequest`. But you would also have to write the logic that binds the parameters to business objects and you'd have to put validation logic in the controller itself. Binding and validation logic really don't belong in the controller.

In the event that your controller will need to perform work based on parameters, your controller class should extend a command controller class such as `org.springframework.web.servlet.mvc.AbstractCommandController`. This controller will automatically bind parameters to a command object and provide hooks for you to plug in validators to ensure that the parameters are valid.

Listing 8.3 shows `DisplayCourseController`, a command controller that is used to display a detail page for a specific course.

**Listing 8.3   A controller to display details of a single course**

```
public class DisplayCourseController
    extends AbstractCommandController {

  public DisplayCourseController() {                      ⟵┐ Set command
    setCommandClass(DisplayCourseCommand.class);          ⟵┘ class
  }

  protected ModelAndView handle(HttpServletRequest request,    ┐ Handle
      HttpServletResponse response, Object command,            │ request
      BindException errors) throws Exception {                 ┘

    DisplayCourseCommand displayCommand =
        (DisplayCourseCommand) command;
                                                           Retrieve course ┐
    Course course = courseService.getCourse(displayCommand.getId());  ⟵┘

    return new ModelAndView("courseDetail", "course", course);
  }

  private CourseService courseService;
  public void setCourseService(CourseService courseService) {
    this.courseService = courseService;
  }
}
```

As with `ListCoursesController`, you'll also need to register `DisplayCourse-Controller` in training-servlet.xml:

```
<bean id="displayCourseController"
    class="com.springinaction.training.mvc.DisplayCourseController">
  <property name="courseService">
    <ref bean="courseService"/>
  </property>
</bean>
```

The `handle()` method of `DisplayCourseController` is the main execution method for `AbstractCommandController`. This method is a bit more interesting than the `handleRequestInternal()` method from `AbstractController`. In addition to an `HttpServletRequest` and an `HttpServletResponse`, `handle()` takes an `Object` that is the controller's command.

A command object is a bean that is meant to hold request parameters for easy access. If you are familiar with Jakarta Struts, you may recognize a command object as being similar to a Struts `ActionForm`. The key difference is that unlike a Struts form bean that must extend `ActionForm`, a Spring command object is a POJO that doesn't need to extend any Spring-specific classes.

In this case, the command object is an instance of `DisplayCourseCommand`, as set in the controller's constructor. `DisplayCourseCommand` is a simple JavaBean with a single property, as follows:

```
public class DisplayCourseCommand {
  public DisplayCourseCommand()  {}

  private Integer id;
  public void setId(Integer id) {
    this.id = id;
  }

  public Integer getId() {
    return id;
  }
}
```

Before the `handle()` method is called, Spring will attempt to match any parameters passed in the request to properties in the command object. Since `Display-CourseCommand` only has an `id` property, this means that if the request has an parameter whose name is `id`, then its value will be set to the command object's `id` property. `DisplayCourseController`'s `handle()` method uses the `id` property of the `DisplayCourseCommand` when looking up the course detail.

Command controllers make it easy to handle requests with request parameters by binding the request parameters to command objects. The request parameters could be given as either URL parameters (as is likely the case with `Display-CourseController`) or as fields from a web-based form.

### 8.3.3 *Processing form submissions*

In a typical web-based application, you're likely to encounter at least one form that you must fill out. When you submit that form, the data that you enter is sent to the server for processing and, once the processing is completed, you are either presented with a success page or are given the form page with errors in your submission that you must correct.

For instance, consider what might happen in the Spring Training application when a new student registers. To begin, students will be given a form to complete where they must enter data about themselves such as their name, address, phone number, etc. When students submit the form, the data that they entered is sent to the server to perform the task of registering them in the Spring Training database.

If everything goes well, they'll receive a page indicating that they are now registered and may begin enrolling in courses. But if a student enters any bad data (perhaps the phone number is in an invalid format), then the form will be redisplayed and the student will have to correct the mistake before resubmitting the form.

When implementing the registration process, you might choose to extend `AbstractController` to display the form and to extend `AbstractCommandController` to process the form. This could certainly work, but would end up being more difficult than necessary. You would have to maintain two different controllers that work in tandem to process student registration. Wouldn't it be simpler to have a single controller handle both form display and form processing?

What you'll need in this case is a form controller. Form controllers take the concept of command controllers a step further by adding functionality to display a form when an HTTP GET request is received and process the form when an HTTP POST is received. Furthermore, if any errors occur in processing the form, the controller will know to redisplay the form so that the user can correct the errors and resubmit.

To illustrate how form controllers work, consider `RegisterStudentController` in listing 8.4.

**Listing 8.4    Registering students through SimpleFormController**

```
public class RegisterStudentController
    extends SimpleFormController {
  public RegisterStudentController() {
    setCommandClass(Student.class);    ⟵ Set command class
  }

  protected void doSubmitAction(Object command)
      throws Exception {
                                                    Process
    Student student = (Student) command;           request
    studentService.enrollStudent(student);
  }

  private StudentService studentService;
  public void setStudentService(StudentService studentService) {
    this.studentService = studentService;
  }
}
```

Although it's not very obvious, `RegisterStudentController` is responsible for both displaying a student registration form and processing the results of that form. The doSubmitAction() method handles the form submission (an HTTP POST request) by passing the command object (which happens to be a Student domain object) to the enrollStudent() method of the injected StudentService reference.

What's not clear from listing 8.4 is how this controller knows to display the registration form. It's also not clear where the user will be taken if the registration is successful. In fact, the doSubmitAction() method doesn't even return a Model-AndView object.

SimpleFormController is designed to keep view details out of the controller's Java code as much as possible. Instead of hard-coding a ModelAndView object, you configure your controller in the context configuration file as follows:

```
<bean id="registerStudentController" class="com.springinaction.
    training.mvc.RegisterStudentController">
  <property name="studentService">
    <ref bean="studentService"/>
  </property>
  <property name="formView">
    <value>newStudentForm</value>
  </property>
  <property name="successView">
    <value>studentWelcome</value>
  </property>
</bean>
```

Just as with the other controllers, the registerStudentController bean is wired with any services that it may need (e.g., studentService). But here you also specify a formView property and a successView property. The formView property is the logical name of a view to display when the controller receives an HTTP GET request or when any errors are encountered. Likewise, the successView is the logical name of a view to display when the form has been submitted successfully. A view resolver (see section 8.4) will use these values to locate the View object that will render the output to the user.

You may have noticed one small limitation with using the doSubmitAction() method. As it spares you from returning a ModelAndView object, it also makes it impossible to send any model data to the view. This may or may not be a problem for you, depending on whether you need to display model data on the success view.

If you need to send data to be displayed by the view, you should override the onSubmit() method instead of doSubmitAction(). For example, suppose that after enrolling the new student you want to send the user to a page where the student's information is displayed. You'll need to send the Student object to the view. To do this, replace the doSubmitAction() from listing 8.4 with the following onSubmit() method:

```
protected ModelAndView onSubmit(Object command,
   BindException errors) throws Exception {

 Student student = (Student) command;
 studentService.enrollStudent(student);

 return new ModelAndView(getSuccessView(),"student", student);
}
```

The onSubmit() method is slightly more complex then doSubmitAction(), but is the only way to go if you need to send model data to the view in a form controller. Like the handler methods from the other controllers, onSubmit() returns a ModelAndView object. But so that you can still configure its success view in the context configuration file, you should call getSuccessView() when setting the view's logical name.

Because of its simplicity, you should favor the doSubmitAction() method over the onSubmit() method unless you need to build your own ModelAndView object to pass model data to the view.

### Validating form input

When RegisterStudentController calls enrollStudent(), it's important to ensure that all of the data in the Student command is valid and complete. You don't want to let students only enter partial information when they register. Nor do you want them to register with an invalid e-mail address or phone number.

The org.springframework.validation.Validator interface accommodates validation for Spring MVC. It is defined as follows:

```
public interface Validator {
  void validate(Object obj, Errors errors);
  boolean supports(Class clazz);
}
```

Implementations of this interface should examine the fields of the object passed into the validate() method and reject any invalid values via the Errors object. The supports() method is used to help Spring determine whether or not the validator can be used for a given class.

StudentValidator (listing 8.5) is a Validator implementation used to validate a Student object.

**Listing 8.5  Validating a Student**

```
public class StudentValidator implements Validator {
  public boolean supports(Class clazz) {
    return clazz.equals(Student.class);
  }

  public void validate(Object command, Errors errors) {
    Student student = (Student) command;
```

```
        ValidationUtils.rejectIfEmpty(
            errors, "login", "required.login", "Login is required");
        ValidationUtils.rejectIfEmpty(
            errors, "password", "required.password",
            "Password is required");
        ValidationUtils.rejectIfEmpty(
            errors, "firstName", "required.firstName",
            "First name is required");
        ValidationUtils.rejectIfEmpty(
            errors, "lastName", "required.lastName",
            "Last name is required");
        ValidationUtils.rejectIfEmpty(
            errors, "address1", "required.address",
            "Address is required");
        ValidationUtils.rejectIfEmpty(
            errors, "city", "required.city", "City is required.");
        ValidationUtils.rejectIfEmpty(
            errors, "state", "required.state", "State is required");
        ValidationUtils.rejectIfEmpty(
            errors, "zip", "required.zip", "Zip is required");
    }
```

**Validate required fields**

```
private static final String PHONE_REGEXP =
"/(\\({0,1})(\\d{3})(\\){0,1})(\\s|-)*(\\d{3})(\\s|-)*(\\d{4})/";

private void validatePhone(String phone, Errors errors) {
  ValidationUtils.rejectIfEmpty(
      errors, "phone", "required.phone", "Phone is required");

  Perl5Util perl5Util = new Perl5Util();
  if(!perl5Util.match(PHONE_REGEXP, phone)) {
    errors.reject("invalid.phone", "Phone number is invalid");
  }
}
```

**Verify phone format**

**Validate required fields**

```
private static final String EMAIL_REGEXP =
  "/^[a-z0-9]+([_\\.-][a-z0-9]+)*@([a-z0-9]+([\\.-][a-z0-9]+)*)
    +\\.[a-z]{2,}$/i";

private void validateEmail(String email, Errors errors) {
  ValidationUtils.rejectIfEmpty(
      errors, "email", "required.email", "E-mail is required");

  Perl5Util perl5Util = new Perl5Util();
  if(!perl5Util.match(EMAIL_REGEXP, email)) {
    errors.reject("invalid.email", "E-mail is invalid");
  }
 }
}
```

**Verify e-mail format**

The only other thing to do is to use the `StudentValidator` with `RegisterStudent-Controller`. You can do this by wiring a `StudentValidator` bean into the `RegisterStudentController` bean:

```
<bean id="registerStudentController" class=
    "com.springinaction.training.mvc.RegisterStudentController">
...
  <property name="validator">
    <bean class="com.springinaction.training.mvc.StudentValidator"/>
  </property>
</bean>
```

When a student registers, if all of the required properties are set and the e-mail and phone number are valid, then `RegisterStudentController`'s `doSubmit-Action()` will be called and the student will be registered. However, if `StudentValidator` rejects any of the fields, then the user will be returned to the form view to correct the errors.

A basic assumption with `SimpleFormController` is that a form is a single page. That may be fine when doing something simple such as registering a student, but what if your forms are complex, requiring the user to answer dozens of questions? In that case, it may make sense to break the form into several subsections and walk them through using a wizard. Let's see how Spring MVC can help you construct wizard forms.

### 8.3.4 Processing complex forms with wizards

Imagine that Spring Training wants to conduct a quality survey among its students after they have completed a course. Among the types of questions asked are ones concerning the quality of the course materials, the effectiveness of the instructor, and the quality of the facilities in which the training was held. This feedback will be used to improve on future course offerings. Your job is to implement this survey as a form to be completed online when students complete the course.

One approach you could take is to throw all of the questions into a single JSP and extend `SimpleFormController` to process and save the data. However, there may be upwards of 40 questions asked on the survey and placing all of those questions on a single page would require users to scroll in their browser to complete it all. If it's hard to use, students will not be as inclined to complete the survey.

Instead of creating one huge survey form, let's break the survey into several subsections and walk the student through the form using a wizard. Suppose that you were to partition the survey questions into four categories:

- General questions, including the title of the course and (optionally) contact information for the student
- Questions regarding the instructor's effectiveness, including an assessment of the instructor's knowledge of the subject matter and willingness to answer questions
- Questions pertaining to the course content and material
- Questions related to the quality and cleanliness of the facilities where the training took place

Breaking it up this way, you are able to step the student through four pages, well defined in purpose, that together complete the entire survey form.

Fortunately, Spring MVC provides org.springframework.web.servlet.mvc. AbstractWizardFormController to help out. AbstractWizardFormController is the most powerful of Spring's controllers. It is a special type of form controller that makes simple work of processing forms that span multiple pages.

### Building a basic wizard controller

To construct a wizard controller, you must extend the AbstractWizardForm-Controller class. FeedbackWizardController (listing 8.6) shows a minimal wizard controller for a feedback survey.

#### Listing 8.6 Receiving student feedback using a wizard controller

```java
public class FeedbackWizardController
    extends AbstractWizardFormController {

  public FeedbackWizardController() {
    setCommandClass(FeedbackSurvey.class);      <-- Set command class
  }

  protected ModelAndView processFinish(HttpServletRequest request,
      HttpServletResponse response, Object command,
      BindException errors) throws Exception {             Finalize form

    FeedbackSurvey feedback = (FeedbackSurvey) command;

    feedbackService.submitFeedback(feedback);    <-- Submit feedback data

    return new ModelAndView("thankyou");     <-- Go to Thank You page
  }

  private FeedbackService feedbackService;
  public void setFeedbackService(FeedbackService feedbackService) {
```

```
        this.feedbackService = feedbackService;
    }
}
```

Just as with any command controller, you must set the command class when using a wizard controller. Here `FeedbackWizardController` has been set to use `FeedbackSurvey` as the command class. `FeedbackSurvey` is just a simple JavaBean that holds survey data.

The only compulsory method of `AbstractWizardFormController` is `process-Finish()`. This method is called to finalize the form when the user has finished completing it (presumably by clicking a Finish button). In `FeedbackWizard-Controller`, `processFinish()` sends the data in the `FeedbackSurvey` object to `submit-Feedback()` on the injected `FeedbackService` object.

Notice, however, that there's nothing in `FeedbackWizardController` that tells you anything about what pages make up the form or in what order the pages appear. That's because `AbstractWizardFormController` handles most of the work involved to manage the workflow of the wizard under the covers. But how does `AbstractWizardFormController` know what pages make up the form?

Some of this may become more apparent when you see how `FeedbackWizard-Controller` is declared in training-servlet.xml:

```
<bean id="feedbackController" class="com.springinaction.
    ➥ training.mvc.FeedbackWizardController">
  <property name="feedbackService">
    <ref bean="feedbackService"/>
  </property>
  <property name="pages">
    <list>
      <value>general</value>
      <value>instructor</value>
      <value>course</value>
      <value>facilities</value>
    </list>
  </property>
</bean>
```

So that the wizard knows which pages make up the form, a list of logical view names is given to the `pages` property. These names will ultimately be resolved into a `View` object by a view resolver (see section 8.4). But for now, just assume that these names will be resolved into the base filename of a JSP (e.g., `general` resolves into `general.jsp`).

While this clears up how `FeedbackWizardController` knows which pages to show, it doesn't tell us how it knows what order to show them in.

### Stepping through form pages

The first page to be shown in any wizard controller will be the first page in the list given to the `pages` property (although this can be overridden by overriding the method). In the case of the feedback wizard, the first page shown will be the `general` page.

To determine which page to go to next, `AbstractWizardFormController` consults its `getTargetPage()` method. This method returns an `int`, which is an index into the zero-based list of pages given to the `pages` property.

The default implementation of `getTargetPage()` determines which page to go to next based on a parameter in the request whose name begins with "_target" and ends with a number. `getTargetPage()` removes the "_target" prefix from the parameter and uses the remaining number as an index into the `pages` list. For example, if the request has a parameter whose name is "_target2", then the user will be taken to the "course" page.

Knowing how `getTargetPage()` works helps you to know how to construct your Next and Back buttons in your wizard's HTML pages. For example, suppose that your user is on the "course" page (index = 2). To create a Next and Back button on the page, all you must do is create submit buttons that are appropriately named with the "_target" prefix:

```
<form method="POST" action="feedback.htm">
...
    <input type="submit" value="Back" name="_target1">
    <input type="submit" value="Next" name="_target3">
</form>
```

When the Back button is clicked, a parameter with its name, "_target1", is placed into the request back to `FeedbackWizardController`. The `getTargetPage()` method will process this parameter's name and send the user to the "instructor" page (index = 1). Likewise, if the Next button is clicked, `getTargetPage()` will process a parameter named "_target3" and decide to send the user to the "facilities" page (index = 3).

The default behavior of `getTargetPage()` is sufficient for most projects. However, if you would like to define a custom workflow for your wizard, you may override this method.

### Finishing the wizard

That explains how to step back and forth through a wizard form. But how can you tell the controller that you have finished and that the `processFinish()` method should be called?

There's another special request parameter called "_finish" that indicates to `AbstractWizardFormController` that the user has finished filling out the form and wants to submit the information for processing. Just like the "_targetX" parameters, "_finish" can be used to create a Finish button on the page:

```
<form method="POST" action="feedback.htm">
  …
    <input type="submit" value="Finish" name="_finish">
</form>
```

When `AbstractWizardFormController` sees the "_finish" parameter in the request, it will pass control to the `processFinish()` method for final processing of the form.

### Canceling the wizard

What if your user is partially through with the survey and decides that they don't want to complete it at this time? How can they abandon their input without finishing the form?

Aside from the obvious answer—closing their browser—you could also add a Cancel button to the form:

```
<form method="POST" action="feedback.htm">
  …
    <input type="submit" value="Cancel" name="_cancel">
</form>
```

As you can see, a Cancel button should have "_cancel" as its name so that, when clicked, the browser will place a parameter into the request called "_cancel". When `AbstractWizardFormController` receives this parameter, it will pass control to the `processCancel()` method.

By default, `processCancel()` throws an exception indicating that the cancel operation is not supported. So, you'll need to override this method so that it (at a minimum) sends the user to whatever page you'd like them to go to when they click Cancel. The following implementation of `processCancel()` sends the user to the home page:

```
protected ModelAndView processCancel(HttpServletRequest request,
    HttpServletResponse response, Object command,
    BindException bindException) throws Exception {

  return new ModelAndView("home");
}
```

If there is any cleanup work to perform upon a cancel, you could also place that code in the `processCancel()` method before the `ModelAndView` is returned.

### *Validating a wizard form a page at a time*

As with any command controller, the data in a wizard controller's command object can be validated using a `Validator` object. However, there's a slight twist.

With other command controllers, the command object is completely populated at once. But with wizard controllers, the command object is populated a bit at a time as the user steps through the wizard's pages. With a wizard, it doesn't make much sense to validate all at once because if you validate too early, you will probably find validation problems that stem from the fact that the user isn't finished with the wizard. Conversely, it is too late to validate when the Finish button is clicked because any errors found may span multiple pages (which form page should the user go back to?).

Instead of validating the command object all at once, wizard controllers validate the command object a page at a time. This is done every time that a page transition occurs by calling the `validatePage()` method. The default implementation of `validatePage()` is empty (i.e., no validation), but you can override it to do your bidding.

To illustrate, suppose that on the "general" page you ask the user for their e-mail address. This field is optional, but if it is entered, it should be in a valid e-mail address format. The following `validatePage()` method shows how to validate the e-mail address when the user transitions away from the "general" page:

```
protected void validatePage(Object command, Errors errors,
    int page) {

  FeedbackSurvey feedback = (FeedbackSurvey) command;
  FeedbackValidator validator =
     (FeedbackValidator) getValidator();

  if(page == 0) {
    validator.validateEmail(feedback.getEmail(), errors);
  }
}
```

When the user transitions from the "general" page (index = 0), the `validate-Page()` method will be called with 0 passed in to the page argument. The first thing `validatePage()` does is get a reference to the `FeedbackSurvey` command object and a reference to the `FeedbackValidator` object. Because there's no need to do e-mail validation from any other page, `validatePage()` checks to see that the user is coming from page 0.

At this point, you could perform the e-mail validation directly in the `validatePage()` method. However, a typical wizard will have several fields that will need to be validated. As such, the `validatePage()` method can become quite unwieldy. We recommend that you delegate responsibility for validation to a fine-grained field-level validation method in the controller's validator object, as we've done here with the call to `FeedbackValidator`'s `validateEmail()` method.

All of this implies that you'll need to set the `validator` property when you configure the controller:

```
<bean id="feedbackController" class="com.springinaction.
         training.mvc.FeedbackWizardController">

  <property name="pages">
    <list>
      <value>general</value>
      <value>instructor</value>
      <value>course</value>
      <value>facilities</value>
    </list>
  </property>
  <property name="feedbackService">
    <ref bean="feedbackServices"/>
  </property>
  <property name="validator">
    <bean class="com.springinaction.training.mvc.
                 FeedbackValidator"/>
  </property>
</bean>
```

An important thing to be aware of is that unlike the other command controllers, wizard controllers never call the standard `validate()` method of their `Validator` object. That's because the `validate()` method validates the entire command object as a whole, whereas it is understood that the command objects in a wizard will be validated a page at a time.

If for some reason you need to perform a wholesale validation of the command object before the `processFinish()` method is called (or any other validation prior to the call to `processFinish()`, for that matter), you should implement the alternate version of `validatePage()`, as follows:

```
protected void validatePage(Object command, Errors errors,
    int page, boolean isFinish) {

  FeedbackSurvey feedback = (FeedbackSurvey) command;
  FeedbackValidator validator =
      (FeedbackValidator) getValidator();

  if(page == 0) {
    validator.validateEmail(feedback.getEmail(), errors);
  }
```

```
    if(isFinish) {
      validator.validate(command, errors);
    }
  }
```

This version of `validatePage()` takes an additional `boolean` argument that is set to `true` if the user has indicated that they have finished with the wizard. (The default implementation of this version of `validatePage()` simply calls the other version.)

### 8.3.5 *Handling multiple actions in one controller*

The controllers you've seen up until now all perform a single task. This may not seem too unusual to you, since this is how controller classes in many web frameworks behave. But one action per controller seems a bit limiting, and you could end up repeating a lot of code between controllers that perform similar or related functionality.

`MultiActionController` is a special type of controller that is able to perform multiple actions, with each action being dispatched to a different method. For example, suppose that you need to revisit `ListCoursesController` from listing 8.2 to return the list of courses, sorted by either the start date or the course name.

One way to have `ListCoursesController` return sorted course lists is to reimplement it as a `MultiActionController`, as shown in listing 8.7.

**Listing 8.7  A multiaction controller that offers three ways to view a course listing**

```
public class ListCoursesController extends MultiActionController {
  public ListCoursesController() {}

  public ModelAndView coursesUnsorted(HttpServletRequest request,      ◁─┐
      HttpServletResponse response) {                        Display unsorted
                                                                course list
    Set courses = courseService.getAllCourses();
    return new ModelAndView("courseList", "courses", courses);
  }
                                                         Display course list
                                                            sorted by date
  public ModelAndView coursesSortedByStartDate(
      HttpServletRequest request, HttpServletResponse response) {   ◁─┘

    List courses = new ArrayList(courseService.getAllCourses());
    Collections.sort(courses, new ByNameComparator());

    return new ModelAndView("courseList", "courses", courses);
  }

  public ModelAndView coursesSortedByName(
```

```
          HttpServletRequest request, HttpServletResponse response) {

    List courses = new ArrayList(courseService.getAllCourses());
    Collections.sort(courses, new ByNameComparator());

    return new ModelAndView("courseList", "courses", courses);
  }

  private CourseService courseService;
  public void setCourseService(CourseService courseService) {
    this.courseService = courseService;
  }

  public class ByDateComparator implements Comparator {
    public int compare(Object o1, Object o2) {
      Course c1 = (Course) o1; Course c2 = (Course) o2;

      return c1.getStartDate().compareTo(c2.getStartDate());
    }
  }

  public class ByNameComparator implements Comparator {
    public int compare(Object o1, Object o2) {
      Course c1 = (Course) o1; Course c2 = (Course) o2;

      return c1.getName().compareTo(c2.getName());
    }
  }
}
```

**Display course list
sorted by name**

Each of the three course listing methods—coursesUnsorted(), coursesSortedBy-Date(), and coursesSortedByName()—perform very similar functionality. But each one produces the course listing in a different sort order. Each of these methods represents an individual action that can be performed by this single controller.

By default, the method chosen is based on the filename portion of the URL. For example, if ListCoursesController is mapped to a URL pattern of "/courses*.htm", then

- "http://.../coursesUnsorted.htm" will be handled by coursesUnsorted().
- "http://.../coursesSortByDate.htm" will be handled by coursesSortByDate().
- "http://.../coursesSortByName.htm" will be handled by coursesSortByName().

Although this is very straightforward, it's not necessarily the most desirable way to choose which method handles the request. You probably will not want to couple the URL directly to the method name.

### Resolving method names

Fortunately, you're not stuck with this approach to method name resolution. `Multi-ActionController` resolves method names based on a method name resolver. The default method name resolver is `InternalPathMethodNameResolver`, which resolves method names based on URL patterns, as shown earlier. But Spring comes with two other method name resolvers:

- `ParameterMethodNameResolver`—Resolves the execution method name based on a parameter in the request
- `PropertiesMethodNameResolver`—Resolves the name of the execution method by consulting a list of key/value pairs

Regardless of which method name resolver you choose, you'll need to wire it into the `methodNameResolver` property of the `MultiActionController` to override the default:

```
<bean id="multiactionController"
    class="com.springinaction.training.mvc.ListCoursesController">
  <property name="methodNameResolver">
    <ref bean="methodNameResolver"/>
  </property>
</bean>
```

Now which method name resolver should you choose?

If you've ever used Struts' `DispatchAction`, you may like `ParameterMethodNameResolver`. `ParameterMethodNameResolver` configures your `MultiActionController` to behave like `DispatchAction`, choosing which method to call based on a parameter passed into the request. Configure `ParameterMethodNameResolver` as follows:

```
<bean id="methodNameResolver" class="org.springframework.web.
       servlet.mvc.multiaction.ParameterMethodNameResolver">
  <property name="paramName">
    <value>action</value>
  </property>
</bean>
```

The `paramName` property indicates the name of the request parameter that will contain the name of the execution method to choose. In this case, it has been set to `action`. As such, if `ListCoursesController` is mapped to a URL pattern of "listCourses.htm", then

- "http://.../listCourses.htm?action=coursesUnsorted" will be handled by `coursesUnsorted()`.

- "http://…/listCourses.htm?action=coursesSortByDate" will be handled by `coursesSortByDate()`.

- "http://…/listCourses.htm?action=coursesSortByName" will be handled by `coursesSortByName()`.

Likewise, it makes it possible to present the choice to the user using an HTML form. For example:

```
<form action="listCourses.htm">
…
Sort by:  <select name="action">
    <option value="coursesUnsorted">Unsorted</option>
    <option value="coursesSortByDate">Date</option>
    <option value="coursesSortByName">Name</option>
  </select>
…
</form>
```

Another approach to method name resolution is to map URL patterns to method names. You can do this using `PropertiesMethodNameResolver`:

```
<bean id="methodNameResolver" class="org.springframework.web.
      servlet.mvc.multiaction.PropertiesMethodNameResolver">
  <property name="mappings">
    <props>
      <prop key="/courseList.htm">coursesUnsorted</prop>
      <prop key="/coursesByDate.htm">coursesSortByDate</prop>
      <prop key="/coursesByName.htm">coursesSortByName</prop>
    </props>
  </property>
</bean>
```

Using `PropertiesMethodNameResolver` is very similar to using `SimpleUrlHandler-Mapping`, except that instead of mapping a URL pattern to a particular controller, `PropertiesMethodNameResolver` goes a step further by mapping the URL to a method in the multiaction controller. `PropertiesMethodNameResolver` is also the most sophisticated of the method name resolvers because it completely decouples the name of the execution method from the view.

The controllers you've seen up until now are all part of the same hierarchy that is rooted with the `Controller` interface. Even though the controllers all get a bit more complex (and more powerful) as you move down the hierarchy, all of the controllers that implement the `Controller` interface are somewhat similar. But before we end our discussion of controllers, let's take a look at another controller that's very different than the others—the throwaway controller.

### 8.3.6 *Working with Throwaway controllers*

One last controller that you may find useful is a *throwaway controller*. Despite the dubious name, throwaway controllers can be quite useful and easy to use. Throwaway controllers are significantly simpler than the other controllers, as evidenced by the ThrowawayController interface:

```
public interface ThrowawayController {
  ModelAndView execute() throws Exception;
}
```

To create your own throwaway controller, all you must do is implement this interface and place the program logic in the excecute() method. Quite simple, isn't it?

But hold on. How are parameters passed to the controller? The execution methods of the other controllers are given HttpServletRequest and command objects to pull the parameters from. If the execute() method doesn't take any arguments, how can your controller process user input?

You may have noticed in figure 8.4 that the ThrowawayController interface is not even in the same hierarchy as the Controller interface. This is because throwaway controllers are very different than the other controllers. Instead of being given parameters through an HttpServletRequest or a command object, throwaway controllers act as their own command object. If you have ever worked with WebWork, this may seem quite natural because WebWork actions behave in a similar same way.

As an illustration, let's rewrite DisplayCourseController from listing 8.3 to be a throwaway controller. The new throwaway DisplayCourseController is shown in listing 8.8.

#### Listing 8.8 Displaying course information using a throwaway controller

```
public class DisplayCourseController
    implements ThrowawayController {

  private Integer id;
  public void setId(Integer id) { this.id = id; }    ◁— Set id

  public ModelAndView execute() throws Exception {
    Course course = courseService.getCourse(id);

    return new ModelAndView("courseDetail", "course", course);
  }

  private CourseService courseService;
  public void setCourseService(CourseService courseService) {
```

Load course
information

```
    this.courseService = courseService;
  }
}
```

Before this new `DisplayCourseController` handles the request, Spring will call the `setId()` method, passing in the value of the `id` request parameter. Once in the `execute()` method, `DisplayCourseController` simply passes `id` to `course-Service.getCourse()`. One thing that remains the same as the other controllers is that the `execute()` method must return a `ModelAndView` object when it has finished.

You also must declare throwaway controllers in the `DispatcherServlet`'s context configuration file. There's only one small difference, as shown here where `DisplayCourseController` is configured:

```
<bean id="displayCourseController"
    class="com.springinaction.training.mvc.DisplayCourseController"
    singleton="false">
  <property name="courseService">
    <ref bean="courseService"/>
  </property>
</bean>
```

Notice that the `singleton` attribute has been set to `false`. This is where throwaway controllers get their name. By default all beans are singletons, and so unless you set `singleton` to `false`, `DisplayCourseController` will end up being recycled between requests. This means its properties (which should reflect the request parameter values) may also be reused. Setting singleton to `false` tells Spring to throw the controller away after it has been used and to instantiate a fresh instance for each request.

There's only one more thing you must do to be able to use throwaway controllers. `DispatcherServlet` knows how to dispatch requests to controllers by using a *handler adapter*. The concept of handler adapters is something that you usually don't need to worry about because `DispatcherServlet` uses a default handler adapter that dispatches to controllers in the `Controller` interface hierarchy.

But because `ThrowawayController` isn't in the same hierarchy as `Controller`, you must tell `DispatcherServlet` to use a different handler adapter. Specifically, you must configure `ThrowawayControllerHandlerAdapter` as follows:

```
<bean id="throwawayHandler"class="org.springframework.web.
    servlet.mvc.throwaway.ThrowawayControllerHandlerAdapter"/>
```

By just declaring this bean, you are telling `DispatcherServlet` to replace its default handler adapter with `ThrowawayControllerHandlerAdapter`. But since you will probably use both throwaway controllers and regular controllers alongside each other in the same application, you will still need DispatcherServlet to use its regular handler adapter as well. So, you must also declare SimpleController-HandlerAdapter as follows:

```
<bean id="simpleHandler" class="org.springframework.web.
    servlet.mvc.SimpleControllerHandlerAdapter"/>
```

Declaring both handler adapters lets you mix both types of controllers in the same application.

Regardless of what functionality your controllers perform, ultimately they'll need to return some results to the user. For example, if a student surfs to the URL that is mapped to ListCoursesController they'll probably expect to see a list of courses in their browser when the controller has finished processing the request.

## 8.4 *Resolving views*

As you saw in the previous section, most of Spring MVC's controllers return ModelAndView objects from their main execution method. You saw how model objects are passed to the view through the ModelAndView object, but we deferred discussion of how the logical view name is used to determine which view will render the results to the user.

In Spring MVC, a view is a bean that renders results to the user. How it performs the rendering depends on the type of view you'll use. Most likely you'll want to use JavaServer Pages (JSP) to render the results, so that's what we'll assume in this chapter. In chapter 9, you'll see how to use alternate views with Spring MVC, such as Velocity and FreeMarker templates or even views that produce PDF and Microsoft Excel documents.

The big question at this point is how a logical view name given to a ModelAnd-View object gets resolved into a View bean that will render output to the user. That's where view resolvers come into play.

A view resolver is any bean that implements org.springframework.web.servlet.ViewResolver. Spring MVC regards these beans as special and consults them when trying to determine which View bean to use.

Spring comes with four implementations of ViewResolver:

- InternalResourceViewResolver—Resolves logical view names into View objects that are rendered using template file resources (such as JSPs and Velocity templates)

- `BeanNameViewResolver`—Resolves logical view names into `View` beans in the `DispatcherServlet`'s application context

- `ResourceBundleViewResolver`—Resolves logical view names into `View` objects contained in a `ResourceBundle`

- `XmlViewResolver`—Resolves `View` beans from an XML file that is separate from the `DispatcherServlet`'s application context

Let's take a look at each of these view resolvers, starting with the one you'll most likely use: `InternalResourceViewResolver`.

### 8.4.1 *Using template views*

Odds are good that most of the time your controllers won't be rendering their output as a result of a custom `View` object. Instead, you'll probably use a template (JSP, Velocity, FreeMarker, etc.) to define how results are presented to your user.

For example, suppose that after `DisplayCourseController` is finished, you'd like to display the course information using the following JSP:

```
<%@ page contentType="text/html; charset=UTF-8" %>
<%@ taglib uri="http://java.sun.com/jsp/jstl/core" prefix="c" %>
<%@ taglib uri="http://java.sun.com/jsp/jstl/fmt" prefix="fmt" %>

<html>
  <head>
    <title>Course: ${course.id}/${course.name}</title>
  </head>

  <body>
    <h2>${course.name}</h2>
    <b>ID: </b>
      <fmt:formatNumber value="${course.id}" pattern="000000"/><br>
    <b>Instructor: </b>
      ${course.instructor.firstName} ${course.instructor.lastName}
      <br>
    <b>Starts: </b>
      <fmt:formatDate value="${course.startDate}" type="date"
        dateStyle="full"/><br>
    <b>Ends: </b>
      <fmt:formatDate value="${course.endDate}" type="date"
        dateStyle="full"/><br>
    <br>
    ${course.description}
    <br>
    <br>
    <a href="enroll.htm?courseId=${course.id}">
        Enroll in course
    </a><br>
```

```
    <a href="listCourses.htm">Return to course list</a>
  </body>
</html>
```

Knowing that `DisplayCourseController`'s concludes with the following return...

```
return new ModelAndView("courseDetail", "course", course);
```

...how can you tell Spring MVC that the logical view name `courseDetail` means to use the JSP page above to render the results?

`InternalResourceViewResolver` resolves a logical view name into a `View` object that delegates rendering responsibility to a template located in the web application's context. It does this by taking the logical view name returned in a `ModelAndView` object and surrounding it with a prefix and a suffix to arrive at the path of a template within the web application.

Let's say that you've placed all of the JSPs for the Spring Training application in the /WEB-INF/jsp/ directory. Given that arrangement, you'll need to configure an `InternalResourceViewResolver` bean in training-servlet.xml as follows:

```
<bean id="viewResolver" class="org.springframework.web.
        servlet.view.InternalResourceViewResolver">
  <property name="prefix"><value>/WEB-INF/jsp/</value></property>
  <property name="suffix"><value>.jsp</value></property>
</bean>
```

When `InternalResourceViewResolver` is asked to resolve a view, it takes the logical view name, prefixes it with "/WEB-INF/jsp/", and suffixes it with ".jsp" to arrive at the path of the JSP that will render the output. It then hands that path over to a `View` object that dispatches the request to the JSP.

So, when `DisplayCourseController` returns a `ModelAndView` object with `courseDetail` as the logical view name, it ends up resolving that view name to the path of a JSP:

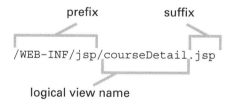

`InternalResourceViewResolver` then loads a `View` object with the path of the JSP. This implies that the course detail JSP must be named "courseDetail.jsp".

By default the `View` object is an `InternalResourceView`, which simply dispatches the request to the JSP to perform the actual rendering. But since

courseDetail.jsp uses JSTL tags, you may choose to substitute `InternalResource-`
`View` with `JstlView` by setting `InternalResourceViewResolver`'s `viewClass` property as follows:

```
<bean id="viewResolver" class="org.springframework.web.
        servlet.view.InternalResourceViewResolver">
  <property name="viewClass">
    <value>org.springframework.web.servlet.view.JstlView</value>
  </property>
  <property name="prefix"><value>/WEB-INF/jsp/</value></property>
  <property name="suffix"><value>.jsp</value></property>
</bean>
```

`JstlView` dispatches the request to a JSP just like `InternalResourceView`. However it also exposes JSTL-specific request attributes so that you can take advantage of JSTL's internationalization support.

Although `InternalResourceViewResolver` is quite easy to use, it may not be the most appropriate view for all circumstances. It assumes that your view is defined in a template file within the web application. That may be the case in most situations, but not always. Let's look at some other ways to resolve views.

### 8.4.2  *Resolving view beans*

As you'll recall from listing 8.2, `ListCoursesController` retrieves a list of available courses using its injected `CourseService`. Once finished, it sends the list of courses to the view to be rendered by returning the following `ModelAndView` object:

```
new ModelAndView("courseList", "courses", courses);
```

When you first looked at listing 8.2, you may have assumed that the `courseList` view would be rendered by a JSP. However, there's nothing about `ListCourses-` `Controller` that implies a JSP view at all. What if instead of rendering an HTML page using a JSP, you wanted to list all of the available courses in a PDF document?

In chapter 9 you'll learn how to extend `AbstractPdfView` to produce PDF documents. But for now, pretend that you've already written `CourseListPdfView`, an extension of `AbstractPdfView` that produces a PDF listing of available courses.

Since the course listing isn't represented by a JSP (or any other resource) in the web application, `InternalResourceViewResolver` isn't going to be of much help. Instead, you're going to have to choose one of Spring's other view resolvers.

`BeanNameViewResolver` is a view resolver that matches logical view names up with names of beans in the application context. To use `BeanNameViewResolver`, simply declare it as a `<bean>` in the context configuration file:

```
<bean id="beanNameViewResolver" class=
    "org.springframework.web.servlet.view.BeanNameViewResolver"/>
```

Now when a controller returns a `ModelAndView` with a logical view name of `courseList`, `BeanNameViewResolver` will look for a bean named `courseList`. This means you must register `CourseListPdfView` in the context configuration file as follows:

```
<bean id="courseList" class=
    "com.springinaction.training.mvc.CourseListPdfView"/>
```

### Declaring view beans in a separate XML file

Another way to resolve View objects by their bean name is to use `XmlFileView-Resolver`. `XmlFileViewResolver` works much like `BeanNameViewResolver`, but instead of looking for `View` beans in the main application context, it consults a separate XML file. To use `XmlFileViewResolver`, add the following XML to your context configuration file:

```
<bean id="xmlFileViewResolver" class="org.springframework.web.
    ➥ servlet.view.XmlFileViewResolver">
  <property name="location">
    <value>/WEB-INF/training-views.xml</value>
  </property>
</bean>
```

By default, `XmlFileViewResolver` looks for `View` definitions in /WEB-INF/views.xml, but here we've set the `location` property to override the default with "/WEB-INF/training-views.xml."

`XmlFileViewResolver` is useful if you end up declaring more than a handful `View` beans in `DispatcherServlet`'s context configuration file. To keep the main context configuration file clean and tidy, you may separate the `View` declarations from the rest of the beans.

### Resolving views from resource bundles

Yet another way of resolving `Views` by name is to use `ResourceBundleViewResolver`. Unlike `BeanNameViewResolver` and `XmlFileViewResolver`, `ResourceBundleViewResolver` manages view definitions in a properties file instead of XML.

By employing properties files, `ResourceBundleViewResolver` has an advantage over the other view resolvers with regard to internationalization. Whereas the other view resolvers always resolved a logical view name to a single `View` implementation, `ResourceBundleViewResolver` could return a different `View` implementation for the same logical view name, based on the user's `Locale`.

For example, suppose that Spring Training, Inc. were to begin offering courses in Paris, France, and Berlin, Germany, in addition to their current selection of courses offered in the United States. Oddly, the French prefer to receive course listings in Microsoft Excel while the Germans prefer their course listing in plain HTML. Meanwhile, American students prefer PDF course listings.

Fortunately, `ResourceBundleViewResolver` can help keep everyone happy. To start, configure `ResourceBundleViewResolver` in training-servlet.xml as follows:

```
<bean id="bundleViewResolver" class="org.springframework.web.
    servlet.view.ResourceBundleViewResolver">
  <property name="basename">
    <value>views</value>
  </property>
</bean>
```

The `basename` property is used to tell `ResourceBundleViewResolver` how to construct the names of the properties files that contain `View` definitions. Here it has been set to `views`, which means that the `View` definitions could be in views.properties (by default), views_en_US.properties (for English-speaking students in the United States), views_fr_FR.properties (for French students), or views_de_DE.properties (for German students).

Next you'll need to set up the properties files for each locale. Starting with the default, let's assume that most of the students will be based in the United States and will prefer PDF course listings. Place the following line in both views.properties and views_en_US.properties:

```
courseList.class=com.springinaction.training.mvc.CourseListPdfView
```

The name of this property can be broken down into two parts. The first part is `courseList`, which is the logical name of the `View` as returned in `ModelAndView`. The second part, `class`, indicates that you are setting the class name of the `View` implementation that should render the output for the `courseList` view (in this case, `CourseListPdfView`).

For our French students, who prefer Excel spreadsheet listings of courses, you'll need to add the following to views_fr_FR.properties:

```
courseList.class=com.springinaction.training.mvc.CourseListExcelView
```

Again, this property tells `ResourceBundleViewResolver` that `CourseListExcelView` is the `View` implementation to use when rendering the output for the `courseList` view.

Finally, for the German students, you'll need to set up views_de_DE.properties to use a JSP-based `View` as follows:

```
courseList.class=org.springframework.web.servlet.view.JstlView
courseList.url=/WEB-INF/jsp/courseList.jsp
```

Here the `courseList.class` property has been set to use a `JstlView`. `JstlView`, like `InternalResourceView`, uses a JSP contained in the web application to render the output to the user. But `JstlView` also adds support for internationalization by taking advantage of JSTL's internationalization support.

Notice that in addition to `courseList.class`, you must also set `course-List.url`. This effectively calls the `setUrl()` method of `JstlView` to specify the location of the JSP file. (This wasn't necessary with `CourseListExcelView` or `CourseListPdfView` because those views aren't template-driven.)

`ResourceBundleViewResolver` offers a powerful way of resolving views based on locale. Instead of merely returning the same view for all users, `ResourceBundle-ViewResolver` makes it possible to offer a different view of the same information based on a user's language and location.

Now that you have seen four different view resolvers that come with Spring, which one do you choose? Let's look at some guidelines that may help you decide.

### 8.4.3 *Choosing a view resolver*

Many projects rely on JSP (or some other template language) to render the view results. Assuming that your application isn't internationalized or that you won't need to display a completely different view based on a user's locale, we recommend `InternalResourceViewResolver` because it is simply and tersely defined (as opposed to the other view resolvers that require you to explicitly define each view).

If, however, your views will be rendered using a custom `View` implementation (e.g., PDF, Excel, images, etc.), you'll need to consider one of the other view resolvers. We favor `BeanNameViewResolver` and `XmlFileViewResolver` over `Resource-BundleViewResolver` because they let you define your `View` beans in a Spring context configuration XML file.

Given the choice between `BeanNameViewResolver` and `XmlFileViewResolver`, we would settle on `BeanNameViewResolver` only when you have a handful of `View` beans that would not significantly increase the size of `DispatcherServlet`'s context file. If the view resolver is managing a large number of `View` objects, we'd choose `XmlFileViewResolver` to separate the `View` bean definitions into a separate file.

In the rare case that you must render a completely different view depending on a user's locale, you have no choice but to use `ResourceBundleViewResolver`.

### *Using multiple view resolvers*

Consider the case where most of an application's views are JSP-based, but only a handful require one of the other view resolvers? For example, most of the Spring

Training application will use JSPs to render output, but (as you'll see in chapter 9) some responses will render PDF and Excel output. Must you choose a BeanName-ViewResolver or XmlFileViewResolver and explicitly declare all of your views just to handle the special cases of PDF and Excel?

Fortunately, you aren't limited to choosing only one view resolver for your application. To use multiple view resolvers, simply declare all of the view resolver beans you will need in your context configuration file. For example, to use both InternalResourceViewResolver (for your JSPs) and XmlFileViewResolver (for everything else) together, declare them as follows:

```
<bean id="viewResolver" class=
    "org.springframework.web.servlet.view.InternalResourceViewResolver">
  <property name="prefix"><value>/WEB-INF/jsp/</value></property>
  <property name="suffix"><value>.jsp</value></property>
  <property name="order"><value>1</value></property>
</bean>
<bean id="xmlFileViewResolver" class=
    "org.springframework.web.servlet.view.XmlFileViewResolver">
  <property name="location">
    <value>/WEB-INF/views.xml</value>
  </property>
  <property name="order"><value>2</value></property>
</bean>
```

Because it's quite possible that more than one view resolver may be able to resolve the same logical view name, you should set the order property on each of your view resolvers to help Spring determine which resolver has priority over the others when a logical view name is ambiguous among more than one resolver. As shown here, the InternalResourceViewResolver has a lower order than the XmlFileViewResolver, so in the event of ambiguity InternalResource-ViewResolver wins.

## 8.5 *Using Spring's bind tag*

Now that you are handling requests and forwarding them to JSPs, you will need to access the model data in order to display it on the page. Fortunately, Spring provides a tag library for doing this very thing. This allows you to not only see your command objects and all of their properties, but any error messages associated with these properties as well.

In order to take advantage of this tag library, you must first register it in your application. Spring comes with a tag library descriptor (TLD) file named spring.tld. Place this file under the WEB-INF directory in your web application. Next, register the tag library in your web.xml file:

```
<taglib>
  <taglib-uri>/spring</taglib-uri>
  <taglib-location>/WEB-INF/spring.tld</taglib-location>
</taglib>
```

The Spring tag library is now ready to be used in your JSPs. The `<spring-bind>` tag is what you will use to access command objects and any error messages associated with them. This tag has only one attribute—`path`—that indicates the bean or bean property being used. For example, to access the `firstName` property of a `Student` object, you would set the `path` attribute to `student.firstName`. This is made available through a `org.springframework.web.servlet.support.Bind-Status` object that is placed in `page` scope with the name `status`. This object has three properties that will be of use to you on a JSP page:

- `expression`—The expression used to retrieve the property. For example, if you are using this tag to access the `firstName` property of a `Student`, the expression property would have a value of `firstName`.

- `value`—The value, as a `String`, of the property. If the property is not a `String`, it will be converted by the `PropertyEditor` associated with the property.

- `errorMessaages`—An array of `Strings` that are the error messages associated with this property.

Listing 8.9 shows how you would use this tag on a form for registering a `Student`.

**Listing 8.9 Populating a form using the `<spring-bind>` tag**

```
<%@ taglib prefix="c" uri="http://java.sun.com/jstl/core" %>
<%@ taglib prefix="spring" uri="/spring" %>
...
<form method="POST" action="/registerStudent.htm">
<spring:bind path="student.firstName">      ◁┐ Bind to firstName       Set input name
First name:                                     property               to status
<input type="text"                                                     expression
       ➡ name="<c:out value="${status.expression}"/>"        ◁┘
       ➡ value="<c:out value="${status.value}"/>">          ◁  Bind input value
</spring:bind>                                                    to status value
...
</form>
...
```

In this example, we use both the `expression` and `value` properties of the status object. Notice that we use the `expression` value to set the name of our form input tag. Doing so will allow Spring to automatically map the form input field to our

Student object when the form is submitted. Using the `value` property as the value of the form element also has its benefits. This property will display the current value of the field, which will likely be the value of that property. However, this could also be a rejected value from a previous form submission, such as a date String improperly formatted. This can be extremely useful so that you can display rejected values to the user to they can see what they did wrong and correct it.

How exactly will users know what they did wrong? This is where the `errorMessages` property comes in. As we said, this is an array `Strings` that are the error messages for a particular property. But perhaps showing an error message for each property is a little too fine grained. You also have the ability to bind to the actual command objects and display all error messages associated with this object, including any errors associated with a particular property. Listing 8.10 shows how you would do this.

---

**Listing 8.10  Displaying error message using `<spring-bind>` tag**

```
<%@ taglib prefix="c" uri="http://java.sun.com/jstl/core" %>
<%@ taglib prefix="spring" uri="http://www.springframework.org/tags" %>
...
<form method="POST" action="/registerStudent.htm">
<spring:bind path="student">      <--  Bind to Student
<c:forEach items="${status.errorMessages}"    <--  Iterate over error messages
     var="errorMessage">
  <font class="error">                         Show error
    <c:out value="${errorMessage}"/><br>       message
  </font>
</c:forEach>      <--  Iterate over error messages
</spring:bind>
...
</form>
...
```

---

Now instead of binding to a specific property, we are binding directly to our command object. This way we can iterate over every error message associated with our `Student` object. This is important because not every error message has to be associated with a particular property.

Now you have a way for accessing your model objects from your JSP with using Spring MVC. Now let's take a look at what to do when things go wrong.

## 8.6 *Handling exceptions*

There's a bumper sticker that says "Failure is not an option: It comes with the software." Behind the humor of this message is a universal truth. Things don't always go well in software. When an error happens (and it inevitably *will* happen), do you want your application's users to see a stack trace or a friendlier message? How can you gracefully communicate the error to your users?

SimpleMappingExceptionResolver comes to the rescue when an exception is thrown from a controller. Use the following <bean> definition to configure SimpleMappingExceptionResolver to gracefully handle any java.lang.Exeptions thrown from Spring MVC controllers:

```
<bean id="exceptionResolver" class="org.springframework.web.
       servlet.handler.SimpleMappingExceptionResolver">
  <property name="exceptionMappings">
    <props>
      <prop key="java.lang.Exception">friendlyError</prop>
    </props>
  </property>
</bean>
```

The exceptionMappings property takes a java.util.Properties that contains a mapping of fully qualified exception class names to logical view names. In this case, the base Exception class is mapped to the View whose logical name is friendlyError so that if any errors are thrown, users won't have to see an ugly stack trace in their browser.

When a controller throws an Exception, SimpleMappingExceptionResolver will resolve it to friendlyError which in turn will be resolved to a View using whatever view resolver(s) are configured. If the InternalResourceViewResolver from section 8.4.1 is configured, then perhaps the user will be sent to the page defined in /WEB-INF/jsp/friendlyError.jsp.

## 8.7 *Summary*

The Spring framework comes with a powerful and flexible web framework that is itself based on Spring's tenets of loose-coupling, inversion of control, and extensibility. In this chapter, you've been taken on a whirlwind tour of all of the moving parts that make up the web layer of a Spring MVC application.

At the beginning of a request, Spring offers a variety of handler mappings that help to choose a controller to process the request. You are given a choice to map URLs to controllers based on the controller bean's name, a simple URL-to-controller mapping, or source-level metadata.

To process a request, Spring provides a wide selection of controller classes with complexity ranging from the very simple `Controller` interface all the way to the very powerful wizard controller and several complex layers in between, letting you choose a controller with an appropriate amount of power (and no more complexity than required). This sets Spring apart from other MVC web frameworks such as Struts and WebWork, where your choices are limited to only one or two `Action` classes.

On the return trip to the client, Spring MVC's view resolvers let you choose a `View` to render the results of the request as output to the user. As with Spring MVC's handler mapping, you are afforded several view resolvers, each providing a different scheme for choosing a `View`, including finding views by the `View` bean's name, from the web application's resource directory, or from a `ResourceBundle`.

All in all, Spring MVC maintains a loose coupling between how a controller is chosen to handle a request and how a view is chosen to display output. This is a powerful concept, allowing you to mix-'n'-match different Spring MVC parts to build a web layer most appropriate to your application.

In the next chapter, we'll build on Spring MVC by taking the view layer beyond JSP. You'll learn how to use alternate template languages such as Velocity and FreeMarker. And you'll also learn how to dynamically produce binary output, including PDF documents, Excel spreadsheets, and images.

*View layer alternatives*

9

**This chapter covers**

- Using Velocity templates
- Integrating with FreeMarker
- Working with Jakarta Tiles
- Generating PDF and Excel files

In October 1908, Henry Ford rolled out the "car for the great multitude": the Model-T Ford. The sticker price: $950. To speed assembly, all Model-Ts were painted black because black paint dried the fastest. Legend quotes Henry Ford as saying "Any customer can have a car painted any color that he wants so long as it is black."[1]

Automobiles have come a long way since 1908. In addition to a dizzying selection of body styles, you also get to choose among several options, including the type of radio, whether or not you get power windows and door locks, and cloth versus leather upholstery. And nowadays any customer *can* have any color that they want … including, but not limited to, black.

In chapter 8 we showed you how to use Spring's MVC and JSP to build the web layer on top of your applications. Certainly, Spring MVC and JSP are a powerful combination and a strong platform to build your web applications upon. But is this the only choice afforded to Spring developers?

Although JSP is commonly used to produce the view of Java-based web applications, JSP is not everyone's choice. Back in JSP's infancy, many developers turned to alternative templating solutions, such as Jakarta Velocity and FreeMarker, when JSP didn't live up to their expectations. Although JSP has grown up in the last few years by adding support for custom tag libraries and virtually eliminating the need for scriptlet code, many of those who shunned it early on still prefer the other options.

JSP also has its limitations. JSP is primarily intended to produce HTML and XML output for web applications. Velocity and FreeMarker, on the other hand, are flexible with regard to the content that they produce and are able to generate virtually any kind of text file. JSP is incapable of producing binary content such as Microsoft Excel spreadsheets, Adobe PDF documents, or images.

Even if you like JSP, you may want to place your JSP pages in a layout framework such as Jakarta Tiles to make your application more aesthetically pleasing.

As it turns out, Spring MVC is very flexible with regard to the content produced. If you aren't a big fan of JSP, you may be delighted to learn Spring comes with view resolvers that enable you to use Velocity or FreeMarker instead. If you need to produce dynamically generated binary content, Spring offers support for generating Excel spreadsheets and PDF documents within Spring MVC.

In this chapter, we'll show you how to configure Spring MVC to

---

[1] Although this quote has been historically attributed to Henry Ford, some question whether or not he ever actually spoke these words. With regard to the historical accuracy of this quote, consider another quote by Henry Ford: "History is more or less bunk."

- Use Velocity or FreeMarker templates instead of JSP
- Use Jakarta Tiles to lay out your application pages
- Produce dynamically created binary Excel spreadsheets, PDF documents, and images

Let's begin by looking at how to swap out JSPs with alternative view-layer languages, starting with Velocity.

## 9.1 Using Velocity templates

Velocity is an easy-to-use template language for Java applications. Velocity templates contain no Java code, making them easy to understand by nondevelopers and developers alike. From Velocity's user guide: "Velocity separates Java code from the web pages, making the web site more maintainable over the long run and providing a viable alternative to JavaServer Pages."

Aside from JSP, Velocity is probably the most popular template language for web-based applications. So it is highly likely that you may want to develop your Spring-based application using Velocity as the view-layer technology. Fortunately, Spring supports Velocity as a view-layer templating language for Spring MVC.

Let's see how to use Velocity with Spring MVC by reimplementing the view layer of the Spring Training application so that it's based on Velocity.

### 9.1.1 Defining the Velocity view

Suppose that you've chosen to use Velocity, instead of JSP, to produce the view for the Spring Training application. One of the pages you'll need to write as a Velocity template is the page that shows a list of available courses. Listing 9.1 shows courseList.vm, the Velocity equivalent of courseList.jsp used to display a list of courses.

**Listing 9.1  A Velocity-based listing of courses**

```
<html>
  <head>
    <title>Course List</title>
  </head>

  <body>
    <h2>COURSE LIST</h2>

    <table width="600" border="1" cellspacing="1" cellpadding="1">
      <tr bgcolor="#999999">
        <td>Course ID</td>
```

```
        <td>Name</td>
        <td>Instructor</td>
        <td>Start</td>
        <td>End</td>
      </tr>
  #foreach($course in $courses)      ⟵ Iterate over all courses
      <tr>
        <td>
          <a href="displayCourse.htm?id=${course.id}">
            ${course.id}      ⟵ Display course ID
          </a>
        </td>
        <td>${course.name}</td>
        <td>${course.instructor.lastName}</td>
        <td>${course.startDate}</td>
        <td>${course.endDate}</td>
      </tr>
  #end     ⟵ Iterate over all courses
    </table>
  </body>
</html>
```

Annotations: "Display course name and instructor" (pointing to the name and instructor lines); "Display dates" (pointing to the startDate and endDate lines).

The first thing you'll probably notice about this template is that there are no template tags. That's because Velocity isn't tag-based like JSP. Instead, Velocity employs its own language—known as Velocity Template Language (VTL)—for control flow and other directives. In courseList.vm, the #foreach directive is used to loop through a list of courses, displaying course details with each iteration.

Despite this basic difference between Velocity and JSP, you'll find that Velocity's expression language resembles that of JSP. In fact, JSP merely followed in Velocity's footsteps when using the ${} notation in its own expression language.

This template demonstrates only a fraction of what you can do with Velocity. To learn more, visit the Velocity home page at http://jakarta.apache.org/velocity.

Now that the template has been created, you'll need to configure Spring to use Velocity templates for the view in MVC applications.

### 9.1.2 Configuring the Velocity engine

The first thing to configure is the Velocity engine itself. To do this, declare a VelocityConfigurer bean in the Spring configuration file, as follows:

```
<bean id="velocityConfigurer" class="org.springframework.
       web.servlet.view.velocity.VelocityConfigurer">
  <property name="resourceLoaderPath">
    <value>WEB-INF/velocity/</value>
  </property>
</bean>
```

VelocityConfigurer sets up the Velocity engine in Spring. Here, we've told Velocity where to find its templates by setting the resourceLoaderPath property. We recommend placing the templates in a directory underneath the WEB-INF directory so that the templates can't be accessed directly.

You can also set other Velocity configuration details by setting the velocity-Properties property. For example, consider the following declaration of VelocityConfigurer:

```
<bean id="velocityConfigurer" class="org.springframework.
    web.servlet.view.velocity.VelocityConfigurer">
  <property name="resourceLoaderPath">
    <value>WEB-INF/velocity/</value>
  </property>
  <property name="velocityProperties">
    <props>
      <prop key="directive.foreach.counter.name">loopCounter</prop>
      <prop key="directive.foreach.counter.initial.value">0</prop>
    </props>
  </property>
</bean>
```

Notice that velocityProperties takes a <props> element to set multiple properties. The properties being set are the same as those that would normally be set in a "velocity.properties" file if this were a typical Velocity application.

By default, Velocity's #foreach loop maintains a counter variable called $velocity-Count that starts with a value of 1 on the first iteration of the loop. But here we've set the directive.foreach.counter.name property to loopCounter so that the loop counter can be referred to with $loopCounter. We've also made the loop counter zero-based by setting the directive.foreach.counter.initial.value property to 0. (For more on Velocity configuration properties, refer to Velocity's developer guide at http://jakarta.apache.org/velocity/developer-guide.html.)

### 9.1.3  *Resolving Velocity views*

The final thing you must do to use Velocity template views is to configure a view resolver. Specifically, declare a VelocityViewResolver bean in the context configuration file as follows:

```
<bean id="viewResolver" class="org.springframework.
    web.servlet.view.velocity.VelocityViewResolver">
  <property name="suffix"><value>.vm</value></property>
</bean>
```

VelocityViewResolver is to Velocity what InternalResourceViewResolver is to JSP. Just like InternalResourceViewResolver, it has prefix and suffix properties that it uses with the view's logical name to construct a path to the template. Here, only the `suffix` property is set with the ".vm" extension. No prefix is required because the path to the template directory has already been set through `VelocityConfigurer`'s `resourceLoaderPath` property.

> **NOTE** Here the bean's ID is set to `viewResolver`. This is significant when `DispatcherServlet` is not configured to detect all view resolvers. If you are using multiple view resolvers, then you'll probably need to change the ID to something more appropriate (and unique), such as `velocity-ViewResolver`.

At this point, your application is ready to render views based on Velocity templates. All you need to do is return a `ModelAndView` object that references the view by its logical name. In the case of `ListCourseController`, there's nothing to do because it already returns a `ModelAndView` as follows:

```
return new ModelAndView("courseList", "courses", allCourses);
```

The view's logical name is "courseList". When the view is resolved, "courseList" will be suffixed with ".vm" to create the template name of "courseList.vm". `Velocity-ViewResolver` will find this template in the WEB-INF/velocity/ path.

As for the "courses" model object, it will be exposed in the Velocity template as a Velocity property. In listing 9.1, it is the collection used in the `#foreach` directive.

### 9.1.4 *Formatting dates and numbers*

Although the application is now set to render Velocity views, we have a few loose ends to tie up. If you compare courseList.vm from listing 9.1 to courseList.jsp, you'll notice that courseList.vm doesn't apply the same formatting to the course's ID and its start and end dates as in courseList.jsp. In courseList.jsp, the course ID is displayed as a six-digit number with leading zeroes and all dates are displayed in "full" format. For courseList.vm to be complete, you'll need to tweak it to format the ID and date properties.

The VTL doesn't directly support date and number formatting. However, Velocity does have date and number utility tools that support formatting. To enable these tools, you'll need to tell the `VelocityViewResolver` the name of the attributes to expose them through. These attributes are specified through `Velocity-ViewResolver`'s `dateToolAttribute` and `numberToolAttribute` properties:

```
<bean id="viewResolver" class="org.springframework.
    web.servlet.view.velocity.VelocityViewResolver">
...
```

```
  <property name="dateToolAttribute">
    <value>dateTool</value>
  </property>
  <property name="numberToolAttribute">
    <value>numberTool</value>
  </property>
</bean>
```

Here, the number tool is assigned to a `numberTool` attribute in Velocity. So, to format the course ID, all you need to do is reference the course ID through the number tool's `format()` function. For example:

```
$numberTool.format("000000", course.id)
```

The first parameter to `format()` is the pattern string. Here we've specified that the course's ID be displayed in a six-digit field with leading zeroes as necessary. The pattern string adheres to the same syntax as `java.text.DecimalFormat`. Refer to the Velocity's documentation for `NumberTool` for more information on this tool's functions.

Likewise, the date tool has been assigned to the `dateTool` attribute. To format the course's start and end dates, you'll use the date tool's `format()` function:

```
$dateTool.format("FULL", course.startDate)
$dateTool.format("FULL", course.endDate)
```

Just as with the number tool's `format()` function, the first parameter is the pattern string. This string adheres to the same syntax as that of `java.text.Simple-DateFormat`. In addition, you can specify one of the standard `java.text.DateFormat` patterns by setting the pattern string to one of `FULL`, `LONG`, `MEDIUM`, `SHORT`, or `DEFAULT`. Here we've set it to `FULL` to indicate the full date format. Refer to Velocity's documentation for `DateTool` for more information on this tool's functions.

### 9.1.5 *Exposing request and session attributes*

Although most data that needs to be displayed in a Velocity template can be passed to the view through the model `Map` given to the `ModelAndView` object, there are times when you may wish to display attributes that are in the servlet's request or session. For example, if a user is logged into the application, that user's information may be carried in the servlet session.

It would be clumsy to copy attributes out of the request or session into the model `Map` in each controller. Fortunately, `VelocityViewResolver` can copy the attributes into the model for you. The `exposeRequestAttributes` and `exposeSession-Attributes` properties tell `VelocityViewResolver` whether or not you want servlet request and session attributes copied into the model. For example:

```
<bean id="viewResolver" class="org.springframework.
       web.servlet.view.velocity.VelocityViewResolver">
  ...
  <property name="exposeRequestAttributes">
    <value>true</value>
  </property>
  <property name="exposeSessionAttributes">
    <value>true</value>
  </property>
</bean>
```

By default, both of these properties are `false`. But here we've set them both to `true` so that both request and session attributes will be copied into the model and therefore be visible in the Velocity template.

### 9.1.6 *Binding form fields in Velocity*

In chapter 8, you saw how to use Spring's `<spring:bind>` JSP tag to bind form fields to properties of a command object. This tag was also useful for displaying field-related errors to the user.

Fortunately, you don't have to give up the functionality that `<spring:bind>` provides if you are using Velocity instead of JSP. Spring comes with a couple of Velocity macros that mimic the functionality of the `<spring:bind>` tag.

For example, suppose that the student registration form from the Spring Training application is written as a Velocity template. Listing 9.2 shows a snippet from registerStudent.vm that demonstrates how to use the `#springBind` macro.

**Listing 9.2   Using `#springBind` in a Velocity template**

```
#springBind("command.phone")     <— Bind status variable
phone: <input type="text"
    name="${status.expression}"     <— Name form field
    value="$!status.value">     <— Display value
<font color="#FF0000">${status.errorMessage}</font><br>     <—┐
                                                              │  Display
#springBind("command.email")     <— Bind status variable     │  error
email: <input type="text"                                     │  messages
    name="${status.expression}"     <— Name form field        │  (if any)
    value="$!status.value">     <— Display value              │
<font color="#FF0000">${status.errorMessage}</font><br>     <—┘
```

The `#springBind` macro takes the path of the field to be bound. It sets a `status` variable in the template that holds the name of the field, the value of the field, and any error messages that may be incurred (perhaps from a validator).

If your error messages contain characters that have special meaning in HTML (e.g., <, >, &), you may want to escape the error messages so that they display correctly in a web browser. If that's the case, then you may want to use the #springBindEscaped macro instead of #springBind:

```
#springBindEscaped("command.email", true)
```

In addition to the field path, #springBindEscaped takes a boolean argument that indicates whether or not to escape the error message. If this argument is true, then the macro will escape HTML-special characters in the error message. If this argument is false, then #springBindEscaped behaves exactly like #springBind, leaving the HTML-special characters "unescaped."

To be able to use the Spring macros in your templates, you'll need to enable the macro using the exposeSpringMacroHelpers property of VelocityViewResolver:

```
<bean id="viewResolver" class="org.springframework.
        ➥ web.servlet.view.velocity.VelocityViewResolver">
   ...
   <property name="exposeSpringMacroHelpers">
     <value>true</value>
   </property>
</bean>
```

By setting the exposeSpringMacroHelpers property to true, you'll ensure that your Velocity templates will have access to the #springBind and #springBind-Escaped macros.

Although Velocity is a widely used alternative to JSP, it is not the only alternate templating option available. FreeMarker is another well-known template language that aims to replace JSP in the view layer of MVC applications. Let's see how to plug FreeMarker into your Spring MVC application.

## 9.2 *Working with FreeMarker*

FreeMarker is slightly more complex than Velocity, but only as the result of being slightly more powerful. FreeMarker comes with built-in support for several useful tasks, such as date and number formatting and white-space removal. These features are only available in Velocity through add-on tools.

You'll soon see how using FreeMarker with Spring MVC isn't much different than using Velocity with Spring MVC. But first things first—let's start by writing a FreeMarker template to be used in the Spring Training application.

### 9.2.1 *Constructing a FreeMarker view*

Suppose that after much consideration, you decide that FreeMarker templates are more suited to your tastes than Velocity. So, instead of developing the view layer of the Spring Training application using Velocity, you'd like to plug FreeMarker into Spring MVC. Revisiting the course listing page, you produce courseList.ftl (listing 9.3), the page that displays a list of courses being offered.

**Listing 9.3 Listing courses using FreeMarker's template language**

```html
<html>
  <head>
    <title>Course List</title>
  </head>

  <body>
    <h2>COURSE LIST</h2>

    <table width="600" border="1" cellspacing="1" cellpadding="1">
      <tr bgcolor="#999999">
        <td>Course ID</td>
        <td>Name</td>
        <td>Instructor</td>
        <td>Start</td>
        <td>End</td>
      </tr>
<#list courses as course>         <-- Loop through all courses
      <tr>
        <td>
        <a href="displayCourse.htm?id=${course.id}">
          ${course.id?string("000000")}    <-- Format the course ID
        </a>
        </td>
        <td>${course.name}</td>
        <td>${course.instructor.lastName}</td>
        <td>${course.startDate?string.long}</td>   | Format
        <td>${course.endDate?string.long}</td>     | the dates
      </tr>
</#list>
    </table>
  </body>
</html>
```

You'll notice that the FreeMarker version of the course listing isn't dramatically different than the Velocity version from listing 9.1. Just as with Velocity (or JSP), the ${} notation is used as an expression language to display attribute values.

But you may also notice that the course ID and dates have extra arguments used to format the fields. FreeMarker, unlike Velocity, has built-in support for formatting numbers and dates.

The courseList.ftl template barely scratches the surface of FreeMarker's capabilities. For more information on FreeMarker, visit the FreeMarker home page at http://freemarker.sourceforge.net.

### 9.2.2 *Configuring the FreeMarker engine*

Just like Velocity, FreeMarker's engine must be configured in order for Spring's MVC to use FreeMarker templates to render views. Declare a `FreeMarkerConfigurer` in the context configuration file like this:

```
<bean id="freemarkerConfig" class="org.springframework.
    web.servlet.view.freemarker.FreeMarkerConfigurer">
  <property name="templateLoaderPath">
    <value>WEB-INF/freemarker/</value>
  </property>
</bean>
```

`FreeMarkerConfigurer` is to FreeMarker as `VelocityConfigurer` is to Velocity. You use it to configure the FreeMarker engine. As a minimum, you must tell FreeMarker where to find the templates. You can do this by setting the `templateLoaderPath` property.

You can configure additional FreeMarker settings by setting them as properties through the `freemarkerSettings` property. For example, FreeMarker reloads and reparses templates if five seconds (by default) have elapsed since the template was last checked for updates. But checking for template changes can be time consuming. If your application is in production and you don't expect the template to change very often, you may want to stretch the update delay to an hour or more.

To do this, set FreeMarker's `template_update_delay` setting through the `freemarkerSettings` property. For example:

```
<bean id="freemarkerConfig" class="org.springframework.
    web.servlet.view.freemarker.FreeMarkerConfigurer">
  ...
  <property name="freemarkerSettings">
    <props>
      <prop key="template_update_delay">3600</prop>
    </props>
  </property>
</bean>
```

Notice that like `VelocityConfigurer`'s `velocityProperties` property, the `freemarkerSettings` property takes a `<props>` element. In this case, the only `<prop>` is one to set the `template_update_delay` setting to 3600 (seconds) so that the template will only be checked for updates after an hour has passed.

### 9.2.3 *Resolving FreeMarker views*

The next thing you'll need to do is to declare a view resolver for FreeMarker:

```
<bean id="viewResolver" class="org.springframework.
    web.servlet.view.freemarker.FreeMarkerViewResolver">
  <property name="suffix"><value>.ftl</value></property>
</bean>
```

`FreeMarkerViewResolver` works just like `VelocityViewResolver` or `Internal-ResourceViewResolver`. Template resources are resolved by prefixing a view's logical name with the value of the `prefix` property and are suffixed with the value of the `suffix` property. Again, just as with `VelocityViewResolver`, we've only set the `suffix` property because the template path is already defined in `FreeMarker-Configurer`'s `templateLoaderPath` property.

#### Exposing request and session attributes

In section 9.1.3, you saw how to tell `VelocityViewResolver` to copy request and/or session attributes into the model map so that they'll be available as variables in the template. You can do the same thing with `FreeMarkerViewResolver` to expose request and session attributes as variables in a FreeMarker template. To do so, set either the `exposeRequestAttributes` or `exposeSessionAttributes` properties (or both) to `true`:

```
<bean id="viewResolver" class="org.springframework.
    web.servlet.view.freemarker.FreeMarkerViewResolver">
  ...
  <property name="exposeRequestAttributes">
    <value>true</value>
  </property>
  <property name="exposeSessionAttributes">
    <value>true</value>
  </property>
</bean>
```

Here, both properties have been set to `true`. As a result, both request and session attributes will be copied into the template's set of attributes and will be available to display using FreeMarker's expression language.

### 9.2.4 *Binding form fields in FreeMarker*

One last thing you may want to do with FreeMarker is to bind form fields to command properties. In chapter 8, you used the JSP `<spring:bind>` tag and in section 9.1.6, you used the #springBind Velocity macro in Velocity to accomplish this. Similarly, Spring provides a set of FreeMarker macros to perform the binding.

The equivalent FreeMarker macros are <@spring.bind> and <@spring.bind-Escaped>. For example, listing 9.4 shows a section of code from registerStudent.ftl that uses the <@spring.bind> directive to bind status information to the form.

**Listing 9.4  Using `<@spring.bind>` in a FreeMarker template**

```
<@spring.bind "command.phone" />       ⟵ Bind status variable
phone: <input type="text"
    name="${spring.status.expression}"   ⟵ Name form field
    value="${spring.status.value}">    ⟵ Display value
<font color="#FF0000">${spring.status.errorMessage}</font><br>  ⟵┐
                                                                   │ Display
<@spring.bind "command.email" />       ⟵ Bind status variable     │ error
    email: <input type="text"                                      │ messages
    name="${spring.status.expression}"   ⟵ Name form field         │ (if any)
    value="${spring.status.value}">    ⟵ Display value             │
<font color="#FF0000">${spring.status.errorMessage}</font><br>  ⟵┘
```

You may have noticed that listing 9.4 is very similar to listing 9.2. But there are two differences. First, instead of using the Velocity #springBind macro, the FreeMarker version uses the <@spring.bind> directive. Also, <@spring.bind> binds the status information to ${spring.status} instead of ${status}.

Just as with Spring's Velocity macros, in order to use these macros you must enable the FreeMarker macros by setting the exposeMacroHelpers property of FreeMarkerViewResolver to true:

```
<bean id="viewResolver" class="org.springframework.
    ➥ web.servlet.view.freemarker.FreeMarkerViewResolver">
...
  <property name="exposeSpringMacroHelpers">
    <value>true</value>
  </property>
</bean>
```

Finally, there's one more thing you'll need to do so that you'll be able to use the FreeMarker macros. Add the following line to the top of all FreeMarker templates that will use the <@spring.bind> or <@spring.bindEscaped> macro:

```
<#import "/spring.ftl" as spring />
```

This line will import the Spring macros for FreeMarker into the template.

## 9.3 *Designing page layout with Tiles*

Up until now, we've kept the look and feel of the Spring Training application very generic. We've focused on how to write Spring-enabled web applications with little regard for aesthetics. But how an application looks often dictates its success. To make the Spring Training application visually appealing, it needs to be placed in a template that frames its generic pages with eye-popping graphics.

Jakarta Tiles is a framework for laying out pieces of a page in a template. Although originally created as part of Jakarta Struts, Tiles can be used with or without Struts. For our purposes, we're going to use Tiles alongside Spring's MVC framework.

Although we'll give a brief overview of working with Tiles, we recommend that you read chapter 11 of *Struts in Action* (Manning, 2002) to learn more about using Tiles.

### 9.3.1 *Tile views*

The template for the Spring Training application will be reasonably simple. It will have a header where the company logo and motto will be displayed, a footer where contact information and a copyright will be displayed, and a larger area in the middle where the main content will be displayed. Figure 9.1 shows a box diagram of how the template will be laid out.

The template, mainTemplate.jsp (listing 9.5), defines this layout. It uses HTML to define the basic layout of a page and uses the `<tiles:getAsString>` and `<tiles:insert>` tags as placeholders for the real content to be filled in for each individual page.

**Figure 9.1  The layout of the Spring Training application template**

---

**Listing 9.5  mainTemplate.jsp, the Spring Training template**

```
<%@ taglib prefix="tiles"
    uri="http://jakarta.apache.org/struts/tags-tiles" %>

<html>
  <head>
    <title><tiles:getAsString name="title"/></title>          Display
  </head>                                                      page title
  <body>
    <table width="100%" border="0">
```

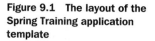

```
      <tr>
        <td><tiles:insert name="header"/></td>
      </tr>
      <tr>
        <td valign="top" align="left">
          <tiles:insert name="content"/>
        </td>
      </tr>
      <tr>
        <td>
          <tiles:insert name="footer"/>
        </td>
      </tr>
    </table>
  </body>
</html>
```

With the template written, the next step is to create a Tiles definition file. A Tiles definition file is XML that describes how to fill in the template. The file can be named anything you want, but for the purposes of the Spring Training application, "training-defs.xml" seems appropriate.

The following excerpt from training-defs.xml outlines the main template (called "template"), filling in each of its components with some default values:

```
<tiles-definitions>
  <definition name="template" page="/tiles/mainTemplate.jsp">
    <put name="title" value="Default title"/>
    <put name="header" value="/tiles/header.jsp"/>
    <put name="content" value="/tiles/defaultContentPage.jsp"/>
    <put name="footer" value="/tiles/footer.jsp"/>
  </definition>
  ...
</tiles-definitions>
```

Here, the header and footer components are given the path to JSP files that define how the header and footer should look. When Tiles builds a page, it will replace the <tiles:insert> tags named header and footer with the output resulting from header.jsp and footer.jsp, respectively.

As for the title and content components, they are just given some dummy values. Because it's just a template, you'll never view the template page directly. Instead, when you view another page that is based on template, the dummy values for title and content will be overridden with real values.

The course detail page is a typical example of the pages in the application that will be based on template. It is defined in training-defs.xml like this:

```
<definition name="courseDetail" extends="template">
  <put name="title" value="Course Detail" />
  <put name="content" value="/tiles/courseDetail.jsp"/>
</definition>
```

Extending `template` ensures that the `courseDetail` page will inherit all of its component definitions. However, it chooses to override the template's `title` component with `Course Detail` so that the page will have an appropriate title in the browser's title bar. And its main content page is defined by courseDetail.jsp, so the `content` component is overridden to be `/tiles/courseDetail.jsp`.

So far, this is a typical Tiles-based application. You've seen nothing Spring-specific yet. But now it's time to integrate Tiles into Spring MVC by performing these two steps:

- Configuring a `TilesConfigurer` to load the Tiles definition file
- Declaring a Spring MVC view resolver to resolve logical view names to Tiles definitions

### Configuring Tiles

The first step in integrating Tiles into Spring MVC is to tell Spring to load the Tiles configuration file(s). Spring comes with `TilesConfigurer`, a bean that loads Tiles configuration files and makes them available for rendering Tiles views. To load the Tiles configuration into Spring, declare a `TilesConfigurer` instance as follows:

```
<bean id="tilesConfigurer" class="org.springframework.
➥     web.servlet.view.tiles.TilesConfigurer">

  <property name="definitions">
    <list>
      <value>/WEB-INF/tiledefs/training-defs.xml</value>
    </list>
  </property>
</bean>
```

The `definitions` property is given a list of Tiles definition files to load. But in the case of the Spring Training application, there's only one definition file: training-defs.xml.

### Resolving Tiles views

The final step to integrate Tiles into Spring MVC is to configure a view resolver that will send the user to a page defined by Tiles. `InternalResourceViewResolver` will do the trick:

```
<bean id="viewResolver" class="org.springframework.
     web.servlet.view.InternalResourceViewResolver">
  <property name="viewClass">
    <value>org.springframework.web.
        servlet.view.tiles.TilesView</value>
  </property>
</bean>
```

Normally, `InternalResourceViewResolver` resolves logical views from resources (typically JSPs) in the web application. But for Tiles, you'll need it to resolve views as definitions in a Tiles definition file. For that, the `viewClass` property has been set to use a `TilesView`.

There are actually two view classes to choose from when working with Tiles: `TilesView` and `TilesJstlView`. The difference is that `TilesJstlView` will place localization information into the request for JSTL pages. Even though we're using JSTL, we're not taking advantage of JSTL's support for internationalization. Therefore, we've chosen `TilesView`.

When `InternalResourceViewResolver` is configured with `TilesView` (or `TilesJstlView`) it will try to resolve views by looking for a definition in the Tiles definition file(s) that has a name that is the same as the logical view name. For example, consider what happens as a result of `DisplayCourseController`. When finished, this controller returns the following `ModelAndView`:

```
return new ModelAndView("courseDetail", "course", course);
```

The logical view name is `courseDetail`, so `TilesView` will look for the view definition in the Tiles configuration. In this case, it finds the `<definition>` named `courseDetail`. Since `courseDetail` is based on `template`, the resulting HTML page will be structured like mainTemplate.jsp (listing 9.5), but will have its `title` set to `Course Detail` and its `content` will be derived from the JSP in /tiles/courseDetail.jsp.

Nothing about the Spring Training controller classes will need to change to support Tiles. That's because the page definitions in training-defs.xml are cleverly named to be the same as the logical view names returned by all of the controllers.

### 9.3.2 *Tile controllers*

Suppose that you'd like to make the Spring Training application a bit more personable by placing a greeting in the header for users who are logged in. The message will greet students by name and give a count of the number of courses they've completed.

One way to accomplish this is to place the following code in each of the controllers:

```
Student student =
    (Student) request.getSession().getAttribute("student");
if(student != null) {
  int courseCount =
      studentService.getCompletedCourses(student).size();

  modelMap.add("courseCount", courseCount);
  modelMap.add("studentName", student.getFirstName());
}
```

This would place the student's first name and course count into the request so that it can be displayed in header.jsp like this:

```
Hello ${studentName}, you have completed ${courseCount} courses.
```

But for this to work on all pages, you'd need to repeat the student lookup code in all of the application's controller classes. There are options to eliminate the redundant code, including placing the lookup code in a base controller class or in a utility class. But all of these options add complexity that you'd like to avoid.

A unique feature of Tiles is that each component on a page can have its own controller. This is a Tiles-specific controller, not to be confused with a Spring MVC controller. Component controllers can be associated with Tiles components so that each component can perform functionality specific to that component.

To include a personal message on each page of the Spring Training application, you will need to build a controller for the header component. HeaderTiles-Controller (listing 9.6) retrieves the number of courses that the student has completed and places that information into the component context for display in the banner.

**Listing 9.6  Retrieving course counts using a Tiles controller**

```
public class HeaderTileController
    extends ComponentControllerSupport {
  protected void doPerform(ComponentContext componentContext,
      HttpServletRequest request, HttpServletResponse response)
      throws Exception {                                              Get Spring
                                                                      application
    ApplicationContext context = getApplicationContext();        ◁┘ context

    StudentService studentService =                                  Retrieve student
        (StudentService) context.getBean("studentService");          service bean

    Student student =
        (Student) request.getSession().getAttribute("student");
```

```
    int courseCount =                                              Get course
        studentService.getCompletedCourses(student).size();       count

    componentContext.putAttribute("courseCount",
        new Integer(courseCount));
    componentContext.putAttribute("studentname",
        student.getFirstName());
    }
}
```

`HeaderTileController` extends `ComponentControllerSupport`, a Spring-specific extension of Tiles' `ControllerSupport` class. `ComponentControllerSupport` makes the Spring application context available via its `getApplicationContext()` method.

`HeaderTileController` makes a call to `getApplicationContext()` and uses the application context to look up a reference to the `studentService` bean so that it can find out how many courses the student has completed. Once it has the information, it places it into the Tiles component context so that the `header` component can display it.

The only thing left to do is to associate this component controller with the `header` component. Revisiting the header definition in training-defs.xml, extract the header definition and set its `controllerClass` attribute to point to the `HeaderTileController`:

```
<definition name=".header" page="/tiles/header.jsp"
    controllerClass="com.springinaction.training.
                    ➥ tiles.HeaderTileController"/>
<definition name="template" page="/tiles/mainTemplate.jsp">
  <put name="title" value="Default title"/>
  <put name="header" value=".header"/>
  <put name="content" value="/tiles/defaultContentPage.jsp"/>
  <put name="footer" value="/tiles/footer.jsp"/>
</definition>
```

Now, as the page is constructed, Tiles will use `HeaderTileController` to set up the component context prior to displaying the `header` component.

## 9.4 *Generating non-HTML output*

Up until now, the views produced by the Spring Training application's web layer have been HTML-based. Indeed, HTML is the typical way to display information on the Web. But HTML doesn't always lend itself to the information being presented.

For example, if the data you are presenting is in tabular format, it may be preferable to present information in the form of a spreadsheet. Spreadsheets may also be useful if you want to enable the users of your application to manipulate the data being presented.

Or perhaps you'd like precise control over how a document is formatted. Formatting HTML documents precisely is virtually impossible, especially when viewed across various browser implementations. But Adobe's Portable Document Format (PDF) has become the de facto standard for producing documents with precise formatting that are viewable on many different platforms.

Spreadsheets and PDF files are commonly static files. But Spring provides view classes that enable you to dynamically create spreadsheets and PDF documents that are based on your application's data.

Let's explore Spring's support for non-HTML views, starting with dynamic generation of Excel spreadsheets.

### 9.4.1 *Producing Excel spreadsheets*

Let's say that Spring Training's course director has asked you to produce a spreadsheet that is a report of all of the courses, including the number of students enrolled in each course. This could end up being a report that she requests often. So you decide to automatically generate it and make it available upon request on the Web so that she can pull it down anytime she wants.

As you'll recall, we've already built `ListCourseController` (listing 8.1), which retrieves a list of courses and sends them to the view named `courseList` for rendering. In chapter 8, we assumed that the `courseList` view was a JSP. But, in fact, there is nothing about `ListCourseController` that specifically states that `courseList` is associated with a JSP. This means that all we need to do is to associate `courseList` to a view that produces Excel spreadsheets.

You're in luck. Spring comes with `org.springframework.web.servlet.view.document.AbstractExcelView`, an abstract `View` implementation that is geared toward generating Excel spreadsheets as views in Spring MVC. All you need to do is subclass `AbstractExcelView` and implement its `buildExcelDocument()` method. Listing 9.7 shows `CourseListExcelView`, a subclass of `AbstractExcelView` that generates a course listing as an Excel spreadsheet.

---

**Listing 9.7   A view that generates a spreadsheet listing of courses**

```
public class CourseListExcelView extends AbstractExcelView {
  protected void buildExcelDocument(Map model, HSSFWorkbook wb,
      HttpServletRequest request, HttpServletResponse response)
      throws Exception {
```

```
Set courses = (Set) model.get("courses");    <— Get courses from model

HSSFSheet sheet = wb.createSheet("Courses");
HSSFRow header = sheet.createRow(0);
header.createCell((short)0).setCellValue("ID");
header.createCell((short)1).setCellValue("Name");
header.createCell((short)2).setCellValue("Instructor");
header.createCell((short)3).setCellValue("Start Date");
header.createCell((short)4).setCellValue("End Date");
header.createCell((short)5).setCellValue("Students");

HSSFCellStyle cellStyle = wb.createCellStyle();
cellStyle.setDataFormat(
    HSSFDataFormat.getBuiltinFormat("m/d/yy h:mm"));

int rowNum = 1;
for (Iterator iter = courses.iterator(); iter.hasNext();) {
  Course course = (Course) iter.next();

  HSSFRow row = sheet.createRow(rowNum++);
  row.createCell((short)0).setCellValue(
      course.getId().toString());
  row.createCell((short)1).setCellValue(course.getName());
  row.createCell((short)2).setCellValue(
      course.getInstructor().getLastName());
  row.createCell((short)3).setCellValue(course.getStartDate());
  row.getCell((short)3).setCellStyle(cellStyle);
  row.createCell((short)4).setCellValue(course.getEndDate());
  row.getCell((short)4).setCellStyle(cellStyle);
  row.createCell((short)5).setCellValue(
      course.getStudents().size());
}

HSSFRow row = sheet.createRow(rowNum);
row.createCell((short)0).setCellValue("TOTAL:");
String formula = "SUM(F2:F"+rowNum+")";
row.createCell((short)5).setCellFormula(formula);
  }
}
```

AbstractExcelView is based on Jakarta POI (http://jakarta.apache.org/poi), an API for generating many of the documents supported by Microsoft Office applications, including Excel spreadsheets. The buildExcelDocument() method takes a java.util.Map, which contains any model objects needed to construct the view and an empty HSSFWorkbook[2] to build the spreadsheet in.

---

[2] In case you're wondering, the "HSSF" in POI's class names is an acronym for "Horrible SpreadSheet Format."

CourseListExcelView starts by retrieving a Set of course objects from the model Map. It then uses the data in the course Set to construct the spreadsheet.

If you've ever used servlets or a servlet-based framework to generate spreadsheets (or any non-HTML content), you know that you have to set the response's content type so that the browser knows how to display the document. For Excel spreadsheets, you would probably set the content type like this:

```
response.setContentType("application/vnd.ms-excel");
```

But using CourseListExcelView, you don't have to worry about setting the content type. CourseListExcelView's default constructor takes care of this for you.

The only thing left to do is to associate CourseListExcelView with a logical view name of courseList. The simplest way to do this is to use a BeanNameViewResolver (see section 8.4.2) and declare the CourseListExcelView bean to have courseList as its id:

```
<bean id="courseList"
    class="com.springinaction.training.mvc.CourseListExcelView"/>
```

Another way is to use ResourceBundleViewResolver. In this case, you would associate CourseListExcelView with a logical name of courseList by placing the following line in the views.properties file:

```
courseList.class=com.springinaction.training.mvc.CourseListExcelView
```

Remember that there's nothing about ListCourseController that is specific to generating spreadsheets. The View object is entirely responsible for determining the type of document that is produced. The controller class is completely decoupled from the view mechanism that will be used to render the output. This is important, because it means that you could plug in a different View object to generate a different type of document. In fact, that's what we'll do next—wire a different View into ListCourseController to generate the course listing in a PDF file.

### 9.4.2 *Generating PDF documents*

Suppose that, instead of an Excel spreadsheet, you need to generate a PDF file that lists courses. Just as you did to generate a spreadsheet, the first thing you'll need to do is to create a View implementation that generates the PDF document.

Spring's org.springframework.web.servlet.view.document.AbstractPdfView is an abstract implementation of View that supports the creation of PDF files as views in Spring MVC. Much as with AbstractExcelView, you'll need to subclass AbstractPdfView and implement the buildPdfDocument() method to construct a PDF document.

CourseListPdfView (listing 9.8) is a subclass of AbstractPdfView that generates a PDF document that has a table listing courses.

**Listing 9.8   Generating a PDF document view**

```
public class CourseListPdfView extends AbstractPdfView {
  protected void buildPdfDocument(Map model, Document pdfDoc,
      PdfWriter writer, HttpServletRequest request,
      HttpServletResponse response) throws Exception {

    Set courseList = (Set) model.get("courses");    ◁— Get course list

    Table courseTable = new Table(5);
    CourseTable.setWidth(90);
    courseTable.setBorderWidth(1);

    courseTable.addCell("ID");
    courseTable.addCell("Name");
    courseTable.addCell("Instructor");
    courseTable.addCell("Start Date");
    courseTable.addCell("EndDate");

    for (Iterator iter = courseList.iterator(); iter.hasNext();) {
      Course course = (Course) iter.next();

      courseTable.addCell(course.getId().toString());
      courseTable.addCell(course.getName());
      courseTable.addCell(course.getInstructor().getLastName());
      courseTable.addCell(course.getStartDate().toString());
      courseTable.addCell(course.getEndDate().toString());
    }

    pdfDoc.add(courseTable);    ◁— Add table to document
  }
}
```

The buildPdfDocument() method is where the PDF document is created. Among other parameters, this method takes a java.util.Map and a com.lowagie.text.Document. Just as with buildExcelDocument() in AbstractExcelView, the Map passed to buildPdfDocument() contains model data that can be used to generate the view.

AbstractPdfView is based on iText, an API for manipulating PDF documents. The Document object passed into buildPdfDocument() is an empty iText document, ready to be filled with content. (For more information about iText, visit the iText home page at http://www.lowagie.com/iText.)

In CourseListPdfView, the buildPdfDocument() method starts by retrieving the courses from the model Map. It then constructs a table with one row per course. Once the table is constructed, it is added to the Document.

Just like AbstractExcelView, AbstractPdfView handles setting the content type for you (in this case, the content type will be set to application/pdf).

Next you must associate CourseListPdfView with a logical view name of courseList. Just as with CourseListExcelView, you have two options. The easiest approach would be to use a BeanNameViewResolver and declare a CourseListPdfView bean in the context configuration file as follows:

```
<bean id="courseList"
    class="com.springinaction.training.mvc.CourseListPdfView"/>
```

Or you could use a ResourceBundleViewResolver, declaring the view in views.properties as follows:

```
courseList.class=com.springinaction.training.mvc.CourseListPdfView
```

### Altering the page size

By default, the Document object passed into the buildPdfDocument() method is configured to be sized A4 (210 x 297mm) with portrait orientation. But you may want to override that by specifying a different size or orientation. To do so, you should override the getDocument() method of AbstractPdfView to return a Document object of your choosing.

For example, the following implementation of getDocument() returns a Document object that uses legal-sized (216 x 356mm) pages:

```
protected Document getDocument() {
    return new Document(PageSize.LEGAL);
}
```

To switch a page's orientation from portrait to landscape, all you must do is call the rotate() method on the PageSize object. For example, use this code to switch the legal-sized document from portrait to landscape:

```
protected Document getDocument() {
    return new Document(PageSize.LEGAL.rotate());
}
```

Now you know how to produce Excel and PDF documents using the custom View implementations that come with Spring. But what if your application requires a different type of document not directly supported by Spring?

### 9.4.3 *Generating other non-HTML files*

Both `AbstractExcelView` and `AbstractPdfView` implement the `View` interface. But if spreadsheets and PDF documents aren't what you need, then you can create your own implementation of the `View` interface.

The `View` interface requires that you only implement a single method, the `render()` method. This method has the following signature:

```
void render(Map model,
            HttpServletRequest request,
            HttpServletResponse response) throws Exception;
```

Let's suppose that your application needs to dynamically produce graphs in the form of JPEG images. Since you'll probably end up creating several different JPEGs, it would be wise to create an abstract implementation of `View` that encapsulates all of the code that is common to all JPEG rendering views. Listing 9.9 shows `AbstractJpegView`, an abstract JPEG rendering `View` that follows the same style as `AbstractPdfView` and `AbstractExcelView`.

**Listing 9.9   An abstract view for rendering JPEG images**

```
public abstract class AbstractJpegView implements View {
  public AbstractJpegView() {}

  public int getImageWidth() { return 100; }

  public int getImageHeight() { return 100; }

  protected int getImageType() {
    return BufferedImage.TYPE_INT_RGB;
  }

  public void render(Map model, HttpServletRequest request,
      HttpServletResponse response) throws Exception {

    response.setContentType("image/jpeg");          ◁— Set content type

    BufferedImage image = new BufferedImage(                    | Create buffered
        getImageWidth(), getImageHeight(), getImageType());     | image

    buildImage(model, image, request, response);    ◁— Draw image

    ServletOutputStream out = response.getOutputStream();
    JPEGImageEncoder encoder = new JPEGImageEncoderImpl(out);   | Encode
    encoder.encode(image);                                      | JPEG
    out.flush();
  }
```

```
    protected abstract void buildImage(Map model, BufferedImage image,
        HttpServletRequest request, HttpServletResponse response)
        throws Exception;
}
```

To use `AbstractJpegView`, you must extend it and implement the `buildImage()` method. For example, if you simply want to render a circle, then `CircleJpegView` (listing 9.10) will do the trick.

**Listing 9.10   A circle-drawing view**

```
public class CircleJpegView extends AbstractJpegView {
    public CircleJpegView() {}

    protected void buildImage(Map model, BufferedImage image,
        HttpServletRequest request, HttpServletResponse response)
        throws Exception {

        Graphics g = image.getGraphics();
        g.drawOval(0,0,getImageWidth(), getImageHeight());      ⟵ Draw a circle
    }
}
```

We'll leave it up to you to find more interesting images to be drawn by extending `AbstractJpegView`. Perhaps `CircleJpegView` will give you a decent start toward drawing a pie graph.

## 9.5 *Summary*

Although JSP is the likely choice for generating views in a Spring MVC application, it is not the only choice. By swapping out view resolvers and view implementations, your application can produce web pages using alternative view layer technologies or even produce non-HTML output.

In this chapter, you learned to replace JSP with Velocity or FreeMarker in your Spring MVC applications. In a similar manner, you saw how to integrate Jakarta Tiles into your Spring MVC application to lay out your application's presentation to be more usable and visually pleasing.

Finally, you saw how to create custom view implementations that produce dynamically generated binary content such as Excel spreadsheets, PDF documents, and images.

While this chapter offered you several choices for an application's view layer, everything you saw worked within a Spring MVC application. But what if you have another MVC framework that you prefer?

In the next chapter, we'll extend the set of choices to other MVC frameworks so that you can use Spring along with your MVC framework of choice.

# 10

# Working with
# other web frameworks

Up until this point, we've been assuming that you'll be using Spring's MVC framework to drive the web layer of your application. While we believe that Spring's MVC is a strong choice, there may be reasons why you prefer another framework. Perhaps you're already heavily invested in another MVC framework and aren't prepared to abandon your familiar MVC framework for Spring. Nevertheless, you would like to use Spring in the other layers of your application to take advantage of its support for declarative transactions, AOP, and inversion of control.

If you're not quite ready to make the jump to Spring's MVC, then you certainly have a huge selection of other MVC frameworks to choose from. In fact, there is a blog[1] that lists over 50 such frameworks! We have neither the space nor the inclination to show you how to integrate Spring with all of them. But we will show you how to integrate Spring into some of the more popular MVC frameworks, including Tapestry and JavaServer Faces. Let's start with the archetypal MVC framework—Jakarta Struts.

## 10.1 *Working with Jakarta Struts*

Despite the seemingly endless barrage of Java-based MVC frameworks, Jakarta Struts is still the king of them all. It began life in May 2000 when Craig McClanahan launched the project to create a standard MVC framework for the Java community. In July 2001, Struts 1.0 was released and set the stage for Java web development for thousands and thousands of projects.

Suppose that you had written the Spring Training application using Struts in the web layer. Had that been the case, you would have written `ListCourseAction` (listing 10.1) instead of `ListCourseController`.

**Listing 10.1   A Struts action that lists courses**

```
public class ListCourseAction extends Action {
  private CourseService courseService;

  public ActionForward execute(
     ActionMapping mapping,
     ActionForm form,
     HttpServletRequest request,
     HttpServletResponse response) throws Exception {

  Set allCourses = courseService.getAllCourses();
```

---

[1]   http://www.manageability.org/blog/stuff/how-many-java-web-frameworks/view

```
    request.setAttribute("courses", allCourses);

    return mapping.findForward("courseList");
  }
}
```

Just as with `ListCourseController`, this action uses a `CourseService` to get a list of all courses. What's missing in listing 10.1 is the part that tells where the `Course-Service` comes from. How can a Struts action get references to beans that are contained in a Spring context?

Spring offers two types of Struts integration that answer that question:

1. Writing Struts actions that extend a Spring-aware base class
2. Delegating requests to Struts actions that are managed as Spring beans

You'll learn how to use each of these Struts integration strategies in the sections that follow. But first, regardless of which approach you take, there's one bit of configuration that you'll need to take care of: telling Struts about your Spring context.

### 10.1.1 *Registering the Spring plug-in*

In order for Struts to have access to Spring-managed beans, you'll need to register a Struts plug-in that is aware of the Spring application context. Add the following code to your struts-config.xml to register the plug-in:

```
<plug-in
    className="org.springframework.web.struts.ContextLoaderPlugIn">
  <set-property property="contextConfigLocation"
      value="/WEB-INF/training-servlet.xml,/WEB-INF/..."/>
</plug-in>
```

`ContextLoaderPlugIn` loads a Spring application context (a `WebApplication-Context`, to be specific), using the context configuration files listed (comma-separated) in its `contextConfigLocation` property.

Now that the plug-in is in place, you're ready to choose an integration strategy. Let's first look at how to create Struts actions that are aware of the Spring application context.

### 10.1.2 *Implementing Spring-aware Struts actions*

One way to integrate Struts and Spring is to write all of your Struts action classes to extend a common base class that has access to the Spring application context.

The good news is that you won't have to write this Spring-aware base action class because Spring comes with `org.springframework.web.struts.ActionSupport`, an abstract implementation of the `org.apache.struts.action.Action` that overrides the `setServlet()` method to retrieve the `WebApplicationContext` from the `Context-LoaderPlugIn`. Then, anytime your action needs to access a bean from the Spring context, it just needs to call the `getBean()` method.

For example, consider the updated version of `ListCourseAction` in listing 10.2. This version extends `ActionSupport` so that it has access to the Spring application context.

**Listing 10.2   A Struts action that lists courses**

```
public class ListCourseAction extends ActionSupport {
  public ActionForward execute(
      ActionMapping mapping,
      ActionForm form,
      HttpServletRequest request,
      HttpServletResponse response) throws Exception {

    ApplicationContext context =
        getWebApplicationContext();       <-- Get Spring context

    CourseService courseService =                   Get courseService
      (CourseService) context.getBean("courseService");   bean

    Set allCourses = courseService.getAllCourses();

    request.setAttribute("courses", allCourses);

    return mapping.findForward("courseList");
  }
}
```

When `ListCourseAction` needs a `CourseService`, it starts by calling `getWebApplicationContext()` to get a reference to the Spring application context. Then it calls the `getBean()` method to retrieve a reference to the Spring-managed `courseService` bean.

The good thing about using this approach to Struts-Spring integration is that it's very intuitive. Aside from extending `ActionSupport` and retrieving beans from the application context, you are able to write and configure your Struts actions in much the same way as you would in a non-Spring Struts application.

But this approach also has its negative side. Most notably, your action classes will directly use Spring-specific classes. This tightly couples your Struts action code with Spring, which may not be desirable. Also, the action class is responsible for looking up references to Spring-managed beans. This is in direct opposition to the notion of inversion of control (IoC).

For those reasons, there's another way to integrate Struts and Spring that lets you write Struts action classes that aren't aware they are integrated with Spring. And you can use Spring's IoC support to inject service beans into your actions so that they don't have to look them up for themselves.

### 10.1.3 *Delegating actions*

Another approach to Struts-Spring integration is to write a Struts action that is nothing more than a proxy to the real Struts action that is contained in the Spring application context. The proxy action will retrieve the application context from the `ContextLoaderPlugIn`, look up the real Struts action from the context, then delegate responsibility to the real Struts action.

One nice thing about this approach is that the only action that does anything Spring-specific is the proxy action. The real actions can be written as just plain subclasses of `org.apache.struts.Action`. Listing 10.3 shows yet another version of `ListCourseAction` that is implemented as a plain Spring-ignorant Struts action.

**Listing 10.3   A Struts action that lists courses**

```
public class ListCourseAction extends Action {
  public ActionForward execute(
      ActionMapping mapping,
      ActionForm form,
      HttpServletRequest request,
      HttpServletResponse response) throws Exception {

    Set allCourses = courseService.getAllCourses();

    request.setAttribute("courses", allCourses);

    return mapping.findForward("courseList");
  }

  private CourseService courseService;
  public void setCourseService(CourseService courseService) {     Inject
    this.courseService = courseService;                           CourseService
  }
}
```

Normally at this point, you'd register this Struts action in struts-config.xml. But instead, we're going to register the proxy action. Fortunately, you won't have to write the proxy action yourself because Spring provides one for you in the `org.springframework.web.struts.DelegatingActionProxy` class. All you'll need to do is set this action up in struts-config.xml:

```
<action path="/listCourses"
     type="org.springframework.web.struts.DelegatingActionProxy"/>
```

But what of `ListCourseAction`? Where does it get registered?

### Wiring Actions as Spring beans

Oddly enough, you don't need to register `ListCourseAction` in struts-config.xml. Instead, you register it as a bean in your Spring context configuration file:

```
<bean name="/listCourses"
     class="com.springinaction.training.struts.ListCourseAction">
  <property name="courseService">
    <ref bean="courseService"/>
  </property>
</bean>
```

Here the bean is named using the `name` attribute instead of the `id` attribute. That's because XML places restrictions on what characters can appear in an `id` attribute and the slash (/) is invalid. The value of the `name` attribute is very important. It must exactly match the `path` attribute of the `<action>` in struts-config.xml. That's because `DelegatingActionProxy` will use the value of the `path` attribute to look up the real action in the Spring context. (This is reminiscent of how you would name beans using `BeanNameUrlHandlerMapping`; see chapter 8.)

You may have noticed that the newest `ListCourseAction` gets a reference to a `CourseService` through setter injection. As far as Spring is concerned, it is just another bean. Therefore, you can use Spring's IoC to wire service beans into the Struts action.

The benefit of using `DelegatingActionProxy` is that you are able to write Struts actions that don't use any Spring-specific classes. Also, your Struts actions can take advantage of IoC to obtain references to their collaborating objects.

The only bad thing about this approach is that it's not entirely intuitive. A quick look at the struts-config.xml file may confuse someone who's not used to this approach because it appears that all paths are mapped to the same action class (in fact, they are).

### Using request delegation

To make action delegation slightly more intuitive, Spring provides `Delegating-RequestProcessor`, a replacement request processor for Spring. To use it, place the following in your struts-config.xml:

```
<controller processorClass=
    "org.springframework.web.struts.DelegatingRequestProcessor"/>
```

Or, if you are using Tiles with Struts:

```
<controller processorClass="org.springframework.web.
    struts.DelegatingTilesRequestProcessor"/>
```

`DelegatingRequestProcessor` (or `DelegatingTilesRequestProcessor`) tells Struts to automatically delegate action requests to Struts actions in a Spring context. This enables you to declare your Struts actions in struts-config.xml with their real type. For example:

```
<action path="/listCourses"
    type="com.springinaction.training.struts.ListCourseAction"/>
```

When a request is received for /listCourses, `DelegatingRequestProcessor` will automatically refer to the Spring application context, looking for a bean named /listCourses (which is presumed to be a Struts action class).

As it turns out, the `type` attribute is ignored completely. This means you can declare your Struts actions in shorthand as follows:

```
<action path="/listCourses"/>
```

Although it's optional, you may still choose to set the `type` attribute so that it's clear which action is mapped to the path.

Struts was among the first of the MVC frameworks for Java and set the stage for many of the frameworks that followed. But it was only the beginning.

## 10.2 Working with Tapestry

Tapestry is another MVC framework for the Java platform that is gathering a large following. One of the most appealing features of Tapestry is that it uses plain HTML as its template language.

While it may seem peculiar that Tapestry uses a static markup language to drive dynamically created content, it's actually a very practical approach. Tapestry components are placed within an HTML page using any HTML tag you want to use (`<span>` is often the tag of choice for Tapestry components). The HTML tag is given a `jwcid` attribute, which references a Tapestry component definition. For example, consider the following simple Tapestry page:

```
<html>
  <head><title>Simple page</title></head>
  <body>
    <h2><span jwcid="simpleHeader">Simple header</span></h2>
  </body>
</html>
```

When Tapestry sees the `jwcid` attribute, it will replace the `<span>` tag (and its content) with the HTML produced by the `simpleHeader` component. The nice thing about this approach is that page designers and Tapestry developers alike can easily understand this HTML template. And even without being processed by the Tapestry engine, it loads cleanly into any HTML design tool or browser.

In this section, we're going to replace Tapestry's default engine with a Spring-aware engine so that Tapestry pages and components can have access to service beans that are managed by Spring. We're going to assume that you are already familiar with Tapestry. If you need to learn more about Tapestry, we recommend *Tapestry in Action* by Howard Lewis Ship (the creator of Tapestry).

### 10.2.1 *Replacing the Tapestry Engine*

Tapestry's engine maintains an object (known as `global`) that is a simple container for any objects you want shared among all Tapestry sessions. It is a `java.util.HashMap` by default.

The key strategy behind Tapestry-Spring integration is loading a Spring application context into Tapestry's `global` object. Once it's in `global`, all pages can have access to Spring-managed beans by retrieving the context from `global` and calling `getBean()`.

To load a Spring application context into Tapestry's `global` object, you'll need to replace Tapestry's default engine (`org.apache.tapestry.engine.BaseEngine`) with a custom engine. Unfortunately, the latest version of Spring that was available while we were writing this does not come with a replacement Tapestry engine. This leaves it up to you to write it yourself (even though it's virtually the same for any Spring/Tapestry hybrid application).

`SpringTapestryEngine` (listing 10.4) extends `BaseEngine` to load a Spring application context into the Tapestry `global` property.

**Listing 10.4  A replacement Tapestry engine that loads a Spring context into `global`**

```
package com.springinaction.tapestry;

import javax.servlet.ServletContext;
import org.apache.tapestry.engine.BaseEngine;
import org.apache.tapestry.request.RequestContext;
```

```
import org.springframework.context.ApplicationContext;
import org.springframework.web.context.support.
        WebApplicationContextUtils;

public class SpringTapestryEngine extends BaseEngine {
  private static final String SPRING_CONTEXT_KEY = "springContext";

  protected void setupForRequest(RequestContext context) {
    super.setupForRequest(context);

    Map global = (Map) getGlobal();

    ApplicationContext appContext =
        (ApplicationContext)
        global.get(SPRING_CONTEXT_KEY);          ◁── Check for Spring context

    if (appContext == null) {
      ServletContext servletContext =
          context.getServlet().getServletContext();
      appContext = WebApplicationContextUtils.              Load
          getWebApplicationContext(servletContext);        context

      global.put(SPRING_CONTEXT_KEY, appContext);
    }
  }
}
```

SpringTapestryEngine first checks global to see if the Spring context has already
been loaded. If so, then there is nothing to do. But if global doesn't already have
a reference to the Spring application context, it will use WebApplicationContext-
Utils to retrieve a web application context. It then places the application context
into global for later use.

Because SpringTapestryEngine uses WebApplicationContextUtils to look up
the application context, you'll need to be sure to load the context into your web
application's servlet context using either ContextLoaderServlet or ContextLoader-
Listener. The following <listener> block in web.xml uses ContextLoaderListener
to load the application context:

```
<listener>
  <listener-class>org.springframework.web.
        context.ContextLoaderListener</listener-class>
</listener>
```

Note that there is one limitation of SpringTapestryEngine as it is written. It
assumes that the global object is a java.util.Map object. This is usually not a

problem as Tapestry defaults `global` to be a `java.util.HashMap`. But if your application has changed this by setting the `org.apache.tapestry.global-class` property, `SpringTapestryEngine` will need to change accordingly.

The last thing to do is to substitute the default Tapestry engine with `Spring-TapestryEngine`. This is accomplished by configuring the `engine-class` attribute of your Tapestry application:

```
<application name="Spring Training"
    engine-class="com.springinaction.tapestry.SpringTapestryEngine">
...
</application>
```

At this point, the Spring application context is available in Tapestry's `global` object ready to be used to dispense Spring-managed service beans. Let's take a look at how to wire those service beans into a Tapestry page specification.

### 10.2.2  *Loading Spring beans into Tapestry pages*

Suppose that you're implementing the course detail page from the Spring Training application as a Tapestry page. In doing so, you would need to create a page specification file for the course detail page and a page specification class that performs the logic behind the page.

The page specification class will need to retrieve course information using the `courseService` bean from Spring. Listing 10.5 shows an excerpt from `Course-DetailPage`.

**Listing 10.5   A course detail page, à la Tapestry**

```
public abstract class CourseDetailPage extends BasePage {
  public abstract CourseService getCourseService();

  private Course course;
  public Course getCourse() { return course; }

  public void displayCourse(int courseId, IRequestCycle cycle) {
    CourseService courseService = getCourseService();

    course = courseService.getCourse(courseId);    <-- Look up course

    cycle.activate(this);    <-- Make this current page
  }
}
```

When the `displayCourse()` method is called (perhaps as the result of clicking on a link from a course listing page), it first calls the `getCourseService()` method to

retrieve a reference to the courseService bean. It then proceeds to use the Course-
Service object to retrieve a Course object.

The big question to ask is where does the CourseService come from? The get-
CourseService() method is abstract, so presumably something will implement
this method. But how will that happen?

The page's specification file clears this up a bit:

```
<page-specification
    class="com.springinaction.training.tapestry.CourseDetailPage">
  <property-specification name="courseService"
      type="com.springinaction.training.service.CourseService">
    global.springContext.getBean("courseService")
  </property-specification>
...
</page-specification>
```

Here, the <property-specification> element performs a type of injection. When
Tapestry loads the application, it will extend CourseDetailPage, implementing
the getCourseService() method to retrieve the courseService bean from the
Spring application context (which was placed into Tapestry's global object by
SpringTapestryEngine).

To complete the story of the course detail page, the following excerpt from
courseDetail.html shows how the template uses Object Graph Navigation Language (OGNL) to display course information from the Course object:

```
<h2><span jwcid="@Insert" value="ognl:course.name">
  Some Course
</span></h2>
<b>ID: </b>
  <span jwcid="@Insert" value="ognl:course.id">00000</span>
<br>
<b>Instructor: </b>
  <span jwcid="@Insert"
      value="ognl:course.instructor.firstName + ' ' +
                 course.instructor.lastName">
    Jim Smith
  </span><br>
<b>Starts: </b>
  <span jwcid="@Insert" value="ognl:course.startDate">
    Start Date
  </span><br>
<b>Ends: </b>
  <span jwcid="@Insert" value="ognl:course.endDate">
    End Date
  </span><br><br>
<span jwcid="@Insert" value="ognl:course.description">
  Description
</span>
```

Although this example shows how to use Spring beans from within a Tapestry page specification, the same technique can be applied to a Tapestry component specification.

Tapestry is gathering a huge following, largely due to its use of HTML as a template language and its event-driven approach to handling interaction between the user interface and the application. Another event-driven approach to MVC is found in the JavaServer Faces specification. The final MVC framework we'll integrate with Spring will be JavaServer Faces.

## 10.3 *Integrating with JavaServer Faces*

JavaServer Faces (JSF) may be a newcomer in the space of Java web frameworks, but it has a long history. First announced at JavaOne in 2001, the JSF specification made grand promises of extending the component-driven nature of Swing and AWT user interfaces to web frameworks. The JSF team produced virtually no results for a very long time, leaving some (including us) to believe it was vaporware. Then in 2002, Craig McClanahan (the original creator of Jakarta Struts) joined the JSF team as the specification lead and everything turned around.

After a long wait, the JSF 1.0 specification was released in February 2004 and was quickly followed by the maintenance 1.1 specification in May 2004. At this time JSF has a lot of momentum and is capturing the attention of Java developers.

In a nutshell, JSF-Spring integration makes Spring-managed beans visible as variables to JSF (as if the Spring beans are configured as JSF-managed beans). We're going to assume that you are already familiar with JSF. If you want to know more about JSF, we recommend that you have a look at Kito D. Mann's *JavaServer Faces in Action* (Manning, 2004).

### 10.3.1 *Resolving variables*

Imagine that long before you ever heard of Spring, you had already developed the Spring Training application using JSF to develop the web layer. As part of the application, you have created a form that is used to register new students.

The following excerpt from the JSF-enabled registerStudent.jsp file shows how JSF binds a Student object to fields in the form:

```
<h:form>
  <h2>Create Student</h2>
  <h:panelGrid columns="2">
    <f:verbatim><b>Login:</b></f:verbatim>
    <h:inputText value="#{student.login}" required="true"/>
```

```
<f:verbatim><b>Password:</b></f:verbatim>
<h:inputText value="#{student.password}" required="true"/>

<f:verbatim><b>First Name:</b></f:verbatim>
<h:inputText value="#{student.firstName}" required="true"/>

<f:verbatim><b>Last Name:</b></f:verbatim>
<h:inputText value="#{student.lastName}" required="true"/>
  ….
  </h:panelGrid>
  <h:commandButton id="submit" action="#{student.enroll}"
      value="Enroll Student"/>
</h:form>
```

Notice that the `action` parameter of the `<h:commandButton>` is set to `#{student.enroll}`. Unlike many other MVC frameworks (including Spring's MVC), JSF doesn't use a separate controller object to process form submissions. Instead, JSF passes control to a method in the model bean. In this case, when the form is submitted JSF will call the `enroll()` method of the `student` bean to process the form. The `enroll()` method is defined as follows:

```
public String enroll() {
  try {
    studentService.enrollStudent(this);
  } catch (Exception e) {
    return "error";
  }

  return "success";
}
```

To keep the `Student` bean as simple as possible, the `enroll()` method simply delegates responsibility to the `enrollStudent()` method of a `StudentService` bean. So, where does the `studentService` property get set?

To find the answer to that question, consider the following declaration of the student bean in faces-config.xml:

```
<managed-bean>
  <managed-bean-name>student</managed-bean-name>
  <managed-bean-class>
    com.springinaction.training.model.Student
  </managed-bean-class>
  <managed-bean-scope>request</managed-bean-scope>
  <managed-property>
    <property-name>studentService</property-name>
    <value>#{studentService}</value>
  </managed-property>
</managed-bean>
```

Here the `student` bean is declared as a request-scoped JSF-managed bean. But take note of the `<managed-property>` element. JSF supports a simple implementation of setter injection. `#{studentService}` indicates that the `studentService` property is being given a reference to a bean named `studentService`.

As for the `studentService` bean, you have declared it as a JSF-managed bean as follows:

```
<managed-bean>
  <managed-bean-name>studentService</managed-bean-name>
  <managed-bean-class>
    com.springinaction.training.service.StudentServiceImpl
  </managed-bean-class>
  <managed-bean-scope>session</managed-bean-scope>
  <managed-property>
    <property-name>studentDao</property-name>
    <value>#{studentDao}</value>
  </managed-property>
</managed-bean>
```

Dependency injection is employed again in the `studentService` bean wiring in a `StudentDao` bean to the `studentDao` property of `studentService`. And if you were to examine the declaration of the `studentDao` bean, you'd find it is injected with a `javax.sql.DataSource`, which itself is also declared as a JSF-managed bean.

Seeing how JSF supports dependency injection, you may be wondering why you would ever want to integrate Spring into your JSF application. It's true that JSF's support for setter injection is not too different from that of Spring's. But remember that Spring offers more than just simple IoC. In particular, Spring's declarative transaction support may come in handy with the `student-Service` bean.

Furthermore, even though JSF is a presentation layer framework, you are declaring service- and data access-layer components in its configuration file. This seems somewhat inappropriate and it would be better to separate the layers, allowing JSF to handle presentation stuff and Spring handle the rest.

### Resolving Spring beans

JSF uses a variable resolver to locate beans that are managed within the JSF application. The JSF-Spring project (a separate project from Spring) provides a replacement variable resolver, `FacesSpringVariableResolver`, that resolves variables from both faces-config.xml and a Spring application context. You can download the JSF-Spring integration package from the project's web site at http://jsf-spring.sourceforge.net. We'll be using JSF-Spring version 2.5 to develop the JSF version of the Spring Training application.

To substitute the default variable resolver with `FacesSpringVariableResolver`, place the following `<variable-resolver>` element in the `<application>` block of faces-config.xml, as follows:

```
<application>
  ...
  <variable-resolver>
    de.mindmatters.faces.spring.FacesSpringVariableResolver
  </variable-resolver>
</application>
```

For `FacesSpringVariableResolver` to be able to resolve Spring-managed beans, you'll also need a `ContextLoaderListener` configured in your application's web.xml file to load the Spring application context:

```
<listener>
  <listener-class>org.springframework.web.
          context.ContextLoaderListener</listener-class>
</listener>
```

By default, `ContextLoaderListener` will load the Spring context configuration file from /WEB-INF/applicationContext.xml. If you have your Spring context defined in a different file, perhaps /WEB-INF/applicationContext-hibernate.xml, then you'll want to add the following servlet context parameter to web.xml:

```
<context-param>
  <param-name>contextConfigLocation</param-name>
  <param-value>/WEB-INF/applicationContext-hibernate.xml</param-value>
</context-param>
```

With `FacesSpringVariableResolver` in place and the application context loaded, you are now ready to wire your service and data access layer beans in Spring.

### Using Spring beans

`FacesSpringVariableResolver` makes the resolving of Spring-managed beans transparent in JSF. To illustrate, recall that the `student` bean is injected with a reference to the `studentService` bean with the following `<managed-property>` declaration in faces-config.xml:

```
<managed-property>
  <property-name>studentService</property-name>
  <value>#{studentService}</value>
</managed-property>
```

Even though the `studentService` bean is now going to reside in a Spring context, nothing needs to change about the existing declaration of the `student` bean.

When it comes time to inject the `studentService` property of the `student` bean, it asks `FacesSpringVariableResolver` for the reference to the `studentService` bean. `FacesSpringVariableResolver` will first look in the JSF configuration for the bean. When it can't find it, it will then look in the Spring application context.

But it will only find the `studentService` bean in the Spring context if you declare it there. So, instead of registering it as a `<managed-bean>` in faces-config.xml, place it in the Spring context definition file as follows:

```
<bean id="studentService"
    class="com.springinaction.training.service.StudentServiceImpl">
  <constructor-arg><ref bean="studentDao"/></constructor-arg>
</bean>
```

Notice that this declaration of `studentService` is no different than how it would be declared in an application that uses Spring MVC. In fact, from the service layer to the data access layer, you will declare your application beans in the Spring application context exactly the same as you would if your application were fronted by Spring MVC. `FacesSpringVariableResolver` will find them as though they are part of the JSF configuration.

Resolving Spring beans as JSF variables is the key part of JSF-Spring integration. But there's one more loose end to tie up with regard to JSF-fronted Spring applications: publishing `RequestHandledEvent`s.

### 10.3.2 *Publishing request handled events*

Sometimes it is necessary for your application to know when a servlet request has been handled. Maybe some postprocessing needs to take place or you have to perform some cleanup once the request is complete.

In a Spring MVC application, `DispatcherServlet` publishes a `RequestHandled-Event` after the request has been handled. Any bean that implements the `ApplicationListener` interface will be given a chance to react to this event.

For example, one of the tidbits of information contained in a `RequestHandled-Event` is how long the request took to process (in milliseconds). Spring comes with `PerformanceMonitorListener`, a bean that listens for `RequestHandledEvent` and logs the processing time for the request.

```
<bean id="performanceListener" class="org.springframework.
    ➥ web.context.support.PerformanceMonitorListener"/>
```

Your application may also have custom beans that implement `ActionListener`. They will also receive a `RequestHandledEvent` whenever a servlet request is completed.

But that's what happens if your application's web layer is based on Spring MVC. If you're using JSF, the JSF implementation won't know to fire a `RequestHandledEvent`.

How can you make sure that a `RequestHandledEvent` is published if your application is fronted by JSF?

The JSF-Spring project comes with `RequestHandledFilter`, a servlet filter that publishes a `RequestHandledEvent` for you once the request is completed. All you need to do is to register this filter in web.xml:

```
<filter>
  <filter-name>RequestHandledFilter</filter-name>
  <filter-class>de.mindmatters.faces.
➥    spring.RequestHandledFilter</filter-class>
</filter>

<filter-mapping>
  <filter-name>RequestHandledFilter</filter-name>
  <servlet-name>FacesServlet</servlet-name>
</filter-mapping>
```

Here the `<filter-mapping>` is configured to filter all requests to the `FacesServlet` (presumed to be the JSF servlet) so that all JSF requests end with a `RequestHandled-Event` being published. You may choose to configure the filter with a `<url-pattern>` instead of `<servlet-name>`. For example:

```
<filter-mapping>
  <filter-name>RequestHandledFilter</filter-name>
  <url-pattern>/faces/registerStudent.jsp</url-pattern>
</filter-mapping>
```

Here, the focus of the filter is tightened to a particular request. Only requests to the student registration page will fire the `RequestHandledEvent`.

You should note that most applications will not require notification of `Request-HandledEvents`. Unless your application includes beans that are `Application-Listeners` and are interested in `RequestHandledEvent`, you do not need to add the `RequestHandledFilter` to web.xml.

## 10.4  *Integrating with WebWork*

WebWork is an open source web framework from Open Symphony that has been popular for quite some time. Despite its name, WebWork is actually a service invocation framework that is not specific to just web applications. It its simplest form, Webwork is based around general-purpose actions. These actions process requests and then return a `String` that indicates the next step in the request chain. This could be another action or a view. However, nothing about this is web specific.

However, for our purposes we will be discussing WebWork in the context of web applications. And we will actually be discussing two different versions of WebWork—

WebWork 1 and WebWork 2. Because both the APIs and Spring's integration are quite different for both versions, we will cover them separately. Let's begin by looking at WebWork 1.

### 10.4.1 *WebWork 1*

As we indicated above, you create a WebWork action that is responsible for handling a web request. In the case of WebWork 1, this will be an implementation of the `webwork.action.Action` interface. This interface has one method: `execute()`. A typical implementation would subclass `webwork.action.ActionSupport` like this:

```
public class HelloAction extends webwork.action.ActionSupport {
  public String doExecute() throws Exception {
    // handle request
    return SUCCESS;
  }
}
```

The WebWork framework gets instances of these `Actions` from a subclass of `webwork.action.factory.ActionFactory`. To integrate WebWork 1 and Spring, you will use an instance of `webwork.action.factory.SpringActionFactory`. However, this class is not included in the most current release (1.4) of WebWork 1. Instead, you will have to download this class and `webwork.action.factory.SpringActionFactoryProxy` from WebWork's CVS located at cvs.sourceforge.net/cvsroot/opensymphony or http://cvs.sourceforge.net/viewcvs.py/opensymphony/webwork/.

From there, configure the `webwork.action.factory` property in the webwork.properties file to use the `SpringActionFactory`:

```
webwork.action.factory=webwork.action.factory.SpringActionFactory
```

Next, load the Spring application context using `ContextLoaderServlet` or `ContextLoaderListener;`

```
<listener>
  <listener-class>org.springframework.web.
      context.ContextLoaderListener</listener-class>
  </listener-class>
</listener>
```

Finally, declare your actions in the Spring configuration file, wiring in properties as you would any other Spring bean:

```
<bean id="someAction" class="com.foo.Action">
  <property name="fooService"><ref bean="fooService"/></property>
</bean>
```

Ta-da! Now WebWork will look for its actions in Spring's application context first. If they are not found there, WebWork will simply fall back to its default behavior and instantiate a new instance of the `Action`. Now let's see how we integrate Spring and WebWork 2.

### 10.4.2 *XWork/WebWork2*

The APIs for WebWork 1 and WebWork 2 are really not that different for actions. In fact, the `Action` interface signature is exactly the same. However, it is now part of another command framework on which WebWork 2 depends—Xwork. The action interface you will use in WebWork 2 is `com.opensymphony.xwork.Action`.

And once again, the classes you need for Spring integration are not included with WebWork's latest release (2.1.6). This time you will need to download the XWork/Spring integration JAR from http://www.ryandaigle.com/pebble/images/webwork2-spring.jar.

The next step is to configure the XWork configuration file, xwork.xml. Here you will notice one important difference between WebWork1 integration and WebWork2 integration. With WebWork 1, we defined our actions in the Spring configuration file. With WebWork 2, we define our actions in xwork.xml, just as we would for a "non-Spring" action:

```
<action name="myAction"
    class="com.foo.Action">
  <external-ref name="someDao">someDao</external-ref>
  <result name="success" type="dispatcher">
    <param name="location">/success.jsp</param>
  </result>
</action>
```

Notice the `external-ref` element. This is actually referencing a Spring bean named `someDao`. The rest of the configurations we are going to cover are what make this "magic" possible. The next step is to tell WebWork how to resolve Spring external references:

```
<package name="default" extends="webwork-default"
    externalReferenceResolver="com.atlassian.xwork.ext.
    SpringServletContextReferenceResolver"/>
```

Now we have a resource resolver capable of resolving external beans to our Spring application context. The final piece of configuration for the xwork.xml file is to add an interceptor that will allow any reference to be resolved as an external resource:

```
<interceptors>
  <interceptor name="reference-resolver" class="com.opensymphony.
    xwork.interceptor.ExtenalReferenceInterceptor">
    <interceptor-ref name="defaultStack">
```

```
      <interceptor-ref name="reference-resolver"/>
    </interceptor>
  </interceptors>
  <default-interceptor-ref name="myDefaultWebStack"/>
```

The last step to this process is to configure our web.xml file. Like WebWork 1, we configure a `ContextLoaderListener` or `ContextLoaderServlet`. But we also need to configure a `com.atlassian.xwork.ext.ResolverSetupServletContextListener`. This is the "bridge"" between WebWork2 and Spring, retrieving Spring's application context on behalf of WebWork.:

```
<listener>
  <listener-class>org.springframework.web.
      context.ContextLoaderListener</listener-class>
</listener>
<listener>
  <listener-class>com.atlassian.xwork.ext.
      ResolverSetupServletContextListener</listener-class>
</listener>
```

And there you have it. WebWork 2 will now be able to resolve references to beans with your Spring application context when it is creating its actions.

## 10.5 *Summary*

Spring MVC is an excellent MVC framework for developing web applications. You may, however, find another MVC framework more to your liking. Fortunately, choosing to use Spring in your service and data access layer doesn't preclude the use of an MVC framework other than Spring MVC.

In this chapter, you saw how to integrate Spring into several prevalent MVC frameworks, including Jakarta Struts, JavaServer Faces, Tapestry, and WebWork. Each of these frameworks offers a different strategy for integration.

With Struts, you actually have two choices. First, you can have your Struts actions become Spring-aware, which provides a straightforward solution but couples your actions to Spring. Alternatively, you can have Struts delegate the handling of actions to Spring beans, giving you a more loosely coupled solution but perhaps a more complex Struts configuration.

Tapestry conveniently comes with built-in hooks for integrating other frameworks. To integrate Spring, we simply replace Tapestry's default engine with a `SpringTapestryEngine` and we are in business.

JSF provides a similar hook. To allow JSF to integrate with Spring, we gave it a `FacesSpringVariableResolver` that lets it resolve beans from both its own internal configuration and Spring's application context.

WebWork provides two solutions, depending on which version you are using. With WebWork 1, you simply include WebWork `Actions` in your Spring configuration file as you would any other bean. With WebWork 2, you actually give WebWork the ability to wire in beans that are configured externally in your Spring configuration file.

So now you know how to develop web applications using Spring in a variety of ways. You can use Spring's MVC framework or use a third-party web framework of your choice to handle requests. You can also integrate with many different view technologies. But no matter what technology you choose, you will need to secure your web application. In the next chapter you will discover how to do this using the Acegi Security System.

# Securing
# Spring applications

11

### This chapter covers

- Introducing the Acegi Security System
- Securing web applications using servlet filters
- Authenticating against databases and LDAP
- Transparently securing method invocations

Have you ever noticed that most people in television sitcoms don't lock their doors? It happens all of the time. On *Seinfeld*, Kramer frequently let himself in to Jerry's apartment to help himself to the goodies in Jerry's refrigerator. On *Friends*, the various characters often entered each others' apartments without warning or hesitation. Even once, while in London, Ross burst into Chandler's hotel room, narrowly missing Chandler in a compromising situation with Ross's sister.

In the days of *Leave It to Beaver*, it wasn't so unusual for people to leave their doors unlocked. But it seems crazy that in a day when we're concerned with privacy and security to see television characters enabling unhindered access to their apartments and homes.

Likewise, when dealing with software systems, it would be unwise to let anyone gain access to sensitive and private information. Users should be challenged to identify themselves so that the application can choose to grant or deny access to restricted information. Whether you are protecting an e-mail account with a username/password pair or a brokerage account with a trading PIN, security is an important *aspect* of most applications.

It is no accident that we chose the word "aspect" when describing application security. Security is a concern that transcends an application's functionality. For the most part, an application should play no part in securing itself. Although you could write security functionality directly into your application's code (and that's not uncommon), it is better to keep security concerns separate from application concerns.

If you're thinking that it is starting to sound like security is accomplished using aspect-oriented techniques, then you're right. In this chapter we introduce you to the Acegi Security System and explore ways to secure your applications using both Spring AOP and servlet filters.[1]

## 11.1 *Introducing the Acegi Security System*

Acegi is a security framework that provides declarative security for your Spring-based applications. It provides a collection of beans that are configured within a Spring application context, taking full advantage of Spring's support for dependency injection and aspect-oriented programming.

When securing web applications, Acegi uses servlet filters that intercept servlet requests to perform authentication and enforce security. And, as you'll find in

---

[1] We're probably going to get a lot of e-mails about this, but we have to say it anyway: servlet filters are a primitive form of AOP. There … we've said it … we feel better now.

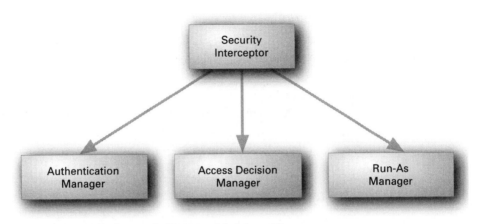

**Figure 11.1  The fundamental elements of Acegi security**

section 11.4.1, Acegi employs a unique mechanism for declaring servlet filters that enables you to inject them with their dependencies using Spring IoC.

Acegi can also enforce security at a lower level by securing method invocations. Using Spring AOP, Acegi proxies objects, applying aspects that ensure a user has the proper authority to call the secured methods.

Regardless of whether you are securing a web application or require method-level security, Acegi applies security using four main components, as shown in figure 11.1.

Throughout this chapter, we'll uncover the details of each of these components. But before we get into the nitty-gritty of Acegi security, let's take a high-level view of the roles that each of these components play.

### 11.1.1  Security interceptors

In order to release a latch and open a door, you must insert a key into the lock that trips the tumblers properly. If the cut of the key is incorrect, the tumblers won't be tripped and the latch will not be released. But if you have the right key, all of the tumblers will accept the key and the latch will be released, allowing you to open the door.

In Acegi, the security interceptor can be thought of as a latch that prevents you from accessing a secured resource in your application. In order to flip the latch and get past the security interceptor you must enter your "key" (typically a username and password) into the system. The key will then try to trip the security interceptor's "tumblers" in an attempt to grant you access to the secured resource.

### 11.1.2 *Authentication managers*

The first of the security interceptor's tumblers to be tripped is the *authentication manager*. The authentication manager is responsible for determining who you are. It does this by considering your *principal* (typically a username) and your *credentials* (typically a password).

Your principal defines who you are and your credentials are evidence that corroborates your identity. If your credentials are good enough to convince the authentication manager that your principal identifies you, then Acegi will know who it is dealing with.

### 11.1.3 *Access decisions managers*

Once Acegi has determined who you are, it must decide whether you are authorized to access to the secured resource. An *access decision manager* is the second tumbler of the Acegi lock to be tripped. The access decision manager performs authorization, deciding whether or not to let you in by considering your authentication information and the security attributes that have been associated with the secured resource.

For example, the security rules may dictate that only supervisors should be allowed access to a secured resource. If you have been granted supervisor privileges, then the second and final tumbler, the access decision manager, will have been tripped and the security interceptor will move out of your way and let you gain access to the secured resource.

### 11.1.4 *Run-as managers*

If you've gotten past the authentication manager and the access decision manager, then the security interceptor will be unlocked and the door is ready to open. But before you twist the knob and go in, there's one more thing that the security interceptor might do.

Even though you have passed authentication and have been granted access to a resource, there may be more security restrictions behind the door. For example, you may be granted the rights to view a webpage, but the objects that are used to create that page may have different security requirements than the webpage. A run-as manager can be used to replace your authentication with an authentication that allows you access to the secured objects that are deeper in your application.

The usefulness of run-as managers is limited in most applications. Fortunately, you don't have to use or fully understand run-as managers to be able to secure your application with Acegi. Therefore, we're going to regard run-as managers as an advanced topic and forego any further discussion of them.

Now that you've seen the big picture of Acegi security, let's back up and see how to configure each of these pieces of Acegi security, starting with the authentication manager.

## 11.2 *Managing authentication*

The first step in determining whether a user should be granted access to a secured resource is to determine the identity of the user. In most applications this means that the user provides a username and password at a login screen. The username (or principal) tells the application who the user claims to be. To corroborate the user's identity, the user also provides a password (or credentials). If the application's security mechanism confirms that the password is good, then the user is assumed to be who they claim to be.

In Acegi, the authentication manager assumes the job of establishing a user's identity. An authentication manager is defined by the `net.sf.acegisecurity.AuthenticationManager` interface:

```
public interface AuthenticationManager {
  public Authentication authenticate(Authentication authentication)
    throws AuthenticationException;
}
```

The `authenticate()` method is given a `net.sf.acegisecurity.Authentication` object (which may only carry the principal and credentials) and attempts to authenticate the user. If successful, the `authenticate()` method returns a complete `Authentication` object, including information about the user's granted authorities (which will be considered by the authorization manager). If authentication fails, an `AuthenticationException` will be thrown.

As you can see, the `AuthenticationManager` interface is quite simple and you could easily implement your own `AuthenticationManager` fairly easily. But Acegi comes with `ProviderManager`, an implementation of `AuthenticationManager` that is suitable for most situations. So instead of rolling our own authentication manager, let's take a look at how to use `ProviderManager`.

### 11.2.1 *Configuring a provider manager*

`ProviderManager` is an authentication manager implementation that delegates responsibility for authentication to one or more authentication providers, as shown in figure 11.2.

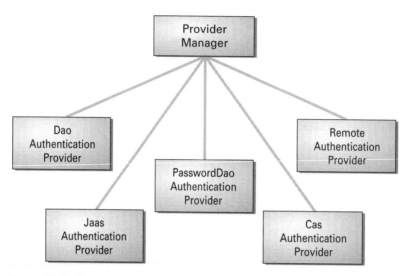

**Figure 11.2** A `ProviderManager` delegates authentication responsibility to one or more authentication providers.

The idea of `ProviderManager` is to enable you to authenticate users against multiple identity management sources. Rather than relying on itself to perform authentication, `ProviderManager` steps one by one through a collection of authentication providers, until one of them successfully authenticates the user (or until it runs out of providers).

You can configure a `ProviderManager` in the Spring configuration file as follows:

```
<bean id="authenticationManager"
    class="net.sf.acegisecurity.providers.ProviderManager">
  <property name="providers">
    <list>
      <ref bean="daoAuthenticationProvider"/>
      <ref bean="passwordDaoProvider"/>
    </list>
  </property>
</bean>
```

`ProviderManager` is given its list of authentication providers through its `providers` property. Typically you'll need only one authentication provider, but in some cases it may be useful to provide a list of several so that if authentication fails against one, another provider will be tried. An authentication provider is defined by the `net.sf.acegisecurity.provider.AuthenticationProvider` interface. Spring comes with several useful implementations of `AuthenticationProvider`, as listed in table 11.1.

**Table 11.1  Acegi's selection of authentication providers**

| Authentication Provider | Purpose |
| --- | --- |
| `net.sf.acegisecurity.adapters.AuthByAdapterProvider` | Authenticating using container adapters. |
| `net.sf.acegisecurity.providers.cas.CasAuthenticationProvider` | Authenticating against Yale Central Authentication Service (CAS). |
| `net.sf.acegisecurity.providers.dao.DaoAuthenticationProvider` | Retrieving user information, including username and password from a database. |
| `net.sf.acegisecurity.providers.jaas.JaasAuthenticationProvider` | Retrieving user information from a JAAS login configuration. |
| `net.sf.acegisecurity.providers.dao.PasswordDaoAuthenticationProvider` | Retrieving user information from a database, but letting the underlying datastore perform the actual authentication. |
| `net.sf.acegisecurity.providers.rcp.RemoteAuthenticationProvider` | Authenticating against a remote service. |
| `net.sf.acegisecurity.runas.RunAsImplAuthenticationProvider` | Authenticating a user who has had their identity substituted by a run-as manager. |
| `net.sf.acegisecurity.providers.TestingAuthenticationProvider` | Unit testing. Automatically considers a `TestingAuthenticationToken` as valid. Should not be used in production. |

You can think of an `AuthenticationProvider` as a subordinate `AuthenticationManager`. In fact, the `AuthenticationProvider` interface has an `authenticate()` method with the same signature as the `authenticate()` method of `AuthenticationManager`.

In this section, we focus on three of the most commonly used authentication providers listed in table 11.1, starting with the simple database authentication using `DaoAuthenticationProvider`.

## 11.2.2  Authenticating against a database

Many applications store user information, including username and password, in a database. If that's your situation, then Acegi has two authentication providers that you may find useful:

- `DaoAuthenticationProvider`
- `PasswordDaoAuthenticationProvider`

Both of these authentication providers enable you to verify a user's identity by comparing their principal and credentials against entries in a database. The

difference is in where the actual authentication takes place. A DaoAuthentication-
Provider uses its DAO to retrieve the username and password, which it then uses
to authenticate the user. PasswordDaoAuthenticationProvider pushes responsibility
for authentication off to its DAO. This is an important distinction that will become
clearer when we discuss PasswordDaoAuthenticationProvider in section 11.2.3.

In this section, we look at using DaoAuthenticationProvider to do simple
authentication against user information kept in some datastore (typically a relational database). In the next section you'll see how to use PasswordDaoAuthenticationProvider to authenticate against an LDAP (Lightweight Directory Access
Protocol) user repository.

### Declaring a DAO authentication provider

A DaoAuthenticationProvider is a simple authentication provider that uses a DAO
to retrieve user information (including the user's password) from a database.

With the username and password in hand, DaoAuthenticationProvider performs authentication by comparing the username and password retrieved from
the database with the principal and credentials passed in an Authentication
object from the authentication manager (see figure 11.3). If the username and
password match up with the principal and credentials, then the user will be
authenticated and a fully populated Authentication object will be returned to the
authentication manager. Otherwise, an AuthenticationException will be thrown
and authentication will have failed.

Configuring a DaoAuthenticationProvider couldn't be simpler. The next XML
excerpt shows how to declare a DaoAuthenticationProvider bean and wire it with
a reference to its DAO.

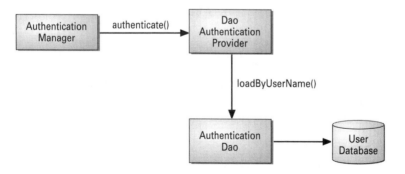

**Figure 11.3**  A DaoAuthenticationManager **authenticates users on behalf
of the authentication manager by pulling user information from a database.**

```
<bean id="authenticationProvider" class="net.sf.acegisecurity.
        providers.dao.DaoAuthenticationProvider">
  <property name="authenticationDao">
    <ref bean="authenticationDao"/>
  </property>
</bean>
```

The `authenticationDao` property is used to identify the bean that will be used to retrieve user information from the database. This property expects an instance of `net.sf.acegisecurity.providers.dao.AuthenticationDao`. The question that remains is how the `authenticationDao` bean is configured.

Acegi comes with two implementations of `AuthenticationDao` to choose from: `InMemoryDaoImpl` and `JdbcDaoImpl`. We'll start by configuring an `InMemoryDaoImpl` as the `authenticationDao` bean and then replace it with the more useful `JdbcDaoImpl`.

### Using an in-memory DAO

Although it may seem natural to assume that an `AuthenticationDao` object will always query a relational database for user information, that doesn't necessarily have to be the case. If your application's authentication needs are trivial or for development-time convenience, it may be simpler to configure your user information directly in the Spring configuration file.

For that purpose, Acegi comes with `InMemoryDaoImpl`, an `AuthenticationDao` that draws its user information from its Spring configuration. You can configure an `InMemoryDaoImpl` in the Spring configuration file as follows:

```
<bean id="authenticationDao" class="net.sf.acegisecurity.
        providers.dao.memory.InMemoryDaoImpl">
  <property name="userMap">
    <value>
      palmerd=4moreyears,ROLE_PRESIDENT
      bauerj=ineedsleep,ROLE_FIELD_OPS,ROLE_DIRECTOR
      myersn=traitor,disabled,ROLE_FIELD_OPS
    </value>
  </property>
</bean>
```

The `userMap` property takes a `net.sf.acegisecurity.providers.dao.memory.UserMap` object that defines a set of usernames, passwords, and privileges. Fortunately, you needn't concern yourself with constructing a `UserMap` instance when wiring `InMemoryDaoImpl` because there's a property editor that handles the conversion of a `String` to a `UserMap` object for you.

Each line of the `userMap` `String` is a name-value pair where the name is the username and the value is a comma-separated list that starts with the user's password and is followed by one or more names that are the authorities (think of *authorities* as *roles*) to be granted to the user.

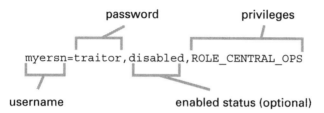

In the declaration of authenticationDao above, three users are defined: palmerd, bauerj, and myersn. Respectively, their passwords are 4moreyears, ineedsleep, and traitor. The palmerd user is defined as having the authorities of ROLE_PRESIDENT, bauerj has been given authorities of ROLE_FIELD_OPS and ROLE_DIRECTOR, and myersn has been given ROLE_CENTRAL_OPS privileges.

Notice that myersn has disabled after the password. This is a special flag indicating that this user has been disabled.

InMemoryDaoImpl has obvious limitations. Primarily, administering security requires that you edit the Spring configuration file and redeploy your application. While this is acceptable (and maybe even helpful) in a development environment, it is probably too cumbersome for production use. Therefore we strongly advise against using InMemoryDaoImpl in a production setting. Instead, you should consider using JdbcDaoImpl.

### Declaring a JDBC DAO

JdbcDaoImpl is a simple, yet flexible, authentication DAO. In its simplest form, all it needs is a reference to a javax.sql.DataSource and can be declared in the Spring configuration file as follows:

```
<bean id="authenticationDao"
    class="net.sf.acegisecurity.providers.dao.jdbc.JdbcDaoImpl">
  <property name="dataSource">
    <ref bean="dataSource"/>
  </property>
</bean>
```

JdbcDaoImpl assumes that you have certain tables set up in your database to store user information. Specifically, it assumes a "Users" table and an "Authorities" table, as illustrated in figure 11.4.

When JdbcDaoImpl looks up user information, it will use "SELECT username, password, enabled FROM users WHERE username = ?" as its query. Likewise,

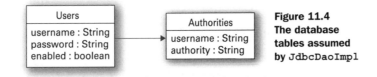

**Figure 11.4
The database
tables assumed
by JdbcDaoImpl**

when looking up granted authorities, it will use "SELECT username, authority FROM authorities WHERE username = ?".

While the table structures assumed by JdbcDaoImpl are straightforward, they probably do not match the tables you have set up for your own application's security. For instance, in the Spring Training application, the Student table holds both a user's username (in the login column) and password. Does this mean that you can't use JdbcDaoImpl to authenticate students in the Spring Training application?

Not at all. But you must tell JdbcDaoImpl how to find the user information by setting the usersByUserNameQuery. The following adjustment to the authenticationDao bean sets it to something more appropriate for the Spring Training application:

```
<bean id="authenticationDao"
    class="net.sf.acegisecurity.providers.dao.jdbc.JdbcDaoImpl">
  <property name="dataSource">
    <ref bean="dataSource"/>
  </property>
  <property name="usersByUserNameQuery">
    <value>SELECT login, password
           FROM student WHERE login=?</value>
  </property>
</bean>
```

Now JdbcDaoImpl knows to look in the Student table for authentication information. However, there's still one thing missing. The Student table has no notion of whether a student is enabled or disabled. In fact, we've been assuming all along that all students are enabled. How can we tell JdbcDaoImpl to make the same assumption?

JdbcDaoImpl also has a usersByUserNameMapping property that takes a reference to a MappingSqlQuery instance. As you may recall from chapter 4, the mapRow() method of MappingSqlQuery maps fields from a ResultSet into a domain object. In the case of JdbcDaoImpl, the MappingSqlQuery given in the usersByUserNameMapping is expected to convert a ResultSet (resulting from running the user query) into a net.sf.acegisecurity.UserDetails object.

UsersByUsernameMapping (listing 11.1) shows a MappingSqlQuery implementation suitable for mapping the results of the student user query into a UserDetails object. It pulls the username and password from the ResultSet, but always sets the enabled property to true.

**Listing 11.1   Mapping results of a student query into a UserDetails object**

```
public class UsersByUsernameMapping extends MappingSqlQuery {
  protected UsersByUsernameMapping(DataSource dataSource) {
    super(dataSource, usersByUsernameQuery);
    declareParameter(new SqlParameter(Types.VARCHAR));
    compile();
  }

  protected Object mapRow(ResultSet rs, int rownum)
      throws SQLException {
    String username = rs.getString(1);      Pull data from
    String password = rs.getString(2);      ResultSet

    UserDetails user = new User(username, password, true,    ⟵ Always
        new GrantedAuthority[]                                 enable User
            {new GrantedAuthorityImpl("HOLDER")});

    return user;
  }
}
```

The only thing left to do is to declare a UsersByUsernameMapping bean and wire it into the usersByUserNameMapping property. The declaration of the authentication-Dao bean that follows wires the usersByUserNameMapping property with an inner bean to use our new user mapping:

```
<bean id="authenticationDao"
    class="net.sf.acegisecurity.providers.dao.jdbc.JdbcDaoImpl">
  <property name="dataSource">
    <ref bean="dataSource"/>
  </property>
  <property name="usersByUserNameQuery">
    <value>SELECT login, password
           FROM student WHERE login=?</value>
  </property>
  <property name="usersByUserNameMapping">
    <bean class=
      "com.springinaction.training.security.UsersByUsernameMapping"/>
  </property>
</bean>
```

You can also change how JdbcDaoImpl queries for authorities granted to a user. In the same way that the usersByUserNameQuery and usersByUserNameMapping properties define how JdbcDaoImpl looks up user authentication information, the authoritiesByUserNameQuery and authoritiesByUserNameMapping properties tell it how to look up privileges for a user. For example, you'd use this code to look up granted authorities from a user_privileges table:

```
<bean id="authenticationDao"
    class="net.sf.acegisecurity.providers.dao.jdbc.JdbcDaoImpl">
  <property name="dataSource">
    <ref bean="dataSource"/>
  </property>
  <property name="usersByUserNameQuery">
    <value>SELECT login, password
           FROM student WHERE login=?</value>
  </property>
  <property name="usersByUserNameMapping">
    <bean class="com.springinaction.training.
       security.UsersByUsernameMapping"/>
  </property>
  <property name="authoritiesByUserNameQuery">
    <value>SELECT login, privilege
           FROM user_privileges where login=?</value>
  </property>
</bean>
```

You could also set a custom MappingSqlQuery to the authoritiesByUserName-Mapping property to customize how the authorities query gets mapped to a net.sf.acegisecurity.GrantedAuthority object. But since the default Mapping-SqlQuery is sufficient for the query given above, we'll just leave it alone.

### Working with encrypted passwords

By default, DaoAuthenticationProvider assumes that the user's password has been stored in clear text (unencrypted). But unencrypted passwords can use a password encoder to encode the password entered by the user before comparing it with the password retrieved from the database. Acegi comes with three password encoders:

- PlaintextPasswordEncoder (default)—Performs no encoding on the password, returning it unaltered.

- Md5PasswordEncoder—Performs Message Digest (MD5) encoding on the password.

- ShaPasswordEncoder—Performs Secure Hash Algorithm encoding on the password.

You can alter DaoAuthenticationProvider's password encoder by setting its passwordEncoder property. For example, to use MD5 encoding use this code:

```
<property name="passwordEncoder">
  <bean class=
    "net.sf.acegisecurity.providers.encoding.Md5PasswordEncoder"/>
</property>
```

You'll also need to set a *salt source* for the encoder. A salt source provides the *salt*, or encryption key, for the encoding. Acegi provides two salt sources:

- ReflectionSaltSource—Uses a specified property of the user's User object to retrieve the salt
- SystemWideSaltSource—Uses the same salt for all users

SystemWideSaltSource is suitable for most situations. The following XML wires a SystemWideSaltSource into the DaoAuthenticationProvider's saltSource property:

```
<property name="saltSource">
  <bean class=
    "net.sf.acegisecurity.providers.dao.SystemWideSaltSource">
    <property name="systemWideSalt">
      <value>123XYZ</value>
    </property>
  </bean>
</property>
```

A ReflectionSaltSource uses some property specific to the user as the salt for the User's password. It is more secure because it means that each user's password will be encoded differently. To wire a ReflectionSaltSource, wire it into the salt-Source property like this:

```
<property name="saltSource">
  <bean class="net.sf.acegisecurity.
    ➥ providers.dao.ReflectionSaltSource">
    <property name="userPropertyToUse">
      <value>userName</value>
    </property>
  </bean>
</property>
```

Here the user's userName property is used as the salt to encrypt the user's password. It's important that the salt be static and never change; otherwise, it will be impossible to authenticate the user.

### Caching user information

Every time that a request is made to a secured resource, the authentication manager is asked to retrieve the user's security information. But if retrieving the user's information involves performing a database query, querying for the same data every time may not result in good performance. Recognizing that a user's information will not frequently change, it may be better to cache the user data upon the first query and retrieve it from cache with every subsequent request.

`DaoAuthenticationProvider` supports caching of user information through implementations of the `net.sf.acegisecurity.providers.dao.UserCache` interface:

```
public interface UserCache {
  public UserDetails getUserFromCache(String username);
  public void putUserInCache(UserDetails user);
  public void removeUserFromCache(String username);
}
```

The methods in the `UserCache` are fairly self-explanatory, providing the ability to put, retrieve, or remove user details from the cache. It would be simple enough for you to write your own implementation of `UserCache`. However, Acegi provides two convenient implementations that you should consider before developing your own:

- `net.sf.acegisecurity.providers.dao.cache.NullUserCache`

- `net.sf.acegisecurity.providers.dao.cache.EhCacheBasedUserCache`

`NullUserCache` does not actually perform any caching. Instead it always returns null from its `getUserFromCache()` method. This is the default `UserCache` used by `DaoAuthenticationProvider`.

`EhCacheBasedUserCache` is a more useful cache implementation. As its name implies, it is based on the open source *ehcache* project. ehcache is a simple and fast caching solution for Java and is the default and recommended cache used by Hibernate. (For more information on ehcache, visit the ehcache website at http://ehcache.sourceforge.net.)

Using ehcache with `DaoAuthenticationProvider` is simple. Simply declare an `EhCacheBasedUserCache` bean:

```
<bean id="userCache" class="net.sf.acegisecurity.
       providers.dao.cache.EhCacheBasedUserCache">
  <property name="minutesToIdle">15</property>
</bean>
```

The `minutesToIdle` property tells the cache how long (in minutes) the user's information should reside in cache without being accessed. Here we've told the cache to remove the user information from cache after 15 minutes of inactivity.

With the `userCache` bean declared, the only thing left to do is to wire it into the `userCache` property on the `DaoAuthenticationProvider`:

```
<bean id="authenticationProvider" class="net.sf.acegisecurity.
     providers.dao.DaoAuthenticationProvider">
  <property name="userCache">
    <ref bean="userCache"/>
  </property>
</bean>
```

### 11.2.3 *Authenticating against an LDAP repository*

`DaoAuthenticationProvider` works by retrieving the user's principal and credentials from a database and comparing them with the principal and credentials provided by the user at login. This is fine if you want the authentication provider to be ultimately responsible for authentication decisions. But it may be that you'd rather delegate authentication responsibility to a third-party system.

For example, it is quite common to authenticate against an LDAP server. In this situation, it is the LDAP server itself that performs the authentication on behalf of the application. The application itself never even sees the user's stored credentials.

`PasswordDaoAuthenticationProvider` is similar in purpose to `DaoAuthenticationProvider` except that its only job is to retrieve user details. The actual authentication is delegated to its DAO. And, as you'll see, in the case of LDAP, the DAO further delegates authentication to the LDAP server.

To use `PasswordDaoAuthenticationProvider`, you'll need to declare it in your Spring configuration as follows:

```
<bean id="authenticationProvider" class="net.sf.acegisecurity.
     providers.dao.PasswordDaoAuthenticationProvider">
  <property name="passwordAuthenticationDao">
    <ref bean="passwordAuthenticationDao"/>
  </property>
</bean>
```

The `passwordAuthenticationDao` property is wired with a reference to a bean of the same name. The bean wired into this property is the DAO that will perform the authentication and retrieve user information. It should implement the `net.sf.acegisecurity.providers.dao.PasswordAuthenticationDao` interface:

```
public interface PasswordAuthenticationDao {
  public UserDetails loadUserByUsernameAndPassword(String username,
      String password) throws DataAccessException,
      BadCredentialsException;
}
```

This interface is similar to the `AuthenticationDao` interface, except that because the DAO will be expected to perform authentication in addition to retrieving user details, its `loadUserByUsernameAndPassword()` method takes a password `String` as an argument and could potentially throw a `BadCredentialsException` if authentication fails.

Unlike many of the other Acegi interfaces you'll see in this chapter, the latest version of Acegi (version 0.6.1) does not come with any useful implementations of the `PasswordAuthenticationDao` interface. But you don't have to go far to find one. At the time we were writing this chapter, Acegi's sandbox in CVS[2] contained `LdapPasswordAuthenticationDao`, an implementation of `PasswordAuthenticationDao` that provides LDAP authentication. It's not yet an official part of Acegi, but if you want to pull it out of the sandbox and give it a spin, all you'll need to do is redeclare the `passwordAuthenticationDao` bean as follows:

```xml
<bean id="passwordAuthenticationDao" class="net.sf.acegisecurity.
    providers.dao.ldap.LdapPasswordAuthenticationDao">
  <property name="host">
    <value>security.springinaction.com</value>
  </property>
  <property name="port">
    <value>389</value>
  </property>
  <property name="rootContext">
    <value>DC=springtraining,DC=com</value>
  </property>
  <property name="userContext">
    <value>CN=user</value>
  </property>
  <property name="rolesAttributes">
    <list>
      <value>memberOf</value>
      <value>roles</value>
    </list>
  </property>
</bean>
```

`LdapPasswordAuthenticationDao` has several properties that guide it in performing authentication against an LDAP server. The only required property is the `host` property, which sets the hostname of the LDAP server. But you'll likely want to adjust one or more of the other properties.

---

[2] cvs.sourceforge.net:/cvs/acegisecurity

The port property indicates the port that the LDAP server is listening on. This defaults to 389 (the well-known port for LDAP), but we've explicitly set it to 389 here for the sake of illustration.

The rootContext indicates the root LDAP context. It is empty by default, so you'll probably want to override it. This diagram illustrates how the rootContext property is used (along with the host and port properties) to construct the provider URL for the LDAP server:

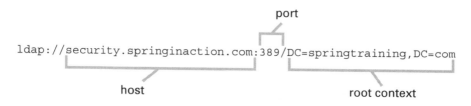

The userContext property specifies the LDAP context where user information is kept. It is CN=Users by default, but we've overridden it here to be CN=user. Both rootContext and userContext are used along with the username to construct the user's principal:

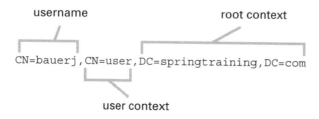

Finally, the rolesAttributes property allows you to list one or more attributes that may be associated with an entry in LDAP where a user's roles are kept. By default this list has a single entry of memberOf, but we've added roles to the list.

One important thing to note about the roles attributes is that when LdapPasswordAuthenticationDao retrieves the attributes from LDAP, it will automatically prefix them with ROLE_. You'll see how this prefix is useful later in section 11.3.2 when we discuss authorization using role voters.

## 11.2.4 *Enabling Single Sign-On with Acegi and Yale CAS*

How many passwords do you have? If you're like most people, you probably juggle a dozen or more passwords for the various systems that you access every day. Keeping track of all of these passwords is a challenge and being forced to log into multiple systems is a nuisance. It would be nice to be able to log in once and have that login automatically authenticate you into all of the systems you use.

Single Sign-On (SSO) is a hot security topic. The name says it all: log in once, access everything. Yale University's Technology and Planning group has created an excellent SSO solution known as the Central Authentication Service (CAS) that works well with Acegi.

The details of setting up and using CAS go well beyond the scope of this book. However, we will discuss the fundamental authentication approach employed by CAS and explore how to use Acegi along with CAS. For more information on CAS, we strongly recommend that you visit the CAS homepage at http://tp.its.yale.edu/tiki/tiki-index.php?page=CentralAuthenticationService.

To understand where Acegi fits within a CAS-authenticated application, it's important to understand how a typical CAS authentication scenario works. Consider the flow of a request to a secured service, as shown in figure 11.5.

When the web browser requests a service ①, the service will look for a CAS ticket in the request to determine whether the user is authenticated. If the ticket is not found, then it means that the user has not been authenticated. As a result, the user is redirected to the CAS login page ②.

From the CAS login page, the user enters his or her username and password. If CAS successfully authenticates the user, then a ticket is created and associated with the requested service. The CAS server then redirects the user to the originally requested service (this time with the ticket in the request) ③.

Again, the service looks for the ticket in the request. This time it finds the ticket and contacts the CAS server to verify that the ticket is valid ④. If CAS responds indicating that the ticket is valid for the service being requested, the service will allow the user access to the application.

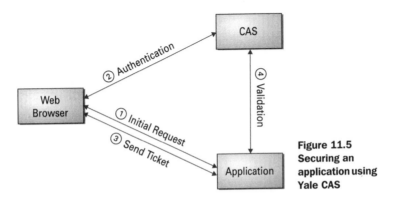

Figure 11.5
Securing an application using Yale CAS

Later, when the user requests access to another CAS-enabled application, that application will contact CAS. Because the user has already logged in before, CAS will respond with a service ticket for the new application without prompting the user to log in again.

One of the key concepts you should understand about CAS is that the secured application never handles the user's credentials. When users are prompted to log into the application, they are actually logging into the CAS server. The application itself never sees a user's credentials. The only form of security that the application does is to verify that the user's ticket is valid by consulting the CAS server. This is a good thing because it means that only one application (CAS) will be responsible for handling user authentication.

When using Acegi with CAS, Acegi takes on the task of verifying a CAS ticket on the behalf of the application. This frees the application itself from being involved in the CAS authentication process.

It accomplishes this using `CasAuthenticationProvider`, an authentication provider that doesn't care about usernames and passwords. Instead it accepts a CAS ticket as its credentials. You configure a `CasAuthenticationProvider` bean in the Spring configuration file:

```
<bean id="casAuthenticationProvider" class="net.sf.acegisecurity.
     providers.cas.CasAuthenticationProvider">
  <property name="ticketValidator">
    <ref bean="ticketValidator"/>
  </property>
  <property name="casProxyDecider">
    <ref bean="casProxyDecider"/>
  </property>
  <property name="statelessTicketCache">
    <ref bean="statelessTicketCache"/>
  </property>
  <property name="casAuthoritiesPopulator">
    <ref bean="casAuthoritiesPopulator"/>
  </property>
  <property name="key">
    <value>some_unique_key</value>
  </property>
</bean>
```

As you can see, `CasAuthenticationProvider` does its job by collaborating with several other beans. The first of these is the `ticketValidator` bean, which is wired into the `ticketValidator` property. It is declared in the Spring configuration file as follows:

```
<bean id="ticketValidator" class="net.sf.acegisecurity.
     providers.cas.ticketvalidator.CasProxyTicketValidator">
```

```
  <property name="casValidate">
    <value>https://localhost:8443/cas/proxyValidate</value>
  </property>
  <property name="serviceProperties">
    <ref bean="serviceProperties"/>
  </property>
</bean>
```

`CasProxyTicketValidator` validates the CAS service ticket by contacting the CAS server. The `casValidate` property specifies the URL on which the CAS server processes validation requests.

The `serviceProperties` bean is a bean that carries important configuration information for CAS-related beans:

```
<bean id="serviceProperties"
    class="net.sf.acegisecurity.ui.cas.ServiceProperties">
  <property name="service">
    <value>https://localhost:8443/training/
            ➡ j_acegi_cas_security_check</value>
  </property>
</bean>
```

The `service` property specifies a URL that CAS should send the user to after login. Later, in section 11.4.3, you'll see how this URL is serviced.

Back on the `casAuthenticationProvider` bean, the `casProxyDecider` property is wired with a reference to the `casProxyDecider` bean, which takes a reference to a bean of the type `net.sf.acegisecurity.providers.cas.CasProxyDecider`. To understand the role of the `casProxyDecider` property, you must understand how CAS supports proxy services.

CAS supports the notion of proxy services that authenticate a user on behalf of another application. A typical example of a proxy service is a portal that authenticates the user on behalf of the portlet applications that it presents. When a user logs into a portal, the portal ensures that the user is also implicitly logged into its applications using proxy tickets.

How CAS deals with proxy tickets is an advanced topic. We refer you to the CAS documentation (http://tp.its.yale.edu/tiki/tiki-index.php?page=CasTwoOverview) for more details on proxy tickets. Suffice it to say that a `CasProxyDecider` decides whether to accept proxy tickets. Acegi comes with three implementations of `CasProxyDecider`:

- `AcceptAnyCasProxy`—Accepts a proxy request from any service
- `NamedCasProxyDecider`—Accepts proxy requests from those in a list of named services
- `RejectProxyTickets`—Rejects all proxy requests

For simplicity's sake, let's assume that your application doesn't involve proxy services. This makes `RejectProxyTickets` the most appropriate `CasProxyDecider` for the `casProxyDecider` bean:

```
<bean id="casProxyDecider" class="net.sf.acegisecurity.
     providers.cas.proxy.RejectProxyTickets"/>
```

The `statelessTicketCache` property exists to help support stateless clients (such as clients of remoting services), which cannot store CAS tickets in `HttpSession`. Unfortunately, even if stateless clients will not access your application, the `statelessTicketCache` property is required. Acegi only comes with one implementation, so declaring a `statelessTicketCache` bean is simple enough:

```
<bean id="statelessTicketCache" class="net.sf.acegisecurity.
     providers.cas.cache.EhCacheBasedTicketCache">
  <property name="minutesToIdle"><value>20</value></property>
</bean>
```

The final bean that `CasAuthenticationProvider` collaborates with is the `casAuthoritiesPopulator` bean. As an SSO implementation, CAS only performs authentication—it plays no part in how authorities are assigned to users. To make up the difference, you'll need a `net.sf.acegisecurity.providers.cas.CasAuthoritiesPopulator` bean.

Acegi comes with only one implementation of `CasAuthoritiesPopulator`. `DaoCasAuthoritiesPopulator` loads user details from a database using an authentication DAO (as discussed in section 11.2.2). Declare the `casAuthoritiesPopulator` bean like this:

```
<bean id="casAuthoritiesPopulator" class="net.sf.acegisecurity.
     providers.cas.populator.DaoCasAuthoritiesPopulator">
  <property name="authenticationDao">
    <ref bean="inMemoryDaoImpl"/>
  </property>
</bean>
```

Finally, the `key` property of `CasAuthenticationManager` specifies a `String` value that the authentication manager will use to identify tokens that it has previously authenticated. You can set this to any arbitrary value.

There's a bit more to SSO with CAS and Acegi than just `CasAuthenticationManager`. We've only discussed how a `CasAuthenticationProvider` performs authentication. In section 11.4.3 you'll see how a user is sent to the CAS login screen when `CasAuthenticationManager` fails to authenticate a user.

But for now, let's look at how Acegi determines whether an authenticated user has the proper authority to access the secured resource.

## 11.3 *Controlling access*

Authentication is only the first step in Acegi security. Once Acegi knows who the user is, it must decide whether to grant access to the resources that it secures. That's where access decision managers come in.

Just as an authentication manager is responsible for establishing a user's identity, an access decision manager is responsible for deciding if the user has the proper privileges to access secured resources. An access decision manager is defined by the `net.sf.acegisecurity.AccessDecisionManager` interface:

```
public interface AccessDecisionManager {
  public void decide(Authentication authentication, Object object,
      ConfigAttributeDefinition config)
      throws AccessDeniedException;
  public boolean supports(ConfigAttribute attribute);
  public boolean supports(Class clazz);
}
```

The `supports()` methods consider the secured resource's class type and its configuration attributes (the access requirements of the secured resource) to determine whether the access decision manager is capable of making access decisions for the resource. The `decide()` method is where the ultimate decision is made. If it returns without throwing an `AccessDeniedException`, then access to the secured resource is granted. Otherwise, access is denied.

### 11.3.1 *Voting access decisions*

It seems simple enough to write your own implementation of `AccessDecisionManager`. But why do something you don't have to do? Acegi comes with three implementations of `AccessDecisionManager` that are suitable for most circumstances:

- `net.sf.acegisecurity.vote.AffirmativeBased`
- `net.sf.acegisecurity.vote.ConsensusBased`
- `net.sf.acegisecurity.vote.UnanimousBased`

These three access decision managers have rather strange names, but they make more sense when you consider Acegi's authorization strategy.

Acegi's access decision managers are ultimately responsible for determining the access rights for an authenticated user. However, they do not arrive at their decision on their own. Instead, they poll one or more objects that vote on whether a user is granted access to a secured resource. Once all votes are in, the decision manager tallies the votes and arrives at its final decision.

What differentiates each of the access decision managers is in how it reckons its final decision. Table 11.2 describes how each of the access decision managers settles on whether access is granted.

**Table 11.2    How Acegi's access decision managers tally votes**

| Access Decision Manager | How It Decides |
|---|---|
| AffirmativeBased | Allows access if at least one voter votes to grant access |
| ConsensusBased | Allows access if a consensus of voters vote to grant access |
| UnanimousBased | Allows access only if no voter votes to deny access |

All of the access decision managers are configured the same in the Spring configuration file. For example, the following XML excerpt configures a UnanimousBased access decision manager:

```
<bean id="accessDecisionManager"
    class="net.sf.acegisecurity.vote.UnanimousBased">
  <property name="decisionVoters">
    <list>
      <ref bean="roleVoter"/>
    </list>
  </property>
</bean>
```

The decisionVoters property is where you provide the access decision manager with its list of voters. In this case, there's only one voter, which is a reference to a bean named roleVoter. Let's see how the roleVoter is configured.

## 11.3.2  Deciding how to vote

Although access decision voters don't have the final say on whether access is granted to a secured resource, they play an important part in the access decision process. An access decision voter's job is to consider the user's granted authorities alongside the authorities required by the configuration attributes of the secured resource. Based on this information, the access decision voter casts its vote for the access decision manager to use in making its decision.

An access decision voter is any object that implements the net.sf.acegisecurity.vote.AccessDecisionVoter interface:

```
public interface AccessDecisionVoter {
  public static final int ACCESS_GRANTED = 1;
  public static final int ACCESS_ABSTAIN = 0;
  public static final int ACCESS_DENIED = -1;
```

```
    public boolean supports(ConfigAttribute attribute);
    public boolean supports(Class clazz);
    public int vote(Authentication authentication, Object object,
        ConfigAttributeDefinition config);
}
```

As you can see the `AccessDecisionVoter` interface is very similar to that of `Access-DecisionManager`. The big difference is that instead of a `decide()` method that returns `void`, there is a `vote()` method that returns `int`. That's because an access decision voter doesn't decide whether to allow access … it only returns its vote as to whether to grant access.

When faced with the opportunity to place a vote, an access decision voter can vote one of three ways:

- *ACCESS_GRANTED*—The voter wishes to allow access to the secured resource.
- *ACCESS_DENIED*—The voter wishes to deny access to the secured resource.
- *ACCESS_ABSTAIN*—The voter is indifferent.

As with most Acegi components, you are free to write your own implementation of `AccessDecisionVoter`. However, Acegi comes with `RoleVoter`, a very useful implementation that votes when the secured resources configuration attributes represent a role. More specifically, `RoleVoter` participates in a vote when the secured resource has a configuration attribute whose name starts with `ROLE_`.

The way that `RoleVoter` decides on its vote is by simply comparing all of the configuration attributes of the secured resource (that are prefixed with `ROLE_`) with all of the authorities granted to the authenticated user. If `RoleVoter` finds a match, then it will cast an `ACCESS_GRANTED` vote. Otherwise it will cast an `ACCESS_DENIED` vote.

The `RoleVoter` will only abstain from voting when the authorities required for access are not prefixed with `ROLE_`. For example, if the secured resource only requires non-role authorities (such as `CREATE_USER`) then the `RoleVoter` will abstain from voting.

You can configure a `RoleVoter` with the following XML in the Spring configuration file:

```
<bean id="roleVoter"
    class="net.sf.acegisecurity.vote.RoleVoter"/>
```

As stated, `RoleVoter` only votes when the secured resource has configuration attributes that are prefixed with `ROLE_`. However, the `ROLE_` prefix is only a default. You may choose to override the default prefix by setting the `rolePrefix` property:

```
<bean id="roleVoter"
    class="net.sf.acegisecurity.vote.RoleVoter">
  <property name="rolePrefix">
    <value>GROUP_</value>
  </property>
</bean>
```

Here, the default prefix has been overridden to be GROUP_. Thus the RoleVoter will now only cast authorization votes on privileges that begin with GROUP_.

### 11.3.3 Handling voter abstinence

Knowing that any voter can vote to grant or deny access or abstain from voting, a question you may have now is what will happen if all voters abstain from voting. Will the user be granted or denied access?

By default, all of the access decision managers deny access to a resource if all of the voters abstain. However, you can override this default behavior by setting the allowIfAllAbstain property on the access decision manager to true:

```
<bean id="accessDecisionManager"
    class="net.sf.acegisecurity.vote.UnanimousBased">
  <property name="decisionVoters">
    <list>
      <ref bean="roleVoter"/>
    </list>
  </property>
  <property name="allowIfAllAbstain">
    <value>true</value>
  </property>
</bean>
```

By setting allowIfAllAbstain to true, you are establishing a policy of "silence is consent." In other words, if all voters abstain from voting, then access is granted as if they had voted to grant access.

Now that you've seen how Acegi's authentication and access control managers work, let's put them to work. In the next section you'll see how to use Acegi's collection of servlet filters to secure a web application. Later, in section 11.5, we'll dig deep into an application and see how to use Spring AOP to apply security at the method-invocation level.

## 11.4 Securing web applications

Acegi's support for web security is heavily based on servlet filters. These filters intercept an incoming request and apply some security processing before the request is handled by your application. Acegi comes with a handful of filters that intercept servlet requests and pass them on to the authentication and access decision managers to enforce security. Depending on your needs, you may use up to six filters to secure your application. Table 11.3 describes each of Acegi's filters.

**Table 11.3  Acegi's servlet filters**

| Filter | Purpose |
|---|---|
| Channel-processing filter | Ensures that a request is transmitted over a secure channel (such as HTTPS) |
| Authentication-processing filter | Accepts authentication requests and pipes them to the authentication manager to perform authentication |
| CAS-processing filter | Accepts CAS service tickets as evidence that Yale CAS has authenticated a user |
| HTTP Basic authorization filter | Processes authentication performed using HTTP Basic authentication |
| Integration filter | Handles storage of authentication between requests (in HTTP Session, for example) |
| Security enforcement filter | Ensures that a user has been authenticated and meets the property authorization requirements to access a secured web resource |

When a request is submitted to an Acegi-secured web application, it passes through each of Acegi's filters in the following sequence (refer to figure 11.6):

1. If a channel-processing filter is configured, it will be the first to handle the request. The channel-processing filter will examine the request's delivery channel (typically either HTTP or HTTPS) and decide if the channel sufficiently meets the security requirements. If not, the request is redirected to the same URL, altering the channel to meet the security requirements.

2. Next, one of the authentication-processing filters (which includes the CAS-processing filter and HTTP Basic authorization filter) will determine whether the request is an authentication request. If so, the perti-

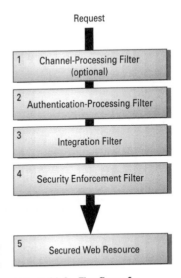

Figure 11.6  The flow of a request through each of Acegi's filters

nent user information (typically username/password) is retrieved from the request and passed on to the authentication manager to determine the user's identity. If this is not an authentication request, the request moves on down the filter chain.

3 The integration filter attempts to retrieve a user's authentication from the location it is kept between requests (typically HTTP Session). If the user's authentication information is found, it is placed into a `Context-Holder` object (which is basically a `ThreadLocal`) for convenient retrieval by all of Acegi's components.

4 Finally, the security enforcement filter makes the final decision as to whether the user is granted access to the secured resource. First, the security enforcement filter will consult the authentication manager. If the user hasn't been successfully authenticated, the security enforcement filter will send the user to an authentication entry point (i.e., a login page). Next, the security enforcement filter will consult the access decision manager to determine if the user has the property authority to access the secured resource. If not, then an HTTP 403 (Forbidden) message is returned to the browser.

5 If the user makes it past the security enforcement filter, then he or she will be granted access to the secured web resource.

We'll explore each of these filters individually in more detail. But before you can start using them, you need to learn how Acegi places a Spring-like twist on servlet filters.

## 11.4.1 *Proxying Acegi's filters*

If you've ever used servlet filters, you know that for them to take effect, you must configure them in the web application's web.xml file, using the `<filter>` and `<filter-mapping>` elements. While this works, it is inconsistent with Spring's way of configuring components using dependency injection.

For example, suppose you have the following filter declared in your web.xml file:

```
<filter>
  <filter-name>Foo</filter-name>
  <filter-class>FooFilter</filter-class>
</filter>
```

Now suppose that `FooFilter` needs a reference to a `Bar` bean to do its job. How can you inject an instance of `Bar` into `FooFilter`?

The short answer is that you can't. The web.xml file has no notion of dependency injection, nor is there a straightforward way of retrieving beans from the

Spring application context and wiring them into a servlet filter. The only option you have is to use Spring's `WebApplicationContextUtils` to retrieve the "bar" bean from the Spring context:

```
ApplicationContext ctx = WebApplicationContextUtils.
    getWebApplicationContext(servletContext);
Bar bar = (Bar) ctx.getBean("bar");
```

But the problem with this approach is that you must code Spring-specific code into your servlet filter. Furthermore, you end up hard-coding a reference to the name of the `Bar` bean.

But Acegi provides a better way through `FilterToBeanProxy`. `FilterToBeanProxy` is a special servlet filter that, by itself, doesn't do much. Instead, it delegates its work to a bean in the Spring application context. The delegate bean implements the `javax.servlet.Filter` interface just like any other servlet filter, but is configured in the Spring configuration file instead of web.xml.

By using `FilterToBeanProxy`, you are able to configure the actual filter in Spring, taking full advantage of Spring's support for dependency injection. As illustrated in figure 11.7, the web.xml file only contains the `<filter>` declaration for `FilterToBeanProxy`. The actual `FooFilter` is configured in the Spring configuration file and uses setter injection to set the `bar` property with a reference to a `Bar` bean.

To use `FilterToBeanProxy`, you must set up a `<filter>` entry in the web application's web.xml file. For example, if you are configuring a `FooFilter` using `FilterToBeanProxy`, you'd use the following code:

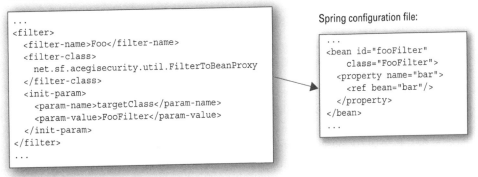

**Figure 11.7** `FilterToBeanProxy` **proxies filter handling to a delegate filter bean in the Spring application context.**

```
<filter>
  <filter-name>Foo</filter-name>
  <filter-class>net.sf.acegisecurity.util.
      FilterToBeanProxy</filter-class>
  <init-param>
    <param-name>targetClass</param-name>
    <param-value>
      FooFilter
    </param-value>
  </init-param>
</filter>
```

Here the `targetClass` initialization parameter is set to the fully qualified class name of the delegate filter bean. When this `FilterToBeanProxy` is initialized, it will look for a bean in the Spring context whose type is `FooFilter`. `FilterToBeanProxy` that will delegate its filtering to the `FooFilter` bean found in the Spring context:

```
<bean id="fooFilter"
    class="FooFilter">
  <property name="bar">
    <ref bean="bar"/>
  </property>
</bean>
```

If a `FooFilter` bean isn't found, an exception will be thrown. If more than one matching bean is found, then the first one found will be used.

Optionally, you can set the `targetBean` initialization parameter instead of `targetClass` to pick out a specific bean from the Spring context. For example, you might pick out the `fooFilter` bean by name by setting `targetBean` as follows:

```
<filter>
  <filter-name>Foo</filter-name>
  <filter-class>net.sf.acegisecurity.
                  util.FilterToBeanProxy</filter-class>
  <init-param>
    <param-name>targetBean</param-name>
    <param-value>fooFilter</param-value>
  </init-param>
</filter>
```

The `targetBean` initialization parameter enables you to be more specific about which bean to delegate filtering to, but requires that you match the delegate's name exactly between web.xml and the Spring configuration file. This creates extra work for you if you decide to rename the bean. For this reason, it's probably better to use `targetClass` instead of `targetBean`.

Regardless of whether you choose `targetClass` or `targetBean`, `FilterToBean-Proxy` must be able to access the Spring application context. This means that the

Spring context has to be loaded using Spring's `ContextLoaderListener` or `ContextLoaderServlet` (see chapter 8).

Finally, you'll need to associate the filter to a URL pattern. The following `<filter-mapping>` ties the `Acegi-Authentication` instance of `FilterToBeanProxy` to a URL pattern of `/*` so that all requests are processed:

```
<filter-mapping>
  <filter-name>Acegi-Authentication</filter-name>
  <url-pattern>/*</url-pattern>
</filter-mapping>
```

`/*` is the recommended URL pattern for all of Acegi's filters. The idea is that Acegi should intercept all requests and then let the underlying security managers decide if and how to secure the request.

> **NOTE** It may be interesting to know that there's nothing about `FilterToBeanProxy` that is specific to Acegi or to securing web applications. You may find that `FilterToBeanProxy` is useful when configuring your own servlet filters. In fact, because it's so useful, there has been some discussion on the Spring developer mailing list to suggest that `FilterToBeanProxy` may move out of Acegi and into the core Spring project in some future release.

Now that you know how to use `FilterToBeanProxy`, you're ready to start using it to setup the web components of Acegi security. Let's start with the filter that is central to Acegi security, the security enforcement filter.

### 11.4.2 *Enforcing web security*

Whenever a user requests a page within your web application, that page may or may not be a page that needs to be secure. In Acegi, a *security enforcement filter* handles the interception of requests, determining whether a request is secure and giving the authentication and access decision managers a chance to verify the user's identity and privileges. It is declared in the Spring configuration file as follows:

```
<bean id="securityEnforcementFilter" class="net.sf.acegisecurity.
      ➥ intercept.web.SecurityEnforcementFilter">
  <property name="securityInterceptor">
    <ref bean="securityInterceptor"/>
  </property>
  <property name="authenticationEntryPoint">
    <ref bean="authenticationEntryPoint"/>
  </property>
</bean>
```

Here the `SecurityEnforcementFilter` has been wired with references to two other beans: `authenticationEntryPoint` and `securityInterceptor`. We'll talk more about the `authenticationEntryPoint` property a little later. For now let's focus on the `securityInterceptor` property.

### Using a filter security interceptor

The `securityInterceptor` property is wired with a reference to a bean of the same name. If you think back to the door lock analogy from earlier in this chapter, the security interceptor is the latch that must be released for the door to be opened. It is what coordinates the efforts of the authentication manager, access decision manager, and run-as manager.

For the purposes of web security, Acegi's `FilterSecurityInterceptor` class performs the job of the security interceptor. It is declared in the Spring configuration file as follows:

```
<bean id="securityInterceptor" class="net.sf.acegisecurity.
        intercept.web.FilterSecurityInterceptor">
  <property name="authenticationManager">
    <ref bean="authenticationManager"/>
  </property>
  <property name="accessDecisionManager">
    <ref bean="accessDecisionManager"/>
  </property>
  <property name="objectDefinitionSource">
    <value>
      CONVERT_URL_TO_LOWERCASE_BEFORE_COMPARISON
      \A/admin/.*\Z=ROLE_ADMIN
      \A/student/.*\Z=ROLE_STUDENT,ROLE_ALUMNI
      \A/instruct/.*\Z=ROLE_INSTRUCTOR
    </value>
  </property>
</bean>
```

The first two properties wired here are references to the authentication manager and access decision manager beans defined earlier in this chapter. The security interceptor will use the authentication manager to determine whether a user has logged in and to obtain the user's granted authorities. It will use the access decision manager to determine whether the use has the proper authorities to access the secured resource.

The `objectDefinitionSource` property tells the security interceptor what authorities are required for the various requests that are intercepted. This property has a property editor that makes it easy to configure it as a String value. The

String is composed of several lines, any of which could be a directive or a URL-to-authority mapping.

As defined above, the first line of the `objectDefinitionSource` value is a directive that indicates that the URL of the request should be normalized to lowercase before comparing it with any of the patterns that follow.

The remaining lines of this property map URL patterns to the authorities that must be granted to the user in order for the user to have access to those URLs. As shown here, the URL patterns are in the form of regular expressions. Therefore, as defined in the `objectDefinitionSource` property of the `security-Interceptor` bean:

- `/admin/reports.htm` will require that the user be granted `ROLE_ADMIN` authority.
- `/student/manageSchedule.htm` will require that the user be granted either `ROLE_STUDENT` or `ROLE_ALUMNI` authority.
- `/instruct/postCourseNotes.htm` will require that the user be granted `ROLE_INSTUCTOR` authority.

If you prefer, you may use Ant-like URL patterns instead of regular expressions by adding a `PATTERN_TYPE_APACHE_ANT` directive to the object definition source. For example, the following definition of `objectDefinitionSource` is equivalent to the one above:

```
<property name="objectDefinitionSource">
  <value>
    CONVERT_URL_TO_LOWERCASE_BEFORE_COMPARISON
    PATTERN_TYPE_APACHE_ANT
    /admin/**=ROLE_ADMIN
    /student/**=ROLE_STUDENT,ROLE_ALUMNI
    /instruct/**=ROLE_INSTRUCTOR
  </value>
</property>
```

As with all of Acegi's filters, the security-enforcement filter is a filter delegate bean that is fronted by `FilterToBeanProxy`. This means that the first step in configuring a security-enforcement filter is to add `<filter>` and `<filter-mapping>` elements for `FilterToBeanProxy` to the application's web.xml file:

```
<filter>
  <filter-name>Acegi-Security</filter-name>
  <filter-class>net.sf.acegisecurity.util.
      FilterToBeanProxy</filter-class>
  <init-param>
    <param-name>targetBean</param-name>
```

```
      <param-value>securityEnforcementFilter</param-value>
    </init-param>
  </filter>
  …
  <filter-mapping>
    <filter-name>Acegi-Security</filter-name>
    <url-pattern>/*</url-pattern>
  </filter-mapping>
```

Notice that the `<filter-mapping>`'s `<url-pattern>` maps the security-enforcement filter to filter all requests. This is typical of Acegi's filters. The idea is to filter all requests and let the security interceptor's object definition source determine whether the filter has any work to do.

> **NOTE** Throughout this section, you'll add several `<filter>` and `<filter-mapping>` elements to the web.xml file, all of them using `FilterToBeanProxy`. Just because they all have the same filter class, do not think of these filters as being replacements for each other. Although all of these filters use the same `FilterToBeanProxy` class, they all serve different purposes and delegate to different beans in the Spring context. Unless otherwise stated, they are all required for Acegi web security to function.

Suppose that a request is submitted for a page that is designated to be secure. If the user has already been authenticated and granted the appropriate privileges, then the security-enforcement filter will allow access to the page. But what if the user hasn't been authenticated yet?

### 11.4.3 *Processing a login*

As you'll recall, the security-enforcement filter was wired with a reference to `authenticationEntryPoint`. When the security-enforcement filter determines that a user hasn't been authenticated, it hands control over to an *authentication entry point*.

The primary purpose of an authentication entry point is to prompt the user to log in. Acegi comes with three authentication entry points:

- `BasicProcessingFilterEntryPoint`—Prompts the user with a browser-driven login dialog by sending an HTTP 401 (Unauthorized) message to the browser

- `AuthenticationProcessingFilterEntryPoint`—Redirects the user to an HTML form-based login page

- `CasProcessingFilterEntryPoint`—Redirects the user to a Yale CAS login page

Regardless of which authentication entry point is used, the user will be prompted to identify him- or herself by providing a username and password. When the user submits the username and password, Acegi will need a way to give its authentication manager a chance to authenticate the user.

The job of handling the authentication request falls to an *authentication-processing filter*. Acegi comes with three authentication-processing filters:

- `BasicProcessingFilter`—Handles Basic authentication requests
- `AuthenticationProcessingFilter`—Handles form-based authentication requests
- `CasProcessingFilter`—Authenticates users based on the presence and validity of a CAS service ticket

As you can see, the three authentication-processing filters mirror the three authentication entry points. In fact, each authentication entry point is paired up with an authentication-processing filter to make up the complete login picture. This is illustrated in figure 11.8.

**Figure 11.8  Authentication entry points and authentication-processing filters work together to authenticate a web user.**

An authentication entry point starts the login process by prompting the user with a chance to log in. After the user submits the requested information, an authentication-processing filter attempts to authenticate the user (with help from the authentication manager).

Let's take a closer look at how this works for each of the three types of authentication available in Acegi, starting with Basic authentication.

### Basic authentication

The simplest form of web-based authentication is known as Basic authentication. The way Basic authentication works is that the server sends an HTTP 401 (Unauthorized) response to the web browser. When the browser sees this response, it realizes that the server needs the user to log in. So, the browser pops up a dialog box to prompt the user for a username and password.

When the user submits the login, the browser sends it back to the server to perform the authentication. If authentication is successful, the user will be sent to the desired target URL. Otherwise, the server may send back another HTTP 401 response and the browser will prompt the user again to log in.

Using Basic authentication with Acegi starts with configuring a `BasicProcessing-FilterEntryPoint` bean:

```
<bean id="authenticationEntryPoint" class="net.sf.acegisecurity.
      ➥ ui.basicauth.BasicProcessingFilterEntryPoint">
  <property name="realmName">
    <value>Spring Training</value>
  </property>
</bean>
```

`BasicProcessingFilterEntryPoint` has only one property. The `realmName` property specifies an arbitrary string that is displayed in the login dialog to give users some indication of what it is that they're being asked to log into.

After the user clicks the OK button in the login dialog, the username and password are submitted via the HTTP header back to the server. At that point `BasicProcessingFilter` picks it up and processes it.

```
<bean id="basicProcessingFilter" class="net.sf.acegisecurity.
      ➥ ui.basicauth.BasicProcessingFilter">
  <property name="authenticationManager">
    <ref bean="authenticationManager"/>
  </property>
  <property name="authenticationEntryPoint">
    <ref bean="authenticationEntryPoint"/>
  </property>
</bean>
```

`BasicProcessingFilter` pulls the username and password from the HTTP header and sends them on to the authentication manager, which is wired in through the `authenticationManager` property. If authentication is successful, an `Authentication` object is placed into the session for future reference. Otherwise, if authentication fails, then control is passed on to the authentication entry point (wired in through the `authenticationEntryPoint` property) to give the user another chance.

Like all of Acegi's filters, `BasicProcessingFilter` needs a corresponding `FilterToBeanProxy` configured in the application's web.xml:

```
<filter>
  <filter-name>Acegi-Authentication</filter-name>
  <filter-class>net.sf.acegisecurity.
            ➥ util.FilterToBeanProxy</filter-class>
```

```
<init-param>
  <param-name>targetBean</param-name>
  <param-value>
    net.sf.acegisecurity.ui.basicauth.BasicProcessingFilter
  </param-value>
</init-param>
</filter>
...
<filter-mapping>
  <filter-name>Acegi-Authentication</filter-name>
  <url-pattern>/*</url-pattern>
</filter-mapping>
```

### Form-based authentication

Although BASIC authentication may be fine for simple applications, it has some limitations. Primarily, the login dialog popped up by the browser is neither user-friendly nor aesthetically appealing. Form-based authentication overcomes this limitation and is more appropriate for most applications. Instead of being presented with a pop-up dialog to log into, a user is prompted to log into a web-based form.

Acegi's `AuthenticationProcessingFilterEntryPoint` is an authentication entry point that prompts a user with an HTML-based login form. You can configure it in the Spring configuration file as follows:

```
<bean id="authenticationEntryPoint" class="net.sf.acegisecurity.
        ui.webapp.AuthenticationProcessingFilterEntryPoint">
  <property name="loginFormUrl">
    <value>/jsp/login.jsp</value>
  </property>
  <property name="forceHttps"><value>true</value></property>
</bean>
```

The `loginFormUrl` property is configured with the URL of a login form. `AuthenticationProcessingFilterEntryPoint` will redirect the user to this URL for the user to login. In this case, it redirects to a JSP file, which might contain the following HTML form:

```
<form method="POST" action="j_acegi_security_check">
  <input type="text" name="j_username"><br>
  <input type="password" name="j_password"><br>
  <input type="submit">
</form>
```

The login form must have two fields named j_username and j_password in which the user will enter the username and password. As for the form's `action` attribute, it has been set to j_acegi_security_check, which will be intercepted by `AuthenticationProcessingFilter`.

`AuthenticationProcessingFilter` is a filter that processes form-based authentication. It is configured in Spring's configuration file as follows:

```
<bean id="authenticationProcessingFilter"
      class="net.sf.acegisecurity.
   ui.webapp.AuthenticationProcessingFilter">
  <property name="filterProcessesUrl">
   <value>/j_acegi_security_check</value>
  </property>
  <property name="authenticationFailureUrl">
   <value>/jsp/login.jsp?failed=true</value>
  </property>
  <property name="defaultTargetUrl">
   <value>/</value>
  </property>
  <property name="authenticationManager">
   <ref bean="authenticationManager"/>
  </property>
</bean>
```

The `filterProcessesUrl` property tells `AuthenticationProcessingFilter` which URL it should intercept. This is the same URL that is in the login form's `action` attribute. It defaults to `/j_acegi_security_check`, but we've explicitly defined it here to illustrate that you can change it if you'd like.

The `authenticationFailureUrl` property indicates where the user will be sent should authentication fail. In this case, we're sending them back to the login page, passing a parameter to indicate that authentication failed (so that an error message may be displayed).

Under normal circumstances, when authentication is successful, `AuthenticationProcessingFilter` will place an `Authentication` object in the session and redirect the user to their desired target page. It knows what the target page is because `SecurityEnforcementFilter` puts the original target URL into the HTTP session before handing control over to the authentication entry point. When `AuthenticationProcessingFilter` successfully authenticates the user, it retrieves the target URL from the session and redirects the user to it.

The `defaultTargetUrl` property defines what will happen in the unusual circumstance where the target URL isn't in the session. This could happen if the user arrived at the login screen through a bookmark or some other means without having gone through `SecurityEnforcementFilter`.

With the `AuthenticationProcessingFilter` defined in Spring, the final thing to do is to configure a `FilterToBeanProxy` that will delegate to the `authenticationProcessingFilter` bean:

```
<filter>
  <filter-name>Acegi-Authentication</filter-name>
  <filter-class>net.sf.acegisecurity.
                    ➥ util.FilterToBeanProxy</filter-class>
  <init-param>
    <param-name>targetClass</param-name>
    <param-value>
      net.sf.acegisecurity.ui.webapp.AuthenticationProcessingFilter
    </param-value>
  </init-param>
</filter>
...
<filter-mapping>
  <filter-name>Acegi-Authentication</filter-name>
  <url-pattern>/*</url-pattern>
</filter-mapping>
```

### CAS authentication

In section 11.2.4 you saw how to configure `CasAuthenticationManager` to authenticate CAS service tickets against a CAS server. But a big unanswered question left from that section is how the user is sent to the CAS login screen in the first place.

Acegi's `CasProcessingFilterEntryPoint` is an authentication entry point that sends the user to the CAS server to log in. You can declare it in the Spring configuration file as follows:

```
<bean id="authenticationEntryPoint" class="net.sf.acegisecurity.
        ➥ ui.cas.CasProcessingFilterEntryPoint">
  <property name="loginUrl">
    <value>https://localhost:8443/cas/login</value>
  </property>
  <property name="serviceProperties">
    <ref bean="serviceProperties"/>
  </property>
</bean>
```

The two properties of `CasProcessingFitlerEntryPoint` are fairly self-explanatory. The `loginUrl` property specifies the URL of the CAS login page while the `serviceProperties` property is a reference to the same `serviceProperties` bean declared in section 11.2.4.

Whether or not the user successfully logs into CAS, you need to be certain that the `CasAuthenticationManager` gets to try to authenticate the CAS ticket before allowing access to the secured resource. `CasProcessingFilter` is an authentication-processing filter that intercepts requests from the CAS server that contain the ticket to be authenticated.

```
<bean id="authenticationProcessingFilter"
    class="net.sf.acegisecurity.ui.cas.CasProcessingFilter">
  <property name="filterProcessesUrl">
    <value>/j_acegi_cas_security_check</value>
  </property>
  <property name="authenticationManager">
    <ref bean="authenticationManager"/>
  </property>
  <property name="authenticationFailureUrl">
    <value>/authenticationfailed.jsp</value>
  </property>
  <property name="defaultTargetUrl">
    <value>/</value>
  </property>
</bean>
```

CasProcessingFilter has the same properties as AuthenticationProcessing-
Filter. But pay particular attention to the filterProcessesUrl property. Here it
is set to /j_acegi_cas_security_check. In section 11.2.4 we set the service property of the serviceProperties bean to a URL that ends with the same pattern.

After a successful login on the CAS server, CAS will redirect the user to a service
URL. In a non-Acegi application, this could be any arbitrary URL of the secured
application. But when securing an application with Acegi, you need to make sure
that the CasAuthenticationManager is invoked to handle the Acegi side of authentication as well as look up the user's authorities.

On the CAS server side, the service property of the serviceProperties bean
tells CAS where to go after a successful login. On the client side, the filterProcessesUrl property makes sure that CasProcessingFilter answers that request
and sends the CAS ticket on to CasAuthenticationManager for authentication.

### 11.4.4 Setting up the security context

During the course of a request, a user's authentication information is carried in a
ContextHolder (which is effectively a ThreadLocal). Each filter in the Acegi filter
chain accesses the user's authentication by retrieving it from the ContextHolder.

But a ThreadLocal does not survive between requests. Therefore, Acegi has to
find some convenient place to store the user's authentication so that it is available
when the next request comes through. That's where Acegi's integration filters go
to work.

An integration filter starts its life by looking for the user's Authentication
object in a well-known location—typically the HTTP session. It then constructs a
new ContextHolder object and drops the Authentication object into it.

After the request completes, the integration filter pulls the `Authentication` object out of the `ContextHolder` and puts it back into the well-known location to await another request.

Acegi comes with several integration filters, but `HttpSessionIntegration-Filter` is the one that is appropriate for most cases. It keeps the `Authentication` object in the HTTP session between requests. You can configure it in the Spring configuration file like this:

```
<bean id="integrationFilter" class="net.sf.acegisecurity.
    ui.webapp.HttpSessionIntegrationFilter"/>
```

Finally, you'll need to configure a `FilterToBeanProxy` filter in web.xml that will delegate to the `integrationFilter` bean:

```
<filter>
  <filter-name>Acegi-Integration</filter-name>
  <filter-class>net.sf.acegisecurity.util.FilterToBeanProxy
      </filter-class>
  <init-param>
    <param-name>targetClass</param-name>
    <param-value>net.sf.acegisecurity.ui.AutoIntegrationFilter
        </param-value>
  </init-param>
</filter>
...
<filter-mapping>
  <filter-name>Acegi-Integration</filter-name>
  <url-pattern>/*</url-pattern>
</filter-mapping>
```

It's important that the `<filter-mapping>` entry be placed after all of the `<filter-mapping>` entries for the other Acegi filters.

### 11.4.5 *Ensuring a secure channel*

There are certain pages within a secure web application that will carry sensitive information. If this information is delivered across an insecure channel (such as HTTP), a risk exists that some nefarious hacker will intercept the data and use it for corrupt purposes.

Common examples of this include a login page or any page where a user's credit card information is entered or displayed. Should the security of this information be compromised, an individual's personal data could be used to make purchases or to assume identity of the user. It's very important that users feel their information remains confidential or else they will no longer use your site. Or worse, they may resort to litigation to ensure that you compensate them for their loss.

HTTPS helps prevent high-tech criminals from intercepting sensitive data over the Internet by encrypting messages sent between server and browser. Using HTTPS is often as simple as using "https://" in a URL instead of "http://". However, this requires that you remember to add that "s" every time you link to a page that displays sensitive data. It seems easy enough, but in our own experience, we've forgotten that "s" more times than we can count.

Acegi provides a solution through its ChannelProcessingFilter. ChannelProcessingFilter ensures that web application pages are delivered over the proper channels (HTTP or HTTPS)—regardless of whether you remember to put "https://" in the link URL.

To use ChannelProcessingFilter, you must start by adding another FilterToBeanProxy configuration to your web application's web.xml file:

```
<filter>
  <filter-name>Acegi-Channel</filter-name>
  <filter-class>net.sf.acegisecurity.util.FilterToBeanProxy
      ➥ </filter-class>
  <init-param>
    <param-name>targetClass</param-name>
    <param-value>
      net.sf.acegisecurity.securechannel.ChannelProcessingFilter
    </param-value>
  </init-param>
</filter>
...
<filter-mapping>
  <filter-name>Acegi-Channel</filter-name>
  <url-pattern>/*</url-pattern>
</filter-mapping>
```

It's very important that the <filter-mapping> for ChannelProcessingFilter appear in the web.xml before any of the other <filter-mapping>s. That's because ChannelProcessingFilter needs to ensure that the request is being sent over the proper channel before allowing any of the other filters to do their work.

Once you've configured the FilterToBeanProxy in web.xml, you'll need to declare the delegate filter bean in the Spring configuration file:

```
<bean id="channelProcessingFilter" class="net.sf.acegisecurity.
      ➥ securechannel.ChannelProcessingFilter">
  <property name="filterInvocationDefinitionSource">
    <value>
      CONVERT_URL_TO_LOWERCASE_BEFORE_COMPARISON
      \A/secure/.*\Z=REQUIRES_SECURE_CHANNEL
      \A/login.jsp.*\Z=REQUIRES_SECURE_CHANNEL
      \A/j_acegi_security_check.*\Z=REQUIRES_SECURE_CHANNEL
      \A.*\Z=REQUIRES_INSECURE_CHANNEL
```

```
      </value>
    </property>
    <property name="channelDecisionManager">
      <ref bean="channelDecisionManager"/>
    </property>
  </bean>
```

The `filterInvocationDefinitionSource` property is where you define which pages must be either secure or insecure. Just as with a `FilterSecurityInterceptor` (section 11.4.2) a property editor interprets this property. The first line indicates that the URL of the request should be converted to lowercase before comparing with the patterns in the lines that follow.

Each line after the first line associates a channel rule with a URL pattern. In this case, we're using regular expressions to define the URL patterns, but just as with the security interceptors, you can also use Ant-like patterns by adding the `PATTERN_TYPE_APACHE_ANT` directive. There are two channel rules that can be applied to a URL pattern:

- `REQUIRES_SECURE_CHANNEL`—Indicates that URLs matching the pattern *must* be delivered over a secure channel (e.g., HTTPS)
- `REQUIRES_INSECURE_CHANNEL`—Indicates that URLs matching the pattern *must* be delivered over an insecure channel (e.g., HTTP)

In this case, we've declared that the login page, the authentication filter (/j_ acegi_security_check), and any page under the "/secure" path must be delivered over a secure channel. Any other URL must be delivered over an insecure channel.

`ChannelProcessingFilter` doesn't work alone when enforcing channel security. It collaborates with a `ChannelDecisionManager`, as referenced by the `channelDecisionManager` property, which will in turn delegate responsibility to one or more `ChannelProcessors`. This relationship is reminiscent of the relationship between an `AccessDecisionManager` and its `AccessDecisionVoters`. Figure 11.9 illustrates this relationship.

The channel decision `manager` is supposed to be responsible for deciding whether the channel of the request's URL meets the channel security rules (defined by the `filterInvocationDefinitionSource` property of the `ChannelProcessingFilter`). However, `ChannelDecisionManagerImpl`, Acegi's only prepackaged implementation of `ChannelDecisionManager`, leaves that decision up to its channel processors.

`ChannelDecisionManagerImpl` iterates over its channel processors, giving them an opportunity to override the channel of the request. A channel processor

**Figure 11.9   A channel-processing filter relies on a channel decision manager to decide whether to switch to/from a secure channel. If a switch is necessary, a channel processor makes the switch.**

examines the request and holds it up to the channel security rules. If the channel processor takes issue with the request's channel, then it will perform a redirect to ensure that the request is sufficiently secure.

Now that you see how all `ChannelProcessingFilter` works, it's time to put all of the pieces together. As you saw earlier, the `channelProcessingFilter`"bean's `channelDecisionManager` property is wired with a reference to a `channelDecision-Manager` bean. The `channelDecisionManager` bean is declared as follows:

```
<bean id="channelDecisionManager" class= "net.sf.acegisecurity.
      securechannel.ChannelDecisionManagerImpl">
  <property name="channelProcessors">
    <list>
      <ref bean="secureChannelProcessor"/>
      <ref bean="insecureChannelProcessor"/>
    </list>
  </property>
</bean>
```

`ChannelDecisionManagerImpl`'s channel processors are provided through its `channelProcessors` property. In this case, we've given it two channel processors, which are declared with the following XML:

```
<bean id="secureChannelProcessor" class="net.sf.acegisecurity.
      securechannel.SecureChannelProcessor"/>
<bean id="insecureChannelProcessor" class=
    "net.sf.acegisecurity.securechannel.InsecureChannelProcessor"/>
```

`SecureChannelProcessor` considers at the channel security rule associated with the request's URL. If the rule is REQUIRES_SECURE_CHANNEL and the request is not secure, then `SecureChannelProcessor` redirects to a secure form of the request. For example, based on the value of `filterInvocationDefinitionSource` given to the `channelProcessingFilter` bean:

- http://www.springinaction.com/training/secure/editCourse.htm will be redirected to https://www.springinaction.com/training/secure/editCourse.htm because it matches a URL pattern that has a REQUIRES_SECURE_CHANNEL rule.

- http://www.springinaction.com/training/j_acegi_security_check will be redirected to https://www.springinaction.com/training/j_acegi_security_check because it matches a URL pattern that has a `REQUIRES_SECURE_CHANNEL` rule.
- http://www.springinaction.com/training/displayCourse.htm will not be redirected because it matches a URL pattern that does not have a `REQUIRES_SECURE_CHANNEL` rule.
- https://www.springinaction.com/training/j_acegi_security_check will be not be redirected because it is already secure.

`InsecureChannelProcessor` is the functional opposite of `SecureChannelProcessor`. Instead of ensuring that a request is delivered over a secure channel, it ensures that a request is delivered over an insecure channel. For example:

- https://www.springinaction.com/training/displayCourse.htm will be redirected to http://www.springinaction.com/training/displayCourse.htm because it matches a URL pattern that has a `REQUIRES_INSECURE_CHANNEL` rule.
- https://www.springinaction.com/training/j_acegi_security_check will not be redirected because it matches a URL pattern that does not have a `REQUIRES_INSECURE_CHANNEL` rule.
- http://www.springinaction.com/training.displayCourse.htm will not be redirected because it matches a URL pattern that has a `REQUIRES_INSECURE_CHANNEL` and it is already insecure.

Before we move past Acegi's support for web-based security, let's see how to use Acegi's tag library to enforce security rules within a page in the web application.

### 11.4.6  Using the Acegi tag library

To call it a tag library is a bit of an overstatement. Actually, Acegi comes with only one JSP tag: the `<authz:authorize>` tag.

While Acegi's security-enforcement filter will prevent users from navigating to a page that they aren't allowed to see, it is often best to not offer a link to the restricted page in the first place. The `<authz:authorize>` tag helps to show or hide web content based on whether the current user is authorized.

`<authz:authorize>` is a flow-control tag that displays its body content when certain security requirements are met. It has three mutually exclusive parameters:

- `ifAllGranted`—A comma-separated list of privileges that the user must all have in order for the tag's body to be rendered
- `ifAnyGranted`—A comma-separated list of privileges that the user must have at least one of in order for the tag's body to be rendered

- ifNotGranted—A comma-separated list of privileges that the user must not have any of in order for the tag's body to be rendered

You can easily imagine how the <authz:authorize> tag may be used in a JSP to limit users' actions based on their granted authorities. For example, the Spring Training application has a course detail page that displays information about a course to the user. It would be convenient for an administrator to be able to navigate directly from the course detail screen to a course edit screen to update the course information. But you wouldn't want that link to appear for anyone except administrative users.

Using the <authz:authorize> tag, you can prevent the link the course edit screen from being rendered except when the user has administrative privileges:

```
<authz:authorize ifAllGranted="ROLE_ADMINISTRATOR">
  <a href="admin/editCourse.htm?courseId=${course.id}">
    Edit Course
  </a>
</authz:authorize>
```

Here we've used the ifAllGranted parameter, but since there's only one authority being checked, ifAnyGranted would've worked just as well.

Web application security is only one side of Acegi's functionality. Now let's examine the other side—securing method invocations.

## 11.5 Securing method invocations

Whereas Acegi used servlet filters to secure web requests, Acegi takes advantage of Spring's AOP support to provide declarative method-level security. This means that instead of setting up a SecurityEnforcementFilter to enforce security, you'll set up a Spring AOP proxy that intercepts method invocations and passes control to a security interceptor.

### 11.5.1 Creating a security aspect

Probably the easiest way to setup an AOP proxy is to use Spring's BeanNameAutoProxyCreator and simply list out the beans that you'll want secured.[3] For instance, suppose that you'd like to secure the courseService and billingService beans:

---

[3] This is only a suggestion. If you prefer one of the other mechanisms for proxying beans (as discussed in chapter 4), such as ProxyFactorybean or DefaultAdvisorAutoProxyCreator, then you are welcome to use those here instead.

# Spring-related projects

```
<target name="war" depends="compile">
  <war destfile="${target.dir}/${ant.project.name}.war"
       webxml="${webapp.dir}/web.xml">
    <lib dir="${spring.lib.dir}"/>
    <lib dir="${app.lib.dir}"/>
    <classes dir="${classes.dir}"/>
  </war>
</target>

...

</project>
```

**Include Spring dependencies**

The Ant build files that accompany the example code for this book will follow this pattern for managing Spring dependencies.

With your build file now in place, there is one final thing you will want to do. When you first start using Spring, one feature you will definitely find useful is logging. The easiest way to set this up is to include a simple log4j configuration file. Assuming the project structure described above, you would create a file located at /src/webapp/WEB-INF/classes/log4j.properties. Listing A.2 shows a simple configuration that logs all Spring messages to the console.

**Listing A.2   Simple log4j.properties file**

```
log4j.appender.stdout=org.apache.log4j.ConsoleAppender
log4j.appender.stdout.layout=org.apache.log4j.PatternLayout
log4j.appender.stdout.layout.ConversionPattern=%d %p %c - %m%n
log4j.rootLogger=INFO, stdoutlog4j.logger.org.springframework=DEBUG
```

Your project is now set up and ready to go. All you have to do is start coding, put Ant to work, and you will have a working Spring application in no time.

- */src/java*—All Java source code files
- */src/webapp*—All web application files, including configuration files and JSPs
- */lib*—Any third-party JAR files not included in the Spring distribution
- */target*—Our WAR file once it is created
- */target/classes*—Our class files once they are compiled

That should do it. We are now ready to set up our build.

## A.4  *Building with Ant*

Most Java applications are built with Apache Ant. If you're using Ant to build your Spring project, you'll need to download the Spring framework for yourself (as described in section A.1) and be sure to add the Spring dependency JAR files to the appropriate places in your Ant's build file.

We recommend declaring an Ant `<path>` element that will contain your application's dependencies, including the Spring JAR files. Listing A.1 shows a small section of an Ant build file that manages Spring dependencies this way.

**Listing A.1   Building a Spring application with Ant**

```
<project name="training" default="init">
  <property name="spring.home"
      location="/opt/spring-framework-1.1.3"/>        Define Spring
                                                        distribution location
  <property name="target.dir" location="target"/>
  <property name="classes.dir" location="${target.dir}/classes"/>
  <property name="src.dir" location="src"/>
  <property name="java.src.dir" location="${src.dir}/java"/>
  <property name="webapp.dir" location="${src.dir}/webapp"/>
  <property name="app.lib.dir" location="lib"/>
  <property name="spring.lib.dir" location="${spring.home}/dist"/>
  <property name="spring.depends.dir"
      location="${spring.home}/lib"/>

  <path id="dependency.path">
    <fileset dir="${spring.lib.dir}" includes="*.jar"/>
    <fileset dir="${spring.depends.dir}" includes="**/*.jar"/>
    <fileset dir="${app.lib.dir}" includes="*.jar"/>
  </path>                                       Include Spring
                                                dependencies
  <target name="compile">
    <mkdir dir="${classes.dir}"/>
    <javac destdir="${classes.dir}"
           classpathref="dependency.path">     Set class path
      <src path="${java.src.dir}"/>            for javac
    </javac>
  </target>
```

**Table A.1 Spring JAR distributions** *(continued)*

| JAR File | Purpose | Depends on |
|---|---|---|
| spring-context.jar | Application context, validation framework, templating support (Velocity, FreeMarker), remoting (JAX-RPC, Hessian, Burlap), EJB support, and scheduling. | spring-core.jar. *Optional: Velocity, FreeMarker, JavaMail, EJB, JAX-RPC, Hessian, Burlap, Quartz* |
| spring-dao.jar | JDBC and DAO support. Transaction infrastructure. | spring-core.jar. *Optional: spring-aop.jar, JTA* |
| spring-orm.jar | Support for ORM frameworks, including Hibernate, JDO, and iBatis. | spring-dao.jar. *Optional: Hibernate, JDO, iBATIS* |
| spring-web.jar | Web application context and utilities. Multipart file upload support. | spring-context.jar, servlet. *Optional: Commons FileUpload, COS* |
| spring-webmvc.jar | Spring's MVC framework. | spring-web.jar. *Optional: JSP, JSTL, Tiles, iText, POI* |
| spring.jar | The entire Spring framework, including everything in the other JAR files. | All of the above |

The choices may seem a bit overwhelming, but it's really quite simple. Each of the first seven JAR files from table A.1 correlate to each of Spring's modules, as discussed in chapter 1. Realizing that not every Spring-enabled application will necessarily use every part of Spring, the Spring team made the smart decision to break up the distribution into seven parts and allow you to choose the parts appropriate for your application. For example, if your application will only use the application context and AOP features in Spring, you will only need spring-core.jar, spring-context.jar, and spring-aop.jar.

In the event that you will use all of the Spring framework in your application, they've also packaged the whole framework in one convenient spring.jar file. You may choose to use this JAR file while learning Spring to avoid the inconvenience of having to keep adding and removing module JAR files from your class path. The remaining instructions will assume that this is the choice you have made.

## A.3 Setting up your project

Once you have downloaded Spring, the next step is to set up the directory structure for your project. If you are like most developers, you probably have a project structure you are already comfortable with. If you do, by all means stick to it. For this example, we are going to build a web application with the following project structure:

If you are reading this book, you are probably doing so because you want to develop your own Spring application. We would be remiss if we did not show you how to get your project up and running. So in this appendix we are going to show you how to begin building your own Spring application, starting with downloading Spring itself.

## A.1 Downloading Spring

Spring comes in the form of one JAR file or a handful of JAR files depending on how you choose to deploy it. To begin using Spring in your application, you must do the following:

1 Download the latest version of Spring from http://www.springframe-work.org. In this book, we assume that you are using the 1.1.3 version of Spring, unless otherwise noted. You'll be given the choice of two zip files: one with dependencies and one without. The one with dependencies is much larger, but includes all of the third-party dependency libraries that Spring relies on. We recommend the one with dependencies, simply because you won't need to hunt down and download any other JAR in order to get started.

2 Unzip the zip file downloaded in step 1 to a directory on your computer (for example, C:\ on Windows or /opt/ on UNIX).

3 Choose the distribution JAR file(s) you will use from the dist directory (for example, C:\spring-framework-1.1.3\dist on Windows or /opt/spring-framework-1.1.3/dist on Unix).

4 Add the Spring JAR file and its dependencies to your build's class path and your application's class path.

## A.2 Choosing a distribution

Spring's libraries are distributed in eight JAR files, as listed in table A.1.

**Table A.1   Spring JAR distributions**

| JAR File | Purpose | Depends on |
| --- | --- | --- |
| spring-core.jar | The core Spring container and utilities. | Commons logging. *Optional: Log4J* |
| spring-aop.jar | Spring's AOP framework and metadata support. | spring-core.jar, AOP alliance. *Optional: CGLIB, Commons Attributes* |

*continued on next page*

# Spring setup

## *11.6 Summary*

Security is a very important aspect of many applications. The Acegi Security System provides a mechanism for securing your applications that is based on Spring's philosophy of loose coupling, dependency injection, and aspect-oriented programming.

You may have noticed that this chapter presented very little Java code. We hope you weren't disappointed. The lack of Java code illustrates a key strength of Acegi—loose coupling between an application and its security. Security is an aspect that transcends an application's core concerns. Using Acegi you are able to secure your applications without writing any security code directly into your application code.

Another thing you may have noticed is that much of the configuration required to secure an application with Acegi is ignorant of the application that it is securing. The only Acegi component that really needs to know any specifics about the secured application is the object definition source where you associate a secured resource with the authorities required to access the resource. Loose coupling runs both ways between Acegi and its applications.

```
<bean id="autoProxyCreator" class="org.springframework.
    aop.framework.autoproxy.BeanNameAutoProxyCreator">
  <property name="interceptorNames">
    <list>
      <value>securityInterceptor</value>
    </list>
  </property>
  <property name="beanNames">
    <list>
      <value>courseService</value>
      <value>billingService</value>
    </list>
  </property>
</bean>
```

Here the auto-proxy creator has been instructed to proxy its beans with a single interceptor, a bean named securityInterceptor. The securityInterceptor bean is configured as follows:

```
<bean id="securityInterceptor" class="net.sf.acegisecurity.
    intercept.method.MethodSecurityInterceptor">
  <property name="authenticationManager">
    <ref bean="authenticationManager"/>
  </property>
  <property name="accessDecisionManager">
    <ref bean="accessDecisionManager"/>
  </property>
  <property name="objectDefinitionSource">
    <value>
      com.springinaction.springtraining.service.
          CourseService.createCourse=ROLE_ADMIN
      com.springinaction.springtraining.service.
          CourseService.enroll*=ROLE_ADMIN,ROLE_REGISTRAR
    </value>
  </property>
</bean>
```

MethodSecurityInterceptor does for method invocations what FilterSecurity-Interceptor does for servlet requests. That is, it intercepts the invocation and coordinates the efforts of the authentication manager and the access decision manager to ensure that method requirements are met.

Notice that the authenticationManager and accessDecisionManager properties are the same as for FilterSecurityInterceptor. In fact, you may wire the same beans into these properties as you did for FilterSecurityInterceptor.

MethodSecurityInterceptor also has an objectDefinitionSource property just as FilterSecurityInterceptor does. But, although it serves the same purpose here as with FilterSecurityInterceptor, it is configured slightly different.

A common theme in the open source world is successful projects beget more successful projects. This is especially true for frameworks. Once a framework hits critical mass and gains wide adoption, supporting projects spring up as complements.

Spring is no different. Over the last year many projects have been developed that are related to Spring. This appendix looks at a few of these projects. This is by no means an exhaustive list of Spring-related projects, but we do examine the projects we feel you will find most beneficial.

## B.1 *AppFuse*

If you have not yet started developing your own Spring application, you may be chomping at the bit to do so. Starting an application from scratch is not easy, especially a full-blown enterprise Java application. It sure would be nice if there were an easy way to bootstrap an application.

Fortunately, Matt Raible was thinking the same thing when he created App-Fuse. AppFuse is a tool for kick-starting a web application. As its name suggests, it is the fuse you ignite to get your project up and going with a bang. But instead of the fuse being attached to a stick of dynamite, it is a fully configured project just waiting for you to give it some code.

To begin using AppFuse, you will need to download it from http://raibledesigns.com/wiki/Wiki.jsp?page=Downloads. As of this writing, AppFuse 1.7 was the latest release.

Once you download AppFuse itself, you will also need a few other applications that are required to build and run your Spring application:

- J2SE 1.4+
- Ant 1.6.2+
- MySQL 3.23.x+
- Tomcat 4.1.x+
- JUnit 3.8.1
- An SMTP mail server

This will provide the infrastructure that will support your web application. All that's left is to add your code—and this is where AppFuse comes to the rescue. As we mentioned, AppFuse comes with a project structure that will contain your files and an Ant build file ready to compile your classes, execute test cases, and deploy your application.

To help with development, the AppFuse website (https://appfuse.dev.java.net/) provides step-by-step tutorials for creating classes for all layers of your application.

Whether you are using Hibernate or iBATIS, Struts or Tapestry, AppFuse will guide you from writing the actual code, to creating test cases, to editing configuration files, to wiring everything together in Spring. When it comes to creating enterprise applications quickly, AppFuse is a quick fuse indeed.

## B.2  Rich Client Project

As you probably have figured out from reading this book, a good portion of the Spring framework is dedicated to simplifying server-side development. The Rich Client Project (RCP) addresses the other side of the equation by creating a framework for developing applications for the client side.

The goal of the RCP is to provide a framework for developers to follow best practices and create Swing applications quickly. Specifically, it aims to

- Provide a means to configure Swing actions in a central location and external to the actual Swing code.

- Provide integration points with existing rich-client projects (much like Spring's support for existing projects, such as Hibernate). This includes integration with two existing layout managers: jgoodies-forms and TableLayout.

- Provide a set of common support classes for common rich client requirements, such as dialogs, wizards, progress bars, and tables.

As of the publishing of this book, RCP was still in the alpha stage. But development is continuing and you can keep an eye on this project at http://sourceforge.net/projects/spring.

## B.3  Spring.NET

Believe it or not, Java is not the only technology out there. Other languages are flourishing in the enterprise development space. In fact, there is also a company in Redmond, Washington, that is staying competitive with a platform of their own. In case you have not seen through our sarcasm yet, we are talking about Microsoft. Specifically, we are referring to their language that mirrors Java: C#.NET.

Recognizing the benefits of a lightweight framework like Spring, some enterprising (pun intended) developers have created a similar framework for the .NET platform, aptly named Spring.NET. The roadmap for Spring.NET is to provide core container services first—namely inversion of control. This will be followed by AOP support and enterprise services.

As of the publishing of this book, Spring.NET has not had a production release. However, in August 2004, the first release candidate was published: Spring.NET 0.6. The features already available include

- Constructor and setter dependency injection
- Singleton and prototype bean support
- Autowiring
- .NET application configuration file support

Spring.NET is still in its early stages but is being actively developed. You can find out the latest status of Spring.NET at its cleverly named website: http://www.springframework.net.

# *index*